Michael Lysander Fremuth | Jörn Griebel
Robert Heinsch (eds.)

Natural Resources and International Law – Developments and Challenges

A Liber Amicorum in Honour of
Stephan Hobe

HART

Nomos

The Deutsche Nationalbibliothek lists this publication in the Deutsche Nationalbibliografie; detailed bibliographic data are available on the Internet at http://dnb.d-nb.de

ISBN: HB (Nomos) 978-3-8487-8441-7
ePDF (Nomos) 978-3-7489-2976-5

British Library Cataloguing-in-Publication Data
A catalogue record for this book is available from the British Library.

ISBN: HB (Hart) 978-1-5099-5283-0

Library of Congress Cataloging-in-Publication Data
Michael Lysander Fremuth | Jörn Griebel | Robert Heinsch
Natural Resources and International Law –
Developments and Challenges
A Liber Amicorum in Honour of Stephan Hobe
Fremuth, Michael Lysander | Griebel, Jörn | Heinsch, Robert (eds.)
321 pp.
Includes bibliographic references.

ISBN 978-1-5099-5283-0 (hardcover Hart)

Onlineversion
Nomos eLibrary

1st Edition 2021

Foreword

It is always a challenge to summarise a decades-long career of a successful and highly esteemed academic in just a few sentences—this also holds true with regard to what Stephan Hobe has achieved during his long and still ongoing career. In more than 35 years of his academic work, our academic mentor has developed a great expertise in a remarkable variety of fields of law, such as German constitutional law, European Union law and public international law (with its special fields of air law, space law, international economic law and international investment law being amongst the many themes of his life). Bringing all these fields of interest and expertise together under one common topic was a great challenge which we tried to address with this *liber amicorum* and a two-day conference that served as the basis for the content of this collection of contributions.

In summer 2017, when the three of us met with our academic teacher at our *alma mater* in Cologne in order to prepare this conference, Stephan Hobe had already designed a conference programme connecting many of his fields of expertise to a particularly challenging problem of mankind, i.e., how to deal with increasingly rare natural resources or commodities, their exploration and exploitation. The conference took place on the 2nd and 3rd of March 2018 in Ladenburg, Germany, and was hosted and financially supported by the Daimler and Benz Foundation. All participants, amongst them many long-time colleagues and friends, contributed to this *liber amicorum* in honour of Stephan Hobe's 60th birthday.

We are very grateful for their support which also expresses their genuine admiration towards Stephan Hobe.

For us as editors of this book, it is equally a pleasure and an honour to thank our teacher Stephan Hobe for the many years of his support while we were young research assistants—more than two decades ago—and for mentoring us on our path of developing into independent scholars ourselves. Becoming an academic in the area of international law is never an easy endeavour, and so we were lucky to take our first steps towards this ambitious goal in cooperation with such a well-versed and well-connected academic teacher.

It does not come as a surprise that all three of us followed Stephan Hobe's academic approach to research and teaching law in one way or another. We tried to become inspiring and energetic law teachers and dedicated researchers by following his stimulating and enthusiastic way of teaching and his contentious and diligent way of conducting research, i.e., keeping the big picture and the underlying conditions in mind, while not losing the necessary focus on particular research questions.

We would like to thank our collaborators at Leiden University, Siegen University and the University of Vienna for supporting us in the process of editing the *liber amicorum*. We would specifically like to mention in alphabetical order: Alla Ershova, Emma Irving, Sharon Pia Hickey, Sofia Larriera Santurio (Leiden University), Stefan Schelhaas, Dominik Schmidt, Christian Schäfer (Siegen University), as well as Roman Friedrich and Magdalena Steringer (University of Vienna). We would also like to extend our gratitude to all the authors for the productive cooperation and the high quality of their contributions, as well as to the Daimler and Benz Foundation for laying the basis for this book by supporting the initial conference.

We hope that this *liber amicorum* is only a first step to honour Stephan Hobe for his life-long achievements. Knowing his energy and dedication to the fields of his expertise, we would not be surprised if another 10, 20 or 30 years of productivity will follow. We are eager to celebrate his future achievements.

Therefore, we believe that for science as well as for Stephan Hobe the following is equally valid:
The sky is not the limit!

Michael Lysander Fremuth, Jörn Griebel, Robert Heinsch

Contents

Energy as a Resource for Sustainable Development. The need for good governance in the energy sector

Charlotte Kreuter-Kirchhof[*]

Abstract

In 2015, the international community recognized energy access as a key resource for sustainable development. At the United Nations Sustainable Development Summit, states agreed upon the goal to grant access to clean energy for all by 2030. Having access to energy will save and significantly improve lives and will lead to broad social and economic benefits. At the same time, clean energy supply is pivotal to combatting climate change. To monitor progress towards reaching the goal of clean energy for all, the General Assembly agreed upon targets and a set of global indicators. With regard to these indicators, progress has been made in some areas. More people have gained access to electricity and to clean cooking fuels and technologies. The share of renewable energy in total final energy consumption grew, albeit only slightly. However, the international community is not on track to meet its goal, most notably in sub-Saharan Africa where progress lags especially behind. The challenge to provide access to clean energy for all offers the opportunity for Africa to leapfrog towards renewable energy systems that avoid carbon emissions. Decentralised energy generation with diversified ownership systems can contribute to achieving these goals. To enable investments in renewable energy generation in Africa, suitable regulatory and policy frameworks are needed.

Overview

---

* The author holds the chair for German and Foreign Public Law, Public International Law and European Law at Heinrich-Heine University Düsseldorf, Germany.

I. Sustainable Development Goals for the energy sector

In 2000, the United Nations agreed upon the Millennium Development Goals (MDG) that set the framework for the international development agenda for the following 15 years. The MDGs ranged from halving extreme poverty to halting the spread of HIV/AIDS and providing universal primary education. By 2015, these targets were not fully achieved, but had galvanized unprecedented efforts and achievements to meet the needs of the world's poorest. For example, the number of people living in extreme poverty has declined by more than half, primary school enrolment reached 91 percent in the developing regions, the global child mortality rate for children under five declined by more than half, maternal mortality declined by 45 percent. New HIV infections fell by approximately 40 percent between 2000 and 2013.[1]

However, the MDGs were not comprehensive enough. They encompassed only some areas of sustainable development. For example, the MDGs did not consider access to clean energy or a specific climate change goal. Moreover, while the MDGS did concentrate on the development of developing countries, they did not sufficiently involve industrialised countries nor contribute enough to form a collaborative partnership of all countries and all stakeholders to foster sustainable development.

In order to react to these findings, but also to build on the success of the MDGs and to continue along the chosen path for sustainable development, the world leaders adopted the Sustainable Development Goals

1 See *United Nations*, The Millennium Development Goals Report (2015), p. 6.

(SDGs) at a historic UN summit in 2015.[2] These SDGs form the Agenda 2030. They go beyond the MDGs and include the goals of ending poverty, protecting the planet and ensuring prosperity for all. These goals – the result of the broadest and most inclusive consultation process in UN history – now address the entire international community and not only the lesser developed states.[3] While the SDGs are not legally binding, states are expected to establish national frameworks for the achievement of the 17 goals. The SDGs also aim for the involvement of the private sector as well as civil society in the process towards sustainable development for all.

The SDGs cover 17 goals for sustainable development which are supported by a list of 169 specific targets to be reached by 2030. Goal number seven sets the aim to *"ensure access to affordable, reliable, sustainable and modern energy for all"* by 2030. This is the first time access to clean energy has been recognized as a central goal in order to achieve sustainable development.[4] The specific targets associated with goal seven are to increase substantially the share of renewable energy, to improve energy efficiency, to enhance international cooperation to facilitate access to clean energy research and technology and to promote investment in energy infrastructure and clean energy technology. These targets recognize increasing the share of renewable energy as well as energy efficiency as integral to sustainable development for all countries. Furthermore, international cooperation is needed to foster energy research and to transfer new (clean) technologies. The targets also emphasize that investment in energy infrastructure and clean energy technology has to be promoted.

These clear targets for the energy sector are interconnected with other Sustainable Development Goals. Recognizing the interdependency of the different development goals is one of the important achievements of the SDGs. Thus, the aim to grant access to clean energy for all has to be seen especially in the context of the goal to *"take urgent action to combat climate change and its impacts"*.[5] Energy supply and combatting climate change are closely interlinked.

---

2 See *United Nations General Assembly*, Transforming our world: the 2030 Agenda for Sustainable Development, A/RES/70/1 of 25 September 2015.

3 See *United Nations General Assembly*, The future we want, A/Res/66/288 of 27 July 2012; *Europäische Union /Agentur für Grundrechte*, Implementing the Sustainable Development Goals in the European Union, 2019; *Duncan / Kotzé*, Sustainable Development Goals, 2018.

4 See *United Nations Development Programme*, UNDP Support to the Implementation of Sustainable Development Goal 7 (2016), p. 4.

5 See Goal 13 of the Sustainable Development Goals.

II. Energy as a resource for sustainable development

Since the establishment of the SDGs, energy access is regarded as one of the key elements for sustainable development. Thus, goal number seven asks the international community to foster access to clean energy for all. Clean energy calls especially for using renewable energy resources. This contributes to sustainable energy supply that serves the needs of the present without compromising the ability of future generations to meet their energy needs.[6]

1. Importance of energy access for sustainable development

Access to reliable electricity allows for clean and safe cooking fuels, charging phones, powering computers, refrigerating food and vaccines, and is necessary for the functioning of essential infrastructure. Providing energy for all would save and significantly improve lives. For example, according to the International Energy Agency, ensuring access to clean cooking fuel for all would lower the premature death toll by 1.8 million people per year in 2030.[7] Having access to energy also leads to broad social and economic benefits. At the same time, clean energy supply is pivotal to saving our earth's atmosphere. In 2015, the international community agreed upon the first universal, legally binding international agreement to combat climate change. The Paris Agreement sets the goal of limiting global warming to well below 2 degrees Celsius above pre-industrial levels and to pursue efforts to limit the temperature increase even further to 1.5 to avoid dangerous anthropogenic climate change. In order to reach this goal, we need to decarbonize the economy and energy systems worldwide. Thus, access to *clean* energy is one of the core elements for sustainable development.[8] It is

---

6 See the definition of sustainable development in *United Nations World Commission on Environment and Development*, Report of the World Commission on Environment and Development: Our Common Future (1987), No. 27.

7 *International Energy Agency*, Energy Access Outlook 2017 – Executive Summary (2017), p. 6.

8 See also *Power for All/Sustainable Development for All*, Why wait? Seizing the energy access dividend (2017), pp. 27, 76.

the "golden thread" connecting economic growth, social equity and environmental sustainability.[9]

2. *Targets to be reached by 2030*

The Sustainable Development Goals call for clean energy for all and set specific targets that are to be achieved. These include:

- ensuring universal access to affordable, reliable and modern energy services;
- increasing substantially the share of renewable energy in the global energy mix;
- doubling the global rate of improvement in energy efficiency;
- enhancing international cooperation to facilitate access to clean energy research and technology, including renewable energy, energy efficiency and advanced and cleaner fossil-fuel technology, and to promote investment in energy infrastructure and clean energy technology; and
- expanding infrastructure and upgrading technology for supplying modern and sustainable energy services for all in developing countries, in particular least developed countries, small island developing states and landlocked developing countries, in accordance with their respective programmes of support.

To monitor progress towards reaching the SDGs' goals and targets, a robust review mechanism for the implementation of Agenda 2030 is indispensable. Therefore, the General Assembly agreed upon a set of global indicators developed by the Inter-Agency and Expert Group on Sustainable Development Goal Indicators.[10] Annually, the Secretary-General of the UN prepares a progress report on the Sustainable Development Goals based on this global indicator framework.[11] In order to review goal num-

9 *International Bank for Reconstruction and Development/World Bank/International Energy Agency*, Global Tracking Framework 2017, Progress toward Sustainable Energy (2017), p. 2.

10 *United Nations General Assembly*, Work of the Statistical Commission pertaining to the 2030 Agenda for Sustainable Development, A/Res/71/313 of 10 July 2017; see also *United Nations*, Global SDG Indicator Database, available under: https://unstats.un.org/sdgs/indicators/database/ (last accessed: 1 April 2020).

11 For the latest report see *United Nations*, The Sustainable Development Goals Report 2019, Report of the Secretary-General on SDG Progress 2019, Special Edition, available under:

ber seven, ensuring access to affordable, reliable, sustainable and modern energy for all, the following indicators have been set:

- proportion of population with access to electricity;
- proportion of population with primary reliance on clean fuels and technology;
- renewable energy share in the total final energy consumption;
- energy intensity measured in terms of primary energy and GDP;
- international financial flows to developing countries in support of clean energy research and development and renewable energy production, including in hybrid systems;
- investments in energy efficiency as a proportion of GDP and the amount of foreign direct investment in financial transfer for infrastructure and technology to sustainable development services.

These indicators serve as the basis for measuring progress towards reaching the goal of clean energy for all.

III. Progress towards universal access to clean energy for all

Looking at the first three indicators, which consider the proportion of population with access to electricity and with primary reliance on clean fuels and technology as well as the renewable energy share in the total final energy consumption, an electricity access gap is clearly visible. This gap is particularly evident when comparing Northern America and Europe with sub-Saharan Africa.

1. Access to electricity

In 2018, 789 million people still lived without electricity,[12] most of them in sub-Saharan Africa.[13] The good news is, that the share of the global population with access to electricity increased from 83 percent in 2010 to 90

https://unstats.un.org/sdgs/report/2019/The-Sustainable-Development-Goals-Report-2019.pdf (last accessed: 28 May 2020).

12 *International Bank for Reconstruction and Development/World Bank et al.*, The Energy Progress Report 2020 – Tracking SDG 7 (2020), p. 4.

13 *United Nations*, Sustainable Development Goals Report 2019 (2019), p. 36.

percent in 2018.[14] Since 2000, nearly 1.2 billion people have gained access to electricity, 500 million of whom live in India.[15] While in Europe and Northern America the entire population has access to electricity, in Latin America and the Caribeean as well as in Eastern Asia and in South-eastern Asia access to electricity exceeded 98 percent in 2018. In Central Asia and Southern Asia, 92 percent of the population had gained access to electricity.[16] In contrast to these positive developments, sub-Saharan Africa poses a severe challenge. One-out-of-two people do not have access to electricity in this region.[17] In 2018, only 44 percent of the population had access, and an estimated 573 million people still lacked electricity.[18] Moreover, recent developments are not very encouraging. Between 2016 and 2018, the number of people in the region lacking access remained almost stable.[19] By 2030, it is estimated that 620 million people will still remain without access to electricity, 85 percent of them living in sub-Saharan Africa.[20] Besides, electricity demand in the sub-Saharan Africa region without South Africa is set to quadruple by 2040.[21]

2. *Reliance on clean fuels and technologies*

The proportion of population with primary reliance on clean fuels and technology is calculated as the number of people using clean fuels and technologies for cooking, heating and lighting.[22] Lack of access to clean cooking fuels and technologies endangers health due to household air pol-

14 *International Bank for Reconstruction and Development/World Bank et al.*, The Energy Progress Report 2020 – Tracking SDG 7 (2020), p. 4.

15 *International Energy Agency*, Energy Access Outlook 2017 – Executive Summary (2017), p. 5.

16 *International Bank for Reconstruction and Development/World Bank et. al.*, The Energy Progress Report 2020 – Tracking SDG 7 (2020), p. 4.

17 *International Energy Agency*, Africa Energy Outlook 2019, p. 113.

18 *United Nations*, Sustainable Development Goals Report 2019 (2019), p. 36.

19 *International Bank for Reconstruction and Development/World Bank et al.*, The Energy Progress Report 2020 – Tracking SDG 7 (2020), p. 4.

20 *International Bank for Reconstruction and Development/World Bank et al.*, The Energy Progress Report 2020 – Tracking SDG 7 (2020), p. 4.

21 *International Energy Agency*, Africa Energy Outlook 2019, p. 113.

22 *United Nations*, Metadata for Goal 7, Ensure access to affordable, reliable, sustainable and modern energy for all, updated on 30 March 2016, p. 5, available under: https://unstats.un.org/sdgs/files/metadata-compilation/ Metadata-Goal-7.pdf (last accessed: 1 April 2020).

lution. Some 4 million premature deaths are caused each year by inhaling carbon monoxide and particulate matter from traditional biomass cook stoves.[23] Worldwide, about 2.8 billion people still lack access to clean and safe cooking fuels, such as gas and electricity. That number remained largely unchanged over the past two decades due to population growth outpacing the number of people gaining access to clean cooking fuels.[24]

In Europe and Northern America, over 95 percent of the population rely on clean fuels and technology,[25] while only 17 percent of the population in sub-Saharan Africa have access to clean fuels and technology.[26] From 2010 to 2018, in Eastern Asia and South-eastern Asia the number of people lacking access to clean fuels decreased from 1.0 billion to 0.8 billion.[27] In sub-Saharan Africa, however, due to a stagnating access rate and rapid population growth the number of people without access to clean fuels increased from 750 million people to 890 million.[28] Sub-Saharan Africa is the only region where the number of people without access to clean cooking facilities continues to rise significantly.[29]

From 2000 to 2014, the proportion of the global population with access to clean and safe fuels increased from 50 to 57 percent.[30] In 2018, 63 percent of the global population had access to clean cooking fuels and technologies.[31] However, current progress is far lower than the annual increase required for universal access by 2030.[32] The slow progress towards clean cooking is a cause for severe concern. Population growth outpaces the number of those gaining access to clean cooking fuels and technologies.[33]

---

23 *United Nations*, Sustainable Development Goals Report 2019 (2019), p. 36.

24 *International Bank for Reconstruction and Development/World Bank et al.*, The Energy Progress Report 2020 – Tracking SDG 7 (2020), p. 6.

25 *United Nations Economic and Social Council*, Progress towards the Sustainable Development Goals, Report of the Secretary-General, Supplementary Information, E/2017/66, revised on 28 September 2017, p. 64.

26 *International Energy Agency*, Africa Energy Outlook 2019. p. 37.

27 *International Bank for Reconstruction and Development/World Bank et al.*, The Energy Progress Report 2020 – Tracking SDG 7 (2020), p. 43.

28 *International Bank for Reconstruction and Development/World Bank et al.*, The Energy Progress Report 2020 – Tracking SDG 7 (2020), p. 43.

29 *International Energy Agency*, Africa Energy Outlook 2019. p. 37.

30 *United Nations*, Sustainable Development Goals Report 2017 (2017), p. 33.

31 *International Bank for Reconstruction and Development/World Bank et al.*, The Energy Progress Report 2020 – Tracking SDG 7 (2020), p. 43.

32 See *United Nations*, Sustainable Development Goals Report 2019 (2019), p. 36; *United Nations*, Sustainable Development Goals Report 2017 (2017), p. 33.

33 *International Bank for Reconstruction and Development/World Bank et. al.*, The Energy Progress Report 2020 – Tracking SDG 7 (2020), p. 43.

Without prompt action, it is estimated that 2.3 billion will still be deprived of access to clean cooking fuels by 2030.[34] Universal access will fall short for this SDG goal by almost 30 percent in 2030.[35]

3. *Renewable energy share in total final energy consumption*

From 2010 to 2016, the share of renewable energy in total final energy consumption grew modestly from 16.6 percent to 17.5 percent. Since 2011, renewable energy resources increased more rapidly than global energy consumption.[36] Most growth in renewable energy has been concentrated in the electricity sector due to the expansion of solar and wind power.[37] However, electricity makes up only 20 percent of the final energy use; 80 percent are consumed in the heat and transportation sectors.[38]

For the indicator "renewable energy share in the total final energy consumption", the comparison of Europe and Northern America with sub-Saharan Africa paints a picture that is contrary to the one observed for the indicators access to electricity and primary reliance on clean fuels. While in sub-Saharan Africa 69 percent of the total final energy consumption comes from renewables,[39] in Europe and Northern America this share is only about 12 percent.[40] It has to be noted, however, that the particularly high share of renewables in sub-Saharan Africa strongly reflects traditional uses of biomass[41] such as wood, charcoal, dung and agricultural waste.[42] In

34 *International Bank for Reconstruction and Development/World Bank et. al.*, The Energy Progress Report 2020 – Tracking SDG 7 (2020), p. 7 und p. 48.

35 *International Bank for Reconstruction and Development/World Bank et. al.*, The Energy Progress Report 2020 – Tracking SDG 7 (2020), p. 43.

36 *International Bank for Reconstruction and Development/World Bank et. al.*, The Energy Progress Report 2020 – Tracking SDG 7 (2020), p. 72.

37 *United Nations*, Sustainable Development Goals Report 2019 (2019), p. 37.

38 *United Nations*, Sustainable Development Goals Report 2019 (2019), p. 37.

39 *International Bank for Reconstruction and Development/World Bank et. al.*, The Energy Progress Report 2020 – Tracking SDG 7 (2020), p. 71.

40 *United Nations Economic and Social Council*, Progress towards the Sustainable Development Goals, Report of the Secretary-General, Supplementary Information, E/2017/66, revised on 28 September 2017, p. 65.

41 For a definition of „traditional uses of biomass" see *International Bank for Reconstruction and Development/World Bank et. al.*, The Energy Progress Report 2020 – Tracking SDG 7 (2020), p. 73.

42 *International Bank for Reconstruction and Development/World Bank/International Energy Agency*, Global Tracking Framework 2017, Progress toward Sustainable Energy, Summary (2017), p. 8. See also *International Bank for Reconstruction and Devel-*

sub-Saharan Africa, bioenergy made up almost 60 percent of primary energy use in 2018.[43] The findings clearly show that the current pace of clean energy progress falls short of what is needed to meet the sustainable energy development goal by 2030.[44] In order to limit global warming to well below 2 degrees Celsius and to pursue efforts to limit the temperature increase even further to 1.5, it is imperative to find a way to increase the share of renewable energy in the electricity, heat and transportation sectors, which together account for 80 percent of global energy consumption. The Secretary General's latest report on the Sustainable Development Goals concludes that *"if Sustainable Development Goals 7, 13 and related Goals are to be met, much higher levels of ambition are required with regard to renewable energy, including transportation and heating"*.[45]

IV. Answering the twin challenges of universal access to energy and climate change in Africa

Currently, Africa is the continent with the least access to energy, but – at the same time – it has a very high potential for renewable energy. Its potential of renewable energy power is by far larger than the current and projected power consumption.[46] Africa emits the least CO_2, but is one of the regions that is the most vulnerable to the adverse effects of climate change. The challenge to provide access to energy for all Africans offers the opportunity for Africa to leapfrog towards renewable energy systems that avoid carbon emissions. Africa has abundant renewable energy resources. These resources, including local geothermal, solar thermal and bioenergy, can be used to grant access to energy also in rural areas.

The African Renewable Energy Initiative (AREI) is committed to accelerating access to renewable energy in Africa. This Africa-owned initiative is

---

opment/World Bank et. al., The Energy Progress Report 2020 – Tracking SDG 7 (2020), p. 73.

43 *International Energy Agency*, Africa Energy Outlook 2019. p. 74.

44 *International Bank for Reconstruction and Development/World Bank/International Energy Agency*, Global Tracking Framework 2017, Progress toward Sustainable Energy, Summary (2017), p. 10.; *International Bank for Reconstruction and Development/ World Bank et. al.*, The Energy Progress Report 2020 – Tracking SDG 7 (2020), p. 71.

45 *United Nations Economic and Social Council*, Report of the Secretary General: Progress towards the Sustainable Development Goals, E/2019/68, 8. Mai 2019, no. 28.

46 *International Energy Agency*, Africa Energy Outlook 2019. p. 72.

led by the African Union's commission, the New Partnership for Africa's Development (NEPAD)'s Agency, the African Group of Negotiators, the African Development Bank, the UN Environment Program (UNEP) and the International Renewable Energy Agency (IRENA). It aims to achieve at least 10 gigawatts of new and additional renewable energy generation capacity by 2020, and to mobilize 300 gigawatts by 2030.[47] This would considerably contribute to closing the energy access gap in Africa. The African Renewable Energy Initiative has two over-arching goals. The first goal is to help achieve sustainable development, enhance well-being and sound economic development by ensuring universal access to sufficient amounts of clean, appropriate and affordable energy. The AREI's second goal is to help African countries leapfrog towards renewable energy systems that support their low carbon development strategies while enhancing economic and energy security.[48] The Initiative aims not only to expand electricity access for households, but also to provide sufficient energy to drive development of the productive sector, thus fostering economic development in the different countries. Thereby, AREI intends to answer the twin challenges for Africa of granting energy access for all and combatting climate change at the same time.

In the energy sector, centralized power plants and transmission grids are the traditional way to grant access to energy. It often takes a long time until large-scale centralized energy projects deliver service. In contrast, decentralised energy based on renewables offers a faster path to energy access for the unelectrified.[49] Solar home systems and mini-grids provide alternatives, particularly for rural areas. Throughout a diversified ownership system, a larger number of households, communities as well as small and medium-sized enterprises can participate in this process towards sustainable development. The people using these alternatives can become prosumers, who consume as well as produce energy. Small and medium-sized enterprises, municipalities and citizens may set up green energy supply systems. Energy cooperatives can foster this process by creating a diversified ownership system. The overall aim must not only be to ensure the bare minimum requirements of electricity access for households and families, but also to allow for a level of energy access that is sufficient to drive the

47 *African Renewable Energy Initiative (AREI)*, Transforming Africa towards a renewable energy powered future with access for all, Summary (August 2016), p. 3.

48 *African Renewable Energy Initiative (AREI)*, Transforming Africa towards a renewable energy powered future with access for all, Summary (August 2016), p. 4.

49 *Power for All*, Decentralised Renewables: The Fast Track to Universal Energy Access (2016), p. 4.

productive sectors including micro-, small- and medium-sized enterprises.[50] Renewable energy resources offer the opportunity for Africa to jump directly to people-centred, distributed renewable energy supply systems and to avoid CO_2 emissions at the same time. Through this integrated approach, the Sustainable Development Goals as well as the goals of the Paris Agreement can be reached through the same means.[51]

Installing renewable energy generation capacity demands specific investments. In 2020, the European Commission and the High Representative for Foreign Affairs and Security Policy proposed a new strategy for Africa to intensify cooperation between the European Union and the African Union. It aims to maximise the benefits of green transition and to increase substantially environmentally, socially and financially sustainable investments that are resilient to the impacts of climate change.[52]

For renewable energies, the initial investment costs are comparably high, while the operation costs tend to be low. Therefore, decentralised clean energy projects for Africa need funding as well as a sound legal framework that guarantees investment security.[53] Suitable regulatory frameworks can accelerate the diffusion of green energy systems in Africa. In order to harness the continent's renewable energy potential, substantial financial resources from private investors, development finance institutions and multilateral development banks are needed. Good investment conditions, including suitable legal frameworks, are a prerequisite for obtaining these financial resources. The African Renewable Energy Initiative aims to strengthen regulatory and policy frameworks in order to enable investments in renewable energy generation in Africa with a vastly expanded and diversified ownership base.[54]

---

50 *African Renewable Energy Initiative (AREI)*, Transforming Africa towards a renewable energy powered future with access for all, Summary (August 2016), p. 4.

51 See *German Federal Ministry for Economic Cooperation and Development*, Green people's energy for Africa (2017), p. 8.

52 See *European Commission / High Representative of the Union for Foreign Affairs and Security Policy*, Joint Communication to the European Parliament and the Council: Towards a comprehensive Strategy with Africa, 9.3.2020, JOIN(2020) 4 final.

53 See *German Federal Ministry for Economic Cooperation and Development*, Green people's energy for Africa (2017), p. 5.

54 *African Renewable Energy Initiative (AREI)*, Transforming Africa towards a renewable energy powered future with access for all, Summary (August 2016), p. 9.

V. Regulatory Indicators for Sustainable Energy (RISE)

The World Bank estimates that more than a trillion dollars of annual investments are needed to achieve the global energy goals.[55] One of the fundamental questions in implementing the clean energy goal is how to generate investment in renewable energies. Energy investment is affected by many factors including market size, country risk and financial markets. In addition, one of the core elements needed to create an investment friendly climate is a robust regulatory framework. By providing investment security and mechanisms to build, finance and run the generation of renewable energies, the right set of policies and regulations can contribute to attracting private investment in the energy sector.

One instrument that allows governments to assess if they have a policy and regulatory framework in place to drive progress on clean energy is the "Regulatory Indicators for Sustainable Energy" (RISE) developed by the World Bank. With 27 indicators, RISE covers 133 countries representing 97 percent of the world population.[56] RISE indicators are one of the results of the "Sustainable Energy for All" initiative (SEforALL) and its knowledge hub. Former UN Secretary-General *Ban Ki-moon* launched this global initiative in 2011 to mobilize action in order to ensure universal access to modern energy services, to double the share of renewable energy in the global energy mix and to double the global rate of improvement in energy efficiency.[57] Thereby, SEforALL contributes to realizing the goal of access to clean energy for all and supports the Paris Agreement.

RISE classifies countries into strong, middling and weaker performers based on their regulatory framework for energy access, energy efficiency and renewable energy. This classification allows policymakers to benchmark and improve their regulatory frameworks.[58] The 27 RISE indicators include the existence, scope and the monitoring of officially approved electrification plans, a framework for grid electrification, minigrids and for stand-alone systems, the affordability of electricity for consumers and the

---

55 *International Bank for Reconstruction and Development/World Bank/International Energy Agency*, Global Tracking Framework 2015, Progress toward Sustainable Energy (2015), p. XIV.

56 See *International Bank for Reconstruction and Development*, RISE - Regulatory Indicators for Sustainable Energy, 2018, p. 5.

57 See *Sustainable Energy for All*, About us, available under: http://www.se4all.org/about-us (last accessed: 1 April 2020).

58 *International Bank for Reconstruction and Development*, RISE - Regulatory Indicators for Sustainable Energy, 2018, p. II.

transparency of the generation companies. Furthermore, it evaluates the national energy efficiency planning, the information provided to consumers about electricity usage, possible incentives from electricity rate structures, financing mechanisms for energy efficiency, energy labelling systems and carbon pricing. With a view to renewable energy, RISE monitors the legal framework for renewable energy, the planning for renewable energy expansion, incentives and regulatory support for renewable energy as well as financial and regulatory incentives.

According to RISE assessments, the good news is that there has been a substantial increase in the number of countries adopting advanced policy frameworks in support of sustainable energy. 44 percent have implemented advanced policy frameworks, while 19 percent still have undeveloped policy frameworks in place.[59] However, in Sub-Saharan Africa, around half of the countries have undeveloped policy frameworks.[60] This result presents a particular challenge as Africa is the least electrified continent and home to about 600 million people without electricity. In 2015, 70 percent of Africa's least electrified nations – those nations with access rates below 20 percent of the population – had barely begun to establish an investment friendly environment for energy access.[61] Some sub-Saharan countries have rather strong policy frameworks in place and are, correspondingly, atop of the list of strong RISE-performers in their region. In 2017, three countries located in sub-Saharan Africa were among the top ten improvers in RISE since 2010.[62] Cote d'Ivoire, for example, has made the fastest progress on sustainable energy policies according to the 2018 RISE index.[63] However, still too many countries especially in sub-Saharan Africa are lagging substantially behind.[64] Agenda 2030 promises to leave no one behind. In order to provide access to clean energy to all Africans by 2030, efforts have to be intensified.

---

59 *International Bank for Reconstruction and Development*, RISE - Regulatory Indicators for Sustainable Energy, 2018, p. 13.

60 *International Bank for Reconstruction and Development*, RISE - Regulatory Indicators for Sustainable Energy, 2018, p. 15.

61 *International Bank for Reconstruction and Development*, RISE 2016, Regulatory Indicators for Sustainable Development, A Global Scoreboard for Policy Makers (2017), p. XVIII.

62 *International Bank for Reconstruction and Development*, RISE - Regulatory Indicators for Sustainable Energy, 2018, p. 19.

63 *International Bank for Reconstruction and Development*, RISE - Regulatory Indicators for Sustainable Energy, 2018, p. 20.

64 *International Bank for Reconstruction and Development*, RISE - Regulatory Indicators for Sustainable Energy, 2018, p. 16.

To implement this, renewable energy generation has to play a major role. It offers the opportunity for Africa to setting up clean energy systems that avoid carbon emissions. It can lead to decentralised energy generation with diversified ownership systems. However, investments in renewables depend on suitable regulatory and policy frameworks for clean energy. One focus of the efforts needed to achieve the goal of clean energy for all should therefore be to strengthen regulatory and policy frameworks to enable investments in renewable energy generation especially in Africa.

VI. Conclusion

The international community is not yet on track to reach the Sustainable Development Goal to grant access to clean energy for all. In some regions of the world, vast improvements have to be made in order to achieve the goal. To tackle this pressing issue and realize the Sustainable Development Goals within the next ten years, investments on scales considerably larger than currently seen must be undertaken. However, and this concerns the African nations more than other regions in the world, money alone will not suffice. Instead, a solid legal framework is needed to warrant investment security, thereby attracting potential investors and giving local communities the ability to run decentralised, self-sufficient mini-grids with diverse ownership systems. Clean energy for all is possible, in dimensions not only satisfying basic needs, but also boosting economic drivers in the world's least developed regions. In order to reach this ambitious goal, the world must continue to recognize the significant role of energy as a key resource for sustainable development.

Securing of Resources as a Valid Reason for Using Force? A Pre-Emptive Defence of the Prohibition on the Use of Force[1]

Heike Krieger and Jonas Püschmann***

Abstract

A growing demand for natural resources embedded in current changes of the international order will put pressure on states to secure the future availability of these resources. Some political discourses suggest that states might respond by challenging the foundations of international law. Whereas the UN Charter was inter alia aimed at eliminating uses of force for economic reasons, one may observe an ongoing trend of securitization of matters of resource supply resulting into the revival of self-preservation doctrines. The chapter will show that those claims lack a normative foundation in the current framework of the prohibition of the use of force. Instead, international law has sufficient instruments to cope with disputes over access to resources by other means than the use of force. The international community, therefore, must oppose claims that may contribute to normative uncertainties and strengthen already existing instruments of pacific settlement of disputes.

Overview

---

1 Sincere thanks to the members of the Berlin Potsdam Research Group "The International Rule of Law – Rise or Decline?" for their valuable feedback on this chapter.

* Prof. Dr., Professor of Public Law and International Law at Freie Universität Berlin; Max Planck Fellow at Max Planck Institute for Comparative Public Law and International Law.

** Ass. iur., Research Fellow at Max Planck Institute for Comparative Public Law and International Law.

I. Introduction

In its 2010 Global Strategic Trends report, the UK Ministry of Defence forecasted that

> *"[t]he issue of energy security is one in which governments, and defence organizations, will increasingly have to be engaged if states are to maintain their standards of living, and to ensure adequate supplies of natural resources, at reasonable prices. States who perceive that energy security is impacting on national survival are likely to challenge conventional interpretations on the legality of the use of force. However, the cornerstone of the UN Charter, which prohibits the threat, or use, of force in international relations, will remain firmly in place".*[2]

In an ambivalent language the report suggests that, in view of a changing security environment, the prohibition on the use of force may undergo interpretative shifts which threaten to affect its normative strength. The general expectation that the prohibition of the use of force, as well as its steering function, will be undermined in years to come is formulated more explicitly in the 2018 Global Strategic Trends report where it is stated that

2 *Development, Concepts and Doctrine Centre*, The DCDC Global Strategic Trends Programme (4th edition 2010), p. 107, available under: https://espas.secure.europarl.europa.eu/orbis/sites/default/files/generated/document/en/GST4_v9_Feb10.pdf (last accessed: 8 August 2020).

> *"[c]hanges to laws governing the use of force in international relations are [...] expected over the coming decades. [...] The general prohibition on the use of force is almost certain to remain in place, but it may be progressively challenged and narrowed in scope. This could in turn lead to increased tensions and a greater tendency to resort to military action to settle disputes"*.[3]

This assessment written for the purposes of strategic government policies reflects current discussions in academic discourse. While most academic observers hold that, despite certain contestations, the prohibition of the use of force remains unchallenged in its legal validity,[4] there are indications for an erosion of the prohibition: Different strands of challenges intersect, seriously threatening to undermine the prohibition on the use of force. From a legal perspective, such a process of norm erosion consists of various legally relevant phenomena which reduce the legal effects of a prohibition. For example, restrictive readings of the constitutive elements of a prohibition as well as extensive readings of its exceptions may reduce its scope and thereby its legal effects.[5]

Pertinent cases concern efforts to establish a broad interpretation of the right of self-defence against non-state actors as an exception to the prohibition on the use of force which threatens to swallow the rule. The same applies to new threats resulting from modern technologies and growing dependency on the cyber-space that have the potential to fundamentally change the prohibition of the use of force in general as the 2018 UK report predicts.[6] Also, more expansive readings of Art. 39 UN Charter will at least

---

3 *Development, Concepts and Doctrine Centre*, Global Strategic Trends – The Future Starts Today (6th edition, 2018), p. 130, available under: https://assets.publishing.service.gov.uk/government/uploads/system/uploads/attachment_data/file/771309/Global_Strategic_Trends_-_The_Future_Starts_Today.pdf (last accessed: 8 August 2020).

4 See *e.g.*, *Marxsen*, Violation and confirmation of the law: the intricate effects of the invocation of the law in armed conflict, in: Journal on the Use of Force and International Law 5 (2018), p. 8; *Gray*, International Law and the Use of Force (4th edition 2018), pp. 26 *et seqq.*; *Henderson*, The Use of Force and International Law (2018), p. 47.

5 *Cf. Krieger/Liese*, A Metamorphosis of International Law?: Value Changes in the International Legal Order From the Perspectives of Legal and Political Science, in: KFG Working Paper Series 27, Berlin Potsdam Research Group "The International Rule of Law – Rise or Decline?" (2019), p. 12; *Aust/Payandeh*, Praxis und Protest im Völkerrecht: Erosionserscheinungen des völkerrechtlichen Gewaltverbots und die Verantwortung der Bundesrepublik im Syrien-Konflikt, in: JuristenZeitung 73 (2018), p. 633 (635 *et seqq.*).

6 *Development, Concepts and Doctrine Centre* (fn. 3).

have an indirect impact on Art. 2 (4) UN Charter by potentially opening more and more policy areas to military solutions.

Within the context of global resource allocation and scarcity, another process of erosion of the prohibition of the use of force starts to emerge. Whilst interstate conflicts arguably always had been linked to resources and securing trade, the acquisition of resources had mostly neither been the primary purpose nor been advanced as a legal justification for a conflict. However, the effects of climate change and a rise of global demand for certain resources may render securing natural resources to a primary reason for waging war. For example, UN-Water reports point out that around four billion people already experience severe physical water scarcity at least one month a year and it is projected that by 2050, 3.1 billion people will live under severe water stress.[7] At the same time, water resources are rarely a domestic good but to a large extent shared among two or more states requiring long-term cooperation.[8] On the demand side, the expected establishment of "new global players" such as China and India with a fast-growing economy as well as a growing population will increase the need for resources. At the same time, for strategic sources, such as oil, the existence of a peak in supply is controversially debated.[9]

While international law has developed frameworks to manage the scarcity of resources through instruments of bi- or multilateral cooperation and peaceful settlement of disputes, where cooperation seems unlikely, violent disputes over territory and investments may rise. According to the 2020 Conflict Barometer of the Heidelberg Institute for International Conflict Research, resources are among the leading causes for conflicts with a total number of 59 conflicts ranging from low-intensity conflicts to fully-

---

7 *UN-Water*, The United Nations Water Development Report 2021: Valuing Water (2021), pp. 13, 45.

8 International river basins cover 45.3 percent of the earth's land surface, affect about 40 percent of the world's population, and account for approximately 80 percent of global river flows, see *FAO*, Transboundary Waters, available under: http://www.fao.org/land-water/water/water-management/transboundary-water-management/en/ (last accessed: 8 August 2020).

9 The so called "Hubbert's peak" refers to the point at which this production rate is at its highest with demand for the resource rising, and after this it predicts a drop in correlation to the increased demand. Nevertheless, the trend towards such a peak had been called into question: *DNV GL*, Energy Transition Outlook 2019 – Oil and Gas (2019), p. 35: "The world's energy landscape is now heading for a peak in oil demand rather than supply."

fledged armed conflicts[10] and have been among the main causes for conflicts in 2019.[11] Parties to such conflicts may try to justify the use of force to secure "their" resources, challenging traditional understandings of the prohibition of the use of force as the prognosis of the 2010 UK Global Strategic Trends report suggests.

This chapter will examine whether there are indications in state practice and legal discourse for a creeping erosion of the prohibition on the use of force in relation to conflicts over natural resources. It will be shown that the absolute prohibition of the use of force under the UN Charter, *inter alia*, was aimed to ban specifically these types of armed conflicts. In a second step, the chapter will analyse how norm erosion is fostered and will assess such processes against the backdrop of the legal framework of the *ius ad bellum*.[12]

II. Banning Resource Conflicts by Banning Measures Short of War

The absolute prohibition of the use of force under the UN Charter and its aim to specifically ban armed conflicts over natural resources must be read against the backdrop of state practice of the late 18th and early 20th century. Access to and securing of resources served, alongside an alleged mission to civilize the world, as an authorization of the use of force towards "non-civilized people".[13] In the context of colonialization, measures to secure resources and foreign investments without an occupation of territory would have likely been characterized as "police measures" or "measures short of war".[14] "Measures short of war" were defined as one-sided acts of war in the sense of material armed clashes without the intention of a state of war.[15] In the form of reprisals, they were seen as a form of self-help that

10 Heidelberg Institute for International Conflict Research, Conflict Barometer 2020 (2021), p. 19.

11 Heidelberg Institute for International Conflict Research, Conflict Barometer 2019 (2020), p. 16.

12 This chapter will limit itself to the *ius ad bellum* framework against state actors, leaving aside especially the *ius ad bellum* relationship to non-state actors and the *ius in bello* framework.

13 *von Bernstorff*, The Use of Force in International Law before World War I, in: European Journal of International Law 29 (2018), p. 233 (245).

14 *von Bernstorff* (fn. 13), pp. 241 *et seq.*, 248.

15 *Neff*, War and the Law of Nations: A General History (2005), pp. 173, 175, 215 *et seqq.*

allowed the resort to military force against unlawful acts.[16] In the form of necessity they served to protect a fundamental value of a state, in particular its survival.[17] These measures were linked to the overall environment of a developing global economy and the spirit of imperialism prevalent in that era.

As an early example, a UK council order of 1795 allowed cruisers to seize and detain all vessels, laden, wholly or in part with corn, flour, meal, and other articles of provisions, which were bound for any port in France, and to send them to ports in the UK where the load could be purchased by the government. The UK justified these measures before a UK-US Maritime Claims Commission, *inter alia*, on the grounds of necessity, since the country was threatened by a scarcity of such resources.[18] Moreover, "Western" countries resorted to armed interventions for the protection of foreign investments in South America and East Asia as "measures short of war", in the form of armed reprisals against alleged wrongdoings.[19] For instance, the US, in defending its influence over the (South)-American states, followed such an interventionist approach formulated by the former US President *Roosevelt* in the so-called Roosevelt-Corollary to the Monroe Doctrine.[20]

After World War I, although the 1928 Briand – Kellogg Pact, in its Art. 1, condemned recourse to war, those measures were not fully outlawed because the pact lacked a definition of self-defence and left its assessment to the invoking state.[21] During the Pact's negotiations, the UK expressly made a reservation for actions against interference in "certain regions of the world the welfare and integrity of which constitute a special

16 *Neff* (fn. 15), p. 226.

17 *Neff* (fn. 15), p. 240.

18 *Wheaton*, Elements of International Law (5th edition 1916), pp. 724 *et seqq.*

19 *von Bernstorff* (fn. 13), p. 242.

20 *Roosevelt*, Annual Message to Congress, 6 December 1904, available under: www.ourdocuments.gov/doc.php?ash=true&doc=56&page=transcript (last accessed: 8 August 2020).

21 This is indicated in the *travaux préparatoires*, see: Note by Mr. Atherton to Sir Austen Chamberlain from 23rd June 1928, available under: http://avalon.law.yale.edu/20th_century/kbbr.asp#no1 (last accessed: 8 August 2020): "Every nation is free at all times and regardless of treaty provisions, to defend its territories from attack or invasion, and it alone is competent to decide whether circumstances require recourse to war in self-defence".

and vital interest for our peace and safety".[22] The motive for this reservation was to make clear that self-defence covers securing access to India via interventions in vital regions such as Egypt, Afghanistan and the Persian Gulf where no other great power should gain influence.[23]

Shortly before and during World War II, the war over resources was finally culminating due to the absence of a clear prohibition. Japan argued that it was being economically strangled by US sanctions resulting from its invasion of Manchuria and French Indochina. It claimed that it was left with no other choice than to preserve its military advantage by attacking the US in Pearl Harbour and was therefore justified to wage war in the Pacific.[24] However, the International Military Tribunal for the Far East rejected this justification.[25] Even before, the Assembly of the League of Nations refused to accept that the Japanese invasion of Manchuria in 1931 in reaction to a Chinese economic boycott of Japan could be considered as legitimate self-defence.[26]

The paradigm shift to an absolute prohibition of the use of force was brought about by the drafters of the UN Charter which aimed at limiting self-defence for economic reasons. In the literature it is argued that the drafters had the Axis powers in mind, and the excuse those states had used. Both powers had made self-defence claims in the World War II: *Lebensraum* in the case of Germany, and access to natural resources in the case of Japan.[27]

Securing access to resources by means of using force against another country would now clearly constitute a violation of the prohibition of the use of force in Art. 2 (4) UN Charter and under customary international

---

22 *Chamberlain*, Note of 19 May 1928, cited after: *Lesaffer*, Kellogg-Briand Pact 1928, in: Wolfrum, Max Planck Encyclopedia of Public International Law (2010), para. 12.

23 *McKercher*, The Second Baldwin Government and the United States, 1924–1929: Attitudes and Diplomacy (1984), pp. 117 *et seq.* citing an explanation of the motivation by former UK Foreign Minister *Chamberlain*.

24 *Röling/Rüter*, The Tokyo Judgement – The International Military Tribunal for the Far East, 29 April 1946 – 12 November 1948, Vol. II (1977), p. 616.

25 *Röling/Rüter*, The Tokyo Judgement – The International Military Tribunal for the Far East, 29 April 1946 – 12 November 1948, Vol. I (1977), pp. 380 *et seq.*; *Brownlie*, The Use of Force in Self-Defence, in: British Year Book of International Law 37 (1961), p. 183 (220).

26 *League of Nations*, League of Nations Assembly Report on the Sino-Japanese Dispute, in: American Journal of International Law 27 (1933), Supplement: Official Documents, p. 119 (145 *et seq.*).

27 *O'Connel/Niyatzmatov*, What is Aggression, in: Journal of International Criminal Justice 10 (2012), p. 189 (193).

law.[28] Art. 2 (4) UN Charter proscribes the "threat or use of force against the territorial integrity or political independence of any state, or in any other manner inconsistent with the Purposes of the United Nations". The use of military force to acquire economic resources or territory of another state clearly constitutes such a case.[29] The historical exception for "measures short of war" that do contain uses of force without the intent of occupation is no longer accepted under the UN Charter. "Territorial integrity or political independence" is not to be understood as restricting the application of the use of force, but setting out examples for certain violations.[30] At an early stage, the ICJ strengthened this understanding and rejected arguments for "measures short of war" in the Corfu Channel Case, arguing that

> *"[…] the alleged right of intervention as the manifestation of a policy of force, such as has, in the past, given rise to most serious abuses and such as cannot, whatever be the present defects in international organization, find a place in international law. [Such] [i]ntervention would be reserved for the most powerful States, and might easily lead to perverting the administration of international justice itself"*.[31]

Thereby, the ICJ acknowledged that "measures short of war" were no longer a permissible exception to the prohibition of the use of force and closed the option for unilaterally securing natural resources or protecting trade interests through military means.

Despite the absolute prohibition of the use of force, attempts to justify military intervention on the basis of securing access to resources continued, following the logic of "measures short of war".[32] In 1956, for example, the nationalization of the Suez Canal resulted in the Suez crisis over securing access to resources through the Suez Canal and finally led to France, the UK, and Israel attacking Egypt. While UN member states accused

---

28 *International Court of Justice*, Judgement of 26 November 1984, Military and Paramilitary Activities in and against Nicaragua (Nicaragua v. United States of America), I.C.J. Reports (1984), pp. 424 *et seq*.

29 See *e.g.*, *Saul/Kinley/Mowbray*, The International Covenant on Economic, Social and Cultural Rights (2014), p. 105.

30 *Cf. Brownlie* (fn. 25), p. 235.

31 *International Court of Justice*, Judgement of 9 April 1949, Corfu Channel Case (United Kingdom of Great Britain and Northern Ireland v. Albania), I.C.J. Reports (1949), p. 35.

32 See *e.g.*, *Brownlie* (fn. 25), p. 213.

France and the UK of a flagrant violation of international law[33] both states argued to have a legitimate claim of securing access to resources. They described their intervention as an "emergency police force" to protect the Suez Canal which did not aim at affecting the sovereignty of Egypt.[34] As another case in point, during the Oil Crisis in 1973, the US publicly considered seizing oil fields in the Persian Gulf. In an interview, US State Secretary *Kissinger* replied to a question, whether the US considered the use of military force in response to the embargo:

> "*I am not saying that there's no circumstance where we would not use force. But it is one thing to use it in the case of a dispute over price; it's another where there is some actual strangulation of the industrialized world*".[35]

This response implied, that there are military options in case of an "actual strangulation".

More specifically, scholars currently observe an all-time high of conflicts over water resources under the keyword "water wars". The term "water wars" usually describes a broad range of conflicts over shared water resources, ranging from a shared ocean, shared rivers or basins to shared groundwater resources. The concept covers military as well as non-military conflicts. Despite criticism that, until now, in modern times, no inter-state conflict had been carried out by military means solely based on access to water,[36] words and behaviour of states suggest the opposite: in 2019, tensions arose again between India and Pakistan over withdrawal from the Indus Water Treaty, governing each nation's share of the transboundary

---

33 See *United Nations General Assembly*, Record of the Meetings, United Nations General Assembly's First Emergency Special Session, 01.11.1957, UN Doc. A/PV.562, *i.a.* paras. 21 (Philippines), 43 (Syria), 186 (Ecuador), 314 (Union of South Africa), 337 (Poland), 352 (Indonesia).

34 See United Nations General Assembly (fn. 33), para. 201.

35 See *Willner*, The 1975 Congressional Feasibility Study on "Oil Fields as Military Objectives": U.S.–Saudi Arabian relations and the repercussions of the 1973 Oil Crisis, in: The Journal of the Middle East and Africa 9 (2018), p. 121 (127).

36 Arguing the last "real" water war broke out 4500 years ago between the Mesopotamian city-states Lagash and Umma, see: *Pacific Institute*, Water Conflict Chronology List, available under: http://www.worldwater.org/conflict/list/ (last accessed: 8 August 2020); *Magsig*, International Water Law and the Quest for Common Security (2015), p. 20; *Neuber/Scheumann*, Kein Blut für Wasser, in: Internationale Politik 3 (2003), p. 31 (31–38); *Kunig*, Konflikte um das Wasser – Was sagt das Völkerrecht (2004), available under: https://www.fu-berlin.de/presse/publikationen/fundiert/archiv/2004_02/04_02_kunig/index.html (last accessed: 8 August 2020).

rivers.[37] Moreover, violent conflicts may be expected between Ethiopia and Egypt over the construction and operation of the Grand Ethiopian Renaissance Dam at the Blue Nile. In all those cases, there is a certain discrepancy between the UN Charter regime and the official rhetoric of certain states which may contribute to processes of norm erosion.

III. Initiating Processes of Norm Erosion

Processes of norm erosion may, *inter alia*, be initiated by certain argumentative techniques, which include arguments of securitization and legitimacy. Securitization can be described as a process of turning something into an existential threat for a community thereby justifying exceptional measures. Turning a policy field into a matter of national security had been the "key to legitimizing the use of force" because "traditionally, by saying 'security', a state representative declares an emergency condition, thus claiming a right to use whatever means are necessary to block a threatening development".[38]

1. Invoking Arguments of Securitization and Legitimacy

In this context, a securitization of access to natural resources arguably takes place. Such a securitization can, for example, be seen in the context of "energy security". States prepare for resource scarcity in think tanks and official publications by turning it into a matter of national security. For this line of argument, they can rely on well-established perceptions. For instance, already in 1984, the ECJ found that petroleum products are of fundamental importance for the existence of a country and therefore affect

---

37 For the latest call in the media to "scrap the Indus Water Treaty" after the armed conflict between India and Pakistan in 2019, see *JhunJhunwala*, Scrap the Indus Water Treaty (2019), available under: http://www.dailyexcelsior.com/a-leaf-from-history-tribute-to-those-who-saved-ladakh/ (last accessed: 8 August 2020): "[…] we should consider using water as an instrument of war. The total river water available in Pakistan is 145 million acre feet (MAF). Of this the Indus river system provides 113 MAF. India allocated the water of three […] rivers totalling 80 MAF to Pakistan under the Indus Water Treaty"; *Prakash*, Abrogate Indus Water Treaty (2019), available under: https://www.thehansindia.com/posts/index/My-Voice/2019-03-06/Abrogate-Indus-Water-Treaty/508347 (last accessed: 8 August 2020).

38 *Buzan/Waever/de Wilde*, Security – A New Framework for Analysis (1998), p. 21.

public security.[39] Today, many national security strategies predict a rise of conflicts due to water scarcity as well as an increased risk for energy security because resources for energy production are imported from countries considered unstable. The strategies often use language that includes the vague possibility of deploying forces or intervening to secure resources.[40]

Securitization is frequently linked to legitimacy arguments which are related to concepts of self-preservation and preserving defence capabilities when it comes to access to natural resources. In the literature, it is already claimed that securing resources, in particular water, is a legitimate ground for using force.[41] Based on just war theories, it has been argued in moral terms that

> *"[g]uided by a broad rationale that a secure state is a morally better alternative to a failed state, which is the presumed outcome of a serious strategic threat, the defence of a resource, even a downstream water supply [...] appears plausible"*.[42]

Arguments of "self-preservation" refer to an overall concept of necessity where all means are valid for a state when the very existence of itself and its

39 *European Court of Justice*, Judgement of 10.07.1984, C-72/83, ECLI:EU:C:1984:256 (Campus Oil Limited), para. 34: "It should be stated in this connection that petroleum products, because of their exceptional importance as an energy source in the modern economy, are of fundamental importance for a country's existence since not only its economy but above all its institutions, its essential public services and even the survival of its inhabitants depend upon them".

40 See *e.g.*, *Henken*, Knapper werdende Rohstoffe – Eine Quelle für Aufrüstungen und Kriegsplanungen, in: *Österreichisches Studienzentrum für Friedens- und Konfliktforschung*, Von kalten Energiestrategien zu heißen Rohstoffkriegen? (2008), pp. 203 *et seq*.; *North Atlantic Treaty Organisation*, Strategic Concept for the Defence and Security of the Members of the North Atlantic Treaty Organisation (2012), paras. 13, 15, 19 (indent 13), available under: https://www.nato.int/strategic-concept/pdf/Strat_Concept_web_en.pdf (last accessed: 8 August 2020); *Germany*, Weißbuch zur Sicherheitspolitik (2016), pp. 41 *et seq*., 50; *UK*, National Security Strategy and Strategic Defence and Security Review (2015), pp. 21, 44; *US*, National Security Strategy (2017), pp. 22 *et seq*.; *France*, Defence and National Security Strategic Review (2017), pp. 29 *et seq*.; *Russia*, Russian National Security Strategy (2016), paras. 13, 57, 61, available under: http://www.ieee.es/Galerias/fichero/OtrasPublicaciones/Internacional/2016/Russian-National-Security-Strategy-31Dec2015.pdf (last accessed: 8 August 2020); *China*, China's Military Strategy (2015), available under: http://www.chinadaily.com.cn/china/2015-05/26/content_20820628.htm (last accessed: 8 August 2020).

41 *Waddington*, Reconciling Just War Theory and Water-Related Conflict, in: International Journal of Applied Philosophy 26 (2012), p. 197 (209).

42 *Waddington* (fn. 41), p. 201.

people are at stake. In this sense, resources such as water are usually tied to the most basic needs of life. Other resources, such as oil, are as well seen to be necessary for manufacturing and transporting goods as well as providing energy.[43] Moreover, in light of the importance of strategic resources, an intervention aimed at the preservation of defence capabilities alludes to a kind of pre-emptive use of force. The rationale behind this argument follows the idea that when a state is deprived of its necessary resources through actions by a third state, this hostile act might aim at lowering the defence capability of the state. As a result, and after a certain time, this third state could then easily take over the other state.[44]

Arguments on the legitimacy of the use of force open space for legal development in this respect. Where states rely on legitimacy arguments they (implicitly) challenge the positive law or claim that under exceptional circumstance the law does not apply to them. Such claims may incite legal developments aimed at reducing the dissonance between legality and legitimacy.[45] However, Art. 2 (4) UN Charter contains an absolute prohibition of the use of force. Since the prohibition is a fundamental principle of international law as *ius cogens*, each exception to it requires high scrutiny to avoid that the prohibition will be deprived of its function. Therefore, one must be cautious about whether existing legal conditions are in general open for broadening exceptions and thereby contributing to processes of norm erosion, even if legitimate grounds could morally justify the use of force. Securing of resources as a legitimate reason for using force may either be justified by a Security Council authorization under Chapter VII (2.), as use of self-defence (3.) or under the concept of necessity (4.).

43 *Waddington* (fn. 41), pp. 201 *et seq*., but arguing that economic hardships are much slower to drive a population to a breaking point than starvation and dehydration.

44 *Cf. Sinnot-Armstrong*, Preventive War, What is it Good For?, in: Shue/Rodin (eds.), Preemption – Military Action and Moral Justification (2007), p. 214.

45 *Marauhn*, The International Rule of Law in Light of Legitimacy Claims, in: Krieger/Nolte/Zimmermann (eds.), The International Rule of Law - Rise or Decline (2019), p. 286, quoting: *Popovsky*, Legality and Legitimacy of International Criminal Tribunals, in: Falk/Juergensmeyer/Popovsky (eds.), Legality and Legitimacy in Global Affairs (2012), p. 407. On dissonance reduction as a driving force for legal change see *Reinold*, The Prohibition on the Use of Force: Plus ça change? Toward a theory of global normative change, in: Krieger/Liese (eds.), A Metamorphosis of International Law, forthcoming.

2. *UN Security Council Authorization under Chapter VII*

The ability of the UN Security Council to authorize military force in disputes over natural resources is the alternative to unilateral and thus more destabilizing measures by states involved in such a conflict. In the exercise of these powers, Security Council involvement in disputes over natural resources may arise at three different stages of conflict.

a) *Disputes over Natural Resources*

In one scenario, conflicts over resources are already in a state of military conflict or are about to develop into this direction. In such cases, the Security Council is acting within its primary responsibility to preserve peace. A case in point is the conflict over the Heglig oil field between Sudan and South Sudan in 2012.[46] Acting under Chapter VII UN Charter, the Security Council adopted Resolution 2046 in which the Council

> "*decided that Sudan and South Sudan shall unconditionally resume negotiations, [...] in consultation with relevant international partners, but within no more than two weeks from the time of adoption of this resolution, to reach agreement on [...inter alia] arrangements concerning oil and associated payments*".[47]

In such a constellation, the Security Council would be the competent body to even authorize the use of force to enforce its resolutions.

In a second scenario, a military conflict is not immediate but a political dispute about the allocation of resources exists. In view of the wide and unspecific concept of "threat" to peace, it remains questionable as to what extent measures under Chapter VII could be taken in such a case. A wide conception of "threat to peace" would involve general threats that entail only a distant risk of leading to armed conflict. In this respect, competencies and functions of the Security Council under Chapter VII of the UN Charter have constantly been widened. Based on a substantive definition of peace, the Security Council has broadened its activities to deal with threats to peace in the early stages of conflict prevention even under Chap-

---

46 On the conflict, see *Johnson*, The Heglig oil dispute between Sudan and South Sudan, in: Journal of Eastern African Studies 6 (2012), p. 561.

47 *United Nations Security Council*, Resolution 2046 adopted on 02.05.2012, UN Doc. S/RES/2046.

ter VII. Since Resolution 688, the determination of a threat to peace moves away from direct threat of inter-state military conflict and covers general risks including the illegal exploitation of resources, for example in cases of trade with conflict diamonds.[48] Therefore, as previous Security Council resolutions clearly dealt with the role of resources in fuelling existing armed conflicts,[49] moving the concept of "threat to peace" further forward would be in line with such a trend.

An early Security Council involvement under Chapter VII of the UN Charter may foster multilateral solutions for resource conflicts because it can serve as a back-up for other dispute settlement fora including bilateral negotiations, arbitration or involvement of other actors such as regional organisations and the World Bank offering good services. Coordinated activities between diverse international institutions may thus efficiently bring together reluctant dispute parties. Apparently, this is, for example, what Egypt aimed to achieve by bringing the matter of the Grand Ethiopian Renaissance Dam to the attention of the Security Council, despite the involvement of the African Union Bureau of the Assembly of Heads of State and Government, arguing that this was

> *"not intended to pre-empt or forestall any negotiations, but to express, at the highest level, the keen interest of the international community in reaching an agreement on GERD and its appreciation of the dangers of acts of unilateralism in this matter."*[50]

However, an involvement of the UN Security Council in political disputes over the allocation of natural resources affects the diluted relationship between Chapter VI and Chapter VII of the UN Charter.[51] Such disputes

---

48 *Cf. i.a. United Nations Security Council,* Resolution 1173, adopted on 12.06.1998, UN Doc. S/RES/1173, on Angola; 1925, adopted on 28.05.2010, UN Doc. S/RES/1925 on the Democratic Republic of the Congo; 1306, adopted on 05.07.2000, UN Doc. S/RES/1306; 1446, adopted on 04.12.2002, UN Doc. S/RES/1446 on Sierra Leone; 1521, adopted on 22.12.2003, UN Doc. S/RES/1521 and 1903, adopted on 17.12.2009, UN Doc. S/RES/1903, both on Liberia.

49 In the context of armed conflicts in Angola, Liberia, Sierra Leonie, Côte d'Ivoire and Cambodia, see *Pertile,* The Changing Environment and Emerging Resource Conflicts, in: Weller (ed.), The Oxford Handbook on the Use of Force in International Law (2015), p. 1091.

50 *United Nations Security Council,* Letter dated 29 June 2020 from the Permanent Representative of Egypt to the United Nations addressed to the President of the Security Council, UN Doc. S/2020/617, p. 6.

51 *Cf. Krisch,* General Framework, in: Simma *et al.* (eds.), The Charter of the United Nations. A Commentary, Vol. II (3rd edition 2012), paras. 20 *et seq.*

will, generally, qualify as a "dispute [...] likely to endanger the maintenance of international peace and security" under Art. 33 UN Charter or as a "situation which might lead to international friction" under Art. 34 UN Charter. While, in its practice, the UN Security Council has rarely made a clear distinction between individual stages of a conflict, the UN Charter wording assumes that the far-reaching Chapter VII powers depend on the existence of a higher risk of military conflict.

Indeed, in cases of disputes over natural resources, a certain restraint in the exercise of Security Council competences under Chapter VII seems appropriate. On the one hand, it is conceivable that the Security Council could, for example, legislatively appropriate a disputed transboundary water system (even in disregard of existing legal frameworks), place it under neutral control till the dispute is settled or even authorize the use of force to enforce the appropriation.[52] On the other hand, considerations of efficiency should not lose out of sight that other actors are primarily competent to deal with non-military disputes over natural resources. Natural resource management is covered by a state's permanent sovereignty over natural resources and primarily falls under the legal framework of international trade, development, and energy law. Ensuring equal access to resources through free trade and resulting disputes belong before the dispute settlement bodies of the WTO.[53]

The administration of transboundary watercourses does not only concern international environmental law but also development law. The World Bank had, for instance, a major influence on the conclusion of the Indus Water Treaty.[54] Accordingly, Art. 2 (3) and 33 (1) UN Charter stipulate that the competences of the Security Council even in the realm of the pacific settlement of disputes are only subsidiary. This "fundamental policy rule" allocates responsibility for dispute settlement between the parties,

---

52 *Cf. Worthen*, Resolving International Water Disputes: Lessons on American and Canadian Federalism, in: Brigham Young University International Law & Management Review 11 (2015), p. 132 (158).

53 For instance, restrictions on the export of rare earth elements by China had been dealt with by the Dispute Settlement Body of the WTO and finally the report had been implemented by China, see: *World Trade Organization*, DS431: China – Measures Related to the Exportation of Rare Earths, Tungsten and Molybdenum (2015), available under: https://www.wto.org/english/tratop_e/dispu_e/cases_e/ds431_e.htm (last accessed: 8 August 2020).

54 *Zawahri*, Third Party Mediation of International River Disputes: Lessons from the Indus River, in: International Negotiation 14 (2009), p. 281 (292).

regional organisations[55] and the UN.[56] After all, an early involvement of the Security Council may question the efficiency of the various tools of dispute settlement as it might entail the search for a "guilty party" to impose sanctions. This may, in turn, undermine the basis for trustful co-operation required for the allocation and administration of a shared resource and even further escalate the dispute at hand. As demonstrated by the 2012 Heglig oil crisis, Chapter VII powers are best employed to bring reluctant parties together for negotiations within the existing legal frameworks for resource allocation and not to create frameworks for such an allocation.

b) *Root Causes of Armed Conflicts – Securitizing Resource Access before the UN Security Council*

In a third scenario, the UN Security Council has dealt with access to resources as a root cause of armed conflict outside specific conflict scenarios. Addressing root causes of armed conflicts has been part of the general development to extend the preventive powers of the Security Council. Thus, already in 1992, the President of the Security Council issued a note on behalf of its members according to which

> "*the absence of war and military conflicts amongst States does not in itself ensure international peace and security. The non-military sources of instability in the economic, social, humanitarian and ecological fields have become threats to peace and security*".[57]

Other more generalized risks such as climate change, drug trafficking as well as health crises, including HIV/AIDS and Ebola, have been addressed in the framework of thematic discussions, statements of the Security Coun-

---

55 *United Nations Security Council*, Letter dated 1 July 2020 from the President of the Security Council addressed to the Secretary-General and the Permanent Representatives of the members of the Security Council, UN Doc. S/2020/636, p. 26: "It is indeed lamentable, to say the least, that the principle of complementarity and subsidiarity between the UN and regional organizations, much talked about in this Council, was ignored when the issue related to the Grand Ethiopian Renaissance Dam (GERD) was unjustifiably brought to its attention. It also contravenes Article 33 of the UN Charter, which stipulates that parties to any dispute, among others, shall first 'resort to regional agencies or arrangements'."

56 *Tomuschat*, Article 33, in: Simma *et al.* (eds.), The Charter of the United Nations. A Commentary, Vol. I (3rd edition 2012), para. 4.

57 *United Nations Security Council*, Note by the President of the Security Council from 31.01.1992, UN Doc. S/1992/23500, p. 3.

cil Presidency or under Arria-Formula meetings.[58] Following the approach to deal with general threats, a securitization of the "access to resources" within the Security Council is evolving, even though, until now, no resolution has been passed. States try to address access to natural resources in meetings on "water and peace"[59] or "climate change"[60] as well as on the "role of natural resources as root causes of conflict".[61] Within the discussions, a wide majority of states would generally welcome the possibility of dealing with this topic in the Security Council. The chair of the Global High-Level Panel on Water and Peace even stated that the

> "*[d]efense of water for the civilian populations by the affected populations themselves is a legitimate form of self-defence and can be legitimately assisted by military means. [...] it should be within the reach of the Security Council to convey a sense of legitimacy to those military actions whose sole purpose is the protection of water sources and installations that are vital for civilian populations*".[62]

Still, dealing with root causes of armed conflicts outside a specific conflict meets strong contestations, in particular by non-Western states. The intensity of such reservations depends on the policy fields concerned.[63]

Strong opposition within the meetings comes from Russia as well as states that can be considered as rising powers in line with their more sceptical view of interventionist policies. Russia,[64] China, and the G-77[65] constantly argue that the topic is out of the scope of the Security Council. Moreover, according to Russia,

> "*[t]o make natural resources a matter of international security, would [...] shift the focus of international efforts towards a subjective search for "guilty*

58 On the development of the practice of the Security Council, *Krisch*, Article 39, in: Simma *et al.* (eds.), The Charter of the United Nations. A Commentary, Vol. II (3rd edition 2012), paras. 30–32.

59 *United Nations Security Council*, Meeting of 20.12.2017, UN Doc. S/PV.8144; Meeting of 22.11.2016, UN Doc. S/PV.7818.

60 *United Nations Security Council*, Meeting of 23 February 2021, UN Doc. S/2021/198; Meeting of 25.01.2019, UN Doc. S/PV.8451; Meeting of 20.07.2011, UN Doc. S/PV.6587; Meeting of 17.04.2007, UN Doc. S/PV.5663.

61 *United Nations Security Council*, Meeting of 16.10.2018, UN Doc. S/PV.8372.

62 *United Nations Security Council*, Meeting of 22.11.2016 (fn. 59), p. 5.

63 *Krisch* (fn. 58), para. 34.

64 *United Nations Security Council* (fn. 61), p. 13.

65 *United Nations Security Council*, Meeting of 25.01.2019 (fn. 60), p. 13, supported by Russia, p. 17, China and G-77, p. 24.

parties" and the subsequent probable imposition of military intervention in the parts of the world concerned".[66]

This securitization would, in the end, in the view of Russia, enable the matter "being regulated pursuant to the top-down principle and could also harm the interests of countries concerned", instead of regulation by "mutually acceptable decisions within specialized organizations".[67] Explicitly referring to processes of securitization, Brazil[68] and India oppose to deal with climate change linked to international peace because, according to India, such a

"securitization [...] has significant downsides. A securitized approach risks pitting States into a competition, when cooperation is clearly the most productive avenue in tackling this threat. Thinking in security terms usually engenders overly militarized solutions to problems that inherently require non-military responses to resolve them. In short, it brings the wrong actors to the table. As the saying goes, if all you have is a hammer, everything looks like a nail".[69]

In view of the contested nature of such a broad understanding of conflict prevention, the question arises as to which legal and policy limitations exist for aligning the matter of resource allocation with efforts to widen the interpretation of "threat to peace". From a systematic perspective, the broadening of Security Council competences to deal with root causes of armed conflicts affects the allocation of competences between UN organs. The Security Council's involvement in issues of resource allocations and scarcity touches upon the relationship between security and development, interfering with the mandate of other UN bodies, in particular the ECOSOC and the General Assembly (Art. 60 UN Charter).

At first glance, it is hard to deny that the massive effects of environmental degradation and resource scarcity on human life and health suggest considering these phenomena as threats to peace. If a country persisted to use or stockpile resources in a manner that threatens human lives and livelihoods of other countries, the magnitude of the threat may allow the

---

66 *United Nations Security Council*, Meeting of 22.11.2016 (fn. 59), p. 21.

67 *United Nations Security Council*, Meeting of 06.06.2017, UN Doc. S/PV.7959, p. 14.

68 *United Nations Security Council*, Meeting of 22.11.2016 (fn. 59), p. 39.

69 *United Nations Security Council*, Meeting of 25.01.2019 (fn. 60), p. 43, supported by Russia, p. 16.

Security Council to act.[70] Accordingly, in June 2020, Egypt requested the Security Council to take action with regard to the developments of the Grand Ethiopian Renaissance Dam, i.e. Ethiopia's announcement to unilaterally fill and operate the dam, arguing,

> "*[...] the unilateral operation of this mega-dam could have disastrous socioeconomic effects that will diminish every dimension of the human security of Egyptians, including food security, water security, environmental security and human health. It will also expose millions to greater economic vulnerability, leading to increasing rates of crime and illegal migration. It would reduce water quality, disrupt the riparian ecosystem, damage biodiversity and aggravate the dangers of climate change. This eventuality represents a serious threat to international peace and security. It could also have serious, if not seismic, political ramifications. Downstream States would find themselves in an intolerable situation and create an atmosphere of animosity between our countries and sow the seeds of discord between our peoples.*"[71]

Nevertheless, some states took a rather cautious stance towards the Security Council's meeting on this issue, highlighting that the Council's involvement "should not set a precedent" or, according to Ethiopia, already sets a bad precedent and "opens Pandora's box".[72]

In particular, ECOSOC and the General Assembly offer fora for negotiation which are, in general, more inclusive than the Security Council whose composition is for reasons of its efficiency non-inclusive. Aware of this critical interplay, the approach of the Security Council already is cautious and debates on threats to peace related to development issues try to be as inclusive as possible, allowing otherwise unrepresented states to be present.[73]

For almost 25 years, efforts within the UN and, in particular, in the Security Council were directed at a change from a "culture of reaction to a

---

70 *Knight*, Global Environmental Threats: Can the Security Council Protect Our Earth?, in: New York University Law Review 80 (2005), p. 1549 (1575).

71 *United Nations Security Council*, Letter dated 29 June 2020 from the Permanent Representative of Egypt to the United Nations addressed to the President of the Security Council, UN Doc. S/2020/617, p. 6. A similar assessment had already been made earlier, cf. *United Nations Security Council*, Letter dated 1 May 2020 from the Permanent Representative of Egypt to the United Nations addressed to the President of the Security Council, UN Doc. S/2020/355, p. 2.

72 *United Nations Security Council*, Letter dated 1 July 2020 from the President of the Security Council addressed to the Secretary-General and the Permanent Representatives of the members of the Security Council, UN Doc. S/2020/636, p. 26.

73 *Krisch*, The Decay of Consent: International Law in an Age of Global Public Goods, in: American Journal of International Law 108 (2014), p. 1 (19).

culture of prevention".[74] Laudable attempts to address root causes of conflict as well as a focus on the presumed efficiency of the Council made concepts of a subsidiary competence of the Council in terms of conflict prevention look outdated. However, recent Security Council debates indicate that states, in particular from the Global South, re-emphasize the subsidiary role of the Council in conflict prevention as well as the immediacy requirement in line with the traditional understanding of the Security Council as a subsidiary organ of last resort. This ensures that the far-reaching powers of the UN Security Council under Chapter VII are still limited to situations where there is an imminent threat of military conflict.

3. *Self-Defence to Secure Resources*

The treatment of access to resources and their steady supply as a vital interest linked to the very existence of states could allow for claims to invoke self-defence. Whereas such claims cannot override the existing normativity of self-defence, they can *de facto* influence the interpretation of Art. 51 UN Charter as subsequent state practice (Art. 31 (3) lit. b VCLT).

a) "Resource-War" Scenarios

Scenarios where a certain deprivation of resources had been called an "act of war" or "aggression" constantly re-emerge in international relations. Especially in the context of water, states employ language reminiscent of Art. 51 UN Charter. The construction of a dam leading to the diversion of a river or reduction of its flow is sometimes seen as a ground to allow for the use of force. For instance, Israel's water plans, especially the National Water Carrier Plan that was designed to carry water from the Jordan River and Sea of Galilee to the Negev, had been considered by the Arab Defence Council in 1960 as "aggressive acts against the Arabs that justify legitimate self-defense by every Arab state".[75] More recently, since 2016, India openly discusses using "water as a weapon" against Pakistan by cutting off the flow of rivers to Pakistan in reaction to terrorist attacks. Pakistan respond-

---

74 *United Nations Secretary General,* Report of the Secretary-General on the work of the Organization, UN Doc. A/54/1 (1999), p. 7, para. 61.

75 *Shemesh,* Prelude to the Six-Day War: The Arab-Israeli Struggle over Water Resources, in: Israel Studies 9 (2004), p. 1 (10).

ed by considering any revocation of the Indus Water Treaty as an "act of war".[76] As well, in 2016, the Parliamentary Assembly of the Council of Europe declared that the deprivation of water by Armenia towards Azerbaijan in the disputed Nagorno-Karabakh region "must be regarded as 'environmental aggression' and seen as a hostile act by one State towards another".[77] Lastly, Ethiopia's plans to construct the Grand Ethiopian Renaissance Dam at the Blue Nile, had been heavily criticised by Egypt due to the possibility of a reduction of the flow of the Nile. In 2013, President Morsi declared: "If a single drop of the Nile is lost, our blood will be the alternative. We are not warmongers, but we will never allow anyone to threaten our security".[78] In 2020, in light of the ongoing tensions, Egypt's Foreign Ministry again confirmed that it "will continue to give the matter the maximum attention [...] defending the interests of the Egyptian people as well as their fate and future, by all available means."[79]

b) Art. 51 UN Charter and Non-Traditional Threats

From a legal perspective, Art. 51 UN Charter requires that "an armed attack occurs". The ordinary meaning of the term "armed" points towards a

76 *Slater*, India wants to use water as a weapon against Pakistan. A 59-year-old treaty stands in the way (2019), available under: https://www.washingtonpost.com/world/2019/02/22/indias-threats-pakistan-offer-hint-future-water-wars/ (last accessed: 8 August 2020). For an overview of the water conflict between India and Pakistan, cf. *Rossi*, Blood, Water, and the Indus Waters Treaty, in: Minnesota Journal of International Law 29 (2020), pp. 103 *et seqq.*

77 Art. 3 of Council of Europe's Parliamentary Assembly Resolution 2085 (2016), Inhabitants of frontier regions of Azerbaijan are deliberately deprived of water, adopted on 26.01.2016.

78 *Pflanz*, Egypt: 'all options open' in Nile dam row with Ethiopia (2013), available under: https://www.telegraph.co.uk/news/worldnews/africaandindianocean/egypt/10113407/Egypt-all-options-open-in-Nile-dam-row-with-Ethiopia.html (last accessed: 8 August 2020).

79 *The Associated Press*, Egypt Vows to Use 'All Means' to Defend Nile Interests After Ethiopia Skips U.S. Talks (2020), available under: https://www.haaretz.com/middle-east-news/egypt/egypt-vows-to-use-all-means-to-defend-nile-interests-after-ethiopia-skips-talks-1.8600505 (last accessed: 8 August 2020). For a more recent analysis of the conflict, cf. *International Crisis Group*, Nile Dam Talks: Unlocking a Dangerous Stalemate (2020), available under: https://www.crisisgroup.org/africa/horn-africa/ethiopia/nile-dam-talks-unlocking-dangerous-stalemate (last accessed: 8 August 2020).

threat of military and kinetic nature.[80] According to the *travaux préparatoires*, an "armed attack" was considered a "clear case of aggression".[81] It is widely accepted and supported by the ICJ that there is a cascading relationship between the use of force and an armed attack. As a minimum, an armed attack would, therefore, involve a certain gravity of the use of force.[82]

A mere deprivation of resources would be non-military in nature. It would first and foremost be considered as an economic measure. Following the *travaux préparatoires* and subsequent UNGA Resolutions, political or economic force is generally not considered to constitute force in the meaning of Art. 2 (4) UN Charter and would violate other norms of international law, such as the principle of non-intervention (Art. 2 (1), 2 (7) UN Charter) or a state's territorial sovereignty. A Brazilian attempt to include "economic measures" into the text of Art. 2 (4) UN Charter had been rejected by two votes to twenty-six at Dumberton Oaks.[83] The same would follow from a systematic interpretation because the UN Charter refers to the term "force" on all other occasions as "armed" force.[84] If then economic coercion would not even amount to use of force, it would also not amount to an armed attack. Thus, the UNGA's Definition of Aggression refers to force as "armed force" and does not list "economic aggression".[85] Correspondingly, a proposal by Bolivia had been rejected within the negotiations to consider as an act of aggression

> *"unilateral action to deprive a state of the economic resources derived from the fair practice of international trade, or to endanger its basic economy,*

---

80 *Zemanek*, Armed Attack, in: Wolfrum, Max Planck Encyclopedia of Public International Law (2013), para. 11.

81 See *e.g.*, *Mori*, Origins of the Right of Self-Defense in International Law: From the Caroline Incident to the United Nations Charter (2018), pp. 225, 229.

82 *International Court of Justice*, Judgement of 27 June 1986, Military and Paramilitary Activities (Nicaragua v. United States of America), I.C.J. Reports (1986), p. 101. The US nevertheless argues, the inherent right of self-defence applies against any illegal use of force, see: *United States Department of Defense*, Law of War Manual (2016), p. 47, para. 1.11.5.2.

83 *United Nations Information Organisation*, Documents of the United Nations Conference on International Organisation, Vol. VI (1945), p. 335; distinguishing "use of force" and "economic measures".

84 Preamble, Arts. 41, 42, 43, 44, 45, 46, 47 UN Charter.

85 See preamble (sixth recital), Art. 1, Art. 3 UNGA Resolution 3314 (1974), Definition of Aggression, adopted on 14.12.1974, UN Doc. A/RES/3314(XXIX).

thus jeopardizing the security of that state or rendering it incapable of acting in its own defence and co-operating in the collective defence of peace".[86]

Nevertheless, these arguments do not imply that force may not at all be exerted by non-military measures. The focus of the classification cannot solely lie on the means used but must take into consideration the scale and effects of measures. For instance, Art. 54 (1) AP I of the Geneva Conventions prohibits starvation as a method of warfare implying that militarily relevant uses of force are not restricted to weapons. Thus, the ICJ in various decisions held that the "use of force" is not restricted to any specific type of weapons.[87] As "force" cannot be interpreted solely within the context of military means available during the draft of the UN Charter, from a teleological view, it must be assessed whether the measure used is comparable by scale and effects to traditional kinetic weapons.[88] Criteria for such "non-military threats" being similar to military threats by scale and effects had been set up by the expert committee of the Tallinn Manual, assessing, inter alia, whether cyber-attacks could amount to a prohibited "use of force". According to Rule 69 of the "Tallinn-Manual", non-military operations would constitute a use of force when its scale and effects are comparable to "traditional operations". Criteria include severity in terms of damage, destruction, harm and death, immediacy of the effects of an attack and directness in terms of the causal connection.[89]

c) "Resource War" Scenarios Are Not Comparable to Traditional Operations

In view of these criteria, resource-wars involving water and/or resource scarcity and deprivation do not amount to use of force, let alone an armed

---

86 *United Nations General Assembly*, Meeting of the Sixth Committee of the General Assembly on 11.01.1952, UN Doc. A/C.6.L.211, cited in Report by the Secretary General on the Question of Defining Aggression, 03.10.1952, UN Doc. A/2211, p. 58.

87 *International Court of Justice*, Judgement of 27 June 1986, Military and Paramilitary Activities (Nicaragua v. United States of America), I.C.J Reports (1986), pp. 103 *et seq.*; Advisory Opinion, 8 July 1996, Legality of the Threat or Use of Nuclear Weapons, I.C.J Reports (1996), p. 244, para. 39.

88 *Krieger*, Krieg gegen anonymous – Völkerrechtliche Regelungsmöglichkeiten bei unsicherer Zurechnung im Cyberwar, in: Archiv des Völkerrechts 50 (2012), p. 1 (9 *et seqq.*).

89 *Schmitt*, The Tallinn Manual 2.0 on the International Law Applicable to Cyber Operations (2nd edition 2017), pp. 334 *et seqq.*

attack in view of their exclusive economic or environmental character. Whilst deprivation of economic resources such as water could meet the threshold of severity because water scarcity could arguably lead to the death of many people, one could already be more sceptical when it comes to the deprivation of other economic resources such as oil. Even though deprivation of the latter could in very extreme situations lead to an economic collapse of industrialized countries and in the end, stop the production of means for a country's existence, such resources in most circumstances can be replaced by other resources. Given that resource scarcity is a problem of availability of resources in one's country, availability of such resources on the global market as well as a state's capacity to acquire such resources must be taken into account: The lack of resources supplied from one country will often open the possibility of either to surrogate resources or to diversify the supplying countries. Thus, all the scenarios set out would likely not reach the comparability-threshold of military threats. Lowering the flow of a shared river by the construction of a dam or diversion of rivers – as it is the case in the India/Pakistan or Egypt/Ethiopia conflict – would not reach the immediacy criterion. First, technical means require large preparation and do not take place from one day to another. Secondly, even if a river would have been fully blocked by a dam and diverted, the effect would not be sudden but occur within weeks, leaving time for a peaceful settlement by relevant regional organisations and UN bodies including the involvement of the Security Council.

Even in cases where the deprivation of resources aims at lowering the defence capabilities of a state, it is hard to argue that the aim to lower defence capabilities would amount to an armed attack just because one state denies access to resources to another state (notwithstanding, that the intention is hard to prove). As such, the immediacy-criterion underlines the *ultima ratio* character of self-defence. As long as there are still pacific means available, self-defence is impermissible.

4. Necessity and the Use of Force

If not covered by the invocation of self-defence, the remaining justification to which official statements occasionally refer is the overall state of necessity which allows for the use of force. Processes of securitization at the national level allude to legitimacy arguments which rely on emergency actions to cope with a threat that touches upon vital interests of states. Policy statements and academic literature sometimes argue that the use of force would be permissible when "vital interests" or the very survival of a state are at stake.[90] This is exemplified by Egypt's declaration following Ethiopia's plans to build a Dam at the Blue Nile that "all options are open" to stop a reduction of "even one drop of Nile water".[91] Here, it can additionally be seen as a worrying trend entailing an escalating potential that Egypt eventually argued before the UN Security Council that:

> *"the unilateral operation of this mega-dam could have disastrous socioeconomic effects that will diminish every dimension of the human security of Egyptians, including food security, water security, environmental security and human health [...] Egypt will uphold and protect the vital interests of its people. Survival is not a question of choice, but an imperative of nature. [...] we believe that justice dictates that Ethiopia respect Egypt's right to life."*[92]

When it comes to other resources than water, the term "economic strangulation" was partly invoked as justification for the use of force. A US-Senate feasibility study in the aftermath of the Oil Crisis argued from an international law perspective, that it is indeed hard to justify any seizure of oil fields.[93] Nevertheless, for allies of the US, the study explicitly mentioned the invocation of "self-preservation" to break an embargo by force and finally found that "[t]hose who view law as flexible instruments may find rationalizations".[94]

In a modern variance, claims of necessity may be bolstered by a state's human rights obligations. The state would justify using force to secure resources by referring to its obligations to provide for its population's basic needs under relevant human rights treaties. For instance, the right to water obliges states, *inter alia* to ensure access to the minimum essential amount of water that is sufficient and safe for personal and domestic uses to pre-

---

90 *Yihdego*, The Blue Nile dam controversy in the eyes of international law: Part 3 (2013), available under: https://globalwaterforum.org/2013/07/02/the-blue-nile-dam-controversy-in-the-eyes-of-international-law-part-3/ (last accessed: 8 August 2020).

91 *Pflanz*, Egypt: 'all options open' in Nile dam row with Ethiopia (2013), available under: https://www.telegraph.co.uk/news/worldnews/africaandindianocean/egypt/10113407/Egypt-all-options-open-in-Nile-dam-row-with-Ethiopia.html (last accessed: 8 August 2020).

92 *United Nations Security Council*, Letter dated 29 June 2020 from the Permanent Representative of Egypt to the United Nations addressed to the President of the Security Council, UN Doc. S/2020/617, p. 6.

93 *Congressional Research Service*, Oil Fields as Military Objective: A Feasibility Study (1975), p. 9.

94 *Congressional Research Service* (fn. 93).

vent disease.[95] To fulfil such obligations towards its population, a state may claim to have no other choice than to use force. Such a line of argument is structurally related to the concept of a Responsibility to Protect or humanitarian intervention and would rely on just war theories mentioned above. However, from the perspective of human rights law, it is hardly conceivable that a positive obligation cumulates into a right, or even an obligation, to use force against other states to provide adequate resources, if it is at all legally coherent with human rights doctrine. From the perspective of the UN Charter, such interpretation would conflict with Art. 103 UN Charter and would most likely face the same normative problems as humanitarian interventions in general or a right to invoke necessity.

The right to invoke necessity as a ground for the use of force refers to the idea of self-preservation and relies on an assumed right of existence of states.[96] Whether a State may use force in accordance with the plea of necessity is highly uncertain and subject to a controversial discussion.[97] In contrast to self-defence, the concept of necessity applies even in view of another state's legal behaviour, since it is grounded solely on the telos of self-preservation.[98] The ICJ Advisory Opinion on the use of nuclear weapons may be regarded as an affirmation of the right of a state to survival. In the Advisory Opinion, the ICJ held, that

> *"it cannot reach a definitive conclusion as to the legality or illegality of the use of nuclear weapons by a State in an extreme circumstance of self-defence, in which its very survival would be at stake".*[99]

But even if such a right would exist, it is more than doubtful that necessity could at all justify a use of force in view of the absolute character of Art 2 (4) UN Charter. As the only exception, where necessity could serve as

---

95 The right to water is implicitly contained in the right to an adequate standard of living (Art. 11 (1) ICESCR) and to the highest attainable standard of health (Art. 12 (1) ICESCR), as well as the right to life and human dignity (Preamble, Art. 6 (1) ICCPR). For the content of the right to water, *cf. i.a. Committee on Economic, Social and Cultural Rights*, General Comment No. 15 (2002), 2003, UN Doc. E/C.12/2002/11, para. 37, lit. a; *Saul/Kinley/Mowbray* (fn. 29), pp. 903 *et seq.*

96 *Fenwick*, International Law (1934), p. 146, cited after *Alder*, The Inherent Right of Self-Defence in International Law (2012), p. 33 at fn. 43.

97 *Cf. Schmitt* (fn. 89), p. 140.

98 *International Law Commission*, Addendum – Eighth report on State responsibility by Mr. Roberto Ago, Special Rapporteur, UN Doc. A/CN.4/318/ADD.5-7, p. 16.

99 *International Court of Justice*, Advisory Opinion, 8.7.1996, Legality of the Threat or Use of Nuclear Weapons, I.C.J. Reports (1996), p. 263, para. 97.

a justification, *Bowett*, for instance, refers to the UK's comment on the Declaration of the Rights and Duties of States. In this comment, the UK claims that there may be exceptions where a state is pursuing a course which leads to the "economic strangulation of another state".[100]

The Articles on the Responsibility of States for Internationally Wrongful Acts (ARSIWA) of the International Law Commission (ILC) formulated in its Art. 25 (1) the invocation of necessity as a circumstance precluding wrongfulness.[101] According to Art. 25 (1) (b) ARSIWA, necessity can only be invoked to sacrifice a lesser good to a greater emergency of a state. In this sense, non-compliance with peremptory norms cannot be justified by a state of necessity, as set out in Art. 26 ARSIWA, because in

> "*view of the compelling reasons which lead to the definitive affirmation of the prohibition of the use of force against the territorial integrity or political independence of any State, it seems […] unconceivable that the legal conviction of States would today accept "necessity" as justification for a breach of that prohibition and, more generally, for an act covered by the now accepted concept of an 'act of aggression'.*"[102]

Notwithstanding the existence of a right to self-preservation in the pre-UN Charter era, today such a notion of self-preservation must be rejected due to the intent to abolish armed reprisals entirely: "Even in instances where a State faces absolute destruction, any forcible response must fall within the requirements of self-defence".[103] Accordingly, the intention to abolish armed reprisals is reflected in Art. 50 (1) (a) ARSIWA.

A precedent for the reasonableness of rebuffing arguments of self-preservation can be seen in the wide denunciation of Japan's justification for the war in the Pacific which was considered as a far-reaching example of an abusive practice. At the time, a counsel at the Tokyo Trials argued:

> "*To deprive a nation of those necessary commodities which enable its citizens and subjects to exist is surely a method of warfare not dissimilar to the vio-*

100 *Bowett*, Self-Defence in International Law (1958), p. 110.

101 Art. 25 (1) ARSIWA: "Necessity may not be invoked by a State as a ground for precluding the wrongfulness of an act not in conformity with an international obligation of that State unless the act: a) Is the only way for the State to safeguard an essential interest against a grave and imminent peril; and b) Does not seriously impair an essential interest of the State or States towards which the obligation exists, or of the international community as a whole".

102 *International Law Commission* (fn. 98), p. 21.

103 *Green*, Self-Preservation, in: Wolfrum, Max Planck Encyclopedia of Public International Law (2009), para. 16.

> *lent taking of lives through explosives and force because it reduces opposition by delayed action resulting in defeat just as surely as through other means of conventional hostilities. It can even be said of a more drastic nature than the blasting of life by physical force, for it aims at the slow depletion of the morale and well-being of the entire civilian population through the medium of slow starvation*".[104]

The judgement in the Tokyo Trials rejected this argument as non-consistent with Japan's own practice and underlined in this sense the abusive nature of such an excuse:

> "*The argument is merely a repetition of Japanese propaganda issued at the time she was preparing for her wars of aggression. It is not easy to have patience with its lengthy repetition at this date when documents are at length available which demonstrate Japan's decision to expand to the North, to the West and to the South at the expense of her neighbors was taken long before any economic measures were directed against her and was never departed from*".[105]

In sum, a concept of necessity that authorizes the use of force outside the UN Charter regime with regard to a resource necessity is neither supported by state practice nor reasonably compliant with the purposes of an abolishment of the use of force in international relations. Such an argument itself follows the principle of "necessity knows no law" and finds itself outside of any legal contexts of justification.[106]

IV. Conclusion

In conclusion, at the level of policy statements there are some indications that processes of securitization involving the securing of natural resources may contribute to an erosion of the prohibition of the use of force. This risk arises in preparation for crises over access to resources and in statements that invoke self-defence or try to revive the concept of necessity on

---

104 Taken from a citation of Judge Pal's (India) Dissenting Opinion, *cf. Röling/Rüter* (fn. 24), p. 616.

105 *Röling/Rüter* (fn. 25), pp. 380 *et seq.*

106 *Cf.* the speech of the Chancellor of the German Empire *Bethmann-Hollweg* at the Reichstag of 4 August 1914, justifying the German invasion of Belgium in World War I: "We are in a state of legitimate defense. Necessity knows no law", cited in: *Editorial Comment*, The Neutrality of Belgium, in: American Journal of International Law 9 (1915), p. 707 (709).

the grounds of survival of the state. This behaviour is taking place in grey areas of interpretation of international law and, therefore, needs strong objection by the international community to prevent such arguments from contributing to interpretative shifts on the basis of subsequent state practice or to the creation of exceptions to the prohibition on the basis of customary international law.

Following the overall duty of peaceful settlement of disputes and the overall need for enduring cooperation to benefit equally from shared water resources, states should support the already existing mechanisms of peaceful settlement.[107] The strength and acceptance of exactly those mechanisms bolster and ensure the prohibition of the use of force. In this sense, it is a worrying and destabilising trend that some of these institutions are called into question.[108] Nevertheless, with an increasing development of global supply chains by permanent installations, such as pipelines between Russia and Europe or the One Belt, One Road Project by China, one cannot foresee what states are willing to do to protect their investments.

New interpretations of the prohibition of the use of force deterring from traditional interpretations always need to balance community interests in the non-use of force and the legitimate security interests of states.[109] Every new exception undermines the function of the prohibition of the use of force as a basic rule of international law and relations. Therefore, one should not risk weakening the prohibition to the use of force. Open it up could lead to a run over natural resources that entails the inherent danger of abuses. As had been said by Kofi Annan with regards to the possibility of pre-emptive attack:

---

107 For an overview, see *Qureshi*, Dispute Resolution Mechanisms: An Analysis of the Indus Waters Treaty, in: Pepperdine Dispute Resolution Law Journal 18 (2018), p. 75 (75 *et seqq.*).

108 After a U.S. campaign to block appointments and reappointments of judges to the WTO Appellate Body, as of 10 December 2019, the Appellate Body was reduced to one member after the second terms of the two remaining three members expired and no longer has the minimum three members needed to hear new appeals; *WTO*, Members urge continued engagement on resolving Appellate Body issues (2019), available under: https://www.wto.org/english/news_e/news19_e/dsb_18dec19_e.htm (last accessed: 8 August 2020). Cf. *Bäumler*, The WTO's Crisis: Between a Rock and a Hard Place, in: KFG Working Paper Series 42, Berlin Potsdam Research Group "The International Rule of Law – Rise or Decline?" (2020), pp. 20 *et seqq*.

109 *Dörr*, Use of Force, Prohibition of, in: Wolfrum, Max Planck Encyclopedia of Public International Law (2015), para. 51.

> *"This logic represents a fundamental challenge to the principles on which, however imperfectly, world peace and stability have rested for the last fifty-eight years. [I]f it were to be adopted, it could set precedents that resulted in a proliferation of the unilateral and lawless use of force, with or without justification".*[110]

The same holds true for any justification of war over resources. Unilateral use of force leads most certainly to an escalation of conflict and thereby to global instability. If then the argument of instability of regions is used to intervene in another country again to secure access to key resources, one may foresee that the prohibition of the use of force becomes blurry and to the end ineffective.

110 *Annan*, The Secretary-General Address to the General Assembly, New York, 23 September 2003, available under: http://www.un.org/webcast/ga/58/statements/sg2eng030923.htm (last accessed: 8 August 2020).

Natural Resources in Times of Occupation

Thilo Marauhn and Barry de Vries

Abstract

The article discusses the use of natural resources in times of occupation. It builds on the examples of the Palestinian Occupied Territories and the Western Sahara. Such situations of prolonged occupation raise questions going beyond the traditional law of occupation. They require a much broader and more comprehensive approach, including the potential application of human rights law. This could mitigate the tensions arising from political stalemate (in achieving an end of occupation) and the need to cater for the local population (where international humanitarian law might benefit from supplementary human rights standards).

Overview

International natural resources law is primarily looked at from the perspective of peacetime international law.[1] However, rules on the use of natural resources in times of occupation go back to 1907, forming part of the Reg-

1 See *e.g.*, *Fischman*, What Is Natural Resources Law?, in: University of Colorado Law Review 78 (2007), p. 717 (717-749); Bungenberg/Hobe (eds.), Permanent sovereignty over Natural Resources (2015); Romanin Jacur/Bonfanti/Seatzu (eds.),

ulations concerning the Laws and Customs of War on Land, annexed to The Hague Convention (IV) respecting the Laws and Customs of War on Land ('Hague Regulations').[2] It is noteworthy that such rules were in place long before debates on the protection of the environment in situations of armed conflict arose.[3] In this chapter we will discuss the application of these rules to two very specific cases, namely the Palestinian Occupied Territories and the Western Sahara. These discussions will raise questions as to the appropriateness of the 1907 rules in situations of prolonged occupation, which may be considered to differ from what the drafters of the rules originally had in mind. Our chapter will shed some light on the challenges arising therefrom and possible solutions thereto.

I. Two Cases to Begin With: The Palestinian Occupied Territories and the Western Sahara

The Palestinian Occupied Territories have been under Israeli occupation since the Six-Day War of June 1967.[4] There have been multiple issues concerning the activities of Israel in these occupied territories with regard to their legality under international humanitarian law.

One of the issues that has been brought up in this regard has been the way water resources have been managed – notwithstanding better proposals to this end.[5] Since the early days of the occupation of Palestinian territories by Israel, water resources have remained controlled by Israeli authorities. The instruments applied arise from a combination of military orders and Israel's effective veto in the Joint Water Committee created in 1995 by

Natural Resource Grabbing: An International Law Perspective, Brill Nijhoff Publishers (2015).

2 Regulations concerning the Laws and Customs of War on Land annexed to The Hague Convention (IV) respecting the Laws and Customs of War on Land The Hague, 18 October 1907, ('Hague Regulations'), Articles 53 and 55.

3 *Bouvier*, Protection of the natural environment in time of armed conflict, in: International Review of the Red Cross 56 (1991), pp. 567-570; *Thadani/Ayyagari*, Law of Armed Conflict and the Environment, in: Environmental Law and Policy Journal 45 (2015), p. 285 (285-286); *Wolfrum*, The Protection of the Environment in Armed Conflict, in: Israel Yearbook on Human Rights 45 (2015), p. 67 (70).

4 *Rubin*, Israel, Occupied Territories, in: Wolfrum (ed.), Max Planck Encyclopedia of International Law (Online Edition www.mpepil.com last update 2009).

5 *Benvenisti*, Collective Action in the Utilization of Shared Freshwater, in: The American Journal of International Law 90 (1996), 384-415.

the Oslo II Accord.[6] It may be argued that this has led to a situation of a deeply inequitable water utilization in the area with significantly more water available for and used by Israel and Israeli settlements, while Palestinian demand for water exceeds the supply.[7] Israel has also denied Palestinians access to other water resources, such as in the Jordan River basin as that has been declared a closed military zone.[8] This situation has been exacerbated by the construction of the wall, which cut of access to many local water sources.[9]

Serious international criticism regarding the wall concerns the hardship caused to the Palestinian residents of the West Bank. Aside from the land requisitions that were needed for the building of the barrier, it cuts through a large number of Palestinian villages. At times farmers are disconnected from their land, or other sources of living, while others are disconnected from friends and family, essential health services, water resources, and educational institutions. Each crossing of the wall for the purposes mentioned is subject to a permit. Israeli authorities have opened crossing points in order to facilitate crossing, but still, hardships are significant.[10] This led to a request made by the United Nations General Assembly ('UNGA') to the International Court of Justice ('ICJ') for an advisory opinion on the following question:[11]

---

6 Appendix 1 Annex III Israeli-Palestinian Interim Agreement on the West Bank and the Gaza Strip, Washington, D.C., September 28, 1995, Article 40.

7 *Scobbie*, Natural Resources and Belligerent Occupation, in: Akram et al. (eds.), International Law and the Israeli-Palestinian Conflict: A Rights-Based Approach to Middle East Peace, Routledge (2010), pp. 243-244; *Beltrán/Kallis*, How Does Virtual Water Flow in Palestine? A Political Ecology Analysis, in: Ecological Economics 143 (2018), p. 17 (17-18).

8 *Scobbie* (fn. 7), p. 244 (reference to both the closed military zone and Israel's pertinent declaration).

9 *Note by the Secretary-General*, Economic and social repercussions of the Israeli occupation on the living conditions of the Palestinian people in the occupied Palestinian territory, including Jerusalem, and of the Arab population in the occupied Syrian Golan, UN Doc. A/62/75, E/2007/13 (3 May 2007) 12, para. 40.

10 *Ahituv*, Fifteen years of separation: The Palestinians Cut Off from Jerusalem by the Wall, available under: https://www.haaretz.com/israel-news/.premium.MAGAZINE-15-years-of-separation-palestinians-cut-off-from-jerusalem-by-a-wall-1.5888001 (last accessed: 6 April 2020).

11 *United Nations General Assembly*, Res ES-10/14, Illegal Israeli Actions in Occupied East Jerusalem and the Rest of the Occupied Palestinian Territory, 8 December 2003, UN Doc. A/Res/ES-10/14. On the ICJ Advisory Opinion see, among others, *Pertile*, Legal consequences of the construction of a wall in the Occupied Palestinian Territory in: The Italian yearbook of international law 14 (2004), pp. 121-161.

"What are the legal consequences arising from the construction of the wall being built by Israel, the occupying Power, in the Occupied Palestinian Territory, including in and around East Jerusalem, as described in the report of the Secretary-General, considering the rules and principles of international law, including the Fourth Geneva Convention of 1949, and relevant Security Council and General Assembly resolutions?"

The case deserves closer consideration below.

A second example concerns the Western Sahara, which has been under Moroccan occupation since 1975. It is located on the Atlantic coast of north-western Africa. The region is sparsely inhabited by nomadic tribes known as Sahrawi. The region was a Spanish colony since the late 19th century, but was evacuated by the Spanish in 1974. This led to competing claims on the territory by both Morocco and Mauritania.[12] When the case was brought before the ICJ in the form of a request for an advisory opinion the Court determined that neither state had a sovereign right to the territory, but that the Sahrawi people were entitled to self-determination.[13] Morocco invaded the territory after the advisory opinion and after fighting with Mauritania and the Sahrawi, took control of most of the territory, which they have maintained since.[14]

Since that time Morocco has placed settlements in the area and there has been a rise of economic activities from foreign companies, especially European business. This is because Western Sahara has a significant amount of natural resources, especially oil, phosphates and fish. The fishing waters in Western Sahara are of increasing importance due to the declining fish stock in the waters of Morocco.[15] More recently this has led to a judgment by the European Court of Justice[16] which will be further discussed later in this chapter.

---

12 *Feinäugle*, Western Sahara (Advisory Opinion), in: Wolfrum (ed.), Max Planck Encyclopedia of International Law (Online Edition www.mpepil.com last update 2007).

13 *International Court of Justice*, Western Sahara Advisory Opinion, I.C.J. Reports (1975), p. 12.

14 *Marauhn*, Sahara, in: Wolfrum (ed.), Max Planck Encyclopedia of International Law (Online Edition www.mpepil.com last update 2010). See also *Simon*, Western Sahara in: Walter/Ungern-Sternberg/Abushov (eds.), Self-Determination and Secession in International Law (2014), pp. 255–272.

15 *Zunes*, Western Sahara, Resources, and International Accountability, in: Global Change, Peace & Security 27(3) (2015), p. 292.

16 *European Court of Justice*, Judgment of 27 February 2018, C-266/16, Western Sahara Campaign UK v. Commissioners for Her Majesty's Revenue and Customs and Secretary of State for Environment, Food and Rural Affairs.

This article will first address applicable rules arising from the laws of war, in particular, the Hague Regulations. We will then analyze the cases of the Palestinian Occupied Territories and the Western Sahara separately. Finally, we will critically review the applicable law.

II. Natural Resources in Occupied Territories in Light of the Law of War

Belligerent occupation refers to a situation where the occupying power has the effective control over a territory without the consent of the sovereign of that territory.[17] During an occupation the original sovereign does not have the powers to effectively govern the territory and for this reason the occupying power is assigned the temporary responsibility to exercise governmental functions. This is, however, necessarily a temporary situation and the underlying rationale is that the sovereignty of the territory remains with the sovereign and that the territory is returned to the ousted sovereign.[18] It is therefore generally prohibited to impose permanent changes on the legal structure pre-existing within the occupied territory.[19]

The state of occupation is governed by a broad set of rules that stem from the 1907 Hague Regulations, the 1949 Fourth Geneva Convention and the 1977 First Additional Protocol. The first question that needs to be answered in any situation is whether or not a territory can be considered as occupied territory. The notion of occupied territory has been defined by Article 42 of the Hague Regulations as follows:

> *"[t]erritory is considered occupied when it is actually placed under the authority of the hostile army. The occupation extends only to the territory where such authority has been established and can be exercised."*

As can be seen from this definition it builds on a pure look at the facts. It is not required for a state to recognize that they are occupying a territory. In order to determine the appropriate legal rules on natural resources in case of occupation it must first be established which legal category specified in the Hague Regulations can be applied. It seems plausible not to de-

---

17 *Benvenisti*, Occupation, Belligerent, in: Wolfrum (ed.), Max Planck Encyclopedia of International Law (Online Edition www.mpepil.com last update 2009).

18 *Longobardo*, State Responsibility for International Humanitarian Law Violations by Private Actors in Occupied Territories and the Exploitation of Natural Resources, in: Netherlands International Law Review 63 (2016), p. 251 (254).

19 *Marauhn*, Konfliktfolgenbewältigung statt Legalisierung Vereinte Nationen (2003), pp. 113-120.

termine these resources as private property unless they are specifically owned by persons. If this was the case, the rules concerning private property would remain in place, meaning that it would be forbidden to destroy such resources except where rendered absolutely necessary by military operations and only war materials could then be seized.[20] It has been argued that under Article 52 of the Hague Regulations natural resources owned by private parties can be exploited as a form of requisition or contribution if it is required by the need of the occupying army.[21]

Most natural resources should, however, be viewed as publicly owned property.[22] The Hague Regulations provide for broader powers over the disposal and use of publicly owned property than privately owned property. Unfortunately, however, the Hague Regulations do not define what is publicly owned property. There are two important provisions in the Hague Regulations that elaborate on the use and disposal of publicly owned properties, namely the first paragraphs of Articles 53 and 55.

Article 53, paragraph 1, stipulates:

> *"An army of occupation can only take possession of cash, funds and realizable securities which are strictly the property of the State, depots of arms, means of transport, stores and supplies, and, generally, all movable property belonging to the State which may be used for military operations."*

Article 55, paragraph 1 provides:

> *"The occupying State shall be regarded only as administrator and usufructuary of public buildings, real estate, forests, and agricultural estates belonging to the hostile State, and situated in the occupied country. It must safeguard the capital of these properties, and administer them in accordance with the rules of usufruct."*

A closer look at these provisions leads to the question as to how natural resources may be considered, whether they are movable or immovable objects.

If natural resources are considered as movable public property the occupying state can take possession of it, but only for military operations. Thus, the state cannot exploit these natural resources for purely economic rea-

---

20 Articles 46 and 53(2) of the Hague Regulations; *Longobardo* (fn. 18), p. 255.

21 *Longobardo* (fn. 18), p. 255; *Dinstein*, The International Law of Belligerent Occupation (2019), pp. 246-249.

22 For a discussion beyond the law of armed conflict see *Lee*, Sovereignty, Ownership of, and Access to Natural Resources, in: Tarlock/ Dernbach (eds.), Environmental Laws and their Enforcement Vol. II (2009), pp. 1-31 (pp. 23-27).

sons. It is because of this that the above provisions specifically refer to such examples as cash, depots of arms, means of transport, stores and supplies. In case of movable public property natural resources can also be taken for the needs of the occupying army, but this should then be proportionate to the territory's resources.[23]

If natural resources are considered as immovable property the occupying power has the obligation to respect the property and can only act as its administrator and usufructuary. The occupying power is entitled to the proceeds or produce that these properties provide.[24] This does not include comprehensive property rights, in particular not title to property. The occupying power can only act as usufructuary. It has the right to exploit natural resources, but it can only do so to a certain level. It cannot exploit these to a level which amounts to the destruction of this property or impairs its value.[25] This means that the occupying power must not act in a wasteful or negligent manner. Because of this the principle of usufruct applies more strictly in the context of non-renewable than renewable natural resources, as the former is more prone to exhaustion, especially in case of long-term occupation.[26] For this reason, it has been argued that, with regard to non-renewable resources, the occupying power can continue the production at pre-occupational levels, but it cannot go beyond this as this would impair the value of the resources.[27]

The question in respect of many natural resources is thus how they should be viewed, and this would generally revolve around whether something has already been extracted or remains *in situ*.[28] Once materials have been extracted they are generally considered to be movable property. As long as they are not extracted they should be regarded as part of the environment and hence considered to be immovable property.[29] This is fairly easy to determine in cases where there is a clear location, such as forests and minerals. It becomes more complex when it concerns natural re-

---

23 Article 52 of the Hague Regulations.

24 *Dinstein* (fn. 21), pp. 232-233.

25 *Longobardo* (fn. 18), p. 255; *Dinstein* (fn. 21), pp. 231-232.

26 *Saul*, The status of Western Sahara as occupied territory under international humanitarian law and the exploitation of natural resources, in: Global Change, Peace & Security 27 (2015) p. 301 (317).

27 *Dinstein* (fn. 21), pp. 233-234.

28 *Scobbie* (fn. 7), p. 234.

29 *Radics/ Bruch*, The Law of Pillage, Conflict Resources, and *Jus Post Bellum, in: Stahn/ Iverson/ Easterday (eds.)*, Environmental Protection and Transitions from Conflict to Peace: Clarifying Norms, Principles, and Practices (2017), pp. 143-168 (p. 155).

sources that can be considered as both movable and immovable property depending on what one considers to be the object.[30] It is these kinds of situations that we will discuss in the cases of Western Sahara and the Occupied Palestinian Territories.

In either case it must be made clear that these goods, whether movable or immovable, may only be exploited to the extent that this is necessary to carry the costs of the occupation itself, or if the property can be used against the occupying state in a military manner. As the International Military Tribunal stated:

> *"[...] under the rules of war, the economy of an occupied country can only be required to bear the expenses of the occupation."*[31]

Natural resources therefore cannot be used in a way that is beneficial for the occupying state's own economy or companies. This does not mean that there is no possibility of exploiting the natural resources when this is not done to offset the costs of military occupation. There is an additional justification for the lawful exploitation of these resources, namely if this is done for the benefit of the local population. This is considered to be the part of the usufructuary duty as it concerns the trustee-role of the occupying power.[32] It must be noted that this relates to the indigenous inhabitants of the territory. It further can be linked to the prohibition of settling the occupier's own population in the territory.

There is another important provision that may be considered applicable in these circumstances. Article 47 of the Hague Regulations prohibits pillaging.[33] This provision is applicable to both public and private property. However, the Hague Regulations themselves do not specify what should be considered as pillaging. A similar prohibition has been included in Article 33 (2) Geneva Convention IV of 1949.[34] In addition, a provision of pillaging has been included in the Rome Statute.[35] These additional provisions in themselves provide limited clarification as to what should be con-

30 *Dinstein* (fn. 21), pp. 235-236.

31 Trial of the Major War Criminals before the International Military Tribunals Judgment 30 September–1 October 1946, p. 239.

32 *Dam-de Jong*, International Law and Governance of Natural Resources in Conflict and Post-Conflict Situations (2015), pp. 229-231.

33 Article 47 of the Hague Regulations: Pillage is formally forbidden.

34 Art. 32 GC IV: Pillage is prohibited.

35 Art. 8(2)(b)(xvi) of the Rome Statute: (2) For the purpose of this Statute, "war crimes" means:
(...)

sidered as pillage. In practice and literature, the term 'pillage' has been defined as the appropriation of property without the consent of the owner.[36] The ICRC commentary on the 1949 Geneva Convention IV highlights that, although Geneva Convention IV focuses on the protection of civilians, the prohibition of pillage protects all property, whether it is private or public.[37] Unlike the provisions of Articles 53 and 55 of the Hague Regulations, pillage requires that the property is appropriated for private or personal use.[38] This would make it difficult to apply to the occupying power when it operates as a government; however, it might be applicable in the circumstances where individuals or companies exploit natural resources. As the occupying state is the power entrusted with the protection of the territory in the case of such pillaging it is possible for the state to be held accountable for either its complicity in the act or for their unwillingness to prevent it.

It has been argued that the exploitation of natural resources would be contrary to the principle of permanent sovereignty over natural resources, that is viewed as part of the right to self-determination.[39] This argument was brought up by the Democratic Republic of the Congo (DRC) in the *Armed Activities* case, but was rejected by the ICJ as not being applicable in the context of exploitation of certain natural resources in the case of occupation as this is governed by international humanitarian law rather than the principle of permanent sovereignty over natural resources.[40] In this case, it was held that the commercial exploitation of natural resources in

(b) Other serious violations of the laws and customs applicable in international armed conflict, within the established framework of international law, namely, any of the following acts:
(…)
(xvi) Pillaging a town or place, even when taken by assault.

36 *Henckaerts/Doswald-Beck (eds.)*, Customary International Humanitarian Law, Volume I: Rules (2005), p. 185.

37 *Pictet (ed.)*, The Geneva Conventions of 12 August 1949: commentary / IV, Geneva Convention relative to the protection of civilian persons in time of war, International Committee of the Red Cross (1958), pp. 226-227.

38 *International Criminal Court*, Elements of Crimes, p. 26.

39 For the principle of permanent sovereignty over natural resources, see *e.g.*, *Schrijver*, Natural Resources, Permanent Sovereignty over, in: in: Wolfrum (ed.), Max Planck Encyclopedia of International Law (Online Edition www.mpepil.com last update 2008); *Tyagi*, Permanent Sovereignty over Natural Resources, Cambridge Journal of International & Comparative Law 4 (2015), p. 588 (588 *et seqq.*).

40 *International Court of Justice*, Armed Activities on the Territory of the Congo (Democratic Republic of the Congo v. Uganda), Judgment, I.C.J. Reports (2005) ('Armed Activities'), p.168, para. 244.

the DRC amounted to pillaging.[41] An important argument for the Court to consider this as pillaging was the fact that such exploitation was not done for the benefit of the local population.[42] It is therefore plausible to consider the commercial exploitation of natural resources as pillaging. There is even the possibility that such activities be considered a grave breach of international humanitarian law and as such as a possible war crime.[43]

The ICJ went even further. In light of Uganda being the occupying power they could be held accountable for the failure to prevent the pillaging:

> *"[...] the fact that Uganda was the occupying Power in Ituri district extends Uganda's obligation to take appropriate measures to prevent the looting, plundering and exploitation of natural resources in the occupied territory to cover private persons in this district and not only members of Ugandan military forces."*[44]

Consequently, even in cases where it is not the occupying power that exploits the resources, but rather private individuals and companies, the occupying power can still be held accountable.[45] Nevertheless, it can be taken from this analysis that the rules concerning the protection of natural resources in international humanitarian law are quite broad and vague. These rules were not intended to be used in the context of natural resources or long-term occupation. They therefore lack much of the specificity necessary to be readily applicable in many of the modern situations of occupation. They may also fail to properly take into account the nature of modern resource extraction.

III. Water and the Occupied Palestinian Territories

As mentioned above there have been significant issues concerning access to water by Palestinians and the manner in which water has been managed by Israel. It must therefore be considered whether the activities by Israel can be seen as being in accordance with the law on occupation.

---

41 Armed Activities, paras. 222–50; *Longobardo* (fn. 18), pp. 257-258.
42 Armed Activities, para. 249.
43 *Longobardo* (fn. 18), p. 257.
44 Armed Activities, para. 248.
45 *Longobardo* (fn. 18), pp. 259-269.

It is clear that water is a natural resource. The question is, however, how it is protected under the law of occupation. A basic distinction must be drawn first between water that comes from wells on private land and the water that is in major basins, such as most importantly the Mountain Aquifer. To begin with, wells on private land should be considered as private property, thus falling within the remit of Article 46 of the Hague Regulations. Hence, they enjoy protection under this provision. The situation for wells on municipal lands and water in major basins is more difficult as these are public along the lines that they do not specifically belong to someone. The primary difficulty lies in the question of whether this public property is to be viewed as movable or immovable. On the one hand, water is liquid and movable, on the other hand, we have to bear in mind the geographical and geological place in the Occupied Territories where the water comes from, and this place is immovable. If we apply a similar perspective as with regard to (other) extractable resources, such as oil and minerals, water basins such as the Mountain Aquifer should be considered as immovable public property.[46]

In essence, this means that Israel needs to act as a usufructuary with regard to these water sources. Israel has the right to use the fruits of the property, but it does not gain the right to ownership and does not have the right to cause harm to the property. While it has been argued that such water in general cannot be used to promote the economy of the occupying state, nor that it can be pumped to the occupying state, the situation with the Mountain Aquifer is somewhat different due to the nature of it as a shared natural resource.

Beyond this, international humanitarian law prohibits the establishment of settlements in the Occupied Territories[47] since these constitute a form of population transfer. Extracting water for the benefit of these settlements contributes to their consolidation, and perpetuates such illegality.

---

46 *El-Hindi*, The West Bank Aquifer and Conventions Regarding Laws of Belligerent Occupation, in: Michigan Journal of International Law 11 (1990), p. 1400 (1410-1413); *Abouali*, Natural Resources under Occupation: The Status of Palestinian Water under International Law, in: Pace International Law Review 10 (1998), p. 411 (472); *Cassese*, Powers and Duties of an Occupant in Relation to Land and Natural Resources (1992) in: Playfair (ed.) International Law and the Administration of Occupied Territory, reprinted in: Antonio Cassese, The Human Dimension of International Law (2008), pp. 261-262.

47 *International Court of Justice*, Legal Consequences of the Construction of a Wall in the Occupied Palestinian Territory, Advisory Opinion, I.C.J. Reports (2004) ('Wall Advisory Opinion'), p. 136, para. 120; *Benvenisti*, The International Law of Occupation (2012), pp. 239-241.

What needs to be taken into account when considering the issue of water within the context of occupation is that not only the law of occupation needs to be considered. Just as important is the right to water which is included in Article 11 of the International Covenant on Economic, Social and Cultural Rights.[48] Read together with Article 2 of the Covenant, this may be taken as imposing an obligation upon states to refrain from any activity or practice that denies or limits equal access to adequate water.

IV. Western Sahara Fisheries

Although the active hostilities between Morocco and the Sahrawi people came to an end in 1991, this does not mean that international humanitarian law is no longer applicable. As long as the occupation continues the rules of international humanitarian law remain applicable.[49]

One of the important natural resources that are being exploited in the area is fish. A 2005 EU-Moroccan Fisheries Partnership Agreement entered into force in February 2007.[50] On the basis of this Agreement European ships enjoyed access to fish in waters falling within the sovereignty or jurisdiction of the Kingdom of Morocco. The term jurisdiction was specifically included to ensure the application of the Agreement to Western Sahara.[51] After its expiration, the Agreement has been tacitly renewed twice, again implicitly referring to Western Sahara. On 24 July 2018, Morocco and the EU initialled a new Sustainable Fisheries Partnership Agreement, which was approved by the Council in March 2019.[52]

The Agreement has received significant criticism not only from Saharawi representatives, but also from European officials and states, as it was considered to be contrary to international law, in particular interna-

48 *Winkler*, The Human Right to Water: Significance, Legal Status and Implications for Water Allocation, Hart Publishing (2014), pp. 41-45.

49 Common Article 2 GC I-IV.

50 Adopted by Council Regulation EC No 764/2006 of 22 May 2006 (OJ L141 of 29 May 2006).

51 Protocol between the European Union and the Kingdom of Morocco Setting out the Fishing Opportunities and Financial Contribution provided for in the Fisheries Partnership Agreement between the European Union and the Kingdom of Morocco, adopted by Council Regulation EC No 764/2006 of 22 May 2006.

52 Council Decision (EU) 2019/441 of 4 March 2019 on the conclusion of the Sustainable Fisheries Partnership Agreement between the European Union and the Kingdom of Morocco, the Implementation Protocol thereto and the Exchange of Letters accompanying the Agreement.

tional humanitarian law. Although such criticism was discussed, the Agreement was adopted. The European Commission specifically rejected the notion that Western Sahara was under occupation. Instead, it argued the territory should be considered as non-self-governing, and should thus be subject to a process of decolonization with Morocco as its *de facto* administrator.[53] The background to this may be that, if conceptually moving from occupation to non-self-governing territory, this seems to open up the door for human rights law and the issue of self-determination rather than international humanitarian law.[54] By way of example, in his report to the UN Security Council of 2002 about oil exploitation in the area, Hans Corell worked from the assumption that the area was a non-self-governing territory rather than occupied territory.[55]

It is our contention that the debate within the European Commission and the legal advice given to the Commission did not sufficiently consider the issue of humanitarian law and rather focused on the issue of human rights law. To date, no state recognizes the claims of Morocco to the territory, and the General Assembly has found the territory to be occupied.[56] Hence, it is our viewpoint that it should be considered as a case of occupation:

1. Even if Western Sahara is to be viewed as a non-self-governing territory, this does not preclude it from being occupied;
2. While Morocco is often considered as the *de facto* administrator of this territory, it has not been recognized as such by the UN, nor has Morocco claimed this status itself;[57]
3. Occupation does not require that the state itself or other states recognize a situation as occupation.

In sum, Western Sahara should clearly be seen as falling within the definition of the Hague Regulations for what occupied territories are. The terri-

53 See Answer Given by High Representative/Vice-President Ashton on behalf of the Commission, Parliamentary Question No. E-000235-14, Mar. 13, 2014, 2014 O.J. (C 288) 1, 197.

54 *Saul* (fn. 26), pp. 302-303; *Smith*, The taking of the Sahara: the role of natural resources in the continuing occupation of Western Sahara in: Global Change, Peace & Security 27(3) (2015), p. 263 (273-274); *Zunes* (fn. 15), pp. 291-292.

55 *Under-Secretary General for Legal Affairs*, Letter dated 29 January 2002 from the Under-Secretary-General for Legal Affairs, the Legal Counsel, addressed to the President of the Security Council, UN Doc. S/2002/161 (2002).

56 G.A. Res. 34/37, UN Doc. A/RES/34/37 (21 November 1979).

57 *Simon* (fn. 12), p. 261; *Kontorovich*, Economic Dealings with Occupied Territories in: Columbia Journal of Transnational Law 53 (2015), p. 584 (613).

tory has been placed under the authority of a hostile army, as can be seen from the initial invasion of the territory. The definition of the Hague Regulations does not require that the territory is a self-governing territory; it only requires that the territory has been placed under the authority of a hostile army.[58] This has been confirmed in the Wall Advisory Opinion, where the argument of Israel that the West Bank was not occupied because it was not sovereign Jordanian territory was rejected by the ICJ.[59] Over the last decades it has been clear that Morocco holds effective governmental and administrative control over most of the territory, with the assistance of its military forces.[60] It has further been argued that, in the case of occupation, effective control needs to be achieved without the consent of the sovereign of that territory.[61] It is this part that could be most difficult to determine the case of Western Sahara. However, when looking at the circumstances by which Morocco gained effective control, it should be seen that this was done without the consent of the sovereign at the time, namely Spain.[62]

If thus Western Sahara is under occupation, the question arises how these natural resources qualify under the law of occupation – movable or not? Should the fish or the fishing waters be considered a natural resource? The answer to this question determines whether or not Morocco can exploit these resources and if so to what extent. If the fish themselves were considered as the natural resource in question, Morocco can only take possession of them if they are to be used for military operations, a possibility that is hardly conceivable. If, however, the fishing waters can be considered as the natural resource, there is the possibility of Morocco acting as a usufruct and allowing limited exploitation of these waters. This then raises the question as to the level to which these waters can be exploited, given that fish is a renewable, but finite natural resource. This does not render the actions of Morocco being in accordance with the law. International humanitarian law requires that the proceeds can only go towards offsetting the costs of the occupation, unless the exploitation is done for the benefit of the local population. In the context of Western Sahara there is a clear profit motive for the actions taken by Morocco without regard to the local

58 *Benvenisti* (fn. 17).

59 Wall Advisory Opinion; *Saul* (fn. 26), pp. 315-316. Even though Spain did not object, this cannot be said to alter the situation as the withdrawal of Spain was done under the threat of force, see *Saul*, pp. 305-316.

60 *Saul* (fn. 26) p. 308.

61 Armed Activities, para. 172.

62 *Saul* (fn. 26).

population.[63] This seems especially true due to the shift in demographics in Western Sahara and the influx of Moroccan settlers in the area assisted by the Moroccan state. At the same time even if one were to argue that Morocco should be able to exploit the stocks of fish, they have not done so in compliance with their usufructuary duty. There are clear indications that their fishing policies are unsustainable. This harms the fish stocks and creates the situation where these might be depleted or at least that their worth is lessened.[64] As the exploitation of these natural resources is not done solely by the Moroccan state itself, but also by different private actors, such as fishing companies, this could be classified as a case of pillage, for which Morocco could be held accountable due to their duty to prevent this from occurring.

Due to the involvement of the EU and European states in the exploitation of the fish stocks in Western Sahara it can be argued quite convincingly that these states are complicit in breaches of humanitarian law, as they profit from the occupation of Western Sahara and the use of its natural resources. Especially, if this exploitation is done in a manner that cannot be said to be sustainable and harms the fish stocks to a degree that deprives them of their renewable potential. By entering into these agreements, it could even be argued that they are complicit in the act of pillage by the private companies that fish in these waters. This might be less applicable in the context of the 2013 Agreement, as this included a specific, albeit vague, reference about benefits for the local population.[65] If it can truly be argued that the profits go towards the local population, it might fall within the exception that has been referred to by the ICJ in *DRC v. Uganda*. The problem with this is that although there has been significant investment in the area, this has mainly gone towards issues of internal security or support for Moroccan settlers, rather than towards the indigenous population.[66]

V. *Issues of Trusteeship*

In light of the difficulty to apply existing standards of international humanitarian law and given the questionable appropriateness of these standards to modern situations, it might be warranted to consider whether a

63 *Saul* (fn. 26), pp. 320-321.
64 *Smith* (fn. 54), p. 280.
65 *Zunes* (fn. 15), p. 294.
66 *Zunes* (fn. 15), p. 295.

different approach might yield better results, especially for the population living under occupation.

A possible approach might be found in the notion of trusteeship. While the formal issue of trusteeship has been relegated to the annals of history since 1994 when the last trusteeship came to an end, the concept has resurfaced in recent years in the context of international environmental law[67] and with regard to UN administered territories in the context of peacekeeping.[68] Whether only the trusteeship concept or the institutional setting thereof should be partially revived is an open question. The object and purpose of such discussions is to ensure the protection and avoid overexploitation of certain areas subject to trusteeship administration. This has mainly focused on those areas that are considered as a common repository of humankind as a whole and therefore the discussion has focused on global commons, such as 'the area', perhaps the oceans as a whole,[69] the atmosphere, Antarctica and outer space.[70]

There is a certain allure to the idea of applying the principles of trusteeship to the protection and exploitation of natural resources in the case of occupation. In a way it is merely an extension of the already existing regime where the occupying state is to act as a usufructuary, which in some regards can already be considered as acting as a trustee. If natural resources are exploited in some way, there is the need that this is done for the benefit of the local population. The occupying power can also be seen as a trustee in the protection of the natural resources from exploitation, as can be seen in *DRC v. Uganda*, they have the responsibility to prevent the exploitation of natural resources by private parties. In many ways the idea

67 *Sand*, The rise of public trusteeship in international environmental law, Environmental Policy and Law 44 (2014), p. 201 (210-218).

68 *Bothe/Marauhn*, The United Nations in Kosovo and East Timor - Problems of a Trusteeship Administration in: Journal of International Peacekeeping 6 (2000), p. 152 (152 *et seqq.*); *Wolfrum*, International Administration in Post-Conflict Situations by the United Nations and Other International Actors, in: Max Planck Yearbook of United Nations Law 9 (2005), p. 649 (672-673).

69 *Sand*, Public Trusteeship for the Oceans, in: Ndiaye/Wolfrum (eds.), Liber Amicorum Judge Thomas A. Mensah: Law of the Sea, Protection of the Marine Environment and Settlement of Disputes (2007), pp. 521-543.

70 *Bosselmann*, Democracy, Sovereignty and the Challenge of the Global Commons in: Westra *et al.* (eds.), The Role of Integrity in the Governance of the Commons, Springer International Publishing (2017), pp. 58-60; *Desai*, On the Revival of the United Nations Trusteeship Council with a New Mandate for the Environment and the Global Commons, in: Yearbook of International Environmental Law 27 (2016), p. 3 (3 *et seqq.*).

of trusteeship is in accordance with how many already view the existing obligations of an occupying power.[71] But by placing the natural resources under trusteeship, which is not the occupying power, might allow for better protection in the interest of the local population and ensuring the sustainable exploitation of renewable but finite resources. Placing it in the hands of a neutral party might also allow the exploitation of resources to be more directly focused on benefiting the local population. This is because, unlike occupation where the occupation itself serves the occupying power, in the case of trusteeship the trustee is considered to act both for the community of states as well as for the benefit of the local population, which in principle should preclude acting in their own interest.[72]

There are, however, significant issues with following such an approach, especially from the viewpoint of self-determination. It could be argued that through the use of trusteeship the UN becomes complicit in the violation of the right to self-determination of those territories that are occupied. This especially is the case in the context of long-standing occupations such as Palestine and Western Sahara. By applying a trusteeship to these territories, the UN could be argued to act in contradiction to the ICESCR, as it goes against the free pursuit of the economic development of the peoples in these territories.

This can be seen as being linked to the perception of trusteeship, which still carries with it some connotation of colonialism.[73] The use of trusteeship could therefore be seen as a form of new colonialism that is, at least implicitly and tacitly, agreed to by the international community. If such a system requires the approval of both states before an occupied territory can be put under trusteeship, this thereby creates an issue for the occupied state as it could be perceived that they are relinquishing their sovereignty over the territory. At the same time, it would be unlikely that the occupying power, at least in the cases discussed here, would agree to such a system, since they do not consider themselves to be an occupying power. While for the question of whether the legal rules of occupation are applicable this lacks stringency, it would prove vital for whether or not the occupying power agrees to the imposition of a trusteeship.

---

71 *Wilde*, From Trusteeship to Self-Determination and Back again: The Role of the Hague Regulations in the Evolution of International Trusteeship, and the Framework of Rights and Duties of Occupying Powers, Loyola of Los Angeles International and Comparative Law Review 31 (2009), p. 85 (100-102); *Benvenisti* (fn. 47), p. 6.

72 *Wolfrum* (fn. 68), p. 672.

73 *Bothe/Marauhn* (fn. 68), p. 218.

VI. Outlook

Looking at difficult situations of prolonged occupation in Palestine or in Western Sahara, these raise questions going beyond the traditional law of occupation. If the interests of the population are to be considered this necessitates a much broader and more comprehensive approach, taking into account human rights law, in particular socio-economic rights. If confined to the application of existing law, there may be a need to supplement the law of war by human rights standards depending on how long occupation has indeed persisted. Such application of human rights standards would not justify or legitimize occupation or even transfer of sovereignty, but it would simply serve to mitigate the tensions arising from political stalemate (in achieving an end of occupation) and the need to cater for the local population (where international humanitarian law might benefit from supplementary human rights standards).

Integrating Sustainable Management of Mineral Resources into International Mining Law

Nico Schrijver[*]

Abstract

Unlike certain other natural resources, mineral resources are not regulated by a specific international convention. Nevertheless, international law is highly pertinent to the regulation of mining and several different branches such as international trade law, law of the sea, human rights law and international environmental law address the management of mineral resources, including their ownership, conservation, exploration, exploitation, marketing and use. This regulation, however, is incomplete and inadequate to guarantee a prudent and rational use and exploitation of the mineral resources in a sustainable manner. Therefore, this contribution calls for a comprehensive and integrated approach to the international regulation of mining in all its different forms and usages.

Overview

---

* Professor Nico Schrijver is State Councillor, Council of State of the Netherlands, and professor emeritus of international law at Leiden University. He also served as Senator in the Dutch parliament, President of the International Law Association (2010-12), President of the *Institut de Droit international* (2017-19) and President of the Royal Netherlands Society of International Law (2003-11). He is a member of the Permanent Court of Arbitration and the Royal Netherlands Academy of Sciences and the author of various books, including *Sovereignty over Natural Resources. Balancing Rights and Duties* (Cambridge, 1997), *Sustainable Development in International Law: Inception, Meaning and Status* (Leiden, 2008) and *Development Without Destruction. The UN and Global Resource Management* (New York, 2010).

I. Introduction

Currently, no specific international convention on mineral resources exists. This in contrast to other specific natural resources, such as fisheries, biological resources, tropical timber and water. Yet, international law is highly pertinent to the regulation of mining. This chapter demonstrates that a host of issues can be identified from an international law point of view which touch upon the use and conservation of mineral resources, including in international economic law, law of the sea, international environmental law and human rights law. However, certain regulatory gaps in the field of mining can also be noted. Therefore, this chapter argues that it would be timely to pursue an integrated and comprehensive approach to the international regulation of mining.[1]

II. Mining and the environment

Mineral resources are non-renewable resources that are consumed as they are used. The quantity of mineral resources on earth is generally considered to be fixed and "finite". Exceptionally, certain mineral resources can be as renewable as living resources such as animals and plants. An example

1 This chapter is dedicated to professor Stephan Hobe, University of Cologne, for his life time contributions to the study of international law, academically as solid as a rock and therefore turning our esteemed colleague into a diamond in the community of international lawyers.

are polymetallic nodules on the deep seabed, which under certain circumstances can grow in approximately fifty years.[2] Minerals have a wide range of uses, ranging from construction (sand, stone), industrial uses (iron, steel), energy (coal, uranium), and stores of value (gold, silver, diamonds). Hence, minerals tend to be highly valuable. Mining can indeed be an important basis for employment and pursuing development. However, it is common knowledge that mining, as well as the processing of minerals, can have many negative impacts. For example, on the environment, on local communities or on the health conditions of workers in the mining industry. As regards the environmental impacts, reference can be made to the often consequent loss of biological diversity, contamination of water, acid mine drainage and air pollution.[3] As regards the impact on the health of workers, it is often a hardship to work in the mining industry: to work with processed mineral resources can be damaging to human health, as evidenced by the frequent problems with asbestos and gold mining. Various ILO Conventions and Recommendations are in place to reduce the negative effects of working in the mining industry on the health of workers.[4]

III. Various forms of mining and places of mining

Mining can take place in an open pit — also called service mining or strip mining — or as shallow or deep underground mining. One can also distinguish mining by reference to the place where it takes place. The first category to mention is mining within the territory of a state. Such territory does not only consist of the land and internal lakes and rivers of a state, but also of the 12 nautical miles (nm) territorial sea and seabed and subsoil thereof. A second category is the marine area under a state's economic jurisdiction, such as the 200-nm Exclusive Economic Zone (EEZ) and the continental shelf, which under certain circumstances can stretch beyond

---

2 See *Sun*, International Environmental Obligations and Liabilities in Deep Seabed Mining, doctoral thesis, Leiden University, Meijers Series, MI-306 (2018); *Li*, Transfer of Technology for Deep Seabed Mining: The 1982 UN Convention on the Law of the Sea and Beyond (1994).

3 See *Kidd*, Minerals, in: Morgera/Kulovesi (eds.), Research handbook on international law and natural resources, (2016) p. 327 (328-331).

4 A prime example is ILO Convention 176 on Safety and Health in Mines, adopted 22 June 1995, entered into force 28 February 1998; 2029 UNTS 207.

200 nm.[5] A third category is the area beyond national jurisdiction. This includes the high seas, the deep-sea bed, and to a certain extent Antarctica, outer space and the celestial bodies. The latter are also popularly referred to as the global commons.[6] Among these, the mineral resources of the deep seabed and Antarctica have received most active attention and regulation.[7] Potential mining in outer space, particularly on the moon, is also a topic of speculation.[8]

IV. Sources of international law for the regulation of mining

Principles and rules pertinent to mining can be found in a variety of sources of international law. These include customary international law, a number of treaties and soft law instruments.

1. Customary international law

Obviously, the principle of state sovereignty and the related principles of territorial jurisdiction and permanent sovereignty over natural resources are of high relevance to mining. They determine where and how mining can take place and who is entitled to do so. Increasingly, a number of principles of international environmental law with a customary international law status are also relevant for the regulation of mining. Reference should be made, first of all, to the prohibition of significant transboundary harm as formulated for the first time in the *Trail Smelter* award in a case (1938-1941) relating to significant environmental harm as a result of transboundary air pollution from the smelting of minerals, particularly for the production of aluminum.[9] Other principles emanate from this general

---

5 See Art. 76 of the UN Convention on the Law of the Sea, 10 December 1982; UN Doc. A/RES/48/263 (17 August 1994); 33 ILM 1309 (1994).

6 See also *Schrijver/Prislan*, From *Mare Liberum* to the Global Commons, Building on the Grotian Heritage, in: Grotiana 30 (2009) p. 168.

7 See *Lodge*, Deep Seabed, in: Rothwell/Elferink/Scott/Stephens (eds.), The Oxford Handbook on the Law of the Sea (2015).

8 *Hobe*, Technological development as a Challenge for the Development of Air and Space Law, in: Cheng (ed.), A New International Legal Order: in Commemoration of the Tenth Anniversary of the Xiamen Academy of International Law (2016), p. 295.

9 *Trail Smelter* (*United States v. Canada*), Award of 16 April 1938 and 11 March 1941, 3 RIAA 1905 (1941).

principle including the principle of prevention, the precautionary approach and the duty of due diligence.[10] Furthermore, in the *Pulp Mills* case, the International Court of Justice also identified the conducting of an environmental impact assessment as a principle under customary international law, where it stated:[11]

> *"[...] a practice, which in recent years has gained so much acceptance among States, that it may now be considered a requirement under general international law to undertake an environmental impact assessment where there is a risk that the proposed industrial activity may have a significant adverse impact in a transboundary context, in particular, on a shared resource."*

2. *Treaty law*

Although no general convention on mining exists, it is notable how many specific multilateral and regional treaties are pertinent to mining. In the context of the Economic Commission for Europe, a number of treaties have been concluded in this field. They include the 1979 Long Range Transboundary Air Pollution Convention and the 1998 Heavy Metals Protocol to it,[12] as well as the 1991 Espoo Convention on Environmental Impact Assessment in a Transboundary Context.[13] A specific convention in the African region is the Minamata Convention on Mercury,[14] a mined substance widely used in artisanal gold mining which has very harmful effects on the environment and human health. Furthermore, there are a number of global treaties. Here reference should be made to the Basel Convention on Hazardous Waste.[15] The General Agreement on Tariffs and

---

10 See *Sands/Peel*, Principles of International Environmental Law (4th edition 2018); *Birnie/Boyle/Redgwell*, International Law and the Environment (3rd edition 2009).

11 *International Court of Justice*, Judgment of 20 April 2010, Case Concerning Pulp Mills on the River Uruguay (Argentina v. Uruguay), ICJ Reports (2010), p. 14.

12 Protocol to the 1979 Convention on Long-Range Transboundary Air Pollution on Heavy Metals, Aarhus, 24 June 1998, entered into force 29 December 2003; 2237 UNTS 4.

13 Convention on Environmental Impact Assessment in a Transboundary Context, Espoo, Finland, 25 February 1991, entered into force on 10 September 1997; 1989 UNTS 309; 30 ILM 802 (1991).

14 Adopted on 10 October 2013 in Kumamoto, Japan, entered into force on 16 August 2017, UN registration no. 54669.

15 Basel Convention on the Control of Transboundary Movement of Hazardous Wastes and their Disposal, adopted on 22 March 1989, entered into force in 1992,

Trade (GATT),[16] now part of WTO law, addresses the issue of exhaustible resources in its Article XX on general exceptions to liberalization of and non-discrimination in international trade, resulting from the necessity "to protect human, animal or plant life or health" (subsection (b)) and relating "to the conservation of exhaustible natural resources" (subsection (g)). The UN Convention on the Law of the Sea also includes an extensive Part XI on the mineral resources of the deep seabed as well as specific provisions for mineral resources in other areas, such as states' EEZ and continental shelf.[17] To this category of global treaties also belongs a number of international environmental treaties, such as the Ramsar Convention on Wetlands,[18] the Convention on World Cultural and Natural Heritage Law,[19] the Convention on Biological Diversity[20] and the three international climate treaties (UNFCCC, Kyoto Protocol and the Paris Agreement).[21]

3. *Soft law instruments*

In various fields of international economic life, self-regulation takes place through voluntary industrial codes. Currently, many multinational corporations have their own codes of conduct and ethical standards which they

---

1673 UNTS 57. Among other forms, it mentions "wastes from mining operations in non-dispersible form" (Annex IX) and asbestos waste (Annex XX).

16 General Agreement on Tariffs and Trade (GATT 1947), Geneva, 30 October 1947, entered into force on 1 January 1948; 55 UNTS 187.

17 United Nations Convention on the Law of the Sea of 10 December 1982, entered into force on 16 November 1994; UN Doc. A/RES/48/263, 17 August 1994; 33 ILM 1309 (1994).

18 Convention on Wetlands of International Importance especially as Waterfowl Habitat, Ramsar, 2 February 1972, entered into force on 21 December 1975; (1972) 996 UNTS 245; 11 ILM 963.

19 Convention for the Protection of the World Cultural and Natural Heritage, adoption in 1972, entered into force in 1975, 1977 UNTS 1.

20 Convention on Biological Diversity (Biodiversity Convention), Rio de Janeiro, 5 June 1992, entered into force on 29 December 1993; 1760 UNTS 79; 31 ILM 822 (1992).

21 United Nations Framework Convention on Climate Change (UNFCCC), New York, 9 May 1992, entered into force on 21 March 1994; 1771 UNTS 107; 31 ILM 851 (1992); Kyoto Protocol to the United Nations Framework Convention on Climate Change, Kyoto, 11 December 1997, entered into force on 16 February 2005; UN Doc. FCCC/CP/L.7/Add.1, 10 December 1997; 37 ILM 22 (1998); Paris Agreement, Paris, 12 December 2015, entered into force 4 November 2016; UN Doc. FCCC/CP/2015/10/Add. 1 (2016).

voluntarily proclaim and seek to comply with. Regularly, these codes are also of an international nature. In the mining field, examples are the Code of Conduct in the Extractive Industries[22] and the Guidelines for Mining and Sustainable Development (adopted in Berlin, 2002).[23] Also, a number of soft law instruments of a general nature are relevant, such as the United Nations Global Compact (launched by former UN Secretary-General Kofi Annan in 2004)[24] and the Standards on Business and Human Rights, commonly known as the Ruggie Principles or the UN Guiding Principles.[25] Moreover, various soft law instruments of a general nature in the international environmental field apply to mineral resources. The most pertinent ones are the Stockholm Declaration of 1972,[26] the UNEP Guidelines on Shared Resources of 1978,[27] the World Charter for Nature of 1981[28] and the Rio Principles of 1992.[29] Furthermore, the ILC Draft Articles on the Prevention of Transboundary Harm do also apply to impacts of mining on the environment of neighbouring states.[30]

---

22 See The Extractive Industries Transparency Initiative (EITI), launched in 2002, available under: https://eiti.org/standard/overview (last accessed: 3 April 2020).

23 See http://www.mineralresourcesforum.org/Berlin/index.htm, including the Berlin II Guidelines for Mining and Sustainable Development (2002).

24 See the website www.unglobalcompact.org (last accessed: 3 April 2020).

25 Guiding Principles on Business and Human Rights: Implementing the United Nations 'Protect, Respect and Remedy' Framework, UN Doc. A/HRC/17/31, 21 March 2011, available under: www.ohchr.org/Documents/Publications/GuidingPrinciplesBusinessHR_EN.pdf (last accessed: 3 April 2020).

26 See UN Doc. A/CONF.48/14/Rev.1, 16 June 1972; text reproduced in 11 ILM 1416 (1972). For a comprehensive analysis of the debates and the text see *Sohn*, The Stockholm Declaration on the Human Environment, in: Harvard International Law Journal 14 (1973) p. 423.

27 Draft Principles of Conduct in the Field of the Environment for the Guidance of States in the Conservation and Harmonious Utilisation of Natural Resources Shared by Two or More States (UNEP 1978) 17 ILM 1097 (1978).

28 World Charter for Nature, UN Doc. A/RES/37/7, 28 October 1982.

29 Declaration of the United Nations Conference on Environment and Development (Rio Declaration), 14 June 1992; UN Doc. A/CONF.151/26 (UNCED); 31 ILM 874 (1992).

30 See Draft Articles on Prevention of Transboundary Harm of Hazardous Activities, in Yearbook of the International Law Commission, 2001, vol. II, Part Two, UN Doc. A/CN.4/SER.A/2001/Add. 1. See also Brunnee, Procedure and Substance in International Environmental Law (2020).

V. Selected chapters of international law pertinent to mineral resources

This section addresses in a non-exhaustive way some key chapters of international law which address mineral resources and their mining.

1. Human rights dimensions of mining

As indicated above, from the principle of sovereignty also follows the principle of permanent sovereignty over natural resources. The latter results from the progressive development of international law during the decolonization period, especially as regards self-determination of peoples and human rights.[31] On the one hand, permanent sovereignty has been formulated in order to underpin the right of colonial peoples to the natural resources within their territory. In this connection, it is also referred to as the principle of economic self-determination, the economic pendant of the principle of political self-determination and the ensuing international law of decolonization.[32] On the other, the principle of permanent sovereignty also served to reserve the natural resources exclusively for newly independent states no matter what treaties or mining concessions had been concluded with metropolitan countries and their companies during the colonial past.

This new law of permanent sovereignty has been most notably formulated in the 1962 UNGA Declaration on Permanent Sovereignty over Natural Resources[33] and subsequently in the identical Articles 1 of the two International Covenants on Human Rights, adopted in 1966.[34] Paragraph 1 of the 1962 UNGA Declaration stipulates that the natural resources of a country must be used in the interest of national development and of the

---

31 See generally Bungenberg/Hobe (eds.), Permanent Sovereignty over Natural Resources (2015) and *Schrijver*, Sovereignty over Natural Resources: Balancing Rights and Duties (1997).

32 See *Anghie*, Imperialism, Sovereignty and the Making of International Law (2004).

33 Declaration on Permanent Sovereignty over Natural Resources, UN Doc. GA Res. 1803 (XVII), 14 December 1962.

34 International Covenant on Economic, Social and Cultural Rights, New York, 16 December 1966, entered into force on 3 January 1976; 999 UNTS 3, 6 ILM 360 (1967); International Covenant on Civil and Political Rights, New York, 16 December 1966, entered into force on 23 March 1976; 999 UNTS 171, 6 ILM 368 (1967).

wellbeing of the people of the state concerned.[35] Building on this stipulation, the identical Articles 1 of the two international human right covenants provide that all peoples have the right to freely dispose of their national resources and that: "In no case may a people be deprived of its means of subsistence". All these documents emphasize, in essence, that the state is not the absolute owner of and master over natural resources within its territory, but rather the custodian of these resources on behalf of its people. This is reflected in various other international legal instruments. Article 22 of the African Charter on Human and Peoples' Rights provides with regard to natural resource sovereignty that: "This right shall be exercised in the exclusive interest of the people".[36] With respect to indigenous peoples, the ILO Convention 169 on Indigenous and Tribal Peoples in Independent Countries, adopted in 1989, formulates the rights of indigenous peoples in respect of their natural resources (including minerals) on their lands.[37] Similarly, Article 26 of the UN Declaration on the Rights of Indigenous Peoples, proclaimed in 2007, provides: "indigenous peoples have the rights to the lands, territories and resources which they have traditionally owned, occupied or otherwise used or acquired".[38] Furthermore, they have also "the right to develop and control territories and resources that they possess by traditional ownership". The same Article 26 also imposes an obligation upon states to "give legal recognition and protection to these lands, territories and resources". Article 10 of the Declaration prohibits forcible removal or relocation of indigenous peoples from their land and territories. Obviously, these provisions apply to mineral resources as well. Apart from peoples' rights, the individual right to health, life, family life, property, cultural rights and the right to religion may also be at stake because their enjoyment can be negatively affected by mining or working in the mining industry.[39] Therefore, the human rights impacts of mining

---

35 See UNGA Declaration on Permanent Sovereignty over Natural Resources (fn. 33), para. 1.

36 African Charter on Human and Peoples' Rights, Nairobi, 27 June 1981, entered into force on 21 October 1986; 1520 UNTS 217; 21 ILM 59 (1982).

37 Art. 15 of ILO Convention 160 Concerning Indigenous and Tribal Peoples in Independent Countries, adopted in 1989, entered into force 5 September 1991, 1650 UNTS 383; 28 ILM 1382 (1989).

38 United Nations Declaration on the Rights of Indigenous Peoples, 13 September 2007, annexed to UNGA Res. A/61/61/295.

39 See also *Francioni*, Natural Resources and human rights, in: Morgera/Kulovesi (eds.), Research handbook on international law and natural resources (2016), p. 66.

within the borders of states are also increasingly the subject of concern and regulation by international legal instruments.

Such basic rules are nowadays also incorporated in the national laws of a number of countries, for example, the South African Minerals and Petroleum Act which provides that the minerals are the common heritage of the peoples of South Africa.[40]

2. *Mineral resources in international economic law*

As noted above, the General Agreement on Tariffs and Trade (GATT), now part of WTO law, addresses the issue of exhaustible resources in its Article XX on General Exceptions. While international trade in minerals is subject to the ordinary GATT and WTO rules, exceptions from the obligations towards liberalization and non-discrimination in international trade can result from the necessity "to protect human, animal or plant life or health" (Art. XX, para. 1 sub (b)) and relate to "the importation of gold and silver" (sub (c)) and "to the conservation of exhaustible natural resources" (sub (g)). The former received recognition in the *Asbestos* case as a justification for a ban on importation of asbestos by France on the basis of the health risks.[41] The latter played a crucial role in two cases before the Dispute Settlement Body of the WTO involving China, respectively *Measures Related to the Exportation of Various Raw Materials*[42] and *Rare Earths*.[43] However, in both cases the justification claimed by China upon the basis of GATT Arti-

40 No. 28 of 2002. Government Gazette, Vol. 448, Cape Town, 10 October 2002. See also the Argentinian Constitution (1853, as reformed in 1994) which grants in section 41 any inhabitant the right to enjoy a healthy and balanced environment, suitable for human development, so that productive activities meet the needs of the present without compromising the needs of future generations to meet their own needs. National Constitution of the Argentine Republic, General Constituent Assembly, City of Santa Fe, 22 August 1994.

41 *World Trade Organisation*, European Communities — Measures Affecting Asbestos and Asbestos-Containing Products, WT/DS135/AB/R, 12 March 2001.

42 *World Trade Organisation*, China — Measures Related to the Exportation of Various Raw Materials, WT/DS394-5-8/R (Panel Report), circulated on 5 July 2011, WT/DS394-5-8/AB/R (Appellate Body Report), circulated on 30 January 2012, adopted on 22 February 2012 (including the Panel Report, as modified by the Appellate Body).

43 *World Trade Organisation*, China — Measures Related to the Exportation of Rare Earths, Tungsten and Molybdenum, WT/DS431-2-3/R (Panel Report), circulated on 26 March 2014, WT/DS431-2-3/AB/R (Appellate Body Report), circulated on 7 August 2014, adopted on 29 August 2014.

cle XX (sub (g)) was ultimately not accepted by the Appellate Body of the WTO.[44] Also the UN Convention on the Law of the Sea includes an extensive Part XI on the mineral resources of the deep seabed ("the Area") as well as specific provisions on mineral resources in other parts, such as those on the EEZ (Part V) and the Continental Shelf (Part VI). In recent years the International Seabed Authority drafted "Regulations on Exploitation of Mineral Resources in the Area", seeking to balance the potential exploitation of the minerals of the deep seabed and the widely felt need to preserve the marine environment, including the fauna and flora of the deep seabed.[45]

3. *Mineral resources and international environmental law*

The only multilateral environmental treaty that specifically addresses mineral resources is the Madrid Protocol on Environmental Protection to the Antarctic Treaty of 1991.[46] It was adopted in response to an outcry of public protest to the Convention on the Regulation of Antarctic Mineral Resource Activities, which was adopted in 1988.[47] Although this convention entailed a number of measures to ensure environmental protection and required decisions on mineral resource activities to be based on adequate information and the precautionary approach, it soon was delegitimized as a result of worldwide protests from many environmental NGOs.[48] Thereupon, the parties to the 1959 Antarctic Treaty framework hastened to adopt the Madrid Environmental Protocol in 1991, which prohibits "any

44 The Panel in *China – Rare Earths* emphasised that "WTO Members' right to adopt conservation programmes is not a right to control the international markets in which extracted products are bought and sold." After examining the nature of the export restraints, the Panel in *China – Rare Earths* concluded that they were inconsistent with China's WTO obligations, which was subsequently upheld by the Appellate Body.

45 See Art. 145 (a)(b) of UNCLOS (fn. 17). For an extensive analysis *Sun* (fn. 2).

46 Madrid Protocol on Environmental Protection of the Antarctic Treaty, adopted in 1991, entered into force 1998, 402 UNTS 5778.

47 Convention on the Regulation of Antarctic Mineral Resource Activities, Wellington, adopted 2 June 1988, not entered into force.

48 See also *Schrijver*, Development without Destruction: The UN and Global Resource Management (2010), pp. 92-93.

activity relating to mineral resources, other than scientific research",[49] and designates Antarctica as "a natural reserve, devoted to peace and science".[50]

Other global environmental treaties do not specifically refer to mineral resources but their principles and rules have in various ways a bearing on mining. For example, the Ramsar Convention on Wetlands,[51] the Convention on World Heritage,[52] the Convention on Biological Diversity[53] and the three international climate treaties mentioned above in section IV.2 (UNFCCC, Kyoto Protocol and the Paris Agreement),[54] all include provisions from which principles and rules emanate regarding duties to take into account with respect to mining activities. Similarly, as regards deep seabed mining, the Seabed Dispute Chamber of ITLOS in its Advisory Opinion on the topic also recognized the precautionary approach, as codified in Principle 15 of the Rio Declaration, to be "an integral part of the due diligence of sponsoring States which is applicable even outside the scope of the regulations".[55] In doing so, there are reflections of core principles of international environmental law, including the no harm principle, due diligence, precaution and prevention: principles which are also recorded in key environmental documents such as the Stockholm Declaration on the Protection of the Human Environment and the Rio Declaration on Environment.[56]

49 See Art. 7 of the Madrid Protocol (fn. 46).

50 See Art. 2 of the Madrid Protocol (fn. 46).

51 Convention on Wetlands of International Importance Especially as Waterfowl Habitat, adoption in 1971, entered into force in 1975, 996 UNTS 245.

52 Convention for the Protection of the World Cultural and Natural Heritage, adoption in 1972, entered into force in 1975, 1977 UNTS 1.

53 Convention on the Conservation of Biological Diversity, adoption in 1992, entered into force in 1993, 1760 UNTS 382.

54 UNFCCC; Kyoto Protocol and Paris Agreement (fn. 21).

55 *International Tribunal for the Law of the Sea*, Advisory Opinion of 1 February 2011, Responsibilities and obligations of States with respect to activities in the Area, ITLOS Reports (2011), para. 131. See also *Freestone*, Responsibilities and Obligations of States Sponsoring Persons and Entities with Respect to Activities in the Area in: American Journal of International Law 105 (2011), p. 755 (758).

56 Stockholm Declaration on the Human Environment, UN Doc. A/CONF.48/14/Rev.1, 16 June 1972; text reproduced in 11 ILM 1416 (1972) and Rio Declaration (fn. 29).

VI. *Conflict minerals*

The proliferation of civil wars in the 1990s and the concentration of such conflicts in mineral-rich countries called into question the relationship between natural resources and stability. The availability of natural resources became increasingly viewed not only as an economic blessing but also as a curse.[57] The conflicts in Angola, Liberia and Sierra Leone, to mention just a few, were caused or at least fueled by access to natural resources. Furthermore, rivalry over natural resources characterized several interstate wars: for instance, the Iraqi invasion of Kuwait in August 1990 was sparked because of the disputed transboundary Rumaila oil field, and a principal reason for Rwandan and Ugandan aggression against the Democratic Republic of Congo (DRC) was to gain access to its extensive gold and diamond mines. The relationship between natural resources and armed conflict has thus received increasing attention from practitioners and social scientists.[58]

One main response was the so-called Kimberley process, which was started in 2000 and was followed up by a debate and resolution of the UN General Assembly: "The Role of Diamonds in Fueling Conflict: Breaking the Link between the Illicit Transaction of Rough Diamonds and Armed Conflict as a Contribution to Prevention and Settlement of Conflict".[59] By 2003, the Kimberley Process resulted in a certification scheme which imposes obligations on participants to certify shipments of diamonds and to prevent "blood diamonds" from entering the legitimate trade market.[60]

Furthermore, in various parts of the world, non-state armed groups – including terrorist organizations such as the Daesh (Islamic State), Al-Qaida, the Taliban, the Lord Resistance's Army and rebel groups in the DRC – operate upon the basis of the revenues of illegal natural resource exploitation in areas under their control. The UN Security Council has prohibited the import and export of commodities, including oil, from a number of non-government controlled areas in certain countries such as Somalia, Libya, Syria and DRC. Similarly, the International Criminal Court has taken up the investigation of serious war crimes "that are committed by means of, or that result in, inter alia, the destruction of the environment,

57 See *Collier*, Plundered Nations and Successes and Failures in Natural Resource Extraction (2011).

58 *Dam-de Jong*, International Law and Governance of Natural Resources in Conflict and Post-Conflict Situations (2015).

59 UN Doc. A/RES/55/56, 29 January 2001. For a recent update see UN Doc. A/RES/73/283, 1 March 2019.

60 See website www.kimberleyprocess.com (last accessed: 3 April 2020).

the illegal exploitation of natural resources or the illegal dispossession of land".[61]

With a view to strengthening its effectiveness in conflict prevention, particularly in Africa, the Security Council passed Resolution 1625 in September 2005, expressing the Council's determination "to take action against illegal exploitation and trafficking of natural resources and high-value commodities in areas where it contributes to the outbreak, escalation or continuation of armed conflict".[62] This policy was reaffirmed in 2006 in Resolution 1653 on the Great Lakes region and in various other country-specific resolutions with respect to Liberia, Libya, Eritrea and the Central African Republic.[63]

In this way, the UN exposed the issue of conflict minerals and formulated policies to address the nexus between armed conflict and natural resource exploitation, especially regarding "blood diamonds", and condemned the illegal exploitation and trade in natural resources by non-state armed groups. The issue of conflict goods also brought urgency to the need to formulate responsible, accountable strategies for mineral resource management, so that a country's natural wealth is harnessed for the benefit of that country's development, rather than being used to finance war.

Individual countries and regional economic organizations have also taken action to address the issue of conflict minerals. The US Congress adopted the Dodd-Frank Act in 2010, which seeks to regulate the activities of US listed companies operating in the DRC. Specifically, under Section 1502 the Act aims to stop US companies from buying natural resources from armed groups operating in the DRC. Especially, Section 1502 anchors in a domestic law an advanced corporate social responsibility to exercise due diligence in the sourcing of minerals extracted and exported from conflict zones in the DRC and nine listed neighbouring countries. Companies have reporting obligations to the US Security and Exchange Commission (SEC) on the way they have performed their due diligence duties with respect to specified minerals such as tin, tungsten, coltan/tantalum (3Ts) and gold, which they have acquired from the DRC and neighbouring countries. These minerals are widely used for consumer goods such as mobile

---

61 *Cf.* Art. 8 on War Crimes, para. 2 (e) (v) on Pillaging, Rome Statute of the International Criminal Court, 17 July 1998, entered into force on 1 July 2002, 2187 UNTS 3.

62 UN Doc. S/RES/1625 (2005), 14 September 2005.

63 See *Dam-de Jong*, Elected Members and Agenda-Setting: The Security Council as Peace Broker, in: Schrijver/Blokker (eds.), Elected Members of the Security Council: Lame Ducks or Key Players? (2020) p. 197.

phones, laptops and the like. In addition, the Act also seeks to wipe out corruption by all parties involved in such natural resource transactions, including the respective governments and their state organs and companies.[64]

The European Union has also adopted a notable EU Conflict Minerals Regulation as a follow-up to Security Council Resolution 1952 (2010) on conflict minerals in the DRC.[65] The EU regulation does not only focus on the Great Lakes region like the Dodd-Frank Act, but more generally applies to all conflict zones that are politically unstable.[66] The EU Regulation applies to a narrower range of companies than the Dodd-Frank Act, namely those who directly import the identified minerals into the EU and to smelters and refiners that process these minerals from conflict affected and high-risk areas. In a way, the EU Regulation builds on the core elements of due diligence as formulated by the OECD.[67] The EU Conflict Minerals Regulation is to become operational by 2021 and is currently being implemented in national legislation by EU member states.

VII. Strategies towards sustainable management of mineral resources

From the review in this chapter it follows that current international law addresses in a variety of its chapters the management of mineral resources, including their ownership, conservation, exploration, exploitation, marketing and use. Several branches of international law are pertinent to this such as international trade law, law of the sea, human rights law and inter-

---

64 See *Brackett/Levin/Melin*, Revisiting the Conflict Minerals Rule, in: Global Trade and Customs Journal 10 (2015), p. 73.

65 UN Doc. S/RES/1951, 24 November 2010.

66 Art. 2 (f) of the EU Conflict Minerals Regulation provides an interesting definition of conflict affected or high-risk areas as "areas in a state of armed conflict or fragile post-conflict areas as well as witnessing weak or non-existent governance and security such as failed States and systematic violations of international law, including human rights abuses." Regulation (EU) 2017/821 of the European Parliament and of the Council of 17 May 2017 laying down supply chain due diligence obligations for Union importers of tin, tantalum and tungsten, their ores, and gold originating from conflict-affected and high-risk areas. OJ L130, Vol 60, 19 May 2017.

67 See *Organisation for Economic Co-operation and Development*, OECD Due Diligence Guidelines for Responsible Business Conduct, 31 May 2018, available under: http://mneguidelines.oecd.org/OECD-Due-Diligence-Guidance-for-Responsible-Business-Conduct.pdf (last accessed: 3 April 2020).

national environmental law. It follows from the analysis in this chapter that current regulation of mineral resources is incomplete and inadequate to ensure a prudent and rational use and exploitation of the mineral resources, both within countries and in the global commons. Similarly, the existing institutions are not sufficiently equipped to curb the alarming rates of resource degradation and to provide functional rather than territorial regimes aimed at an integrated ecosystem approach for sustainable development.

Obviously, this calls for a comprehensive approach and integrative decision-making, which builds upon the interrelatedness of these various individual chapters of international law. In a way this could well be said to form the quintessential meaning of the principle of the sustainable use of mineral resources so as to ensure that their exploitation and use is compatible with the need to protect and improve the human environment for the benefit of their population, as advocated by the Stockholm Declaration.[68] In a more prescriptive sense, Principle 4 of the Rio Declaration on Environment and Development demands that "environmental protection shall constitute an integral part of the development process and cannot be considered in isolation from it".[69]

In view of all of this, the international community should ideally take on the drafting of a global convention on mineral resources. This would provide a proper opportunity to identify, develop and record a comprehensive approach to mining in all its different forms and usages. Some inspiration could well be drawn from other global conventions, most notably the Convention on Biological Diversity, the Water Resources Convention and the World Fisheries Agreement. However, it is a hard fact of life that such a treaty-making project is a very cumbersome, if not a nearly impossible exercise. Even in the unlikely case that such a project was to succeed, the experience of the Water Resources Convention or, for that matter, the Moon Agreement, show that ratifications may stall at relatively low numbers. Rather than taking on the Tantalus labour of drafting a global convention on mineral resources, it could be more prudent and rewarding to seek to update and refine existing soft law instruments, thereby soliciting the views of all relevant actors and stakeholders (including States, international organisations, business associations, and local communities) through appropriate processes for participation and dialogue. Building on the Berlin Guidelines for Mining and Sustainable Development could serve as a logi-

68 *Cf.* Principle 13 of the Stockholm Declaration (fn. 56).
69 Principle 4 of the Rio Declaration (fn. 29).

cal anchor point.[70] Indeed, the principal task at hand for international mining law is perhaps not so much the drafting of a new legal instrument but rather how to design, agree on and apply a multidimensional framework for the development of mineral resources in a sustainable manner. Such a task would need to encompass the entire mine life cycle – from early prospection and the study of economic, social and environmental impacts, to the final stage of mine closure with physical and social rehabilitation plans, with full access to information, dialogue and local participation in decision-making throughout.[71] This could well provide a feasible way of integrating sustainable management of mineral resources into international mining law.

70 See http://www.mineralresourcesforum.org/Berlin/index.htm, including the Berlin II Guidelines for Mining and Sustainable Development (2002). See also *Starke*, Breaking New Ground: Mining, Minerals and Sustainable Development (2016).

71 See *Bastida*, Integrating Sustainability into Mining Law: The Experience of Some Latin American Countries, in: Schrijver/Weiss (eds.), International Law and Sustainable Development: Principles and Practice (2004), p. 575.

Extractives for Development: Orientation and Activities of German Development Cooperation in the Mining Sector

*Leopold von Carlowitz**

Abstract

This contribution focuses on the relationship between German development cooperation and the extractives sector. The author starts with the phenomenon of the resource curse and then reviews the main national and international policy documents that guide German development cooperation. He also analyses the most relevant human rights due diligence instruments relating to conflict minerals and provides an overview of the extractives-related programs of Germany's main development agency GIZ. While German development cooperation in the sector traditionally has a strong focus on transparency issues including support to the Extractive Industries Transparency Initiative, programming is increasingly focusing on sustainable supply chains and related multi-stakeholder processes. The author appreciates that the German Government has revised its Natural Resource Strategy in early 2020. It thereby strengthened transparency and sustainability aspects in the context of securing sufficient supply of natural resources for German industry. The revision reflects the universal approach of the Agenda 2030 holding both developing and developed countries alike responsible for sustainable development. Noting growing consumer awareness and concern over the social and environment costs of Western "externalization societies", the author is calling for multi-stakeholder collaboration to ensure responsible consumer and production patterns in mining.

* *Leopold von Carlowitz* worked as Senior Advisor for the GIZ Sector Program "Extractives for Development" until Oct. 2020 where he was responsible for the work stream "sustainability standards, human rights, conflict minerals and resource conflicts". The views expressed in this article are his personal views and do not necessarily reflect the position of German development cooperation. The author is grateful to *Katharina Bockisch* for her support in writing this article.

Leopold von Carlowitz

Overview

I. Introduction

The extractive industry plays an important role in many developing countries all over the world. Nonetheless, many resource-rich countries do not benefit from the abundance of their raw materials. Their *per capita* income is below global average. It is estimated that by 2030, 75 % of the world's poor will live in resource-rich countries.[1] In many cases, this is due to governance issues: According to the 2017 Resource Governance Index, only 19 out of the 81 assessed resource-rich countries possess a good or satisfactory

1 Compare *International Monetary Fund*, James Cust on Oil Discoveries: Managing Expectations (23 February 2018), available under https://www.imf.org/en/News/Podcasts/All-Podcasts/2018/02/23/james-cust-on-oil-discoveries (last accessed: 1 April 2020).

governance system.[2] Resource governance and/or natural resource management is thus a concern of development cooperation.

Resource-rich countries in the Global North, like Norway, Canada or previously Saxony, have demonstrated that a wealth of natural resources can be used for the benefit of their nations and populations. According to the Addis Ababa Agenda on Financing for Development, the world leaders also stipulated that developing countries should contribute to their own development by tapping their own natural resources.[3] This makes the topic even more prominent for development cooperation.

At the outset of this overview article, the author sketches the most prominent challenges related to natural resources before reviewing the main policy papers that guide German development cooperation in the extractives sector. In the light of their present-day relevance, the recently adopted EU Regulation on Conflict Minerals[4] and the OECD Due Diligence Guidance for Responsible Supply Chains of Minerals from Conflict-Affected and High Risks Areas[5] are also discussed. In the second part of the paper, the author describes on extractives-related activities of the Deutsche Gesellschaft für Internationale Zusammenarbeit (GIZ) generally seen as the primary implementing agency of German development cooperation.[6] Primary focus lies on the Sector Program "Extractives for Development", jointly implemented by GIZ and the Federal Institute of Geosciences and Natural Resources (BGR). A brief overview is also given of the resource governance projects in partner countries presently running.

---

2 *Natural Resource Governance Institute*, 2017 Resource Governance Index (2017), pp. 4-5, available under: https://resourcegovernance.org/sites/default/files/documents/2017-resource-governance-index.pdf (last accessed: 1 April 2020).

3 *United Nations*, Addis Ababa Agenda of the Third International Conference on Financing for Development (2015), available under: http://www.un.org/esa/ffd/wp-content/uploads/2015/08/AAAA_Outcome.pdf (last accessed: 1 April 2020).

4 Regulation (EU) 2017/821 of the European Parliament and of the Council of 17 May 2017 laying down supply chain due diligence obligations for Union importers of tin, tantalum and tungsten, their ores, and gold originating from conflict-affected and high-risk areas, OJ L 130, 19.5.2017, p. 1.

5 *OECD*, OECD Due Diligence Guidance for Responsible Supply Chains of Minerals from Conflict-Affected and High-Risk Areas (3rd edition 2016), available under: http://www.oecd.org/daf/inv/mne/OECD-Due-Diligence-Guidance-Minerals-Edition3.pdf (last accessed: 1 April 2020).

6 A central actor in the field of mining-related development cooperation is also the BGR. This central geoscientific authority is subordinate to the Federal Ministry for Economic Affairs and Energy (BMWi) and provides advice to the German Government in all geo-relevant questions. At present, the BGR implements 10 technical cooperation projects in different partner countries, mainly in Africa and Asia.

II. The Resource Curse

In the Global South, many resource-rich countries are unable to take advantage of the benefits of their natural resources. They suffer from a phenomenon known as "the resource curse" that describes a plethora of economic, social, environmental and governance related problems in connection with extractive industries.[7]

Originally linked to the "Dutch Disease", the phenomenon addresses the dependency of a national economy in a resource-rich country on the extractive industry.[8] While the extractive sector flourishes (even though commodity prices usually fluctuate), other economic sectors decline dramatically. A strong extractive sector tends to increase the value of the national currency significantly. This makes all export products very expensive for other countries with a weaker currency. Thus, the resource-rich country exports less products and its economy primarily focuses on the extractive sector, unless other economic sectors are strengthened actively and the economy is diversified.

Many resource-rich countries are grappling with weak governance structures in general but also with respect to the extractive sector. Weak governance provides a perfect breeding ground for corruption, smuggling and corresponding impunity. A prominent challenge in this context is transfer pricing inside multinational companies. They use methods of pricing transactions between their own branches or companies controlled by them to avoid paying taxes.[9] This happens easily in developing countries that lack effective monitoring and do not possess adequate analytical and enforcement capacities.

Another important issue is conflict financing through the exploitation of natural resources. Especially in the Democratic Republic of Congo

---

7 Compare *Natural Resource Governance Institute*, The Resource Curse, The Political and Economic Challenges of Natural Resource Wealth, NRGI Reader (March 2015), available under: https://resourcegovernance.org/sites/default/files/nrgi_Resource-Curse.pdf (last accessed: 1 April 2020).

8 For more information, see *Ismael*, The Structural Manifestation of the 'Dutch Disease': The Case of Oil Exporting Countries, IMF Working Paper WP/10/103 (April 2010), pp. 4 et seqq, available under: https://www.imf.org/~/media/Websites/IMF/imported-full-text-pdf/external/pubs/ft/wp/2010/_wp10103 .ashx (last accessed: 1 April 2020).

9 *Readhead*, Preventing Tax Base Erosion in Africa: A Regional Study of Transfer Pricing Challenges in the Mining Sector, Natural Resource Governance Institute (July 2016), *passim*, available under: https://resourcegovernance.org/sites/default/files/documents/nrgi_transfer-pricing-study.pdf (last accessed: 1 April 2020).

(DRC) and the wider Great Lakes Region, the so-called conflict minerals tin, tantalum, tungsten and gold (3TG) have been used to finance warlords and rebels. They thus helped to prolong and sustain armed conflicts. Natural resources including diamonds and oil also fueled violent conflicts in other countries such as Angola, Sierra Leone, Colombia, Venezuela, Libya and Iraq. In various processes, the international community addressed the issue and tried to stop the trade and import of conflict minerals.

Insufficient resource governance is not just problematic in the context of armed conflict. Also in a "peaceful" environment, mining can lead to significant environmental damage and incur serious violations of labor and human rights. A weak state is unable to protect its population from such infringements and damages caused by or related to the extractive sector.

A special human rights issue exists when indigenous peoples are concerned.[10] In many countries, indigenous people are discriminated against and lack the ability to claim their rights to preserve their culture, language and land. Governments too often force indigenous peoples to leave their land needed for mining activities with almost no compensation. As consequence, conflicts erupt between indigenous peoples, the government and the extractive companies.[11]

The principle of Free, Prior and Informed Consent (FPIC) is meant to prevent such developments. Mentioned in several international instruments, including the ILO Convention on Indigenous and Tribal Peoples in Independent Countries No. 169[12] and the UN Declaration on the Rights of Indigenous People[13], FPIC seeks to integrate and protect indigenous peoples' interests in decision-making processes relating to national and international investments including mining. The exact scope of the

---

10 For an overview, see *O'Faircheallaigh*, Mining, development and Indigenous peoples', in: Lodhia (ed.), Mining and Sustainable Development, Current Issues (2018), p. 125 (125 *et seqq.*).

11 *Katz-Lavigne*, Property rights and large-scale mining: overlapping claims at and around mining sites at the Democratic Republic of Congo and Zambia, Third World Thematics 1 (2016), p. 202.

12 Art. 6, 15 and 16 ILO Convention concerning Indigenous and Tribal Peoples in Independent Countries (1989), available under: http://ilo.org/dyn/normlex/en/f?p=NORMLEXPUB:12100:0::NO::P12100_ILO_CODE: C169 (last accessed: 1 April 2020).

13 Art. 19 and 32 UN Declaration on the Rights of Indigenous People (2007), available under: https://www.un.org/esa/socdev/unpfii/documents/DRIPS_en.pdf (last accessed: 1 April 2020).

right to FPIC remains disputed. However, the principle is gaining ground and has been included in various international sustainability initiatives.[14]

III. *Relevant Policy Papers*

German development policy relating to the extractives is guided by multiple policy papers. Among them are the following: the Agenda 2030 (1.), the German Natural Resource Strategy (2.), the Development Policy on Raw Materials (3.), the Africa Mining Vision (4.), the Marshall Plan for Africa (5.) and the National Action Plan for Business and Human Rights (6.).

1. *Agenda 2030*

The 2030 Agenda for Sustainable Development of the UN is a global action plan that entered into force in 2016. It contains 17 Sustainable Development Goals (SDGs) accompanied by 169 targets aiming to realize economic, social and environmental dimensions of sustainable development by 2030.[15]The SDGs are global in nature and universally applicable, taking into account different national realities, capacities and levels of development and respecting national policies and priorities. Expanding the scope of their predecessor, the Millennium Development Goals, the Agenda embraces sustainable development as the organizing principle for global cooperation and applies to both, developing and developed countries alike.[16]

A mapping of the linkages between mining and the SDGs demonstrates that the extractive sector has the potential to contribute to all of the 17

---

14 *Franks*, Mountain Movers: Mining, Sustainability and the Agents of Change (2015), p. 35.

15 *United Nations General Assembly*, Transforming our world: the 2030 Agenda for Sustainable Development, A/RES/70/1 of 25 September 2015, available under: https://www.un.org/ga/search/view_doc.asp?symbol=A/RES/70/1&Lang=E (last accessed: 1 April 2020); for a more detailed analysis including the drafting history, see *Sachs*, The Age of Sustainable Development (2015), pp. 481-511.

16 *Sustainable Development Solutions Network*, Getting Started with the Sustainable Development Goals, A Guide for Stakeholders (December 2015), available under: http://www.sustainablesids.org/wp-content/uploads/ 2018/06/getting-started-guide-FINAL-PDF-.pdf (last accessed: 1 April 2020).

goals.[17] When managed properly, the sector can create jobs, spur innovation and bring investment and infrastructure at a game-changing level. SDG 1 (End Poverty), SDG 8 (Decent Work and Economic Growth) and SDG 9 (Infrastructure, Innovation and Industrialization) are particularly relevant in this context. If managed poorly, as discussed above, mining will often have many negative impacts on the environment, affected communities and on public governance in general. Mining is thus relevant for a number of other goals, including SDG 6 (Clean Water and Sanitation), SDG 7 (Energy Access and Sustainability), SDG 13 (Climate Action) and SDG 15 (Life on Land).

The Agenda also includes goals of a more general nature which are of great relevance to German development cooperation in the extractive sector. These are SDG 12 (Responsible Consumption and Production), SDG 16 (Peace, Justice and Strong Institutions) and SDG 17 (Partnerships for the Goals).

Goal 12 intends to ensure sustainable consumption and production patterns, a goal that also applies to the extractive sector. Two of the eight targets for this goal are particularly relevant for development cooperation: By 2030, states intend to achieve the sustainable management and efficient use of natural resources (target 12.2). And they wish to encourage companies, especially large and transnational companies, to adopt sustainable practices and to integrate sustainability information into their reporting cycle (target 12.6). These targets relate to the implementation of responsible sourcing practices. This means integrating environmental and social considerations as well as requirements in public and private sector procurement processes. It also involves collaboration to establish codes of conduct and sourcing principles including best practices across the entire mining value chain.[18]While these targets address primarily the private sector, the public sector can support these efforts by complementary development

---

17 *Columbia Center on Sustainable Investment et al.*, Mapping Mining to the Sustainable Development Goals: An Atlas (July 2016), p. 3, available under: https://www.undp.org/content/dam/undp/library/Sustainable%20Development/Extractives/Mapping_Mining_SDGs_An_Atlas_Executive_Summary_FINAL.pdf (last accessed: 1 April 2020).

18 Compare *Columbia Center on Sustainable Investment et al.*, Mapping Mining to the Sustainable Development Goals: An Atlas (July 2016), p. 52, available under: https://www.undp.org/content/dam/undp/library/Sustainable%20Development/Extractives/Mapping_Mining_SDGs_An_Atlas_Executive_Summary_FINAL.pdf (last accessed: 1 April 2020).

projects, capacity-building, consumer awareness-raising, creation of roundtables, etc.

Goal 16 is by nature more oriented toward the public sector and institutions: States shall promote peaceful and inclusive societies for sustainable development, provide access to justice for all and build effective, accountable and inclusive institutions at all levels. This goal has various relevant targets for the mining sector, particularly with a view on conflict financing through natural resources and on corruption-related issues: States are to significantly reduce violence and related death rates everywhere (target 16.1) and to promote the rule of law at the national and international levels and ensure equal access to justice for all (target 16.3). By 2030, they shall significantly reduce illicit financial and arms flows, strengthen the recovery and return of stolen assets and combat all forms of organized crime (target 16.4); substantially reduce corruption and bribery in all their forms (target 16.5); and develop effective, accountable and transparent institutions at all levels (target 16.6). Transparency and participation are the focus of two further targets, *i.e.* to ensure responsive, inclusive, participatory and representative decision-making at all levels (target 16.7); and to ensure public access to information and protect fundamental freedoms, in accordance with national legislation and international agreements (target 16.10). Companies can contribute to realizing this goal by preventing mining-related company-community conflict; implementing human rights impact assessments; respecting the rights of indigenous peoples including FPIC; and by participating in conflict-free mineral certification schemes.[19]

Another more general goal is central to international development cooperation. This is Goal 17 which calls for “Partnerships for the Goals” to strengthen the means of implementation and revitalize the global partnership for sustainable development. The scale and ambition of Agenda 2030 is so large that States alone will not be able to advance it. Instead, intensive global engagement is sought bringing together governments, the private sector, civil society, the UN system and other actors, mobilizing all available resources. The extractive sector and its revenues play a significant role in achieving target 17.1: In order to improve domestic capacity for tax and other revenue collection domestic resource mobilization shall be strengthened through international support to developing countries. German de-

19 *Columbia Center on Sustainable Investment et al.*, Mapping Mining to the Sustainable Development Goals: An Atlas July 2016), p. 64, available under: https://www.undp.org/content/dam/undp/library/Sustainable%20Development/Extractives/Mapping_Mining_SDGs_An_Atlas_Executive_Summary_FINAL.pdf (last accessed: 1 April 2020).

velopment cooperation also focuses on targets 17.16 and 17.17 relating to the establishment and support of multi-stakeholder partnerships. They are to mobilize and share knowledge, expertise, technology and financial resources to support the achievement of the SDGs. States shall encourage and promote effective public, public-private and civil society partnerships, building on the experience and resourcing strategies of existing partnerships.

2. *German Natural Resource Strategy*

The German Natural Resource Strategy is the primary strategy paper of the German Federal Government relating to the extractive industries. In January 2020, the German lead Ministry for natural resources, the Federal Ministry of Economic Affairs (BMWi), published a revised strategy which addresses the German industry's needs to ensure sufficient supply of natural resources for its production.[20] This revision is based on a predecessor version dated 2010.[21] The strategy reconfirms that it is in principle a private sector responsibility to make sure Germany's resource needs are met. However, the Federal Government introduced a set of measures to support a sustainable supply and to ensure the competitiveness of German industry. Within EU trade policy, the Federal Government intends to push for a reduction of extractives-related trade barriers such as export tariffs by producer countries. The Government also seeks to support the industry in diversifying its sources for resource supply; to strengthen a sustainable resource sector by promoting recycling and increased energy efficiency; to improve cooperation with resource-rich partner countries; and to invest in innovative technologies and research. Among other things, it created the German Resource Agency (DERA) to monitor resource markets to provide support to German companies in their activities to ensure sufficient sup-

20 *Bundesministerium für Wirtschaft und Energie*, Rohstoffstrategie der Bundesregierung, Sicherung einer nachhaltigen Rohstoffversorgung Deutschlands mit nicht-energetischen mineralischen Rohstoffen (January 2020), available under: https://www.bmwi.de/Redaktion/DE/Downloads/P-R/rohstoffstrategie-der-bundesregierung.pdf?__blob=publicationFile&v=8 (last accessed: 1 April 2020).

21 *Bundesministerium für Wirtschaft und Technologie*, Rohstoffstrategie der Bundesregierung, Sicherung einer nachhaltigen Rohstoffversorgung Deutschlands mit nicht-energetischen mineralischen Rohstoffen (October 2010), available under: http://www.rohstoffwissen.org/fileadmin/downloads/160720.rohstoffstrategie-der-bundesregierung.pdf (last accessed: 1 April 2020).

ply. In the 2020 revision, the Government takes stock of these approaches and updates its policy in the light of current challenges in the sector. Among these are market changes due to disruptive technologies, trade disputes, high market power of individual actors and increasing demands relating to social and environmental concerns.[22]

Already in the 2010 strategy, the Government emphasized its view that sustainable development and social and economic progress is impossible without good governance, respect for human rights and without due regard to ecological and social standards. German industry should act in accordance with internationally recognized instruments and initiatives like the OECD Guidance for Multinational Companies.[23] The revised 2020 strategy gives considerably more prominence to issues related to responsible sourcing of minerals than its predecessor version. It contains a whole chapter on sustainability and transparency in the extractives sector. In this context, the Government explicitly states the private sector's responsibility to consider the conditions under which natural resources are exploited, especially in fragile States with particular threat to human rights. The Government declares its support to responsible sourcing and transparency in mineral supply chains. Its support is to consist of a "smart mix" of voluntary initiatives and regulatory measures, including accompanying development activities, both on a national and international level.[24] The National Action Plan for Business and Human Rights, OECD Due Diligence Guidance, EU Regulation on Conflict Minerals, and Extractive Industries Transparency Initiative (EITI) are all dealt with in sub-chapters. With this increased emphasis on responsible mineral supply chains and transparent resource governance, the German Government includes and embraces in its

---

22 *Bundesministerium für Wirtschaft und Energie*, Rohstoffstrategie der Bundesregierung, Sicherung einer nachhaltigen Rohstoffversorgung Deutschlands mit nicht-energetischen mineralischen Rohstoffen (January 2020), p. 2, available under: https://www.bmwi.de/Redaktion/DE/Downloads/P-R/rohstoffstrategie-der-bundesregierung.pdf?__blob=publicationFile&v=8 (last accessed: 17 April 2020).

23 *Bundesministerium für Wirtschaft und Technologie*, Rohstoffstrategie der Bundesregierung, Sicherung einer nachhaltigen Rohstoffversorgung Deutschlands mit nicht-energetischen mineralischen Rohstoffen (October 2010), p. 8, available under: http://www.rohstoffwissen.org/fileadmin/downloads/160720.rohstoffstrategie-der-bundesregierung.pdf (last accessed: 1 April 2020).

24 *Bundesministerium für Wirtschaft und Energie*, Rohstoffstrategie der Bundesregierung, Sicherung einer nachhaltigen Rohstoffversorgung Deutschlands mit nicht-energetischen mineralischen Rohstoffen (January 2020), p. 32, available under: https://www.bmwi.de/Redaktion/DE/Downloads/P-R/rohstoffstrategie-der-bundesregierung.pdf?__blob=publicationFile&v=8 (last accessed: 1 April 2020).

Natural Resource Strategy key concerns of German development cooperation that will be further discussed below.

3. *Development Policy on Raw Materials*

Complementary to the (first) Natural Resource Strategy, the Federal Ministry of Economic Cooperation and Development (BMZ) issued a strategy paper in 2010, setting out Germany's development policy in the raw materials sector.[25] The primary objective of German development cooperation is to make use of the sector's potential to reduce poverty and to promote sustainable development in producer countries. Wealth in natural resources shall lead to broad and diversified economic development, provided the raw materials sectors in developing and industrialized countries are organized in accordance with economic, ecological and social principles of sustainability.[26] The policy applies a holistic approach covering the entire extractive industry's value chain from exploration, licensing, extraction, processing, trade, revenue collection to recycling and the rehabilitation of mining sites.

Particular importance is placed on good governance and transparency, as well as on anti-corruption measures, as a basis for a setting within which internationally recognized social and environmental standards are implemented and human rights protected. Another key approach is to strengthen structures for economic diversification and increased local linkages and value production. This may include micro-credits for small-scale miners and other local entrepreneurs. A viable local economy should be promoted by a development-friendly money and fiscal policy that counteracts unstainable extractives-related currency increases and debt crises.[27]

---

25 *Bundesministerium für wirtschaftliche Zusammenarbeit und Entwicklung*, Entwicklungspolitisches Strategiepapier, Extraktive Rohstoffe, BMZ-Strategiepapier 4/2010 (2010), available under: http://www.bgr.bund.de/DE/Themen/Zusammenarbeit/TechnZusammenarbeit/Downloads/R&E_Strategiepapier_ExtraktiveRohstoffe.pdf?__blob=publicationFile&v=1 (last accessed: 1 April 2020).

26 *Bundesministerium für wirtschaftliche Zusammenarbeit und Entwicklung*, Entwicklungspolitisches Strategiepapier, Extraktive Rohstoffe, BMZ-Strategiepapier 4/2010 (2010), p. 7, available under: http://www.bgr.bund.de/DE/Themen/Zusammenarbeit/TechnZusammenarbeit/Downloads/R&E_Strategiepapier_ExtraktiveRohstoffe.pdf?__blob=publicationFile&v=1 (last accessed: 1 April 2020).

27 *Bundesministerium für wirtschaftliche Zusammenarbeit und Entwicklung*, Entwicklungspolitisches Strategiepapier, Extraktive Rohstoffe, BMZ-Strategiepapier 4/2010 (2010), p. 8, available under: http://www.bgr.bund.de/DE/Themen/Zusam

Resource-rich partner countries of German development cooperation shall create efficient legal, institutional and economic framework conditions that allow and ensure sustainable natural resource management. This includes efficient tax administrations, public finance institutions, and independent audit capacities to ensure that revenues are at least partially used for the benefit of the local population and that illegal practices such as transfer pricing are minimized. As will be further discussed below, the transparency initiative EITI plays an important role in this context.

Besides providing assistance in establishing the appropriate regulatory and institutional environment, it is crucial to strengthen human capacities in relevant public authorities and in civil society. For example, many developing countries do not possess the technical expertise to analyze and evaluate existing deposits, to process and track tax revenues, or to negotiate mining concessions to their benefit. The BMZ thus makes capacity development a centerpiece of its activities.[28]

Sustainable management of natural resources requires the extractive industries to operate with due regard to ecological and social risks. Economic gains should be weighed against the costs and damages that occur to affected communities as result of mining. International sustainability standards and certification systems are an important instrument to be used in this cost-benefit-analysis.[29] Companies are to apply due diligence practices, especially with respect to applicable human rights standards and to the financing of conflicts through conflict minerals.

One area of particular concern is artisanal and/or small-scale mining (ASM). In many resource-rich areas this mostly informal way of extracting raw materials is the most important source of livelihood. In stark contrast to industrial large-scale mining, this form is very labor intensive. It is estimated that worldwide about 20 million people work in ASM, often women and children. About 100 million people are estimated as being depen-

---

menarbeit/TechnZusammenarbeit/Downloads/R&E_Strategiepapier_ExtraktiveRohstoffe.pdf?__blob=publicationFile&v=1 (last accessed: 1 April 2020).

28 *Bundesministerium für wirtschaftliche Zusammenarbeit und Entwicklung*, Entwicklungspolitisches Strategiepapier, Extraktive Rohstoffe (2010), p. 9, available under: https://foes.de/pdf/Strategiepapier299_04_2010.pdf (last accessed: 1 April 2020).

29 *Bundesministerium für wirtschaftliche Zusammenarbeit und Entwicklung*, Entwicklungspolitisches Strategiepapier, Extraktive Rohstoffe (2010), p. 14, available under: https://foes.de/pdf/Strategiepapier299_04_2010.pdf (last accessed: 1 April 2020).

dent on ASM.[30] This relevance for developing countries makes ASM an important focus of German development interventions, be it with measures to implement environmental and social standards or with formalization programs or micro-credits.

Managing natural resources sustainably also involves using them more efficiently and promoting circular economies through recycling. All these aspects drive German development cooperation in their extractives-related projects and policies.

It is expected that, reacting to the revision of the Natural Resource Strategy, the BMZ will also revise its strategy paper in due course.

4. *Africa Mining Vision*

The Africa Mining Vision (AMV) is a pan-African strategy for the development of the continent's extractive industries. Referred to as *"Africa's own response to tackling the paradox of great mineral wealth existing side by side with pervasive poverty"*[31], the strategy provides orientation for German development cooperation to increase African ownership in development activities in African partner countries.

The AMV was adopted by African Heads of State at the African Union (AU) summit in 2009.[32] It provides a "holistic" roadmap for an extractives sector based on the principles of good governance, transparency and sustainability.[33] The strategy emphasizes the need for broad economic development for the continent as a whole. Through the numerous linkages between mining, social issues and the environmental dimension, the extractives sector exerts a greater influence on the reality of people's lives than most other economic sectors. Recognizing this fact, the AMV addresses a wide range of issues, including better data availability, fair contract negoti-

---

30 *Bundesministerium für wirtschaftliche Zusammenarbeit und Entwicklung*, Entwicklungspolitisches Strategiepapier, Extraktive Rohstoffe (2010), p. 14, available under: https://foes.de/pdf/Strategiepapier299_04_2010.pdf (last accessed: 1 April 2020).

31 *African Union*, AMV – Africa Mining Vision, available under: https://au.int/en/ti/amv/about (last accessed: 1 April 2020).

32 *African Union*, Africa Mining Vision (February 2009), available under: http://africaminingvision.org/amv_resources/AMV/Africa_Mining_Vision_English.pdf (last accessed: 1 April 2020).

33 *Cust*, The Role of Governance and International Norms in Managing Natural Resources, in: Addison/Roe (eds.), Extractive Industries: The Management of Resources as a Driver of Sustainable Development (2018), p. 395 (413).

ations, administrative and governance capacity building, more efficient use of resource wealth, expansion of energy and transport infrastructure, development of local economic cycles, and social and environmental sustainability in small-scale mining.

The AU commissioned the African Minerals Development Centre (AMDC) with implementing the Strategy.[34] Any AU member state may request support from the AMDC, which was established specifically to provide strategic and operational support for the Vision. At country level, tailor-made reform programs, *i.e.* Country Mining Visions, are developed and implemented in accordance with national priorities and at times with support of German development cooperation.

5. *Marshall Plan for Africa*

The "Marshall Plan for Africa" denotes a recent BMZ strategy towards better development cooperation with African States.[35] The goal is to establish cooperation based on key values and common interests. Intending to abandon the former philosophy of donors and recipients, the "Marshall Plan" calls for the responsibility of the African States for their development and new forms of cooperation through "reform partnerships". Development cooperation is to follow new rules. This would involve *i.a.* converting free trade into fair trade and adhering to international environmental and social standards.[36] The "Marshall Plan" is termed a "contract for the future" between Africa and Europe and based on three pillars: (1) Economy, Trade and Employment, (2) Peace and Security, (3) Democracy and Rule of Law. Altogether the plan lists more than 100 ideas for reforms grouped under these pillars.

---

34 *Frank*, Mountain Movers: Mining, Sustainability and the Agents of Change (2015), p. 70.

35 *German Federal Ministry for Economic Cooperation and Development*, Africa and Europe – A New Partnership for Development, Peace and a Better Future, Cornerstones of a Marshall Plan with Africa (2017), available under: https://www.bmz.de/en/publications/type_of_publication/information_flyer/information_brochures/Materialie270_africa_marshallplan.pdf (last accessed: 1 April 2020).

36 *German Federal Ministry for Economic Cooperation and Development*, Africa and Europe – A New Partnership for Development, Peace and a Better Future, Cornerstones of a Marshall Plan with Africa (2017), p. 13, available under: https://www.bmz.de/en/publications/type_of_publication/information_flyer/information_brochures/Materialie270_africa_marshallplan.pdf (last accessed: 1 April 2020).

Although the plan does not contain a specific chapter on natural resources, they are referred to throughout the document, in particular in the context of the first and third pillar. Matching the above-mentioned Development Policy on Raw Materials, the plan states the need to reduce Africa's dependence on natural resources and to promote economic diversity. At the same time, its wealth in natural resources is mentioned as one of the great potentials of the continent. Among the various ideas the plan proposes to support the private sector in its efforts to establish sustainable supply chains and to promote local content and linkages.[37] In the context of democracy and the rule of law, the plan demands transparency in the extractives sector and in public finance, as well as efforts to stop illicit financial flows and aggressive tax evasion. It also proposes to support African States in the mobilization of domestic resources for development.[38]

6. *National Action Plan for Business and Human Rights*

In its "Renewed EU Strategy 2011-2014 for Corporate Social Responsibility", the European Commission called upon all EU Member States to develop national action plans for the implementation of the UN Guiding Principles on Business and Human Rights.[39] These principles stipulate the "protect, respect and remedy framework" for human rights in a business context.[40] In 2016, the German Government adopted its National Action

---

37 *German Federal Ministry for Economic Cooperation and Development*, Africa and Europe – A New Partnership for Development, Peace and a Better Future, Cornerstones of a Marshall Plan with Africa (2017), pp. 17-18, available under: https://www.bmz.de/en/publications/type_of_publication/information_flyer/information_brochures/Materialie270_africa_marshallplan.pdf (last accessed: 1 April 2020).

38 *German Federal Ministry for Economic Cooperation and Development*, Africa and Europe – A New Partnership for Development, Peace and a Better Future, Cornerstones of a Marshall Plan with Africa (2017), pp. 22-23, available under: https://www.bmz.de/en/publications/type_of_publication/information_flyer/information_brochures/Materialie270_africa_marshallplan.pdf (last accessed: 1 April 2020).

39 *European Commission*, A Renewed EU Strategy 2011-14 for Corporate Social Responsibility, Communication from the Commission to the European Parliament, the Council, the European Economic and Social Committee and the Committee of the Regions, COM(2011) 681 final (25 October 2011).

40 *United Nations*, Guiding Principles on Business and Human Rights, Implementing the United Nations "Protect, Respect and Remedy" Framework (2011), available under: https://www.ohchr.org/Documents/Publications/GuidingPrinciplesBusinessHR_EN.pdf (last accessed: 1 April 2020).

Plan on Business and Human Rights (NAP) to spell out in detail the human-rights related obligations and responsibilities for the State and for private businesses in respect of human rights along global supply and value chains.[41] Besides, the action plan intends to ensure policy coherence in Germany as well as present and future competitiveness of the German economy.

Human rights due diligence stands at the center of the NAP. The German Government expresses its expectation of all enterprises to carry out due diligence in the appropriate form within their supply and value chains, especially when active in countries with weak rule of law.[42] The plan describes in detail the various elements of human rights due diligence: Besides a public declaration to respect human rights, enterprises shall establish procedures for human rights risk assessments that also includes human rights impacts from actions by their suppliers. They shall also integrate in their business practices various measures to mitigate potential damages and introduce reporting and complaints mechanisms.[43]

The NAP includes various key areas of action both addressed to the State and to private business. For the State this includes human rights-related recommendations concerning public procurement, public subsidies and parastatal enterprises. As to development cooperation, the plan reaffirms that human rights are its guiding principle and works to protect and promote human rights on all levels.[44] German development cooperation is explicitly held to actively foster dialogue between the public authorities,

41 *Auswärtiges Amt*, Nationaler Aktionsplan Umsetzung der VN-Leitprinzipien für Wirtschaft und Menschenrechte 2016-2020 (2015), available under: https://www.auswaertiges-amt.de/blob/297434/8d6ab29982767d5a31d2e85464461565/nap-wirtschaft-menschenrechte-data.pdf (last accessed: 1 April 2020).

42 *Auswärtiges Amt*, Nationaler Aktionsplan Umsetzung der VN-Leitprinzipien für Wirtschaft und Menschenrechte 2016-2020 (2015), p. 7, available under: https://www.auswaertiges-amt.de/blob/297434/8d6ab29982767d5a31d2e85464461565/nap-wirtschaft-menschenrechte-data.pdf (last accessed: 1 April 2020).

43 *Auswärtiges Amt*, Nationaler Aktionsplan Umsetzung der VN-Leitprinzipien für Wirtschaft und Menschenrechte 2016-2020 (2015), pp. 8-10, available under: https://www.auswaertiges-amt.de/blob/297434/8d6ab29982767d5a31d2e85464461565/nap-wirtschaft-menschenrechte-data.pdf (last accessed: 1 April 2020).

44 *Auswärtiges Amt*, Nationaler Aktionsplan Umsetzung der VN-Leitprinzipien für Wirtschaft und Menschenrechte 2016-2020 (2015), p. 14, available under: https://www.auswaertiges-amt.de/blob/297434/8d6ab29982767d5a31d2e85464461565/nap-wirtschaft-menschenrechte-data.pdf (last accessed: 1 April 2020); see also *Bundesministerium für wirtschaftliche Zusammenarbeit und Entwicklung*, Menschenrechte in der deutschen Entwicklungspolitik, Konzept, BMZ-Strategiepapier 4/2011 (2011), available under: https://www.bmz.de/de/mediathek/publikationen/

private business, trade unions and civil society on relevant topics such as work safety and employment conditions in partner countries. Further, development projects should be carried out, possibly with these stakeholders, that improve the human rights situation in partner countries. Special mention is made of environmental protection and social and labor standards along the entire supply chain of enterprises, areas with great relevance for the extractive industry.[45] Through capacity-building measures, producer countries are to be assisted in introducing and monitoring environmental and social standards. The NAP refers to the positive experiences made with multi-stakeholder initiatives in relevant business sectors, such as the Alliance for Sustainable Textiles, in developing appropriate solutions and monitoring processes. Thus far, there is no national multi-stakeholder initiative in the extractives sector yet, but as described further below, some initiatives exist on the European or global level.

As the UN Guiding Principles on Business and Human Rights, also the NAP contains a chapter on business activities in conflict areas where the risk of serious human rights violations is particularly high. The two legal instruments described in the following section, *i.e.* the OECD Due Diligence Guidance and the EU Regulation on Conflict Minerals play an important role in this context. As specific measure the German Government declares its aim to prevent that the proceeds from the sale of the 3TG minerals finance armed conflict in conflict areas. The Government promotes in this plan compulsory due diligence rules that are proportionate and not overly bureaucratic, especially for small and medium-sized enterprises.[46] Extensive discussions around the monitoring and implementation of the NAP have revealed different positions within the German Government. The Chancellor's Office and the BMWi have indicated their resistance to compulsory due diligence rules, particularly if introduced as German (not EU) legislation. This position stands in sharp contrast to an advance made by the BMZ and the Federal Ministry of Labour and Social Affairs (BMAS)

---

archiv/reihen/strategiepapiere/Strategiepapier303_04_2011.pdf (last accessed: 1 April 2020).

45 *Auswärtiges Amt*, Nationaler Aktionsplan Umsetzung der VN-Leitprinzipien für Wirtschaft und Menschenrechte 2016-2020 (2015), p. 19, available under: https://www.auswaertiges-amt.de/blob/297434/8d6ab29982767d5a31d2e85464461565/nap-wirtschaft-menschenrechte-data.pdf (last accessed: 1 April 2020).

46 *Auswärtiges Amt*, Nationaler Aktionsplan Umsetzung der VN-Leitprinzipien für Wirtschaft und Menschenrechte 2016-2020 (2015), p. 22, available under: https://www.auswaertiges-amt.de/blob/297434/8d6ab29982767d5a31d2e85464461565/nap-wirtschaft-menschenrechte-data.pdf (last accessed: 1 April 2020).

who introduced the idea of a binding due diligence law, either in Germany or on an EU level. A non-paper with the basic principles ("Eckpunktepapier") on a German due diligence law was supposed to be presented to Cabinet in March 2020. The non-paper was withdrawn from the agenda due to other priorities during the Corona crisis. At the time of writing it is not clear when the issue will be re-opened.

IV. Human Rights Due Diligence and Conflict Minerals

Major international legal instruments aiming to curb the damaging effects of the sourcing of and trade with conflict minerals used to finance and prolong the Congo war. Following the precedent of the Kimberly Process Certification Scheme, a multi-stakeholder process established in 2003 to stop the trade with conflict diamonds,[47] the OECD issued a non-binding but widely accepted due diligence standard for responsible mineral supply chains. Moreover, the US Government and the European Union adopted binding legislation on conflict minerals, *i.e.* the Dodd Frank Act and the EU Regulation on Conflict Minerals. The OECD Guidance and the EU Regulation are central legal instruments for German development cooperation.

1. OECD Due Diligence Guidance

The OECD Due Diligence Guidance for Responsible Supply Chains of Minerals from Conflict-Affected and High-Risk Areas[48] is a voluntary initiative to promote responsible corporate governance in the supply chains of mineral resources originating from areas affected by or at risk of conflict. Its objective is to help companies respect human rights and avoid contributing to conflict through responsible sourcing practices. Mineral

---

47 For an overview, see *Bone*, The Kimberly Process Certification Scheme: The Primary Safeguard for the Diamond Industry, in: Lujala/Rustad (eds.), High-Value Natural Resources and Post-Conflict Peacebuilding (2012), p. 189 (189-194).

48 *OECD*, OECD Due Diligence Guidance for Responsible Supply Chains of Minerals from Conflict-Affected and High-Risk Areas (3rd edition 2016), available under: http://www.oecd.org/daf/inv/mne/OECD-Due-Diligence-Guidance-Minerals-Edition3.pdf (last accessed: 1 April 2020).

supply chains shall be made transparent and corporate engagement in the minerals sector sustainable.[49]

The Guidance was developed between 2009 and 2011 as part of an OECD-run multi-actor process. Its implementation is supported by an OECD working group in which Germany actively participates. While not imposing any legal obligations on companies, the Guidance enjoys widespread acceptance, having been approved by the OECD Investment Committee and OECD Development Assistance Committee, embraced by a UN Security Council resolution, and endorsed by all Member States of the International Conference on the Great Lakes (ICGLR).[50]

The Guidance provides a due diligence framework for all minerals from conflict and high-risk areas but contains two supplements with specific requirements for the conflict minerals gold as well as tin, tantalum and tungsten. In October 2019, the London Metals Exchange (LME) adopted the OECD Due Diligence Guidance for its own responsible sourcing requirements for all LME-listed brands.[51] The Guidance defines due diligence as an on-going, proactive and reactive process through which companies can ensure that they respect human rights and do not contribute to conflict. Risk-based due diligence refers to the steps companies should take to identify and address actual or potential risks in order to prevent or mitigate adverse impacts associated with their activities or sourcing decisions.[52] In its first Annex, the Guidance spells out these five steps in detail. It recommends companies to (1) establish strong company management systems,

---

49 For a good overview, see: *Rüttinger et al.*, OECD-Leitlinien für die Erfüllung der Sorgfaltspflicht zur Förderung verantwortungsvoller Lieferketten für Mineralien aus Konflikt- und Hochrisikogebieten, UmSoResss Steckbrief, Adelphi (February 2016), available under: https://www.umweltbundesamt.de/sites/default/files/medien/378/dokumente/steckbrief_oecd_final.pdf (last accessed: 1 April 2020).

50 *United Nations Security Council*, Resolution 1952 (2010), S/Res/1952 of 29 November 2010, paras. 7 and 8, available under: http://www.un.org/ga/search/view_doc.asp?symbol=S/RES/1952%282010%29 (last accessed: 1 April 2020); *International Conference on the Great Lakes Region*, Lusaka Declaration of the ICGLR Special Summit to Fight Illegal Exploitation of Natural Resources in the Great Lakes Region (15 December 2010), para. 12, available under: https://www.oecd.org/daf/inv/mne/47143500.pdf (last accessed: 1 April 2020).

51 *London Metal Exchange*, LME sets out responsible sourcing requirements, available under: https://www.lme.com/News/Press-room/Press-releases/Press-releases/2019/10/LME-sets-out-responsible-sourcing-requirements (last accessed: 1 April 2020).

52 *OECD*, OECD Due Diligence Guidance for Responsible Supply Chains of Minerals from Conflict-Affected and High-Risk Areas (3rd edition 2016), p. 13, available under: http://www.oecd.org/daf/inv/mne/OECD-Due-Diligence-Guidance-Minerals-Edition3.pdf (last accessed: 1 April 2020).

(2) identify and assess risk in the supply chains, (3) design and implement a strategy to respond to identified risks, (4) carry out independent third-party audit of supply chain due diligence at identified points in the supply chain and (5) report on supply chain due diligence.[53]

2. *EU Regulation on Conflict Minerals*

As a reaction to the American Dodd Frank Act, Section 1502,[54] the EU adopted in 2017 its Regulation No. 2017/821 laying down supply chain due diligence obligations for Union importers of tin, tantalum and tungsten, their ores, and gold originating from conflict-affected and high-risk areas[55]. The Dodd Frank Act of 2012 obligated US stock-listed companies to disclose information on their imports of 3TG originating from the DRC and its neighboring countries. In hindsight, one can argue that the Act was an important measure to curb illegal sourcing of the 3T minerals tin, tantal and tungsten (not gold) and related conflict financing.[56] During the initial years after adoption, the Act, however, also led to a de facto embargo of Congolese products and thereby caused intended harm to the Congolese economy.[57] In its Conflict Minerals Regulation, the EU is trying to avoid such unintended consequences by making its geographical scope

53 *OECD*, OECD Due Diligence Guidance for Responsible Supply Chains of Minerals from Conflict-Affected and High-Risk Areas (3rd edition 2016), Annex I, Five-Step Framework for Risk-Based Due Diligence in the Mineral Supply Chain, pp. 17-19, available under: http://www.oecd.org/daf/inv/mne/OECD-Due-Diligence-Guidance-Minerals-Edition3.pdf (last accessed: 1 April 2020).

54 Dodd-Frank Wall Street Reform and Consumer Protection Act, Section 1502, H.R. 4171, 21 July 2010, also available under: https://www.gpo.gov/fdsys/pkg/PLAW-111publ203/pdf/PLAW-111publ203.pdf (last accessed: 1 April 2010).

55 Regulation (EU) 2017/821 of the European Parliament and of the Council of 17 May 2017 laying down supply chain due diligence obligations for Union importers of tin, tantalum and tungsten, their ores, and gold originating from conflict-affected and high-risk areas, OJ L 130, 19.5.2017, p. 1.

56 *Koch/Kingsbergen*, Exaggerating Unintended Effects? Competing Narratives on the Impact of Conflict Minerals Regulation, in: Resources Policy 57 (2018), p. 255 (258-259). The situation is different for gold where conflict trade is thriving, compare *The Sentry*, The Golden Laundromat, The Conflict Gold Trade from Eastern Congo to the United States and Europe (October 2018), available under: https://cdn.thesentry.org/wp-content/uploads/2018/10/GoldenLaundromat_Sentry_Oct2018-final.pdf (last accessed: 1 April 2020).

57 *Stoop/Verpoorten/van der Windt*, More Legislation, More Violence? The Impact of Dodd-Frank in the DRC, PLOS ONE 13(8) (2018), pp. 4-5, available under: https:

universal, *i.e.* by prescribing due diligence requirements to all conflict-affected and high risks areas worldwide.

From 1 January 2021, due diligence requirements apply to all EU importers of the 3TG conflict minerals. This covers EU-based smelters, refiners, traders, banks, and manufacturers that import these minerals and metals to the EU.[58] The current status reflects a compromise in a longer struggle in the regulatory process between the European Parliament and the European Council as to the Regulation's binding nature for the upstream and downstream sectors. The Parliament succeeded in making the due diligence requirements compulsory for the upstream sector including trade and import. Two years after entry into force, *i.e.* 2023, the Regulation's effectiveness will be evaluated, a process that might lead to widening the scope to the downstream sector including European manufacturers. It is also conceivable that the scope of minerals will be expanded.

The Regulation's due diligence requirements are based on the OECD Guidance and apply directly to approximately 600 to 1,000 EU importers. These are determined by specific volume thresholds for the different minerals and metals involved. Those below the threshold are exempted. It is estimated that about 95 per cent of all EU imports are covered and that about 500 smelters and refiners will be indirectly affected irrespective of their seat in- or outside the EU.

At the time of writing, various issues relevant for the Regulation's implementation are still under development. For example, the OECD set up an independent group of experts to produce a (non-exhaustive) list of conflict-affected and high-risk areas. Further, the Regulation foresees that companies may use their own existing due diligence schemes provided their recognition by the European Commission. According to Art. 8 (2) of the Regulation, the Commission shall adopt delegated acts setting out the methodology and criteria for the assessment of existing due diligence schemes.

//journals.plos.org/plosone/article/file?id=10.1371/journal.pone.0201783&type=printable (last accessed: 1 April 2020).

58 For a good overview, see *European Network for Central Africa et al.*, Advice Note to Companies, Member States, and the European Commission, Implementation of the EU Regulation laying down supply chain due diligence obligations for Union importers of tin, tantalum and tungsten, their ores, and gold origination from conflict-affected and high-risk areas (2018), p. 4, available under: https://www.eurac-network.org/sites/default/files/kcfinder/files/Civil%20society%20note%20on%20EU%20responsible%20mineral%20sourcing%20regulation.pdf (last accessed: 1 April 2020).

Even though the Regulation will be directly applicable in EU Member States, the German Government has adopted an Implementation Law in March 2020.[59] The Law names the BGR as competent national authority to control compliance with the Regulation. It regulates cooperation with the customs authorities and authorizes enforcement actions in case of non-cooperation by companies to allow inspections, to comply with reporting requirements and to disclose requested information.

While the BMWi is lead Ministry for the implementation of the Regulation, the matter of also of high interest to the BMZ who supports accompanying measures like the European Partnership for Responsible Minerals (EPRM) described further below.

V. GIZ Development Programs in the Extractive Sector

The GIZ has both sectoral and global programs that pursue particular sectoral policies beyond a particular geographical scope. The agency also implements bilateral and regional projects and programs located in the partner countries of German development cooperation. The extractives sector is dealt within a Sector Program "Extractives for Development" as well as in to date 13 bilateral, regional and global programs worldwide. These are briefly introduced in the following section.

1. Sector Programme "Extractives for Development"

The Sector Program is jointly implemented by GIZ and BGR who match their respective expertise in two program components, *i.e.* policy advice and project piloting. Program advisers provide constant and comprehensive policy advice to the BMZ concerning resource governance and other mining-related matters. They thereby help the Ministry to shape the national and international development agenda in the extractive sector by

59 *Bundesregierung*, Entwurf eines Gesetzes zur Durchführung der Verordnung (EU) 2017/821 des Europäischen Parlaments und des Rates vom 17. Mai 2017 zur Festlegung von Pflichten zur Erfüllung der Sorgfaltspflichten in der Lieferkette für Unionseinführer von Zinn, Tantal, Wolfram, deren Erzen und Gold aus Konflikt- und Hochrisikogebieten sowie zur Änderung des Bundesberggesetzes, BT-Drs. 19/15602 of 2 December 2019. Law adopted by the German Bundestag on 5 March 2020, available under: http://dip21.bundestag.de/dip21/btd/19/156/1915602.pdf (last accessed: 1 April 2020).

adding their own impetus and innovations. In its piloting component, the Program supports partner countries in establishing an extractive sector in accordance with the principles of sustainability, both at national and local level. Aiming to tab the sector's development potential and to reduce social, environmental and human rights risks associated with the extractive sector, the Program develops new approaches in line with the above-mentioned development policies and pilots them in practice. The results of this work are evaluated and then incorporated into German development cooperation in the extractive sector.[60] The topics covered run the gamut from national sector policy, transparency and good financial governance, human rights and conflict minerals, supply chain management, climate, digitalization, gender and local economic development. Pilot projects mostly involve studies and research on relevant topics, various capacity building measures to selected stakeholders, support to bilateral and regional programs in various forms.

A prominent issue at present is how to handle the proliferation of sustainability initiatives in the extractives sector. These initiatives aim at making mining and metals supply chains more sustainable through laws and regulations, standards and certification schemes. Since the various metals and minerals involve different issues and challenges in their supply and value chains, commodity-specific standards have multiplied since the 1990s. This makes it difficult for business and politics to navigate and to apply them. To make standard systems more effective and widely understood, the knowledge gap between experts and users should be reduced. Moreover, efforts need to be made to include those stakeholders particularly affected by mining activities, such as indigenous peoples, in standard-setting and impact measuring. Furthermore, there is a need to enhance the interoperability of different sustainability initiatives, *e.g.* through cross-referencing or cross-recognition of different standards with respect to particular topics. To this end, the Sector Program collaborates with prominent partners such as the University of Queensland, the ISEAL Alliance and the Aluminium Stewardship Initiative.[61] A collaboration also exists with the NGO Resolve to put interoperability into practice by introducing a so-

60 For more information, see *German Federal Ministry for Economic Cooperation and Development*, Extractives and Development Sector programme, available under: http://www.bmz.de/rue/en/index.html (last accessed: 1 April 2020).

61 For example, the Sector Program commissioned research in collaboration with the ISEAL Alliance: *Rusillo/Carey*, Creating Value Together. Interoperability: Opportunities, Challenges and Ways Forward for Metals, Minerals and Mining Sustainability Standards, White Paper commissioned by Deutsche Gesellschaft für In-

called "Climate Smart Widget". This tool is a plug-in device for existing sustainability standards intended to streamline emissions-related reporting and target-setting.[62]

Two international development policy fora are of particular relevance for the Program's work: This is the Intergovernmental Forum on Mining, Minerals, Metals and Sustainable Development (IGF) and the OECD Policy Dialogue on Natural Resource-based Development. Established in 2005, the IGF is a global cooperation platform for governments of industrialized and developing countries serving as a forum for dialogue on mining and mineral resources. Representatives of mining ministries and other ministries from over 50 member countries, including Germany, meet once a year to share their experiences in the extractive sector. The aim of IGF is to increase the mining sector's contribution to sustainable development and poverty reduction worldwide. The Sector Program is one of IGF's donors and cooperates financially and in terms of content as it prepares an Artisanal and Small-scale Mining Guidance (ASM Guidance), a guide for governments on how best to deal with the issues of artisanal and small-scale mining with a focus on development.

The OECD founded its Policy Dialogue on Natural Resource-based Development in 2013. The Forum provides a platform for developing countries and industrialized nations to share their experience concerning the possibilities of utilizing natural resources for inclusive and broad-based growth. German commitment centers mainly around the CONNEX Negotiation Support Forum, a space established to build a common knowledge base to bridge asymmetries of information relating to natural resource contracts and to negotiate better deals for developing countries.

---

ternationale Zusammenarbeit (2018), available under: https://aluminium-stewardship.org/wp-content/uploads/2019/08/2018-10_giz_creating_value_together.pdf (last accessed: 1 April 2020); in collaboration with the Centre for Social Responsibility in Mining, University of Queensland: *Mori Junior/Sturman/Imbrogiano*, Leveraging greater impact of mineral sustainability initiatives: An assessment of interoperability (2017); *Sturman et al.*, Monitoring Impact of Mineral Sustainability Standards to Align with the Sustainable Development Goals (2018); and with the Aluminium Stewardship Initiative: *Annandale/Meadows/Ota*, Indigenous Peoples' Participation in Sustainability Standards for Extractives (March 2018), available under: https://aluminium-stewardship.org/wp-content/uploads/2018/08/GIZ_Indigenous_Peoples_Participation_Susty_Standards_Extractives.pdf (last accessed: 1 April 2020).

62 Compare Resolve Website at: https://www.resolve.ngo/climate_smart_widget.htm# (last accessed: 1 April 2020).

2. CONNEX

As stated above, revenues from the extractive sector have the potential to contribute to the sustainable development of resource-rich countries. As a prerequisite, the underlying contracts governing resource extraction should be fair, *i.e.* maximizing private sector contributions to national development while at the same time creating attractive conditions for investment. Many developing countries negotiate their investment contracts and licenses with international mining companies and investors without having the necessary expertise. They do not negotiate on an equal footing, a situation that often leads to one-sided "unfair" contracts robbing the country and its population of its wealth.

In 2014, the G7 launched the CONNEX Initiative to counteract imbalances in the relationship between partner countries and investors when negotiating resource contracts.[63] Advisory services are provided on an *ad hoc* basis for complex contract negotiations and to provide needs-oriented support to partner countries. CONNEX consists of three different components: Besides advisory services based on careful selection of experts and a code of conduct, the initiative offers capacity-building in connection with specific negotiations on relevant topics. It also provides access to numerous resources via the Negotiation Support Portal, on online information tool. The initiative is managed by a CONNEX Support Unit as an implementation structure mainly for the assignment and secondment of experts.

With the support of the Sector Programme "Extractives for Development", BMZ has taken a lead role in establishing CONNEX. From the outset the initiative's pilot activities have been implemented by the Sector Programme, and from August 2017 by its offspring, the Global Programme "CONNEX Support Unit", in more than 12 countries in Africa and Central Asia.

63 For more information, see the CONNEX website at: https://www.connex-unit.org (last accessed: 1 April 2020).

3. Support to International Sustainability Standards and Multi-Stakeholder Partnerships

a) Extractive Industries Transparency Initiative (EITI)

Promoting transparency in the extractive sector, especially in the revenue flows from mining companies to state institutions, is an important goal of German development cooperation. It is thus not surprising that the EITI[64] stands at the fore of German development cooperation. Using national multi-stakeholder processes to verify and crosscheck payments received by Governments with those made by companies, the EITI aims to ensure the transparent disclosure of public revenues from the extractive sector.[65] Helping to prevent corruption related to royalty payments or taxes, this approach intends to increase those revenues and to foster civil society participation in the usage of their country's resource wealth. The multi-stakeholder verification process followed by an annual report gives citizens an instrument with which they can effectively hold companies and governments to account.

The EITI is at times called the "mother of all multi stakeholder processes". It has an international board that consists of 21 members representing implementing and supporting countries, civil society organizations, industry and institutional investors. The board is responsible for setting, monitoring and assessing progress relating to the EITI Standard that EITI Members and Candidates need to abide to. At present, 48 countries implement the EITI standard or are working towards full implementation.[66] The EITI status of five additional countries was suspended for reasons of political instability or lack of effort.

German development cooperation has significantly supported EITI politically, financially and technically since its establishment in 2003. This has included assistance to national EITI processes through bilateral and re-

---

64 See EITI website at: https://www.eiti.org (last accessed: 1 April 2020); for an analysis of the Initiative's impact, see *Cust*, The Role of Governance and International Norms in Managing Natural Resources, in: Addison/Roe (eds.), Extractive Industries: The Management of Resources as a Driver of Sustainable Development (2018), p. 395 (406-411).

65 *Frank*, Mountain Movers: Mining, Sustainability and the Agents of Change (2015), p. 117.

66 See *EITI*, Countries, available under: https://www.eiti.org/countries (last accessed: 1 April 2020).

gional GIZ programs as well as support to the international EITI secretariat and to the EITI trust fund administered by the World Bank.

The Sector Program promotes the dissemination and further development of the initiative and its Standard. This includes training courses for national EITI secretariats, state actors and civil society in partner countries on how to implement EITI as well as M&E-related efforts.

b) *European Partnership for Responsible Minerals (EPRM)*

Another important, more recent multi-stakeholder initiative with which the Sector Program closely cooperates is the European Partnership for Responsible Minerals (EPRM) established in 2016. The EPRM is an accompanying measure to the EU Regulation on Conflict Minerals and aims to create better living conditions for mineworkers and local mining communities.[67] The Partnership works to increase the number of mines in conflict-affected and high risk areas that adopt responsible mining practices. A central concern is to ensure market access for such mines and to promote coalitions between downstream, midstream and upstream actors to produce and source responsible minerals throughout a transparent supply chain. The EPRM consists of a project implementation fund focused on upstream projects in conflict-affected and high risk areas as well as of a dialogue and information component mainly directed at companies affected by the EU Regulation and other relevant downstream actors.

In January 2020, the BMZ became full EPRM member after supporting the partnership for two years through in kind contributions and working hours of the Sector Program. This has included active participation in tender processes for EPRM pilot projects in the field, efforts to establish a knowledge platform for downstream companies ("EPRM Due Diligence Hub") and assistance in developing an M&E system.

---

67 See EPRM website at: https://europeanpartnership-responsibleminerals.eu/about-eprm (last accessed: 1 April 2020).

c) Global Battery Alliance

GIZ has also become a member of the recently established Global Battery Alliance (GBA).[68] This nascent multi-stakeholder initiative is a project of the World Economic Forum launched at the UN Sustainable Development Impact Summit in New York in September 2017.

The GBA is intended as a global platform for inclusive, sustainable and innovative battery value chains. The growing importance of electromobility creates a growing demand of new battery technologies, requiring increased efforts for sustainable and innovative development of battery technologies. To this end, the platform will mobilize interested partners from the public and private sectors and civil society to share knowledge, coordinate their activities and generate project financing. The GBA has three workstreams, the first concentrating on raw material supply (with special focus on cobalt), the second on circular economy, and the third on unlocking innovation. The Sector Program has been considering to support the GBA secretariat with seconded personnel.

4. Bilateral and Regional Development Projects

The extractives also feature in bilateral and regional development cooperation. With its portfolio "natural resource governance", GIZ supports governments of resource-rich countries in developing and implementing political structures and processes that create an environment conducive to managing natural resources responsibly. Participation and involvement of civil society and the private sector in these processes is promoted as much as possible.

GIZ defines natural resource governance as the *"manner in which governments manage and regulate the extraction of natural resources but also how they mobilize and distribute public revenue and mitigate the environmental and social costs of extracting natural resources."*[69] To improve extractives-related governance GIZ mainly offers policy, process or technical advice and capacity development along the entire value chain. Main addressees are government institutions such as mining, energy or finance ministries, tax authori-

---

68 See GBA website at: https://www.weforum.org/global-battery-alliance/home (last accessed: 1 April 2020).

69 See *GIZ*, Resource governance in the extractive sector, available under: https://www.giz.de/fachexpertise/html/60074.html (last accessed: 1 April 2020).

ties or geodetic services, but also relevant civil society organizations or, at times, companies. Aiming to strengthen regional cooperation and harmonization GIZ also supports relevant regional organizations such as the ICGLR or the Central African Economic and Monetary Community (CEMAC).

Depending on the individual needs of the partner countries (or regional organizations) extractives-related development programs cover a wide range of services and issues.

In May 2020, GIZ was implementing 10 bilateral and regional programs in addition to 3 global programs operating on behalf of BMZ mainly in Central and Western Africa and Central Asia but in Latin America.[70] The total budget is about 88 million EUR for the running project period. These programs include the development of natural resource sector strategies and mining legislation, various forms of capacity development and institution-building, the development and support to local content policies and of community development agreements, support to national EITI processes and to contract negotiations, as well as the promotion and support to multi-stakeholder dialogues around mining.

---

70 In May 2020, the following GIZ programs were commissioned on behalf of BMZ: Africa: Integrated Economic Development in the Extractives Sector, Democratic Republic of Congo (01/2019-12/2021); Good Governance in the Extractive Sector, Mauretania (03/2019-02/2021), Support to the International Conference on the Great Lakes Region (ICGLR), regional programme for ICGLR member states (01/2017-06/2022); Regional Resource Governance in the Fragile States of West Africa, regional programme for Liberia, Sierra Leone, Guinea and Coté d'Ivoire (01/2019-3/2022). Central Asia: Promotion of Mineral Governance, Afghanistan (02/2018-11/2020); Academic Mining Education, Afghanistan (01/2017-05/2020); Integrated Mineral Resource Initiative, Mongolia (08/2017-07/2020); German-Mongolian Institute for Resources and Technology, Mongolia (07/2019-06/2022). Latin America: Regional Cooperation to Promote Sustainable Mining, regional programme for Chile, Columbia, Peru, Bolivia and Equador (08/2019-09/2022); Strengthening Environmental Regulation and Resource Efficiency in the Mining Sector in Chile and Columbia (04/2019-03/2022). Global: Extractives for Development (09/2018-08/2021); CONNEX Support Unit (08/2017-08/2020); Support of EITI Germany (07/2019-12/2022). Until 2020, GIZ has run two additional resource governance projects: Good Financial Governance, Ghana (05/2015-03/2019); Strengthening Mineral Resource Governance, Mali (01/2017-12/2019). At the time of writing, a further project is planned for Mongolia towards the end of 2020: another project scheduled for the end of this year: Good Governance in the Extractive Sector, Mongolia (estimated 09/2020-08/2023).

VI. Conclusion

In line with *Jared Diamond's* argument that innovative technologies such as those in the metals industry are an important factor in human development,[71] German development cooperation believes that the abundance of natural resources can and should be of benefit for developing countries and their populations. For such progress to happen good natural resource governance is key. Ensuring the fair distribution of revenues derived from natural resources and fighting extractives-related corruption remain among the major concerns in this context. As does the need to achieve economic diversification and local content in extractives-dominated economies. As described above, these issues are central to the German Development Policy on Raw Materials.

The global demand for raw materials is increasing and political instability rising in many resource-rich countries. Violent conflicts concerning natural resources are likely to grow in number. At the same time, the social and environmental costs of the capitalist "externalization societies" are becoming more and more a source of concern in the Global North.[72] It is a positive sign that the present Minister of Development Cooperation stated that the topic of supply chains is a BMZ priority in the next years. In his opening speech to Parliament in March 2018, the topic featured several times and he stated that "*we must not build our future prosperity on the backs of the slave laborers in the mines of Africa.*"[73] It is equally encouraging that the revised German Natural Resource Strategy recognizes the extractive industry's responsibility to source responsibly and to promote sustainable supply chains in line with applicable international standards. The revised Strategy is a step in the right direction, even if civil society groups have criticized it for insufficient incentives promoting a future-oriented industrial policy and for lacking specificity how the Government will actually support responsible sourcing.[74] More emphasis and detail on responsible

---

71 *Diamond*, Guns, Germs and Steel (1997), pp. 239 *et seq*.

72 *Lessenich*, Neben uns die Sintflut, Die Externalisierungsgesellschaft und ihr Preis (2016), pp. 183 *et seqq*.

73 *Deutscher Bundestag*, Stenographischer Bericht, 22. Sitzung (21 March 2018), p. 1894, available under: http://dip21.bundestag.de/dip21/btp/19/19022.pdf (last accessed: 1 April 2020).

74 See for example: *AK Rohstoffe*, Stellungnahme zur Rohstoffstrategie, AK Rohstoffe Newsletter #27, available under: http://ak-rohstoffe.de/ak-rohstoffe-newsletter-27-fokus-auf-rohstoffstrategie/ (last accessed: 1 April 2020).

mining can be expected in a new BMZ policy on raw materials that will be produced in due course.

The internet and a more connected world make it easier for consumers to inform themselves about social and environmental risks and costs relating to the extraction of natural resources. These days, consumers seem to care more about global production chains more than previously.[75] In the context of German development cooperation, consumers are at times even referred to as an ally in development. Companies on the other hand appear to care more about social and environmental risks of their operations. In line with the Agenda 2030 it seems to be a good moment for governments, private sector and civil society to work together and ensure that sustainable natural resource management does not remain a promise but practice.

75 *Baker*, The rise of the conscious consumer: why businesses need to open up, Guardian online (2 April 2015), available under: https://www.theguardian.com/women-in-leadership/2015/apr/02/the-rise-of-the-conscious-consumer-why-businesses-need-to-open-up (last accessed: 1 April 2020).

Resources and Trade Law

Hans-Georg Dederer[*]

Abstract

The overall thesis of this contribution is that world trade law, when applied in harmony with environmental, human rights and developmental concerns and related legal frameworks, is an essential, if not the most important, instrument to create and ensure *"fair conditions and opportunities for the sharing and securing of resources"*[1]. For the purposes of our analysis, we define "resources" as "natural resources". Natural resources share some peculiarities which clearly show the need for cross-border trade in resources, for their conservation and sustainable use, for the protection of the environment during, *e.g.*, exploration and extraction of natural resources, and for the taking into account of economic and social development interests of both developing and developed states. In order to cope with the negative consequences arising from those peculiarities, states tend to adopt measures which, however, may interfere with international trade. The focus of this article, therefore, is on the legal disciplines imposed on members of the World Trade Organization (WTO) by the WTO's rules on trade in goods with the aim of ensuring, as far as possible, free world trade.

Overview

---

* Prof. Dr., Chair of Constitutional and Administrative Law, Public International Law, European and International Economic Law, University of Passau.

1 See the title of the concluding remarks by *Stephan Hobe* and *Christian Tams* according to the programme of the Ladenburg Symposium on 2-3 March 2018.

I. Introduction

"Resources and Trade Law" seem to coalesce quasi by nature. From time immemorial, natural resources have been traded among peoples and nations.[2] Today, our heavily interconnected and interdependent world depends more than ever before on the unimpeded transboundary flow of natural resources. Facilitation of cross-border trade through *"substantial reduction of tariffs and other barriers to trade and [...] elimination of discriminatory treatment in international trade relations"*[3] is the very objective of the WTO system which, despite the rise of regional free trade agreements (FTAs), still represents the most comprehensive multilateral effort to trade liberalization in the world. This is why current trends towards re-nationalization, *i.e.* national policies of a roll-back of multilateralism, are so extremely alarming.

Severe obstacles to world trade are not limited to rude forms of blazing populist neo-protectionism, though. Rather, in particular with regard to natural resources, serious well-founded concerns have prompted national

2 Concerning the ancient world see, *e.g.*, contributions, in: *Olshausen/Sauer* (eds.), Die Schätze der Erde – Natürliche Ressourcen in der antiken Welt (2012).

3 Preamble, para. 3, of the Marrakesh Agreement Establishing the World Trade Organization (Marrakesh Agreement) of 1994; similarly Preamble, para. 3, of the General Agreement on Tariffs and Trade (GATT) of 1947.

governments to adopt laws and regulations which, at least *de facto* or indirectly, interrupt the unhindered transboundary movement of natural resources. Among these concerns are environmental, human rights, and economic and social development concerns. In fact, many, if not most, interstate conflicts between WTO members regarding international trade in resources[4] are centered on disputes arising from national measures which were taken with the objective of environmental or human rights protection, or for economic and social development purposes, but have resulted in adverse effects on the import or export of natural resources.

These antagonizing concerns, *i.e.* free trade concerns on the one side and environmental, human rights and development concerns on the other side, have to be weighed against one another with a view to striking a fair balance. Since all those concerns have also gained firm recognition in modern public international law without subordinating *a priori* some of these concerns under the other concerns. Hence, none of the concerns, and neither any of the international legal regimes governing them, exists in *"clinic isolation"*[5]. Rather, for reasons of coherence, but also for reasons of legitimacy and, thus, acceptance, of the international legal order, tensions between the aforementioned concerns have to be levelled out through harmonization as far as possible.

II. Notion of "Resources"

For the purpose of this contribution, the term "resources" is limited to, or synonymous with, "natural resources". A "natural resource", in turn, is a substance which exists as such and out of itself in, and through, nature.[6] Accordingly, *e.g.*, agricultural products being cultivated by man will not be considered to be "natural resources".[7] "Natural resources" may be living

4 For a concise overview of WTO cases related to natural resources see *Kulovesi*, International trade: Natural resources and the World Trade Organization, in: Morgera/Kulovesi (eds.), Research Handbook on International Law and Natural Resources (2016), p. 46 (at 54 *et seqq.*).

5 *Appellate Body*, Report of 29 April 1996, WT/DS2/AB/R, *US – Gasoline*, p. 17.

6 For a more elaborate definition, see *World Trade Organization*, World Trade Report 2010, Trade in natural resources (2010), pp. 46-47.

7 Since agricultural products are cultivated and, hence, "artificial" whereas natural resources are created by nature itself; see *World Trade Organization*, World Trade Report 2010, Trade in natural resources (2010), p. 46. Correspondingly, some substances which belong to the category of so-called "primary commodities" (such as corn, coffee, cocoa, or sugar) do not constitute "natural resources" either. Fish and

matter, *i.e.* biological resources (including genetic resources), or non-living matter, *i.e.* fossil, metallic, mineral or freshwater resources.[8]

What is more important for a legal analysis under WTO law, however, is whether "natural resources" are "goods" or "products"[9] In short, for purposes of trade law, a "natural resource" as defined *supra* is a "good" or "product" when it is, as a matter of fact, traded in markets.

Nevertheless, even if a "natural resource" is not, and, by its nature (*e.g.*, soil, air), cannot be, a "good" or "product" traded across borders, it may be of normative significance under WTO law. Since, *e.g.*, it may form part of the environment protected by a domestic measure which adversely affects international trade contrary to GATT rules, but which may be possibly justified under the GATT's general exceptions clause.[10]

III. Peculiarities of natural resources

Natural resources, within the aforementioned meaning, share certain distinctive peculiarities.[11] First, natural resources are unevenly distributed among states. Indeed, it is a well-known geographical phenomenon that some natural resources may be found, or be extractable, in a few countries only whereas other countries suffer from a serious or complete lack of those resources. This, in turn, entails the necessity to import and, hence, to trade such natural resources across borders.

Second, natural resources are, in general, exhaustible. Even so-called renewable resources, in particular biological resources, *i.e.* living matter such as fish, are usually finite resources which may get depleted through overex-

---

forestry products are "natural resources" within the meaning of our definition only if taken from natural stocks, *i.e.* not if grown in aquaculture or plantations respectively; for a slightly differing view see *World Trade Organization*, World Trade Report 2010, Trade in natural resources (2010), p. 46.

8 Of course, some of these substances may need to be processed in order to become tradable goods. As far as such processing is restricted to a certain minimum degree, they shall still be treated as "natural resources", see *World Trade Organization*, World Trade Report 2010, Trade in natural resources (2010), p. 46. *E.g.*, cut trees are "natural resources" even if their branches and twigs have been sawn off so as to enable transport of the trunks.

9 Accordingly, we will revisit this legal issue in some more depth later on (see *infra* at V.2.a)).

10 See *infra* at V.2.e)).

11 For a full description of these features see *World Trade Organization*, World Trade Report 2010, Trade in natural resources (2010), pp. 46-54.

ploitation. This is why any, or almost any, natural resource may become, or already is, scarce and in urgent need of effective conservation so as to be available for future generations as well.

Third, exploration, exploitation, extraction and use of natural resources may go along with negative externalities, *e.g.* damage to the environment or to human health. From an economic point of view, such externalities should be internalized, *i.e.* reflected, in the end, in the prize of a "good" or "product" to be paid by the consumer. This, in turn, requires adoption of some kind of regulatory measures which may result in obstacles to international trade. An example may be an import prohibition of natural resources which have not been extracted in accordance with certain environmental standards.

Fourth, markets for natural resources may experience high price volatility. A well-known example is the world market price for crude oil oscillating between steep increases and equally steep slides. Extreme price volatility may severely affect, and even cause economic shocks to, either countries supplying the relevant natural resource or countries in demand of that resource.

Finally, fifth, some national economies, especially of developing states, are dominated by natural resources. The economic situation of such resource-rich countries is, typically, characterized by natural resources forming the biggest share in total merchandise export. This dependency of national income on exports of only one or a few natural resources makes their economies extremely vulnerable, *e.g.*, in case of extreme price volatilities on the world markets.

IV. Resource-related measures affecting trade

In order to react to uneven geographical distribution, exhaustibility, negative externalities, price volatility and market dominance of natural resources, states may adopt certain measures. Such resource-related measures may be differentiated, from an international trade law perspective, into border measures and domestic measures.

Border measures are to take effect at the border, *i.e.* on exportation or on importation. Examples are export taxes[12], import tariffs[13], or export quotas[14]. In contrast, domestic measures take effect behind the border. Nevertheless, they may affect international trade. Due to states' creativity, domestic measures may take a broad variety of forms, among them, *e.g.*, consumption taxes[15], labelling requirements[16] or exploration subsidies[17].

Interestingly, in the field of natural resources, border measures and domestic measures may have the same effects in economic terms. *E.g.*, an import tariff imposed by a resource-poor state may yield the same effects as a consumption tax within that state. Both measures will raise the price of the resource on the internal market.[18] Albeit, both measures are regulated differently under word trade law.[19]

---

12 Export taxes may lead, *e.g.*, to higher prices on the world market and, hence, allow resource-rich countries to benefit from uneven geographic distribution of the natural resource, see *World Trade Organization*, World Trade Report 2010, Trade in natural resources (2010), p. 126.

13 Import tariffs may be, *e.g.*, a means of shifting rents from a resource-exporting country to a resource-importing country and, thus, a measure in reaction to the uneven geographic distribution of natural resources, see *World Trade Organization*, World Trade Report 2010, Trade in natural resources (2010), pp. 123-124.

14 Export quotas may be, *e.g.*, a measure to counter the problem of exhaustibility of natural resources, see *World Trade Organization*, World Trade Report 2010, Trade in natural resources (2010), p. 129.

15 Consumption taxes may be, *e.g.*, a means to internalize environmental costs resulting, *e.g.*, from damage to the environment during extraction or use of natural resources, see *World Trade Organization*, World Trade Report 2010, Trade in natural resources (2010), p. 136.

16 Labelling requirements may be, *e.g.*, a means to deal with environmental problems associated with the extraction of natural resources by channelling consumers' preferences towards environment-friendly products, see *World Trade Organization*, World Trade Report 2010, Trade in natural resources (2010), p. 138.

17 Exploration subsidies may be, *e.g.*, a means to induce enterprises to invest in the discovery of deposits of natural resources, *World Trade Organization*, World Trade Report 2010, Trade in natural resources (2010), p. 130.

18 *World Trade Organization*, World Trade Report 2010, Trade in natural resources (2010), p. 124.

19 An import tariff will be subject to the disciplines under Article II:1(a), (b) first sentence, GATT (see *infra* V.2.c)), whereas a consumption tax may be regulated by Article III:2, first sentence, GATT.

V. WTO law

1. WTO system

For the purposes of this article, the notion of "trade law" extends to the law of the WTO only.[20] The WTO is an international organization established by the Marrakesh Agreement of 1994. Accordingly, the Marrakesh Agreement lays down the WTO's institutional and procedural framework. The WTO's substantive law, *i.e.* the trade rules which govern border or domestic measures adopted by the WTO members, is laid down in numerous separate agreements related to goods[21], services[22] and intellectual property rights[23].

---

20 Of course, FTAs are going to play an increasingly important role in the field of international trade, including trade in natural resources. In fact, some of these agreements, in particular the more modern ones, take into account the need for, *e.g.*, environmental protection or sustainable development. For an overview see, *e.g.*, *United Nations Environment Programme/International Institute for Sustainable Development* (eds.), Trade and Green Economy: A Handbook (3rd edition 2014), pp. 123 *et seqq.* Indeed, in this handbook it is stated that, *e.g.*, recent FTAs concluded between the EU and other states, or groups of states, *"include provisions on [...] the prudent use of natural resources such as timber and fish"*, *United Nations Environment Programme/International Institute for Sustainable Development* (eds.), Trade and Green Economy: A Handbook (3rd edition 2014), p. 126. Another interesting example is the US-Peru FTA which *"establishes procedures for regular audits of timber producers and exporters, as well as verification procedures to ensure that timber exports from Peru to the United States comply with Peruvian environmental laws and standards"* (*United Nations Environment Programme/International Institute for Sustainable Development* (eds.), Trade and Green Economy: A Handbook (3rd edition 2014), p. 127). However, as these examples demonstrate, any FTA, and there are close to 600 of them (*United Nations Environment Programme/International Institute for Sustainable Development* (eds.), Trade and Green Economy: A Handbook (3rd edition 2014), p. 58), forms a legal universe of its own. Hence, with regard to trade in goods, unless FTAs are not simply referring to the pertinent WTO agreements related to trade in goods or are, at least, drafted along the line of WTO rules on trade in goods, each FTA would have to be analysed apart for its individual trade in goods regime and its relevance for trade in natural resources and associated environmental, or human rights or development, concerns. This may well be considered a worthwhile task but cannot be accomplished in the context of this contribution.

21 Among them the GATT. For a full list of agreements related to goods see Annex IA to the Marrakesh Agreement.

22 GATS (General Agreement on Trade in Services).

23 TRIPS (Agreement on Trade-Related Aspects of Intellectual Property Rights).

Specifically with regard to natural resources, a special kind of source of WTO law has proven to be of, probably unanticipated, importance: the accession protocols entered into by new WTO member states. These protocols are characterized by their "WTO plus" regulatory approach, *i.e.* acceding states were urged to enter into commitments exceeding those laid down in the original WTO agreements.[24] The two WTO cases at hand are *China – Raw Materials*[25] and *China – Rare Earths*.[26]

2. GATT

Concerning natural resources, the WTO agreements on trade in goods are of primary importance.[27] This article focusses on the most fundamental agreement on trade in goods,[28] *i.e.* the GATT.[29]

---

24 See, e.g., *Ehring*, Nature and Status of WTO Accession Commitments: "WTO-Plus" Obligations and Their Relationship to Other Parts of the WTO Agreement, in: Cremona *et al.* (eds.), Reflections on the Constitutionalisation of International Economic Law, Liber Amicorum for Ernst-Ulrich Petersmann (2013), p. 337 (337 *et seqq.*); *Qin*, "WTO-Plus" Obligations and Their Implications for the World Trade Organization Legal System, in: Journal of World Trade 37 (2003), pp. 483 *et seqq.*.

25 *Appellate Body*, Report of 30 January 2012, WT/DS394/AB/R, WT/DS395/AB/R, WT/DS398/AB/R, *China – Raw Materials*.

26 *Appellate Body*, Report of 7 August 2014, WT/DS431/AB/R, WT/DS432/AB/R, WT/DS433/AB/R, *China – Rare Earths*.

27 However, the GATS may be applicable as well. Since quite some services are related, *e.g.*, to the conservation, management, exploration, exploitation, extraction, transport and sale of natural resources, see *World Trade Organization*, World Trade Report 2010, Trade in natural resources (2010), p. 162. Supply of such services may depend on the establishment of a commercial presence in another state (so-called mode 3 supply of services, see Articles I:2(c), XXVIII(d) GATS; see *World Trade Organization*, World Trade Report 2010, Trade in natural resources (2010), p. 165).

28 Other agreements, *e.g.*, the SCM Agreement (Agreement on Subsidies and Countervailing Measures) or the Anti-Dumping Agreement are highly relevant as well, of course. An important resource-related issue within the WTO are, *e.g.*, fisheries subsidies. The aim was to negotiate an agreement on fisheries subsidies by 2019, see *World Trade Organization*, Fisheries Subsidies, Ministerial Decision of 13 December 2017, WT/MIN[17]/64, WT/L/1031 of 18 December 2017. However, as at the end of March 2020, negotiators have been unable to agree on a consolidated text.

29 Of course, other multilateral WTO agreements on trade in goods, such as the Agreement on Technical Barriers to Trade (TBT Agreement) or the Agreement on the Application of Sanitary and Phytosanitary Measures (SPS Agreement), may be

a) Applicability of the GATT

A preliminary question is whether, in an individual case of a natural resource, the GATT is applicable at all. The GATT applies to "goods" or "products" respectively. Natural resources are "goods" or "products" if they have a *"commercial value"* and *"can be shipped across a frontier for the purposes of a commercial transaction"*.[30] This may hold true for extracted or harvested or captured natural resources, but not for natural resources which are still fully embedded in their natural environment.[31] Accordingly, domestic measures such as prohibitions or restrictions on the extraction, harvesting or capture of natural resources are not governed by the GATT.[32] This can be considered an important expression of the "permanent sovereignty"[33] of states over their natural resources.[34]

---

applicable as well, see *World Trade Organization*, World Trade Report 2010, Trade in natural resources (2010), pp. 170-171. In the *EC – Seal Products* case, *e.g.*, the TBT Agreement was invoked by the complainants and applied by the Panel. However, on appeal, the Appellate Body *"reversed the Panel's finding that the EU Seal Regime constitutes a technical regulation subject to the disciplines of the TBT Agreement"*, see *Appellate Body*, Report of 22 May 2014, WT/DS400/AB/R, WT/DS401/AB/R, *EC – Seal Products*, para. 5.70. Recently, on 22 February 2018, Viet Nam filed a request for consultation with the United States with regard to measures adversely affecting fish imports from Viet Nam, see DS549, *US – Certain Measures Concerning Pangasius Seafood Poducts from Viet Nam*. In its request, Viet Nam relied extensively on violations of the SPS Agreement.

30 Quotes from *European Court of Justice*, Judgment of 9 July 1992, Case C-2/90, ECLI:EU:C:1992:310, *Commission/Belgium*, paras. 23, 26. These criteria derived from the ECJ's jurisprudence can be also used to define the GATT terms "goods" or "products".

31 See, however, *Appellate Body*, Report of 19 January 2004, WT/DS257/AB/R, *US – Softwood Lumber IV*, para. 67, according to which the term "goods" within the meaning of the SCM Agreement may extend to "standing, unfelled trees". This obvious deviation from the legal terminology used under the GATT can be best explained by the object and purpose of the SCM Agreement, see *Appellate Body*, Report of 19 January 2004, WT/DS257/AB/R, *US – Softwood Lumber IV*, para. 64.

32 Whereas border measures such as export bans or quotas are, see Article XI:1 GATT. From an economic point of view, both kinds of measures may have equivalent effects, though.

33 Concerning the principle of "permanent sovereignty over natural resources", see *United Nations*, General Assembly resolution 1803 (XVII) of 14 December 1962. For an in-depth analysis of the principle see the seminal monograph by *Schrijver*, Sovereignty over Natural Resources: Balancing Rights and Duties (1997), *passim*.

34 See, *e.g.*, *Crosby*, Background to WTO Rules and Prodution/Trade Restrictions in the Field of Energy, in: Pauwelyn (ed.), Global Challenges at the Intersection of Trade, Energy and the Environment (2010), p. 83 (83 *et seq.*).

b) Non-discrimination

i. Example: the Most-Favored Nation (MFN) discipline

One of the most fundamental non-discrimination clauses of the GATT[35], indeed, a *"cornerstone of the GATT and [...] one of the pillars of the WTO trading system"*[36], is the most-favored nation (MFN) clause of Article I.[37] Since its *"fundamental purpose"* is *"to preserve the equality of competitive opportunities for like [...] products"*[38] originating in, or destined for, all other WTO members. In relation to natural resources, Article I:1 GATT stipulates that, if a WTO member grants an advantage to natural resources originating in, or destined for, another state,[39] that advantage has to be granted to like natural resources originating in, or destined for, all other WTO members.[40] Such an advantage may be an exemption to an import ban on natural resources, as was the case in *EC – Seal Products*.[41] Another example of an

---

35 *Cf. Appellate Body*, Report of 22 May 2014, WT/DS400/AB/R, WT/DS401/AB/R, *EC – Seal Products*, para. 5.86.

36 *Appellate Body*, Report of 31 May 2000, WT/DS139/AB/R, WT/DS142/AB/R, *Canada – Autos*, para. 69.

37 Another equally fundamental non-discrimination clause is the national treatment (NT) clause of Article III GATT.

38 *Appellate Body*, Report of 22 May 2014, WT/DS400/AB/R, WT/DS401/AB/R, *EC – Seal Products*, para. 5.87.

39 Which may be another WTO member state or any third state. See *Appellate Body*, Report of 22 May 2014, WT/DS400/AB/R, WT/DS401/AB/R, *EC – Seal Products*, para. 5.86.

40 With regard to the distinction between border measures and domestic measures (*supra* IV.), Article I:1 GATT applies to both kinds of measures, *i.e.* the measure which grants the advantage may be a border measure or a domestic measure alike, see *Van den Bossche/Zdouc*, The Law and Policy of the World Trade Organization (4th edition 2017), p. 312.

41 The EC – Seal Products case concerned a ban on import and sale of seal products – with the exception of such seal products resulting from seals caught in a traditional manner by indigenous peoples. In practice, the exception allowed for import and sale of seal products from Greenland but not from Canada and Norway. In other words, the exception granted a "market access advantage" to seal products from Greenland which, contrary to Article I:1 GATT, had not been accorded "immediately and unconditionally" to like seal products from Canada and Norway. Although the EC had drafted the exception in an origin-neutral way, it resulted in a *de facto* discrimination of like Canadian and Norwegian seal products and was, therefore, correctly held to be in violation of Article I:1 GATT. *Cf. Appellate Body*, Report of 22 May 2014, WT/DS400/AB/R, WT/DS401/AB/R, *EC – Seal Products*, para. 5.95.

advantage in the field of natural resources is the access to an eco-label, as was the case in *US – Tuna II (Mexico)*.[42]

ii. "Likeness" and NPR-PPMs

MFN treatment is owed to "like" resources only.[43] In this regard, concerning the concept of "likeness", a still unresolved and, therefore, heavily disputed issue is the NPR-PPM controversy, *i.e.* the controversy whether process and production methods (PPMs) make resultant products unlike even if the PPMs are not product-related (NPR). This ongoing debate is of relevance in the field of natural resources as well because natural resources may be, *e.g.*, extracted, harvested or caught using PPMs which do not conform to certain environmental, human rights, developmental or public morals standards adopted by some, but not all, WTO members. If the PPMs are not product-related (NPR), the extracted, harvested or caught natural resource is physically indistinguishable from a natural resource resulting from PPMs being in full compliance with said environmental, human rights, developmental or public morals standards. *E.g.*, products from seals killed by commercial hunters cannot be distinguished physically from products of seals killed by indigenous peoples, such as the Inuit, using traditional hunting techniques. Are the seals products *"like"* or *"unlike"*? The former, *i.e.* likeness, still seems to be the prevailing view.[44] Indeed, the Panel in *EC – Seal Products* held that *"the type or purpose of the seal hunt does not affect in any way the final product's physical characteristics, end-*

42 *Appellate Body*, Report of 20 November 2015 (Article 21.5), WT/DS381/AB/RW, *US – Tuna II (Mexico)*, para. 7.236, holding that *"access to the dolphin-safe label constitutes an "advantage" on the US market for tuna products by virtue of that label's "significant commercial value."*

43 With regard to WTO case law, the "likeness" test under Article I:1 GATT has to be distinguished from the "likeness" tests under both Article III:2 GATT and Article III:4 GATT; for a discussion of this doctrinal problem see, *e.g.*, *Van den Bossche/Zdouc*, The Law and Policy of the World Trade Organization (4th edition 2017), pp. 316-318. "Likeness" should be interpreted and applied in light of Article I:1's object and purpose which is to prohibit discriminatory measures and to ensure equality of competitive opportunities, *cf. Appellate Body*, Report of 22 May 2014, WT/DS400/AB/R, WT/DS401/AB/R, *EC – Seal Products*, para. 5.82.

44 See *Van den Bossche/Zdouc*, The Law and Policy of the World Trade Organization (4th edition 2017), p. 318.

use, or tariff classification" and that, therefore, seal products are "like" irrespective of the type or purpose of the seal hunt.[45]

iii. Irrelevance of legitimate regulatory distinctions

Equally important, the Appellate Body in the *EC – Seal Products* case held that inconsistency with the MFN clause of Article I:1 GATT does not require to demonstrate that the discrimination, *i.e.* "*the detrimental impact of a measure on competitive opportunities for like imported products*", "*does not stem exclusively from a legitimate regulatory distinction*"[46]. In other words, environmental, human rights, developmental or public morals (such as, *e.g.*, animal welfare) concerns must not be taken into account even if such concerns provided the rational basis for a "legitimate regulatory distinction" between like imported natural resources.[47]

iv. The Kimberley Waiver

However, an important human rights related exception to Article I:1 GATT applies with regard to a peculiar kind of natural resource, namely rough diamonds. Whether they have been extracted, *e.g.*, in violation of international labor standards or, *e.g.*, for the purpose of financing atrocious civil wars also concerns non-product-related characteristics only, since all these circumstances of diamond extraction do not affect the physical properties of rough diamonds. Concerning so-called "conflict diamonds", the WTO has waived,[48] at least until the end of the year 2024,[49] the application of the most-favored nation principle with regard to measures adopted by certain states in accordance with the Kimberley Process Certification

45 *Panel*, Report of 25 November 2013, WT/DS400/R, WT/DS401/R, *EC – Seal Products*, paras. 7.139-7.140, 7.594.

46 *Appellate Body*, Report of 22 May 2014, WT/DS400/AB/R, WT/DS401/AB/R, *EC – Seal Products*, para. 5.90.

47 Rather, the right doctrinal place for such arguments is the General Exceptions clause, see *infra* V.2.e).

48 See *World Trade Organization*, General Council Decision of 15 May 2003, Waiver Concerning Kimberly Process Certification Scheme for Rough Diamonds, WT/L/518.

49 *World Trade Organization*, General Council Decision of 26 July 2018, Extension of Waiver Concerning Kimberly Process Certification Scheme for Rough Diamonds, WT/L/1039.

Scheme (KPCS)[50] the purpose of which is to inhibit trade in these diamonds. Accordingly, the instrument of a waiver of GATT obligations[51] such as the MFN clause of Article I:1 GATT may be used to balance human rights concerns with the interest in free trade.

c) Tariff bindings

i. Export tariffs

The GATT does not rule out tariffs altogether. Rather, a WTO member may impose import tariffs insofar as they do not exceed the tariff bindings laid down in the schedules of concessions (Article II:1(a) and (b), first sentence, GATT).[52] The issue of whether, at least, Article II:1(a) GATT also applies to export tariffs is still contentious.[53] However, very generally speaking, the WTO multilateral agreements on trade in goods including the GATT neither prohibit nor specifically regulate export tariffs, duties or taxes.[54] In contrast, WTO accession protocols, such as the Protocol on Accession of the People's Republic of China[55] may rule out export tariffs on the

---

50 Concerning the KPCS, see, *e.g.*, *Meessen*, Kimberley as a Means of Promoting Good Governance: The Role of Business, in: Hobe/Bungenberg (eds.), Permanent Sovereignty over Natural Resources (2015), p. 173 (173 *et seqq.*).

51 Concerning the legal basis of such waivers see Article IX:3 and 4 Marrakesh Agreement in conjunction with Understanding in Respect of Waivers of Obligations under the General Agreement on Tariffs and Trade 1994.

52 According to the WTO's own analyses, *"tariff protection in the natural resources sector is generally lower than for overall merchandise trade"* with *"[t]he only possible exception [being] fisheries"*, *World Trade Organization*, World Trade Report 2010, Trade in natural resources (2010), p. 114. This corresponds to the WTO's historic view according to which *"[t]he history of natural resources in the [GATT] and the WTO is generally one of progressive market openness"*, *World Trade Organization*, World Trade Report 2010, Trade in natural resources (2010), p. 163.

53 *Van den Bossche/Zdouc*, The Law and Policy of the World Trade Organization (4th edition 2017), p. 471.

54 *Van den Bossche/Zdouc*, The Law and Policy of the World Trade Organization (4th edition 2017), p. 472. Nevertheless, export taxes must be adopted and applied in conformity with WTO law, *e.g.*, and in particular, with the MFN clause of Article I:1 GATT, *Van den Bossche/Zdouc*, The Law and Policy of the World Trade Organization (4th edition 2017), p. 471; *Marceau*, WTO and Export Restrictions, in: Journal of World Trade 50 (2016), p. 563 (at 566, 570).

55 See *World Trade Organization*, Decision of 10 November 2001, Accession of the People's Republic of China, WT/L/432.

basis of their so-called "WTO plus" regulatory approach.[56] In the area of natural resources, it is the *China – Raw Materials*[57] and the *China – Rare Earths*[58] cases in which the prohibition of, or, rather, the obligation to eliminate,[59] export taxes surfaced.[60]

ii. Border tax adjustments

By way of exception to Article II:1(b), first sentence, GATT, tariff bindings do not affect the right of importing states to enact so-called "border tax adjustments", *i.e.* on importation a state may impose *"charges equivalent to an internal tax"* (Article II:2[a] GATT). Such an internal tax may be, *e.g.*, a *"carbon tax"*, *i.e.* a tax related to CO_2 emissions. The purpose of such internal taxes is to reduce CO_2 emissions. Reductions of CO_2 emissions do not only mitigate global warming and, thus, climate change, but contribute to the conservation and sustainable use of natural resources (*e.g.*, fossil fuels or the atmosphere[61]) as well. In order not to disadvantage its own economy, but also to overcome the free rider problem,[62] a state imposing a "car-

---

56 See *supra* V.1. and *Van den Bossche/Zdouc*, The Law and Policy of the World Trade Organization (4th edition 2017), pp. 472-473; *Marceau*, WTO and Export Restrictions, in: Journal of World Trade 50 (2016), p. 563 (576 *et seqq).*

57 *Appellate Body*, Report of 30 January 2012, WT/DS394/AB/R, WT/DS395/AB/R, WT/DS398/AB/R, *China – Raw Materials*.

58 *Appellate Body*, Report of 7 August 2014, WT/DS431/AB/R, WT/DS432/AB/R, WT/DS433/AB/R, *China – Rare Earths*.

59 See Paragraph 11.3 of the Protocol on Accession of the People's Republic of China stipulating that *"China shall eliminate all taxes and charges applied to exports unless specifically provided for in Annex 6 of this Protocol or applied in conformity with the provisions of Article VIII of the GATT 1994."*

60 Further cases against China are pending: DS508, *China – Raw Materials II (US)* (which concerns a US complaint with regard to export duties on antimony, cobalt, copper, graphite, lead, magnesia, talc, tantalum, and tin); DS509, *China – Raw Materials II (EU)* (which concerns a complaint by the EU with regard to export duties and other export restrictions for antimony, chromium, cobalt, copper, graphite, indium, lead, magnesia, talc, tantalum and tin).

61 The atmosphere can be considered a natural resource which exercises the function of a natural "waste dump" for the deposition of all kinds of man-made emissions among them CO_2 emissions or ozone depleting gaseous substances.

62 Which may result from the fact that an internal "carbon tax" contributes to the mitigation of climate change as well as to the conservation and the sustainable use of natural resources (such as fossil fuels or the atmosphere) which benefits everyone everywhere in the world, *i.e.* also those countries which do not burden their economy and population with such a tax.

bon tax" may be allowed to charge imports from other countries with an equivalent duty if the requirements laid down in Article II:2(a) GATT are met.[63]

d) Prohibition of non-tariff barriers

Article XI:1 GATT rules out import or export prohibitions or restrictions other than tariffs. Hence, *e.g.*, export taxes imposed on the export of natural resources, *e.g.*, are not governed by Article XI:1 GATT. In other respects, the scope of the prohibition of non-tariff barriers to trade is very broad, though. It applies, roughly speaking, to import or export measures which limit the quantity of imported or exported natural resources.[64] This also holds true for "zero quotas", *e.g.*, import bans as was the case in *US – Shrimp*.[65] On the other hand, measures restricting or prohibiting the extraction, harvest or catch of natural resources do not constitute a non-tariff barrier to trade within the meaning of Article XI:1 GATT.[66]

An explicit exception to the general prohibition of non-tariff barriers may be also applicable in the field of natural resources. According to Article XI:2(a) GATT,[67] if a particular natural resource is essential to a WTO member state, it may prohibit or restrict the export of that resource, though only temporarily and only for the purpose of preventing or relieving critical shortages.[68] In addition, any such export prohibition or restriction must apply, and be applied, in a non-discriminatory manner to all

---

63 Otherwise, the "carbon tax" may be justifiable under Article XX(b), (g) GATT. For an in-depth discussion of the complex legal issues associated with "carbon taxes" see *Pauwelyn*, Carbon leakage measures and border tax adjustments under WTO law, in: van Calster/Prévost (eds.), Research Handbook on Environment, Health and the WTO (2013), p. 448 (448 *et seqq.*).; *Trebilcock*, International Trade Law (2015), pp. 174-176; see also *Marceau*, WTO and Export Restrictions, in: Journal of World Trade 50 (2016), p. 563 (584).

64 *Appellate Body*, Report of 30 January 2012, WT/DS394/AB/R, WT/DS395/AB/R, WT/DS398/AB/R, *China – Raw Materials*, para. 320.

65 *Panel*, Report of 15 May 1998, WT/DS58/R, *US – Shrimp*, para. 7.16.

66 Even though, from an economic point of view, the effects of such measures may be similar to export bans or quotas (see *supra* in and at fn. 32-34).

67 Concerning Article XI:2(b) GATT with regard to export prohibitions on unprocessed salmon and herring (pre-WTO) *GATT Panel*, Report of 22 March 1988, L/6268 – 35S/98, *Canada – Herring and Salmon*, para. 4.3.

68 For a thorough interpretation of this provision, especially with regard to natural resources, see *Appellate Body*, Report of 30 January 2012, WT/DS394/AB/R, WT/DS395/AB/R, WT/DS398/AB/R, *China – Raw Materials*, paras. 308 *et seqq.*

other states no matter whether they are WTO members or not (Article XIII:1 GATT).[69]

e) General exceptions

Under the general exceptions clause of Article XX GATT,[70] WTO members have retained their "right to regulate", *i.e.* their right to adopt generally applicable measures which pursue legitimate public policy objectives.[71] Especially, Article XX GATT allows WTO member states to take measures related to some of the distinctive peculiarities of natural resources,[72] *e.g.*, exhaustibility, negative externalities or price volatility.

E.g., an import prohibition on natural resources caught contrary to animal welfare standards may be allowed under Article XX(a) GATT,[73] export duties on natural resources the extraction of which pollutes the environment and, as a result, endangers human health may be justifiable under Article XX(b),[74] an import ban on natural resources which implements an export prohibition under a treaty of international environmental law may

69 *Cf. Mavroidis*, Trade in Goods (2007), pp. 63-64.

70 Interestingly, the general exceptions clause of Article XX GATT may be inapplicable with regard to "WTO-plus" obligations laid down WTO accession protocols. Ultimately, the availability of Article XX GATT depends on how the "WTO plus" obligations have been framed in the respective protocol. See *Appellate Body*, Report of 30 January 2012, WT/DS394/AB/R, WT/DS395/AB/R, WT/DS398/AB/R, *China – Raw Materials*, para. 307, stating that, on the basis of a thorough interpretation of Paragraph 11.3 of the Protocol on Accession of the People's Republic of China, China could not have recourse to Article XX GATT in order to justify the imposition of export duties on certain metals.

71 Within the context of Article XX GATT, the legitimate public policy objectives are addressed in paragraphs (a)-(j).

72 See *supra* III.

73 Concerning "seal welfare" as a "public morals" concern within the meaning of Article XX(a) GATT, see *Panel*, Report of 25 November 2013, WT/DS400/R, WT/DS401/R, *EC – Seal Products*, para. 7.631; *Appellate Body*, Report of 22 May 2014, WT/DS400/AB/R, WT/DS401/AB/R, *EC – Seal Products*, para. 5.199.

74 Concerning *"mining and production of rare earths, tungsten, and molybdenum"* causing *"grave harm to the environment"* and, consequently, to *"human, animal or plant life or health"* within the meaning of Article XX(b) GATT, see *Panel*, Report of 26 March 2014, WT/DS431/R, WT/DS432/R, WT/DS433/R, *China – Rare Earths*, para. 7.156. Concerning protection of "dolphin life or health", see (pre-WTO) *GATT Panel*, Report of 16 June 1994, DS29/R, *US – Tuna (EEC)*, para. 5.30, which was, however, not adopted.

be based on Article XX(d),[75] or an export quota on natural resources aiming at their conservation may be permitted by Article XX(g).[76]

Article XX(h) may justify export restrictions on natural resources implementing "intergovernmental commodity agreements" concluded for the purpose of stabilizing prices on the world market.[77] Article XX(i) may be invoked to vindicate export restrictions on natural resources which have

---

75 Since *"law[s] and regulations"* within the meaning of Article XX(d) GATT may include international treaty rules *"that have been incorporated into the domestic legal system of a WTO Member or have direct effect according to that WTO Member's legal system"*, *Appellate Body*, Report of 6 March 2006, WT/DS308/AB/R, *Mexico – Taxes on Soft Drinks*, para. 79. *E.g.*, an import ban on specimen of species threatened with extinction may be considered a measure implementing the obligation of treaty parties to the Convention on International Trade in Endangered Species of Wild Fauna and Flora (CITES, UNTS vol. 993, p. 243) *"not [to] allow trade in specimens of species included in Appendices I, II and III except in accordance with the provisions of the present Convention"* (Article II CITES) if, *e.g.*, specimen listed in Appendix I CITES have been exported without *"prior grant [...] of an export permit"* (Article III[2], first sentence, CITES).

76 Concerning "conservation measures on rare earths" which may include "export quotas" that could be covered by Article XX(g) GATT, see *Panel*, Report of 26 March 2014, WT/DS431/R, WT/DS432/R, WT/DS433/R, *China – Rare Earths*, para. 7.377. Concerning conservation of "sea turtles" see *Appellate Body*, Report of 12 October 1998, WT/DS58/R, *US – Shrimp*, para. 134. Concerning the conservation of "tuna stocks" see (pre-WTO) *GATT Panel*, Report of 22 December 1981, L/5198 – 29S/91, *US – Canadian Tuna*, para. 4.9. Concerning conservation of "salmon and herring stocks" see (pre-WTO) *GATT Panel*, Report of 22 March 1988, L/6268 – 35S/98, *Canada – Herring and Salmon*, para. 4.4. Concerning conservation of "dolphin stocks", see (pre-WTO) *GATT Panel*, Report of 16 June 1994, DS29/R, *US – Tuna (EEC)*, para. 5.13, which was, however, not adopted. It has to be noted here that a shortage of an "exhaustible natural resource" within the meaning of Article XX(g) GATT can be, depending on the circumstances of the individual case, "critical" within the meaning of Article XI:2(a) GATT, *i.e.* a measure adopted in accordance with Article XI:2(a) GATT "might operate simultaneously" with another measure adopted in accordance with Article XX(g) GATT, *Appellate Body*, Report of 30 January 2012WT/DS394/AB/R, WT/DS395/AB/R, WT/DS398/AB/R, *China – Raw Materials*, para. 337. In contrast, generally, one and the same trade restrictive measure cannot be justified both under Article XI:2(a) GATT and Article XX(g) GATT. *Cf. Panel*, Report of 5 July 2011, WT/DS394/R, WT/DS395/R, WT/DS398/R, *China – Raw Materials*, para. 7.300, stating that *"the reach of Article XI:2(a) would not be the same as that of Article XX(g); they are intended to address different situations and thus must mean different things."*

77 *World Trade Organization*, World Trade Report 2010, Trade in natural resources (2010), p. 176. Such "intergovernmental commodity agreements" have, however, never been submitted, in accordance with Article XX(h) GATT, for approval or

been adopted in order to secure essential quantities of the relevant resource to domestic industries.[78] Finally, Article XX(j) may support transitional export restrictions on natural resources which have become temporarily scarce.[79]

f) Trade and development

WTO members may grant preferential treatment to developing countries both under Part IV of the GATT entitled "Trade and Development" and under the so-called "Enabling Clause" which is a permanent waiver decision concerning the MFN treatment clause of Article I.[80] The purpose of such preferential treatment of developing states may be, *e.g.*, to overcome their (continued) problem of market dominance,[81] *i.e.* the problem that national economies of developing countries (still often) excessively depend on the export of a few natural resources.[82]

---

rejection by the Contracting Parties to the GATT or to the WTO respectively, see *Weiss*, Internationale Rohstoffmärkte, in: Tietje (ed.), Internationales Wirtschaftsrecht (2nd edition 2015), p. 296 (301).

78 In times of a governmental program which stabilizes the domestic price of the resource below world prices, *World Trade Organization*, World Trade Report 2010, Trade in natural resources (2010), p. 174.

79 *World Trade Organization*, World Trade Report 2010, Trade in natural resources (2010), p. 168.

80 *GATT*, Differential and More Favourable Treatment Reciprocity and Fuller Participation of Developing Countries, Decision of 28 November 1979, L/4903. The EU, *e.g.*, has implemented the Enabling Clause by creating its own Generalised Scheme of Preferences (GSP), see Regulation (EU) No 978/2012 of the European Parliament and of the Council of 25 October 2012 applying a scheme of generalised tariff preferences and repealing Council Regulation (EC) No 732/2008, OJ L 303, 31.10.2012, p. 1.

81 Tackling the problem of developing countries' excessive dependency on exports of one or a few natural resources was at the heart of international efforts to negotiate and adopt so-called international commodity agreements. Generally speaking, and this seems to be the prevailing view, see, *e.g.*, *Herdegen*, Internationales Wirtschaftsrecht (11th edition 2017), pp. 226 *et seqq.*, the success of international commodity agreements *"was mixed at best"*, *World Trade Organization*, World Trade Report 2010, Trade in natural resources (2010), p. 163.

82 *Cf.* Article XXXVI:5 GATT in conjunction with the ad note to Article XXXVI defining the term "diversification". *Cf.* also *World Trade Organization*, World Trade Report 2010, Trade in natural resources (2010), pp. 174-175.

VI. Conclusions

Resources are scarce. All national economies are in need of them. International trade makes resources available to all states. World trade law of the WTO ensures free trade and, consequently, global availability of resources. On the other hand, exploration, extraction, transport and use of resources may conflict with environmental, human rights or developmental concerns. Hence, states may adopt measures pursuing legitimate environmental, human rights or developmental objectives. Such measures may prove to be trade-restrictive and, therefore, *prima facie* incompatible with WTO law. However, WTO law provides rules, instruments and mechanisms which allow for the harmonization of trade and international trade law, on the one side, with opposed concerns and international rules relating to such concerns, on the other side. Accordingly, fairness regarding the *"conditions and opportunities for the sharing and securing of resources"*[83] can effectively be brought about through WTO law but will, ultimately, depend on correlating WTO law adequately with other areas of international law, such areas as will be discussed in other contributions of this volume.

83 See the title of the concluding remarks by *Stephan Hobe* and *Christian Tams* according to the programme of the Ladenburg Symposium on 2-3 March 2018.

Resource Mining and Human Rights

Michael Lysander Fremuth[*]

Abstract

Human rights have become a cross-sectional topic in international, supranational and domestic law, affecting all branches of societal life. Accordingly, resource mining is not beyond the ambit of human rights law which can entail different related dimensions: First, human rights can grant titles to undertake business activities such as the exploitation of natural resources by mining activities. Bearers of such rights can be individuals and corporations, as well as groups, including indigenous peoples or the people as a whole. In this dimension, human rights might provide for rights to resource mining. Second, the extractive industries are regarded as having an especially high potential for inflicting harm on various human rights of the concerned workers, as well as of uninvolved persons. In particular, the rights of children (child labour), workers and women, as well as rights concerning the environment might be at stake. In this dimension, human rights might become the antagonists of resource mining, what might request limitations and regulation. Third, the protection of human rights might face specific difficulties with regard to resource mining as states on whose territory such activities take place might be unwilling or too weak to effectively protect human rights. As companies themselves are still not directly bound by international human rights law, questions of their home states' responsibilities – including of extraterritorial nature – acquire more and more relevance.

---

* Michael Lysander Fremuth is Professor at the Department of Constitutional and Administrative Law of the University of Vienna and Scientific Director of the Ludwig Boltzmann Institute of Fundamental and Human Rights, Vienna. He wishes to thank *Anna Makrypidi*, *Magdalena Steringer* and *Roman Friedrich* for their helpful assistance in finalising this article.

Overview

I. Introduction

The legal recognition of human rights and their "positivation"[1] can be regarded as a revolution in the history and as a cornerstone of modern public international law.[2] The compliance with human rights and their protection no longer forms part of the states' internal affairs (*domaine réservé*), rather human rights constitute a common concern of the international community[3] that – as a cross-cutting issue – is intertwined with all branches of society, national and international law. Furthermore, human rights are linked with the idea of sustainability and development[4] as it is the case for natural resources development.[5] Thus, it is hardly surprising that resource mining has become integrated in a larger human rights discourse with increasing attention.[6]

Natural resources are of the utmost importance in political and economic terms. Depending on the specific conditions in each country and, thereby, to a staged degree, they form the basis for national wealth, contributing to the gross domestic product.[7] Furthermore, natural resources are indispensable for many branches of economy – *i.e.* rare earth for the

1 The term is used to describe the transformation of a human right as an idea, a concept or an unwritten rule to positive law.

2 *Fremuth*, Menschenrechte: Grundlagen und Dokumente, (2019), pp. 1, 8.

3 On "basic rights of the human person" as *erga omnes* obligations *cp. International Court of Justice*, Barcelona Traction (Belgium v. Spain), I.C.J. Reports 1970, p. 3 paras. 33 *et seq.*; *Beitz*, Human Rights as a Common Concern, in: The American Political Science Review 95 (2001), p. 269 (269 *et seqq.*).

4 *Cp.* the concise comparison between the Sustainable Development Goals and Human Rights by the Office of the United Nations High Commissioner for Human Rights, available under https://www.ohchr.org/Documents/Issues/MDGs/Post2015/SDG_HR_Table.pdf (last accessed: 9 April 2020) and demonstrating that any of the SDGs correlates to a human rights guarantee.

5 *Ezirigwe*, Human rights and property rights in natural resources development, in: Journal of Energy & Natural Resources Law 35 (2017), p. 201 (202 *et seq.*).

6 *Gilbert*, Natural Resources and Human Rights: An Appraisal (2018); *de Schutter*, Transnational Corporations and Human Rights (2006), p. 263 *et seq*; *Cotula*, Human Rights, Natural Resource and Investment Law in a Globalised World: Shades of Grey in the Shadow of the Law (2012).

7 *National Research Council*, Assigning Economic Value to Natural Resources (1994); *Rostow*, The Stages of Economic Growth: A Non-Communist Manifesto (1960), pp. 4–16; but also see the "resource curse" concept, *Prebisch*, The Economic Development of Latin America and its Principal Problems (1950); and *Singer*, US Foreign Investment in Underdeveloped Areas: The Distribution of Gains between Investing and Borrowing Countries, in: American Economic Review, Papers and Proceedings 40 (1950), p. 473 (473 *et seqq.*).

production of IT-devices and smartphones, petroleum for the entire transportation sector – and can, accordingly, be regarded as drivers of economic globalization meeting a high dependency in many countries. Because of the high rents and significant revenues that can be achieved with natural resources, governments, financial institutions, and private companies have their own interests, partly conflicting with more general public interests. Finally, the exploitation and the use of natural resources can come into conflict with the ideas of sustainability and a "green economy" as supported by the UN Sustainable Development Goals[8] and the Paris Climate Accord.[9] Due to their sketched importance as well as the skewed geographical distribution of natural resources, resources-related questions have a sensitive political character within states and for international relations,[10] including the distribution of wealth and trade-related issues.[11]

The human rights dimensions of resource mining in this article will be addressed from three different angles: *First*, human rights can serve as legitimating underpinnings, *i.e.* as titles invoked to justify resource mining (see II.). *Second*, resource mining might have a specific detrimental impact on various human rights due to its conditions, impacts, and hazards. Accordingly, resource mining can be analysed as an infringement of human rights (see III.). *Third*, the question of responsibilities concerning the protection of human rights deserves an intensified discussion with regard to the prominent role played by transnational corporations and artisanal miners as well as concerning the exterritorial protection afforded to human rights (see IV.). Finally, the author will offer some conclusions and present an outlook (see V.).

---

8 *UN General Assembly*, Transforming our world: the 2030 Agenda for Sustainable Development, UN Doc. A/RES/70/1 of 25 September 2015, pp. 13 *et seqq*.

9 Alternatively known as the Paris Agreement or the Paris Accord, C.N.63.2016, which entered into force on 4 November 2016. More details available: https://unfccc.int/process-and-meetings/the-paris-agreement/the-paris-agreement.

10 *Ross*, How do Natural Resources Influence Civil War?, Evidence from Thirteen Cases, in: International Organization 8 (2004), p. 35 (35 *et seqq*.); *Le Billon*, The Political Ecology of War: Natural Resources and Armed Conflict, in: Political Geography 20 (2001), p. 561 (561 *et seqq*.).

11 *WTO*, Trade in Natural Resources, World Trade Report 2010 of 23 July 2010; *WTO*, China – Raw Materials, Reports of the Panel of 5 July 2011 (WT/DS394/R; WT/DS395/R; WT/DS398/R), Reports of the Appellate Body of 30 January 2012 (WT/DS394/AB/R; WT/DS395/AB/R; WT/DS398/AB/R).

II. Resource Mining and its Human Rights Underpinnings

The first human rights dimension of resource mining can be identified as the question of who is entitled to the ownership, exploitation, extraction, and use of natural resources. An answer should differentiate between a collective dimension (permanent sovereignty over natural resources and community rights, see 1.) and an individual dimension (right to property, see 2.) before addressing the relation between the two dimensions (see 3.).

1. The Collective Dimension: Permanent Sovereignty over Natural Resources and Community Rights

The starting point should be the permanent sovereignty over natural resources – a principle that emerged in the course of de-colonisation and the debate about a new international economic order.[12] It marks a reaction to the claim to ownership over natural resources and to their exploitation by former colonial powers disrespecting historic titles to land and its resources, as well as the needs of the local communities. By now, the principle of sovereignty of natural resources in its essence can be regarded to form part of customary international law.[13] Due to that principle, nations and people have the right to dispose freely of their wealth and natural resources. Whereas states as legal persons can invoke their territorial and economic sovereignty in that respect,[14] the entitlement of people reveals a human rights approach that is rooted in the collective right to self-determination.[15] That right is recognized by Article 1 paras. 1 and 2 of both UN Covenants on Human Rights[16] and finds its strongest and most detailed foundation in the African Charter on Human and Peoples' Rights, which

12 *Hossain*, Permanent Sovereignty over Natural Resources in International Law: Principle and Practice (1984); *Tyagi*, Permanent Sovereignty over Natural Resources, in: Cambridge Journal of International and Comparative Law 4 (2015), p. 588 (588 *et seqq.*).

13 *International Court of Justice*, Armed Activities on the Territory of the Congo (Congo v. Uganda), I.C.J. Reports 2005, p. 168 para. 244; Bungenberg/Hobe (eds.), Permanent Sovereignty over Natural Resources (2015), p. 10 *et seq*.

14 *Ezirigwe* (fn. 5), p. 204.

15 Among others: Para. 2 A/RES/15/1514 of 14 December 1960 (Declaration on the Granting of Independence to Colonial Countries and Peoples); Art. 1 (2) A/RES/41/128 of 4 December 1986 (Declaration on the Right to Development).

16 International Covenant on Civil and Political Rights (ICCPR), 999 UNTS 171; International Covenant on Economic, Social and Cultural Rights, 993 UNTS 3.

contains the right to self-determination (Article 20 para. 1) and concretizes the free disposition of wealth and natural resources in Article 21. There, the peoples' right to natural resources is designed as an absolute right and states are regarded as custodians of this exclusive interest of their people. Natural resources are also covered by the still controversial[17] right to (economic) development, enshrined in Article 22 of the African Charter and also recognized by the UN General Assembly.[18] In the African context, it should serve as an instrument to ensure "that the material wealth of the countries is not exploited by aliens to no or little benefit to the African countries".[19] The right of people to development, self-determination, and the free disposal of their wealth and natural resources is, though in less detail, also explicitly recognized by the Salvador Protocol to the American Convention on Human Rights (Preamble), the Arab Charter on Human Rights (Preamble, Article 1) and has been accepted and applied by the European Court of Justice, although European human rights law does not explicitly acknowledge the right to self-determination.[20]

The right to wealth and national resources has a specific dimension with regard to indigenous peoples, who by very definition have a specific and distinct affinity to nature, as well as to the land they (traditionally) occupy and its resources.[21] Indigenous communities have been held to fall under the term 'people' for the purpose of the right to (economic) self-determination.[22] The rights of indigenous peoples concerning land and natural re-

---

17 *Bunn*, The Right to Development and International Economic Law (2012); *Kirchmeier*, The Right to Development: Where do we stand? State of Debate of the Right to Development (2006), Friedrich-Ebert-Stiftung Occasional Papers. Nr. 23 (2006); on the draft convention on the right to development as propsed by the *UN Human Rights Council* (A/HRC/WG.2/21/2) see *Schrijver*, A new Convention on the Human Right to Development: Putting the Cart Before the Horse?, in: Netherlands Quarterly of Human Rights 38 (2020), pp. 84–93.

18 A/RES/41/128 of 4 December 1986 (Declaration on the Right to Development); Art. 1., A/RES/70/1 of 25 September 2015 (Transforming our world: the 2030 Agenda for Sustainable Development).

19 Guidelines for National Periodic Reports to the African Commission, Sec. III para. 6.

20 *European Court of Justice*, C-104/16 P, ECLI:EU:C:2016:973 (Front Polisario), paras. 86–108.

21 *Human Rights Committee*, General Comment No. 23 (1994): Art. 27 (Rights of Minorities), CCPR/C/21/Rev.1/Add.5, para. 7; Art. 13 para. 1 ILO-Indigenous and Tribal Peoples Convention No. 169; Preamble and Art. 3 of the UN Declaration on the Rights of Indigenous Peoples.

22 *Strydom*, Environment and Indigenous Peoples, in: MPEPIL online, January 2013, para. 5; Art. 7 para. 1 ILO-Indigenous and Tribal Peoples Convention No. 169.

sources have been stipulated in the Indigenous and Tribal Peoples Convention, 1989 No. 169, of the International Labour Organization (ILO), regarded as the most important international treaty concerning indigenous peoples. Art. 14 of the Convention recognizes ownership and possession of these peoples over the land which they traditionally occupy, and Art. 15 addresses their rights to the natural resources pertaining to their lands, which shall be especially safeguarded. The Convention falls short of establishing an absolute right over natural resources. Rather, Art. 15 para. 1 guarantees the right of indigenous peoples to participate in the use, management, and conservation of the resources. If the state retains ownership of the land's resources (*i.e.* where no legal title to property of the land and its resources held by the indigenous peoples exists), according to para. 2, the state should consult them to what degree their interests would be prejudiced before the exploration or exploitation of the resources is undertaken or permitted. Only "wherever possible" shall the peoples participate in the benefits of such activities, but they shall receive fair compensation for any damages that they may sustain. They should generally not be removed from the land, which they occupy, and are entitled to safe appropriate compensation if relocation is unavoidable (Art. 16). Governments are asked to prevent unauthorised intrusion upon or use of the indigenous peoples' lands and establish adequate penalties (Art. 18). Indigenous industries and subsistence economy, having a strong relation to the land and its resources – such as fishing, trapping, and gathering – shall be strengthened and promoted (Art. 23). The relevance of the ILO Convention No. 169, which entered into force on 5 September 1991, is limited, as it has been ratified by twenty-three countries only.[23] In contrast, one hundred and forty-four states voted in favour of the UN Declaration on the Rights of Indigenous Peoples (UNDRIP),[24] and even the four opposing states which have huge communities of indigenous people (Australia, Canada, New Zealand, United States) later endorsed UNDRIP. That resolution contains several references to the indigenous peoples' land, territories and resources, among them protection from relocation (Art. 10), protection of archaeological and historical sites (Art. 11 para. 1), the conservation of their vital

23 See *International Labour Organization*, NORMLEX, ratifications by conventions, available under: https://www.ilo.org/dyn/normlex/en/f?p=NORMLEXPUB:11300:0::NO::P11300_INSTRUMENT_ID:312314 (last accessed: 9 April 2020); most recently, Luxembourg on 5. June 2018 has ratified the Convention 169, that entered into force on 5 June 2019.

24 *UN General Assembly*, UN Doc. A/RES/61/295 of 13 September 2007, United Nations Declaration on the Rights of Indigenous Peoples.

medicinal plants, animals and minerals (Art. 24 para. 1), and the right to maintain and strengthen their distinctive relationship with their traditionally owned or otherwise occupied and used lands, territories, and other resources (Art. 25). Regarding the latter, Art. 26 postulates a far-reaching right to own, use, develop, and control the lands, territories, and resources; states are asked to provide for legal recognition and protection. States shall obtain the free and informed consent of the indigenous people prior to the approval of any project affecting them, in particular concerning the development, utilization, or exploitation of resources (Art. 32 para. 2). Without that consent, a right to redress might emerge (Art. 28). Even though the issue of indigenous peoples remains controversial under public international law, it is held that their land rights might have attained the status of customary international law.[25] Whether free, prior, and informed consent already amounts to an obligation under current international law, is, however, unclear.[26]

Such a collective human rights approach can be invoked to require that natural resources, as well as their exploitation and extraction, are used to the benefit of the people concerned – be it a national people or a group within the state (such as an indigenous peoples' group). States do not only have a right but an obligation to act as custodians and to enforce their permanent sovereignty over national resources in this respect. In fulfilling this obligation, they enjoy a margin of discretion and can claim exclusive legal dominion over natural resources. States can differentiate between the ownership over the land on the one hand, and over the resources beneath on the other hand. Furthermore, states are entitled to establish their own legal regimes concerning the grant of property rights and licences concerning natural resources.[27]

---

25 *Strydom* (fn. 22), para. 4.

26 According to *T. Ward*, The Right to Free, Prior, and Informed Consent: Indigenous Peoples' Participation Rights within International Law, in: Northwestern Journal of International Human Rights 10 (2011), p. 54 (84 *et passim*), states at a minimum obligation have to engage in good faith obligations with indigenous peoples.

27 *Amaza*, The Concept of Human Rights and Property Rights in Natural Resources Development, in: International Energy Law Review 35 (2017), p. 272 *et seqq*.

2. *The Individual Dimension: Property Rights to Resource Mining*

The individual dimension of human rights to resource mining should be addressed under the premise of the right to property. This human right is acknowledged by Article 17 Universal Declaration of Human Rights but has not been enshrined in either of the two UN Covenants on Human Rights. Thus, the recognition and status of property as a human right remains controversial.[28] Since most regional human rights documents meanwhile contain the right to property[29] and since it has been introduced in later international human rights documents,[30] a general recognition of a human right to property can at least be assumed.[31] Holders of the right to property might be private individuals or – given that high investment costs are factually more important for the question of resource mining – legal entities.[32] However, property remains a particular human right, which means that its understanding might vary pursuant to different legal traditions, cultures and social orders.[33] That is of particular importance, as its content depends to a high degree on the respective legal order entailing repercussions on the guarantee of property itself (definition of property by the respective legal order). Furthermore, as the public or general interest is a well-accepted broad restriction of the right to property, infringements can be justified more easily compared to other human rights.[34]

Accordingly, within a legal order, titles to permit resource mining might be established and subsequently protected as human rights. Property concerning natural resources can be classified as private, quasi-private,

28 *Howard-Hassmann*, Reconsidering the Right to Own Property, in: Journal of Human Rights 12 (2013), p. 180 (180 *et seqq.*); *Alvarez*, The Human Right of Property, in: University of Miami Law Review 72 (2018), p. 580 (584).

29 Art. 1 of Additional Protocol No. 1 to the ECHR, Art. 14 of the AfrCHR, Art. 21 of the ACHR, General Principle 17 of the ASEAN Human Rights Declaration, Art. 25 of the ArabCHR.

30 Art. 5 International Convention on the Elimination of All Forms of Racial Discrimination, 660 UNTS 195; Art. 17 Convention on the Elimination of All Forms of Discrimination against Women, 1249 UNTS 13.

31 See *Sprankling*, The International Law of Property (2014), pp. 203 *et seq.*, 347 *et seq.*

32 See *e.g.*, Art. 1 of the First Additional Protocol to the ECHR.

33 *McLaughlin Mitchell/Ring/Spellman*, Domestic Legal Traditions and States' Human Rights Practices, in: Journal of Peace Research 50 (2013), p. 189 (189 *et. seqq.*).

34 See *Dagan*, The Social Responsibility of Ownership, in: Cornell Law Review 92 (2007), p. 1255 (1255 *et seqq.*) on various forms of social-obligation dimensions of ownership.

public-private and common.[35] Human rights-based property titles might derive from the ownership of the land if it legally includes the exploitation of resources beneath the surface (property of land). However, most states claim property over subsoil assets so that landowners might only attain limited property rights, according to the definition in the respective national law.[36] If a legal order reserves ownership over natural resources to the public, states often opt for a model of granting licences to private persons. Licences constitute an official authorization by the state to the licensee to do something on the land that would otherwise constitute as trespass of the law and the rights of the state.

In human rights jurisprudence holding a licence has been equated to the legal term 'possessions', where there is a legal foundation for predictable and warranted expectations.[37] So, even under these circumstances the licensee might invoke a right to property against an infringement of his (contractual) rights as granted by the licence. In case of a foreign investor, international investment law might provide an additional form of protection (besides domestic remedies). Due to their contractual relations, an investor's property rights can be protected, so that a state, when carrying out an expropriation, is obliged to pay prompt, adequate, and effective compensation. As expropriation does not need to be formal and can also be indirect, a far-reaching level of protection is guaranteed by the possibility to access an international arbitrational tribunal. Finally, the international minimal standard under customary international law provides protection for foreign investments in the case of expropriation.[38] In conclusion, also individual (= private) rights to natural resources enjoy protection under international (human rights) law.

3. The Relation between Human Rights Titles and their Limits

As shown, human rights titles to resource mining might have a collective, as well as an individual dimension. Due to the principle of permanent sovereignty over natural resources and the peoples' right to self-determina-

35 *Ezirigwe* (fn. 5), p. 206.

36 *Venables*, Using Natural Resources for Development: Why Has It Proven So Difficult?, in: Journal of Economic Perspectives 30 (2016), p. 161 (162).

37 *European Court of Human Rights*, Guide on Article 1 of Protocol No. 1 to the European Convention on Human Rights (August 2019), paras. 9, 36–39.

38 *Kriebaum/Reinisch*, Property, Right to, International Protection (2019), Max Planck Encyclopedia of International Law online, paras 9 *et seqq*.

tion, states have a broad margin of appreciation when establishing their legal regimes on resource mining as the realization of their sovereignty and the claims of their people. However, tensions and conflicts might emerge if a state fails to meet its main obligation to strike a fair balance between competing rights and interests. *First*, the legal regime and practice on resource mining might disregard the interest of the 'people', leading to a conflict between the permanent sovereignty over natural resources of the state on the one hand, and of the people on the other hand, including their right to self-determination. In particular, when states ignore increasing legal claims[39] to democracy, participation and the sharing of benefits, conflicts – as within Sudan finally leading to the secession of South-Sudan – are likely to emerge.[40] *Second*, even if resource mining within a State is democratically legitimized and supported by the majority of citizens, it might conflict with the human rights titles to natural resources of specific groups (such as indigenous peoples) and individuals directed against the state. As the individual right to property depends on the configuration and specification of the domestic legal order, it can be argued that it provides for the weakest claim to resource mining. However, remedial action programs, as well as land reforms and reallocation to disadvantaged groups that include discriminatory expropriation without compensation, might amount to a violation of individual human rights.[41] *Third*, group rights and individual rights can compete each other. A state might violate group rights by granting mining rights to individuals and companies disregarding the group's claims to their rights to land and a safe environment. *Finally*, some argue that other individual human rights, such as the right to food, water, and an adequate standard of living, might be invoked by indi-

---

39 *Christiano*, Self-Determination and the Human Right to Democracy, in: Cruft/Liao/Renzo (eds.), Philosophical Foundations of Human Rights (2015), p. 459 (459 *et. seqq.*); Human Right to Democracy?, in: Cruft/Liao/Renzo (eds.), Philosophical Foundations of Human Rights (2015), p. 481 (480 *et. seqq.*); *Fahner*, Revisiting the Human Right to Democracy: A Positivist Analysis, in: The International Journal of Human Rights 21 (2017), p. 321 (*et. seqq.*).

40 *Sorens*, Mineral Production, Territory and Ethnic Rebellion: The Role of Rebel Constituencies, in: Journal of Peace Research 48 (2011), p. 571 (571 *et. seqq.*); *Ross* (fn. 10), p. 35 (37 *et seqq.*).

41 *Vyver*, The Protection and Promotion of a People's Right to Mineral Resources in Africa: International and Municipal Perspectives, in: Law and Development Review 11 (2018), p. 739 (741 *et seqq.*).

viduals to enable them to claim a fair share of natural resources.[42] This could lead to a potential and further conflict between individual rights to national wealth and resources, and the rights of land- and mine-owners and holders of concessions.

The instrument to be used for the purpose of striking a fair balance between these competing claims is resource regulation and management, which can be a very delicate task, as shown, for example, by South Africa. During Apartheid, most mines were owned by companies from abroad and the majority of South Africans was prevented from being owners of productive resources. After Apartheid, the Mineral and Petroleum Resources Development Act (MPRDA)[43] was enacted in 2002.[44] The law acknowledges that South Africa's mineral and petroleum resources belong to the nation, calling them the common heritage of all of the people of South Africa, and determining that the State is the custodian thereof (Preamble, Art. 3). Furthermore, it reaffirms the State's commitment to promoting equitable access, employment and the welfare of all South Africans, as well as security of tenure regarding prospecting, exploration, mining and production operations. Deviating from traditional common law principles under which the owner of the land is at the same time the owner of the land's resources and entitled to make use of them (*cuius est solum, eius est usque ad coelum et ad inferos*),[45] the MPRDA establishes a system by which any rights regarding natural resources are solely granted by the state.[46] This can include prospecting rights, mining rights, exploration rights or production rights, each of which is declared to constitute a "limited real right". The rights granted are confined to a specific person for a predetermined period of time, requiring an application that shows that the applicant is also will-

---

42 *Committee on Economic, Social and Cultural Rights*, General Comment No. 22 (1999), The Right to Adequate Food (Art. 11), UN Doc. E/C.12/1999/5, paras. 26 *et seq*.

43 Mineral and Petroleum Resources Development Act (Act No. 28) of 10 October 2002, Government Gazette Vol. 448, No. 23922.

44 For a short introduction *Badenhorst*, New Order Rights to Minerals in South Africa: Ten Years after Mayday, in African Journal of International and Comparative Law 26 (2018), p. 366 (366 *et seqq*.)

45 *Cp. Blackstone*, Commentaries on the Laws of England (1753), Vol. 1 Book II Ch. II, p. 16 *et seqq.* calling that principle an "every day's experience in the mining countries".

46 The impact on ownership is disputed, see *Badenhorst* (fn. 44), p. 372 *et seqq.*; it is even held that mineral and petroleum form a category of *res publicae*, *cp*. H. Mostert/A. Pope (eds.), The Principles of The Law of Property in South Africa (2010), p. 272.

ing and able to fulfil various social and environmental objectives, *inter alia* the empowerment of women and black people, training skills, and supporting the local communities. The MPRDA and the potential expropriation of land are highly topical and controversial,[47] reflecting the difficulties resource regulation can be accompanied by.

III. Resource Mining and Human Rights Violations

The second human rights dimension of resource mining concerns its detrimental impact on the full enjoyment of human rights. It can be held that the extractive industry poses a specific threat to human rights (see 1.) and that, generally, all human rights can be impaired (see 2.). An exemplification should differentiate between small-scale artisanal mining and large-scale corporate mining.

1. Specific Risks posed by the Extractive Industry

The extractive industry and oil, gas and mining companies are held to be responsible for the most and the gravest business-related human rights violations (up to 30%).[48] This is owed to various characteristics of this industry: *First*, extraction by its very nature means hard and hazardous work,[49] carried out underground in pits or even underwater, with materials and instruments prone to injuring human health. *Second*, many of the world's re-

---

47 *Vyver* (fn. 41), pp. 739 *et seqq*. On the economic impact of the connected Minerals and Petroleum Resources Royalty Act of 2008, that intends to compensate South Africa as owner of mineral resources by payments of mining companies for the depletion of non-renewable resources, see *Zwan/Nel*, The Impact of the Minerals and Petroleum Resources Royalty Act on the South African Mining Industry: A Critical Analysis, Meditari Accountancy Research 18 (2010), p. 89 (89 *et seqq*.).

48 See *Paré/Chong*, Human rights violations and Canadian mining companies: exploring access to justice in relation to children's rights, in: The International Journal on Human Rights 21 (2017), p. 908 (908 *et seqq*.); *Handelsman*, Human Rights in the Minerals Industry, MMSD, Report No. 9 (2002); *European Commission/IHRB*, Oil and Gas Sector Guide on Implementing the UN Guiding Principles on Business and Human Rights (2014), available under: https://www.ihrb.org/uploads/reports/EC-Guide_OG.pdf (last accessed: 9 April 2020).

49 *International Labour Organization*, Hazardous Work, available under: https://www.ilo.org/global/topics/safety-and-health-at-work/areasofwork/hazardous-work/lang--en/index.htm (last accessed: 9 April 2020).

sources are located in Low- and Middle-Income Countries with weak, often not democratically legitimized governments and institutions, suffering from corruption and a lack of legislation or enforcement. Concerned states often do not act as agents and defenders of human rights. Rather, they are responsible for, ignorant towards, or complicit in human rights violations. *Third*, the increasing global competition for natural resources might make it difficult for home states to force their transnational corporations and trading partners to protect human rights, as well as the environment abroad and to fight corruption. If other states do not value these objectives, a home state acting unilaterally would risk a competitive disadvantage, thus bearing the risk of a potential race to the bottom with regard to human rights standards.

2. *Examples of Human Rights Violations*

Generally, all human rights – in an individual and collective dimension, of civil and political, as well as economic, social and cultural character – can be impaired by resource mining[50] at all of its stages: be it licensing and exploration, construction, operation, or the closure of mines. The respective rights subject to potential infringement and the severity of the infringement might depend on whether an enterprise, oftentimes transnational corporations (TNC),[51] is acting or whether small-scale mining is being carried out by individuals. The estimated number of artisanal miners is up to 100 million[52], mostly within the framework of casual industry. The subsequent examples of human rights violations are based on inquiries and studies by states, human rights NGOs, special representatives, treaty bodies, and the ILO.

Already at the prospecting or exploration stage, measures have to respect the rights of affected groups, in particular the right of indigenous peoples to free, prior, and informed consent, as well as effective participation of traditional communities in the planning, exploration, extraction,

---

50 *Cp. Ezirigwe* (fn. 5), pp. 207 *et seq.*

51 *Deng/Higgs/Chen*, Redefining Transnational Corporations, Transnational Corporations Review 1 (2009), p. 69 (69 *et seqq.*); for a differentiation between trans- and multinational corporations *cp. Drucker*, The Global Economy and the Nation-State, in: Foreign Affairs 76 (1997), p. 159 (167 *et seq.*).

52 *World Bank*, Brief: Artisanal and Small-Scale Mining (2011); available under: https://www.worldbank.org/en/topic/extractiveindustries/brief/artisanal-and-small-scale-mining (last accessed: 9 April 2020).

and use of resources.[53] This right is regularly violated, *e.g.* by Suriname towards the Maroon and Amerindian people,[54] as well as by Uganda towards indigenous landowners in the Karamoja region.[55] The construction of mines could lead to forceful evictions and dispossessions, often accompanied by the use of excessive force, unlawful arrest, torture, and even killings. People are often resettled without adequate housing, access to water, food, and work. It is estimated that in Odisha, a state in India which is rich in resources, 300.000 people suffered from this fate between 1960 and 1990.[56] Australia is facing criticism due to a gold mining project in New South Wales threatening the cultural and spiritual sites of the Wiradjuri, an Aboriginal group. Mozambique applied a resettlement program between 2009 and 2011 that removed self-sufficient farming communities from the Tete province to arid land causing disruptions in access to food, water and work.[57]

In particular, by operating a mine, the rights to health, physical integrity and life can be affected in various ways. People might be harmed as a result of the instruments used or the materials and harmful substances they are exposed to. It is, for example, common to use cyanide to dissolve metals from their ores and even mercury is still in use in artisanal mining to wash out minerals.[58] These chemicals are highly toxic and dangerous to

53 *Cp.* ILO Convention, Art. 1; Art. 27 ICCPR, Art. 15 ICESCR which nominate the right to one's own culture.

54 See case of *Inter-American Court of Human Rights*, Judgment of 28 November 2007 (Preliminary Objections, Merits, Reparations, and Costs), Inter-Am. Ct. H.R. (ser. C) No. 174, paras. 131, 136.

55 See *Powell*, Karamoja: A literature review, Safer World Report. (2010).

56 *Garada*, Coal Mining Environment and Health Problems: A Case of MCL Affected Households at Talcher, Odisha (India), in: Journal of Humanities and Social Science 20 (2015), p. 89 (89 *et seqq.*).

57 *Human Rights Watch*, "What is a House without Food?" – Mozambique's Coal Mining Boom and Resettlements (May 2013), pp. 4 *et seqq.*

58 Cremers/Kolen/de Theije (eds.), Small-Scale Gold Mining in the Amazon The Cases of Bolivia, Brazil, Colombia, Peru and Suriname, Cuadernos del CEDLA (2013), pp. 8 *et seqq.*, available under: https://globalinitiative.net/wp-content/uploads/2018/01/Small-Scale-Gold-Mining.pdf (last accessed: 29 January 2020). See also *Vertié*, The nexus of illegal Gold Mining and Human Trafficking in Global Supply Chaines, Lesons from Latin America (July 2016), p. 9 *et seqq.*, available under: https://globalinitiative.net/wp-content/uploads/2018/01/The-nexus-of-illegal-gold-mining.pdf (last accessed: 29 January 2020).

the central nervous system and healthy heart function.[59] Noise, high temperatures, fumes, and respirable dust represent further common problems. Silicosis is a lung disease caused by the inhalation of crystalline silica and it may progress to tuberculosis, the "typical disease" of the poor.[60] Skin diseases are also common, in particular among artisanal miners who often work without any protection.[61] Furthermore, in artisanal mining bladder infections often affect women washing the minerals in cold water.[62] In the long term, many of these mining-related diseases may lead to death. Miners can be killed straight away if rocks fall down, pits collapse, or the air supply fails. Such events are, not exclusively but particularly, a problem in artisanal mining. In contrast, damage to the environment – the contamination of soil, water and air, the excessive use of scarce water resources – is often the result of corporate large-scale mining.[63] These risks continue even after mines have been abandoned because of Acid Mine Drainage, the outflow of acidic water from metal mines or coal mines that are no longer administered and protected against natural forces.[64] The rights to water and food as well as the rights to health, physical integrity, and life can be affected by the environment being polluted. All workers have a right to fair wages and equal remuneration (Art. 7 (a) (i) ICESCR) so that they can afford a decent living (Art. 7 (a) (ii) ICESCR). For this purpose, people also have the right to form trade unions and to strike (Art. 8 ICESCR). States have to recognize these rights and provide a corresponding legal framework. These undertakings can be difficult – as was displayed by a strike in

---

59 *United States Environmental Protection Agency*, Health Effects of Exposures to Mercury, available under: https://www.epa.gov/mercury/health-effects-exposures-mercury.

60 *The International Federation of Red Cross and Red Crescent Societies* (IFRC), Tuberculosis, available: https://www.ifrc.org/en/what-we-do/health/diseases/tuberculosis/. See also The National Institute for Occupational Safety and Health (NIOSH), Mining Topic: Respiratory Diseases, Centers for Disease Control and Prevention (10 February 2019), available: under https://www.cdc.gov/niosh/mining/topics/RespiratoryDiseases.html (last accessed: 9 April 2020).

61 *Chou/Harper*, Toxicological Profile for Arsenic (2007), U.S. Department of Health and Human Services, Public Health Service,Agency for Toxic Substances And Disease Registry, pp. 3, 4, 214, 254, 315.

62 *Hayduk/Ritzel*, Diseases and Injuries among Coal Miners as Reported in a Rural Hospital, in: Journal of Occupational Accidents 10 (1988), p. 84 (84 *et seqq.*).

63 *Kemp/Bond/Franks/Cote*, Mining, Water and Human Rights: Making the Connection, in: Journal of Cleaner Production 18 (2010), p. 1552 *et seqq.*

64 *Modoi/Roba/Török/Ozunu*, Environmental Risks Due To Heavy Metal Pollution Of Water Resulted From Mining Wastes in New Romania, in: Environmental Engineering & Management Journal 13 (2014), p. 2325 (2336 *et seqq.*).

2012 which escalated in the platinum mining industry of South Africa. During the so-called "Marikana massacre"[65] leaders of the bigger, ANC-related National Mineworker Union and police forces shot down several mineworkers on strike, while mineworkers are also assumed to have committed violent acts themselves. In the end, around 34 miners died, 78 were injured, and 150 detained workers claimed to have been beaten while in police custody. *Cyril Ramaphosa*, the incumbent president of South Africa and former union leader, is said to have asked the police to move in instead of negotiating with the mineworkers.[66]

Another problem, in particular with artisanal (private) mining, is child labour.[67] In the Philippines, for instance, over 18.000 children (14% of all those living in mining areas) are assumed to work in gold mining.[68] Children are more vulnerable than adults because of their physical development and, thus, their rights to health and life are more gravely affected. They often work for too long and carry too heavy loads leading to pain and physical deformity. Children work both above and under the ground. When working underground in the tunnels and mineshafts, they risk death from explosions, rock falls, and tunnel collapse. The air they breathe is always filled with dust and sometimes toxic gases. Above ground, children dig, crush, mill, and haul ore – often under the dangerous hot sun. Some stand for hours in water, digging sand or silt from riverbeds and then carrying bags of mud on their heads or backs to sieving and washing

65 *Chinguno*, Marikana Massacre and Strike Violence Post-apartheid, in: Global Labour Journal 4 (2013), pp. 160–166.

66 *Thomas*, "Remember Marikana": Violence and Visual Activism in Post-Apartheid South Africa, in: ASAP/Journal, Volume 3(2) (May 2018), p. 401 (401 *et seqq.*); *Head*, Marikana: What was Cyril Ramaphosa's role?, The South African (16.08.2018), available under: https://www.thesouthafrican.com/news/marikana-what-did-cyril-ramaphosa-do/ (last accessed: 10. Febuary 2019).

67 For more information on the problem of child labour see *International Labour Organization*, Child Labour, available under: https://www.ilo.org/global/topics/child-labour/lang--en/index.htm; specifically in mining: https://www.ilo.org/ipec/areas/Miningandquarrying/MoreaboutCLinmining/lang--en/index.htm (last accessed: 9 April 2020).

68 *Cp. Human Rights Watch*, "What ... if Something Went Wrong?" Hazardous Child Labor in Small-Scale Gold Mining in the Philippines (September 2015); *IPEC and AsiaDEV*, In Search for the Pot of Gold: A Case Study of the Experiences of the ILO-IPEC Programme on the Elimination of Child Labour in Small-scale Mining Communities in the Province of Camarines Norte (2003).

sites. In all mining sites, there is risk of falling down in open shafts or into pits that are scattered around the areas.[69]

Furthermore, the specific rights of children, enshrined *i.a.* in the Convention on the Rights of the Child,[70] often remain unfulfilled *e.g.* the right to physical, moral and social development (Art. 6 (2), Art. 27, Art. 29 (1a), Art. 32), the right to be protected from exploitation and abuse (Art. 19, Art. 32) and the right to education (Art. 28). Children in Low- and Middle-Income Countries often have to work to support their families or to earn enough money to pay school fees even where fees are contrary to the right to free and compulsory primary education (Art. 14 ICESCR Art. 28 para. 1 (a)). Finally, in some mines, private security personnel or even state forces are used to oversee and control workers, force them to work and to suppress the expression of their free will and participation in political discourse.[71] The prohibition on the use of torture, freedom of expression and assembly might also need to be discussed in that respect.

In conclusion, a state engaged in resource mining through the granting of licences and permissions has to protect the rights of the people to self-determination (concerning wealth and national resources), as well as the individual human rights of affected persons. Corrupt governments and officials are likely to disregard this obligation as their personal economic interest will often prevail over public interests.[72]

IV. Resource Mining and Human Rights Responsibilities

The exemplified widespread violations of human rights by resource mining activities insistently raise the delicate question of responsibilities. A question that can be answered only with a brief overview. In the following, it shall be discussed who is an addressee of international human rights law and what instruments for the protection of human rights exist. As regards the duty bearers of international human rights it is necessary to differentiate between the state and other entities exercising public authority on the

69 As reported by the *International Labour Organization*, International Program on the Elimination of Child Labour (IPEC) (June 2006).

70 Convention on the Rights of the Child, 1577 UNTS 3 (1989).

71 *Narvdez González/Valencia*, Improving Human Rights in the Orivate Security Industry: Envisioning the Role of ICoCA in Latin America, in: Business and human rights journal 4 (2019), p. 79 (79 *et seqq.*).

72 *Bhattacharyya/Hodler*, Natural resources, Democracy and Corruption, in: European Economic Review 54 (2010) p. 608 (608 *et seqq.*)

one hand, and private persons on the other hand. While private business actors are not directly bound by international human rights law, 'soft' steering instruments have been developed within the last decades to ensure that they respect human rights (1.). In the end, though, it is the states (2.) and other entities of public authority (3.) which – as addressees of human rights – have to respect and protect them against private abuses. Due to the human rights situation in many countries where resource mining takes place, the controversial topic of extraterritorial obligations of states deserves closer attention. Three instruments have gained particular relevance in this context: 1. reporting obligations to inform a broader public about the human rights compliance of a company, so that NGO, shareholders or consumers can exert pressure; 2. legislation to ensure that human rights are protected by applying due diligence, in particular extraterritorially, in supply chains; and 3. domestic tort law, which might offer remedies and compensation even for human rights violations abroad.[73]

1. *Private Persons and Transnational Corporations in Particular*

As resource mining is mostly conducted by private companies, the easiest way to protect human rights from abuses would be to directly bind these business actors to respect human rights. However, the idea of private persons being directly bound by human rights under international law has not prevailed so far. Rather, it is part of the states' obligations to transform human rights into domestic law and thereby make them applicable and enforceable.

a) *Private Persons as Addressees under International Human Rights Law?*

It is notable that some human rights instruments mention duties owned to the community[74] or provide for human obligations.[75] Some conceptions of human rights are based on the idea of mutual obligations between human

---

73 See *Krajewski*, Regulierung transnationaler Wirtschaftsbeziehungen zum Schutz der Menschenrechte: Staatliche Schutzpflichten jenseits der Grenze?, in: Krajewski (ed.), Staatliche Schutzpflichten und unternehmerische Verantwortung für Menschenrechte in globalen Lieferketten (2018), p. 97 (126 *et seqq.*) for a concise overview.

74 Art. 29 (1) Universal Declaration of Human Rights.

75 See African Charter on Human and Peoples' Rights, Chapter II ("Duties").

beings rather than on legal entitlements.[76] However, it is still the dominant view that on the international level private persons are holders and beneficiaries of human rights but not obligated addressees.[77] Private persons are not parties to human rights treaties and whenever public international law addresses and obliges them directly, it is explicitly written down – as *e.g.* in the case of international criminal law.[78] Furthermore, if private persons were directly bound, there is the fear of trade-offs and states adopting a 'barter-approach', *i.e.* to make the enjoyment of human rights conditional upon respecting them – which in the end could endanger the idea of human rights as subjective rights and their overall protection. Accordingly, private artisanal miners might invoke human rights (*e.g.* the right to property or right to work) to justify their behaviour even if they voluntarily endanger their health or life. Moreover, parents are not prevented from forcing their children to work and restricting their school attendance by virtue of international human rights law *itself*. Instead, according to their duty to protect (see below 2.) states are asked to enact and enforce national law to protect human rights against private behaviour, *e.g.* the rights of children towards their parents, and even against the will of the concerned persons, *e.g.* against "voluntarily" self-exploitation and overworking.

The debate on human rights obligations for private persons has developed with regard to TNC. They are a cornerstone of economic globalization and major actors in the natural resources business. Therefore, their activities can entail a severe factual impact on several human rights. TNC have increasingly become engaged in contracts with states protecting their investments and providing for investor-state dispute settlement. This raises the issue of their recognition as partial subject of public international law.[79] Furthermore, many TNC possess an economic potency that might

---

76 *Beddard*, Duties of Individuals under International and Regional Human Rights Instruments, in: The International Journal of Human Rights 3 (1999), p. 30 (30 *et seqq.*); *Lohmann*, Individual Human Rights and Obligations Towards Communities, in: Fudan Journal on the Humanities and Social Sciences 8 (2015), p. 387 (388 *et seq.*).

77 *Fremuth* (fn. 2), pp. 19 *et seqq.*

78 *Cp.* Art. 25 para. 1 of the Rome Statute of the International Criminal Court, 2187 UNTS 3 (1998), establishing individual criminal responsibility (though only of natural persons).

79 *Walter*, Subjects of International Law (May 2007), in: Max Planck Encyclopedia of Public International Law, para. 19, available under: www.mpepil.com (last accessed: 9 April 2020).

outperform the national budget of smaller states,[80] enabling them to impose conditions for investments on governments and shield themselves from effective measures to protect human rights relating to their business activities. From a liberal perspective, it has been argued that the social responsibility of business is confined to increasing its benefits in the interests of their owners and shareholders.[81] Even though the protection of human rights by enterprises has been called a "sound business practice" as violations might cause delays, block projects, and increase costs,[82] that perspective has been regarded as unsatisfactory. "With power comes responsibility" is the main rationale behind a movement tracing back to the 1970s for requiring corporate social responsibility and due diligence from TNC,[83] which denotes a process through which corporations identify, prevent, and mitigate actual or potential adverse impacts on human rights, the environment, and other goods and interests and account for how the impacts are addressed.[84]

b) Non-Binding Instruments on Corporate Social Responsibilities

Correspondingly, several recommendations and guidelines for business actors on how to protect human rights and apply due diligence within their activities have been developed. The OECD adopted Guidelines for Multi-

---

80 See *Business Insider*, 25 giant companies that are bigger than entire countries (2018), available under: https://www.businessinsider.de/25-giant-companies-that-earn-more-than-entire-countries-2018-7?r=US&IR=T (last accessed: 9 April 2020); *Kordos/Vojtovic*, Transnational Corporations in the Global World Economic Environment, in: Procedia – Social and Behavioral Sciences 230 (2016), p. 150 (152).

81 *Friedman*, The Social Responsibility of Business is to Increase its Profits, in: The New York Times Magazine (13 September 1970), p. 32.

82 *Business & Human Rights Resource Centre*, Business unusual: Mining in the aftermath of Marikana (February 2015), available under: https://www.business-humanrights.org/sites/default/files/Mining-Indaba-brief-Feb-2015.pdf (last accessed: 9 April 2020), estimates that the strike action in 2012-13 in South Africa cost $1.5 billion and that delays of mining projects absent prior consent by communities can amount to an average of $20 million per week.

83 *Nolan*, With Power Comes Responsibility: Human Rights and Corporate Accountability, in: University of New South Wales Law Journal 28 (2005), p. 581 (581 *et seqq.*).

84 Cp. *OECD*, Guidelines for Multinational Enterprises (2011), Chap. II paras. A 11, A 12.

national Enterprises (1976, last revised in 2011)[85] and the ILO a Tripartite Declaration of Principles Concerning Multinational Enterprises (1977, last revised in 2017)[86]. With regard to the extractive industries and its specifics, the OECD in 2017 adopted Due Diligence Guidance for Meaningful Stakeholder Engagement in the Extractive Sector[87] to implement the Guidelines for Multinational Enterprises. The recommendations contained are not legally binding but intend to reflect a common position and commitment of the OECD members. They offer practical guidance, *i.a.* to mining enterprises, to address challenges related to stakeholder engagement and to help in developing a due diligence policy within the concerned companies in order to avoid and address adverse impacts of extractive activities. The guidelines concern corporate planning at the organisational level, make concrete recommendations to on-the-ground-personnel and provide a monitoring and evaluation framework. The situation of vulnerable groups, such as indigenous people, women, workers, and artisanal miners, is specifically addressed as well as the differences between the mining sector and the oil and gas sector.

Other approaches have been taken as well. In 2000, the UN Global Compact[88] became operational. It is the largest corporate social responsibility initiative asking companies to commit themselves to ten UN principles in the areas of human rights, labour standards, environmental protection and anti-corruption.[89] Taking part in the UN Global Compact is, however, voluntary and merely offers small economic incentives. A company complying with the principle is allowed to use the Global Compact Logo for its advertisement, which is designed to create competitive advantages. In 2003, a working group produced a draft called "Norms on the Re-

---

85 *OECD*, Guidelines for Multinational Enterprises (2011), available under: http://www.oecd.org/daf/inv/mne/48004323.pdf (last accessed: 9 April 2020).

86 *International Labour Organization*, Tripartite Declaration of Principles concerning Multinational Enterprises and Social Policy (5th edition March 2017), available under: https://www.ilo.org/empent/Publications/WCMS_094386/lang--en/index.htm (last accessed: 9 April 2020).

87 *OECD*, Due Diligence Guidance for Meaningful Stakeholder Engagement in the Extractive Sector (2017), available under: https://www.oecd-ilibrary.org/docserver/9789264252462-en.pdf?expires=1579523445&id=id&accname=guest&checksum=DD43BE0219F5AE79C5FC897F1EF8413B (last accessed: 9 April 2020).

88 *United Nations,* Global Compact, Guide to Corporate Sustainability (2014), available under: https://www.unglobalcompact.org/docs/publications/UN_Global_Compact_Guide_to_Corporate_Sustainability.pdf (last accessed: 9 April 2020).

89 *Williams*, The UN Global Compact: The Challenge and the Premise, in: Business Ethics Quarterly 14 (2004), p. 755 (755 *et seqq.*).

sponsibilities of Transnational Corporations with regard to Human Rights".[90] However, the Human Rights Commission, the competent sub-organ at the time, did not approve this draft which provided for a legally binding human rights treaty for enterprises. Instead, in 2005 a special representative for business and human rights, *John Ruggie*, was appointed by the UN Secretary General. He developed the UN framework for human rights and business activities (the UN Guiding Principles[91]), endorsed by the Human Rights Council in 2011[92] and based on three pillars: protect, respect, and remedy.

The first pillar is the *responsibility to protect*. It addresses states which have the obligation and primary responsibility to promote and protect human rights. That is, obviously, nothing new. Under human rights law, there is a "trinity" of state obligations: *i.e.* to respect, to protect, and to fulfil human rights (see below 2.). In theory, all human rights problems with respect to resource mining could be solved on this basis. States must not violate human rights themselves *("respect")*. Thus, and for instance, individuals must not be expelled from their land where this land is to be used for mining activities. A state-run mining company must organize its activities so that life, health and physical integrity are not impaired and working conditions, including labour rights, have to meet international requirements. The duty to *protect* requires states to ensure the enjoyment of human rights in polygonal private relationships. That is of particular importance in business sectors where TNC possess ample money, resources and power, whereas individuals, in particular in countries of low and middle income, have few "weapons" to oppose them with. In these situations, states are seen as the guardians of human rights. Consequently, they have to adopt policies, regulations, legislation and enforcement mechanisms as means to strike a balance between conflicting claims and to settle the imbalance between TNC and individuals. That includes provisions protecting the life and health of workers, the environment, as well as prohibiting child labour and ensuring fair wages so that workers and their families can

---

90 *Weissbrodt/Kruger*, Norms on the Responsibilities of Transnational Corporations and Other Business Enterprises with regard to Human Rights, in: American Journal of International Law 97 (2003), p. 901 (901 *et seqq.*).

91 *OHCHR*, Guiding Principles on Business and Human Rights (2011), available under: https://www.ohchr.org/documents/publications/guidingprinciplesbusinesshr_en.pdf (last accessed: 9 April 2020); *Mares*, The UN Guiding Principles on Business and Human Rights (2012).

92 *United Nations Human Rights Council*, Human rights and Transnational Corporations and other Business Enterprises, UN Doc. A/HRC/RES/17/4 of 16 June 2011.

make a living. The duty to protect implies a mandate for states to establish a just and effective legal order within their borders. This can also require legislation to address small-scale mining and to protect artisanal miners from themselves and children from their parents. States can also cooperate to address the adverse impacts of resource activities as they do in the Kimberley process (see below 3. lit c.).

We do not live in an ideal world though. National legislation and implementation are often noticeably poor, in particular in Low- and Middle-Income Countries that might be rich with resources but at the same time rich with corrupt politicians or despotic leaders who care little for their people. And that is when the second pillar of the *Ruggie*-Framework comes into play, namely the *responsibility to respect human rights*. As stated, this is already a core *obligation* of states. The second pillar complements this obligation by way of imposing a *responsibility* to respect human rights on private business enterprises. They are not just obliged to respect and obey the national law of their host state but have a responsibility of their own regarding human rights, irrespective of the state's national law and its flaws. The Guidelines substantiate this responsibility by stating that the companies have to show due diligence and to undertake *i.a.* a human rights impact assessment. The very idea is: Do not impair human rights through your business activities. Where a state fails to provide an adequate and effective legal order or where a regulation is insufficient, companies could be expected to do more, like establishing voluntary standards and audit-schemes, as was partly done *e.g.* by Rio Tinto and Freeport in Indonesia under Suharto. Furthermore, companies must not become accomplices to states committing human rights violations, be it the unlawful deprivation of land, the excessive use of force of security personnel or the persecution of trade unionists. An example is the Niger Delta, where the company Shell is not only accused of being responsible for human rights violations as a result of oil spills but it is also alleged to have helped the Nigerian government to persecute and in the end execute leaders of the protesting *Ogoni* people.[93] Likewise, the German automotive industry is still under suspicion of having in the past collaborated with the military juntas in Argentina and Chile when they were taking action against political opponents and

93 *Coomans*, The Ogoni Case before the African Commission on Human and Peoples' Right, in: The International and Comparative Law Quarterly 52 (2003), p. 749 (749 *et seqq.*).

trade unionists.[94] This is obviously not in line with enterprises' own responsibility to respect human rights.

The third pillar is the *remedy pillar* providing for equitable, fair, and transparent access to effective grievance mechanisms. Both states and enterprises have to provide victims with judicial and non-judicial mechanisms to remedy business-related violations of human rights. The states are already obliged to provide effective remedies, explicitly instructed by human rights law (*e.g.* Art. 2 (3) ICCPR) and as an emanation of the general duty to protect and fulfil. Additionally, if companies realize that they have caused or contributed to human rights violations they are expected to provide for remediation by participating in legitimate processes and by establishing and participating in effective operational-level grievance mechanisms (*e.g.* dialogue, mediation, ombudspersons) for individuals and communities that may be adversely harmed. Judicial and non-judicial mechanisms are not mutually exclusive and due to high costs, the lack of a functioning judicial system, (assumed) structural bias against victims or because of a cultural approach to solve disputes, non-judicial mechanisms might be in the interest of the victim of human rights abuses. Effective remedies might – depending on the circumstance of a concrete case – take the form of apologies, the guarantee of a cessation of human rights violating activities, as well as financial compensation and restitution.

However, the remedy pillar seems to be the weakest one: There is no 'hard' legal obligation, the language is ambiguous, and the home state of the company is not adequately included in the remedies-regime. As only states can establish predictable, neutral, judicially binding procedures and enforcement mechanisms, the main burden again rests on them. Thus, the remedy-pillar should be understood to constitute a business-addressed request to cooperate in good faith.

The status of the UN Guiding Principles falls short of legal obligations in a strict sense, proven, *i.a.*, by the description as "*responsibility* to respect" instead of establishing a "duty" for companies. However, they concretize the obligations already existing for states with regard to business activities. In this respect the Guidelines are not entirely new but built up on the trinity of states' duties towards human rights and can be regarded as an advancement concerning private business companies. By spelling out their responsibilities towards human rights, the guidelines provide orientation

94 *BBC News*, Car firm probes Argentina missing case (28 October 2002), available under: http://news.bbc.co.uk/2/hi/europe/2369923.stm (last accessed: 9 April 2020).

for doing business and might evolve into a global standard for action, accountability, and assessment.[95] They already have contributed to the (further) development of other standards on business and human rights on the global and regional level.[96] Irrespective of the complementary roles attributed to states and business companies, for the present, it is the states that have the main duty and responsibility to ensure human rights concerning resource mining. To remind companies of their responsibilities in addition to the states' duties and irrespective of domestic law can, however, be seen as another achievement of the guidelines.

c) *Open-ended Intergovernmental Working Group on Transnational Corporations and other Business Enterprises with respect to Human Rights*

Bearing in mind its approval of the above addressed UN Guiding Principles on Business and Human Rights, the Human Rights Council established in June 2014 an open-ended intergovernmental working group on transnational corporations and other business enterprises with respect to human rights.[97] The respective resolution reaffirms "that transnational corporations and other business enterprises have a responsibility to respect human rights" and describes the mandate of the working group as to "elaborate an international legally binding instrument to regulate, in international human rights law, the activities of transnational corporations and other business enterprises" (para. 1). A first draft was published on 16 July 2018,[98] a second on 16 July 2019[99] and negotiations are ongoing. Many civil society actors expected this treaty to provide for a direct legal obligation

95 *OHCHR*, Frequently Asked Questions about the Guiding Principles on Business and Human Rights (2014), p. 7.

96 For a brief overview *cp. OHCHR*, Frequently Asked Questions about the Guiding Principles on Business and Human Rights (2014), pp. 15 *et seq.*

97 *United Nations Human Rights Council*, UN Doc. A/HRC/RES/26/9 of 14 July 2014.

98 *OEIGWG*, Legally Binding Instrument to Regulate, in International Human Rights Law, the Activities of Transnational Corporations and other Business Enterprises, ZERO DRAFT 16.7.2018, available under: https://www.ohchr.org/Documents/HRBodies/HRCouncil/WGTransCorp/Session3/DraftLBI.pdf (last accessed: 9 April 2020).

99 *OEIGWG*, Legally Binding Instrument to Regulate, in International Human Rights Law, the Activities of Transnational Corporations and other Business Enterprises,OEIGWG CHAIRMANSHIP REVISED DRAFT 16.7.2019, available under: https://www.ohchr.org/Documents/HRBodies/HRCouncil/WGTransCorp/OEIGWG_RevisedDraft_LBI.pdf (last accessed: 9 April 2020).

on transnational corporations to respect human rights. The two drafts represented so far fall short of such an approach, however. They rather stick with the recognized understanding according to which private persons are not directly bound by human rights law. The second draft of 16 July 2019 merely mentions the responsibility of all business enterprises to respect all human rights and stresses "that the primary obligation to respect, protect, fulfil and promote human rights and fundamental freedoms lie with the state, and that states must protect against human rights abuse by third parties [...]" (Preamble). Accordingly, the general task of the envisaged instrument is to strengthen the legal obligations imposed on states with regards to their duty to protect, *i.e.* regulating and forcing business actors to respect human rights through domestic law. While international core human rights treaties cover human rights generally,[100] address discriminated or vulnerable groups,[101] or condemn specific behaviour violating human rights,[102] the discussed instrument would, once in force, become a human rights treaty dealing with a specific sector (business activities) as a potential cause for human rights infringements but not proscribing any specific behaviour.

In essence, the draft requires ratifying states to ensure by their domestic laws that all persons conducting business activities respect human rights and take appropriate actions to prevent human rights violations or abuses, in particular by undertaking human rights due diligence, which is extended even to contractual relationships (Art. 5 draft). In occupied or conflict-affected areas human rights due diligence measures have to be enhanced to prevent human rights violations or abuses (para. 3 lit. e) – that could be of particular importance for the extractive sector. Furthermore, states have to provide for a comprehensive and adequate system of criminal, civil, or administrative legal liability for human rights violations in the context of business activities including a list of criminal offences (Art. 6 draft). According to Art. 4 draft, victims who suffered or are alleged to have suffered

100 In particular the International Covenant on Civil and Political Rights and the International Covenant on Economic, Social and Cultural Rights.

101 International Convention on the Elimination of All Forms of Racial Discrimination, 660 UNTS 195; Convention on the Elimination of All Forms of Discrimination against Women 1249 UNTS 30; Convention on the Rights of the Child, 1577 UNTS 3; Convention on the Rights of Persons with Disabilities, 2515 UNTS 3.

102 Convention against Torture and Other Cruel, Inhuman or Degrading Treatment or Punishment, 1465 UNTS 85; International Convention for the Protection of All Persons from Enforced Disappearance, 2716 UNTS 3; Convention on the Prevention and Punishment of the Crime of Genocide, 78 UNTS 277.

human rights violations or abuse shall be granted access to effective judicial protection and remedies including corresponding rights (*e.g.* they shall be freed from the obligation to reimburse the other party even if the claim failed; a reversal of the burden of proof shall apply when necessary). Art. 7 draft provides, *i.a.*, for extraterritorial jurisdiction, and Art. 10 draft contains a far-reaching obligation to recognize foreign decisions.

The attempt to establish a treaty on human rights and business is facing opposition, criticism and many controversies,[103] which can only be briefly addressed here. First, the second draft no longer confines its scope of application to transnational but rather addresses all business activities. This is a substantial deviation from the mandate conferred by the Human Rights Council which was restricted to business activities of transnational character.[104] The application would be of a tremendous scope and have an unpredictable impact on domestic economic orders. Furthermore, the treaty is intended to "cover all human rights" (Art. 3 para. 3), a term that might be concretized by the referral in the preamble to international human rights treaties. Yet, the preamble also refers to declarations of disputed content (*e.g.* the right to development) and there is simply no common understanding what forms part of "all international human rights" as shown by the different ratification status of even the most prominent human rights treaties. Accordingly, the UN Guiding Principles take a more reluctant approach, referring to "internationally recognized human rights". For a state ratifying the treaty on business and human rights, that could mean an obligation to protect human rights against private persons which have not been consented to before. Finally, several delegations complained that many provisions of the draft remained too vague, including those articles establishing state obligations and having consequences for business actors. While in particular NGOs demanded more far-reaching provisions in accordance with existing human rights law (*e.g.* on indigenous peoples), business organizations considered the already enshrined obligations as going too far. While the negotiations continue, the biggest challenge for the legally binding instrument might be the lack of – at least sufficient – sup-

103 On the latest debate *cp.* draft report on the fifth session of the open-ended intergovernmental working group on transnational corporations and other business enterprises with respect to human rights, paras. 20 *et seq.*, available under: https://www.ohchr.org/Documents/HRBodies/HRCouncil/WGTransCorp/Session5/IGWG_5th_DraftReport.docx) (last accessed: 9 April 2020).

104 Resolution 26/9 referred to "transnational corporations and other business enterprises" but defined other business enterprises in footnote 1 as such "that have a transnational character in their operational activities […]".

port by those states and organizations (including the EU)[105] which form the world's major economies and which have mostly already voted against the resolution establishing the entire process.[106] Finally, even *John Ruggie*, father of the UN Guiding Principles, is highly sceptical towards the value and effectiveness of an overarching "business and human rights" treaty, assuming it will remain a symbolic gesture.[107]

2. *The State as Primary Addressee of Human Rights Obligations*

When it comes to the "positivation" and the effective enforcement of human rights, the states and other entities endowed with public authority are in demand.

A philosophical approach to human rights qualifies them as pre-state rights, meaning they do not depend on formal recognition or acknowledgment in order to require state compliance.[108] According to its more pragmatic approach, international law confines itself to asking whether states are bound to human rights either as parties to international treaties or by customary international law.[109] Some fundamental human rights, including the right to self-determination, are even owed towards the internation-

---

105 See, however, *European Parliament*, Resolution of 25 October 2016 on corporate liability for serious human rights abuses in third countries (2015/2315(INI)), para. 12, requesting the EU and the Member States to constructively engage in these negotiations. Further supporting resolutions have been adopted meanwhile, *cf. European Parliament* Resolution of 4 October 2018 on the EU's input to a UN Binding Instrument on transnational corporations and other business enterprises with transnational characteristics with respect to human rights (2018/2763(RSP)), para. 12. It has to be borne in mind, though, that the EU has not obtained a formal negotiation mandate so far.

106 *Cp. Werdelin*, A UN Treaty on Business and Human Rights: Bridging the Gap for Corporate Responsibility (2016), pp. 19 *et seq.*; *Wijekoon/Congiu/Marculewicz*, United Nations Takes Another Step in Developing a Treaty on Business and Human Rights, Littler Insight (5 November 2019), available under: https://www.littler.com/publication-press/publication/united-nations-takes-another-step-developing-treaty-business-and-human (last accessed: 9 April 2020).

107 *Ruggie*, A UN Business and Human Rights Treaty Update (1 May 2014), available under: https://www.business-humanrights.org/sites/default/files/media/un_business_and_human_rights_treaty_update.pdf (last accessed: 9 April 2020).

108 *Fremuth* (fn. 2), pp. 13 *et seq.*

109 *Henkin*, The Age of Rights (1990), pp. 1 *et seq.*; 31 *et seqq.*

al community as a whole.[110] Accordingly, states are the addressees of human rights obligations under public international law,[111] and these obligations extend to all branches of the state in a horizontal and vertical direction. The obligations also encompass various forms of jurisdiction: in addition to personal jurisdiction, authority is exercised within a state's territory, as well as within the exclusive economic zone which grants the coastal state exclusive rights to exploit the natural resources there and to regulate resource mining in accordance with international law of the sea.[112]

a) *The Trinity of Human Rights Duties in general*

Human rights obligations have been classified as a trinity of duties, comprising the duty to respect, to protect and to fulfil.[113]

Respecting human rights requires states not to violate them by themselves, including by state-run companies. This duty also has an external dimension. States are bound to human rights in their international relations[114] and must not lend their hand to human rights violations;[115] as such, they have to consider human rights impacts, *e.g.* when negotiating a treaty. Bilateral investment treaties and comprehensive free trade agreements can cover questions of resource mining (protection of investments of mining companies and mining-related trade and services) and should, therefore, contain explicit clauses on human rights protection. The recent-

110 *International Court of Justice*, Barcelona Traction, paras. 33 *et seqq*.; Armed Activities, para. 64 (on the prohibition of genocide); Construction of a Wall, paras. 88, 155 *et seqq*.; East Timor (Portugal v. Australia), I.C.J. Reports 1995, p. 102, para. 29.

111 On the addressees of human rights obligations *cp. Kälin/Künzli*, Universeller Menschenrechtsschutz (2018), pp. 83 *et seq*., 146 *et seq*.; whether other subjects under public international law, in particular international organisations, are bound by human rights, remains disputed, *cp. Kälin/Künzli*, pp. 95 *et seq*.

112 Art. 56 *et seqq.* United Nations Convention on the Law of the Sea, 1833 UNTS 3.

113 *Fremuth* (fn. 2), pp. 18 *et seq*.

114 With respect to the EU, see Art. 21 TEU; 205 TFEU; *Kälin/Künzli* (fn. 111), pp. 150 *et seqq*; *Zagel*, International Organisations and Human Rights: The Role of the UN Covenants in Overcoming the Accountability Gap, in: Nordic Journal of Human Rights 38 (2018), p. 74 (74 *et. seqq.*).

115 Figuratively speaking the German *Federal Constitutional Court*, BVerfGE 140, p. 317 (359).

ly agreed United States-Mexico-Canada-Agreement[116] (replacing NAFTA) can be invoked as an example. Art. 32.5 contains a general exception from trade related obligations in recognition of indigenous peoples' rights. It has been favoured by Canada – which recognizes protections of indigenous peoples' rights in its constitution (Art. 25; 35) and in self-governance agreements – and states:

> "*Provided that such measures are not used as a means of arbitrary or unjustified discrimination against persons of the other Parties or as a disguised restriction on trade in goods, services, and investment, this Agreement does not preclude a Party from adopting or maintaining a measure it deems necessary to fulfill its legal obligations to indigenous peoples.*"

Besides, states are obliged to *protect* individuals and groups against human rights abuses by other states and non-state actors, in particular in relations between private persons that are not directly bound by international human rights law (see. 1.). The protect-pillar requires states to prevent, investigate, punish, and redress human rights abuses through policies, legislation, regulation and adjudication. Particularly necessary is a transformation of human rights into legal rights and obligations under domestic law and an effective enforcement of that law. National criminal law (as an imperative sanction for human rights abuses), as well as national tort law (as providing damages for people suffering from human rights abuses) play a pivotal role. That is of importance for the mining industry where powerful companies encounter groups or individuals which are often disadvantaged and without political or financial means to enforce their rights themselves.

Finally, to *fulfil* their human rights obligations states must take positive action to facilitate and progressively realize the enjoyment of basic human rights. This obligation of conduct might entail campaigning for human rights and education, providing systems and services (minimum wage or health care), as well as effective remedies by an effective judicial system including legal aid for impoverished victims of human rights violations.

These state-related human rights duties require an indiscriminate application and, therefore, claim relevance for resource mining and its potential detrimental impact on human rights as well. Accordingly, within states that have a good human rights record, resource mining does not pose fur-

---

116 Agreement between the United States of America, the United Mexican States, and Canada (USMCA) of 10 December 2019, available under: https://ustr.gov/trade-agreements/free-trade-agreements/united-states-mexico-canada-agreement/agreement-between (last accessed: 9 April 2020).

ther problems. But while the application of human rights law to resource mining is not questioned, the factual situation makes the difference. Many natural resources are located in states with weak institutions, facing problems of high inequalities and corruption and not abiding by the rule of law. Furthermore, the competition for finite natural resources might ease the pressure on these states for reforms towards a stricter compliance with human rights obligations as purchasers of natural resources may pay less attention to the human rights situation on site. Accordingly, the expectation of international law towards states as protectors of human rights might encounter a host state of mining activities which is unable or unwilling to effectively protect human rights in that specific industry. Therefore, the home state of companies working in these states and its obligation to protect increasingly becomes the focus of attention.

b) On the Extraterritorial Protection of Human Rights

Traditionally, states have to protect human rights within their scope of jurisdiction which is foremost a territorial concept. With regard to business activities in particular, the question of extraterritorial obligations acquired increasing attention. This concerns the question how the home state can ensure the protection of human rights abroad and whether it is obliged to do so with regards to 'its' companies having their registered office (seat), central administration or their principal place of business in its territory.[117]

i. Reporting Obligations

As a 'soft' steering instrument states might oblige companies to (merely) report on their human rights policies and the measures adopted to prevent abuses. Such a moderate approach does not authoritatively sanction misbehaviour but rather intends to create a solid decision-making basis for share- and stakeholders. Specifically, a 'naming and shaming' approach is assumed to enable consumers to consider the information provided when

117 For such a general determination where a company is domiciled *cp.* Art. 63 para. 1 Regulation (EU) No. 1215/2012 of the European Parliament and of the Council of 12 December 2012 on jurisdiction and the recognition and enforcement of judgments in civil and commercial matters (Brussels I-Regulation), OJ L 351, 20 December 2012, p. 1.

deciding upon purchasing a product or service. *E.g.* the Modern Slavery Act of 26 March 2015[118] in the United Kingdom is intended to fight slavery, servitude and forced or compulsory labour and human trafficking by criminal law, preventive measures, an independent anti-slavery commissioner, as well as measures to protect victims. Initially, the law did not cover slave labour abroad. Responding to much criticism, the law was amended by a supply chain clause according to which companies with a certain turnover have to report annually on slavery and human trafficking (part. 6, 54 (4)). They have to report on the steps taken to ensure that slavery and human trafficking is not taking place in their business activities, including in their supply chain or to declare that they have not taken such steps. If the organisation has a website, it must publish it there, otherwise it has to provide a copy of the statement to anyone who makes a written request (paras. (7) and (8)). The act itself does not impose material obligations on respective companies, it rather entrusts share- and stakeholders, as well as the market, with potential reactions to a company's statement. Actually, in the context of human rights and environmental debates, companies doing business in natural resources and mining face increasing criticism and are exposed to pressure from civil society. Yet, there are no penalties enshrined in the Modern Slavery Act for non-compliance with the reporting obligations.

ii. Domestic Legislation to protect Human Rights abroad

In order to grant a stronger instrument for the protection of human rights abroad, states could enact legislation and regulation to ensure that their companies respect and protect human rights even in their business activities abroad. In particular, rules of mandatory due diligence obligations can be established that also cover subsidies, business partnerships, and the entire supply chain.

In March 2017 – after a partly affirmative decision by the *Conseil Constitutionnel* –[119] the French *Loi relative au devoir de vigilance des sociétés mères et*

---

118 The Modern Slavery Act of 26 March 2015; see *Haynes*, The Modern Slavery Act (2015): A Legislative Commentary, in: Statute Law Review 37 (2016), p. 33 (33 *et seqq.*).

119 *Conseil Constitutionnel*, Décision no. 2017-750 DC of 23 March 2017, available under: https://www.conseil-constitutionnel.fr/sites/default/files/as/root/bank_mm/decisions/2017750dc/2017750dc.pdf (last accessed: 9 April 2020).

entreprises donneuses d'ordre entered into force.[120] This law constitutes one of the first and most advanced responses to the UN Guiding Principles, as well as to the standards of the OECD,[121] and it might inspire answers on many remaining legal questions.[122] Companies with at least 5.000 employees in France or at least 10.000 employees in the companies branches in France and abroad are obliged to develop an 'oversight plan' (*plan de vigilance*) and to implement it effectively, *i.e.* the company has to adopt reasonable oversight measures to identify risks and to prevent serious harm to human rights and the environment. The law has a very broad material scope, covering a company's own activities, as well as those of companies it controls, of subcontractors, and of suppliers in an established commercial relationship. Furthermore, the plan has to be published and included in the annual management report. If companies do not perform their duties, they can be ordered to comply and periodic penalty payments might be imposed. The legal option of a civil fine up to 10 million Euros, however, has been nullified by the *Conseil Constitutionnel* as this punitive sanction has not been defined with sufficient clarity and precision.[123] The responses related to the reporting by the share- and stakeholders, as well as the broader public (soft steering by 'naming and shaming') will contribute to the effectiveness of the law. In particular, the companies can be held liable for violations of their vigilance obligations under general French tort law to complement the preventive approach of the law with rights of victims to remedies.

In the Netherlands, the child labour due diligence law (*wet zorgplicht kinderarbeid*) has been adopted on 24 October 2019 (coming into force not before 1 January 2020, see Art. 12).[124] It intends to oblige companies that offer goods or services to Dutch consumers to detect and prevent child

---

120 Loi relative au devoir de vigilance des sociétés mères et entreprises donneuses d'ordre of 27 March 2017, available under: https://www.legifrance.gouv.fr/eli/loi/2017/3/27/2017-399/jo/texte (last accessed: 9 April 2020).

121 *Cp.* the explanatory note of the proposal, Assemblée Nationale, no. 2578 of 11 February 2015, available under: http://www.assemblee-nationale.fr/14/pdf/propositions/pion2578.pdf (last accessed: 9 April 2020).

122 For an intense discussion of the law see the *dossier thématique* compiling various articles published in the Revue Internationale de la Compliance et de l'Éthique des Affaires provided by the website Business & Human Rights in Law, available under: http://www.bhrinlaw.org/frenchcorporatedutylaw_articles.pdf (last accessed: 9 April 2020).

123 *Conseil Constitutionnel*, Décision no. 2017-750 DC of 23 March 2017, paras. 8–14.

124 Wet van 24 oktober 2019 houdende de invoering van een zorgplicht ter voorkoming van de levering van goederen en diensten die met behulp van

labour in their supply chains by establishing a duty of care (*zorgplicht*, Art. 5). Victims as well as stakeholders can file a complaint with a regulator if there is evidence of non-compliance (Art. 3 para. 2). The regulator might impose fines and even criminal sanctions are available in cases of repetition (Art. 7). The Dutch law is the latest example of a legal incorporation of due diligence obligations of business actors into domestic law, which – compared with other regulations – goes even further when it comes to enforcement (regulator's fines and criminal sanctions). Even though currently confined to child labour, it might be a template for further regulation of business and human rights.[125]

From 2015 until 2020, a public initiative was pending in Switzerland (the so called '*Konzernverantwortungsinitiative*') which intended to establish a responsibility of multinational companies with regards to human rights and the environment. The Swiss Constitution should have been amended (Art. 101a)[126] in order to oblige the confederation to enact a law (derogating foreign law, lit. d) forcing companies to respect internationally recognized human rights and environmental standards even when acting abroad, as well as ensuring that companies under their control (*de jure* or *de facto*) respect these standards (lit. a). Small and medium companies should have been exempted from the initiative's scope with a reverse exemption for those companies operating in high risk sectors such as the mining industry or trade in raw materials (lit. b). The companies would have had to carry out 'appropriate due diligence', which includes the identification of impact, the taking of preventing measures and accountability for the actions taken (lit. b). If a company could not prove that it took all due care in the sense of lit. b, it should have been liable for damage as a result of human rights violations, including those caused by companies un-

---

kinderarbeid tot stand zijn gekomen, published in Staatsblad 2019, p. 401 of 13 November 2019. (Translated: Act of 24 October 2019, which is introducing a duty of care to prevent the supply of goods and services created with the aid of child labour, published in Bulletin of Acts and Decrees 2019, p. 401 of 13 November 2019.).

125 For a first appraisal see *Hoff*, Dutch child labour due diligence law: a step towards mandatory human rights due diligence, OxHRH Blog (10 June 2019), available under: http://ohrh.law.ox.ac.uk/dutch-child-labour-due-diligence-law-a-step-towards-mandatory-human-rights-due-diligence/ (last accessed: 9 April 2020).

126 For further information see the fact-sheet of the initiative. *Swiss Coalition for Corporate Justice (SCCJ)*, The initiative text with explanations, available under: https://corporatejustice.ch/wp-content/uploads//2018/06/KVI_Factsheet_5_E.pdf (last accessed: 9 April 2020).

der their control (lit. c). The initiative has met with criticism claiming that it will cause high costs and endanger Switzerland as business location.[127] After the approval of a counter proposal by the Swiss National Council, a parliamentary compromise could have been found to prevent the initiative from being brought to popular vote.[128] In the end, however, a public vote was held on 29 November 2020. Even though the initiative was supported by a public majority (50,7 %), it fell slightly short to gain the majority of the cantons as the second requirement necessary for the amendments of the Swiss constitution.

To hold national companies responsible even for activities abroad and committed by subsidiaries or contractors is not a violation of international law. Admittedly, a state is not allowed to impose its law on other sovereign states, but to enact laws addressing companies located within a state's own borders does not as such constitute an act of "legal imperialism".[129] Furthermore, states are not entitled to enforce their laws within the territories of another State without the latter's consent.[130] But if the regulations are enforced towards companies within their home State's territory, it does not pose legal problems concerning the sovereignty of other states. However, the extension of national law to situations of an extraterritorial character, *i.e.* the jurisdiction to prescribe and to adjudicate, also requires a jus-

---

127 *Bohrer*, Konzernverantwortungsinitiative: schädlich für die Schweiz, in: Neue Zürcher Zeitung (22 April 2019), available under: https://www.nzz.ch/meinung/kolumnen/unternehmensverantwortung-was-nun-ld.1468626 (last accessed: 9 April 2020).

128 *Cp. Werro*, JETL 10 (2019), p. 166 (166 *et seqq.*), defending the initiative and the counter proposal against the criticism and calling them moderate. In September 2019, the Swiss Council of States postponed the debate so that a public vote may take place end of 2020 only, *cp.* the critical comment by *Schick*, Der Ständerat kuscht vor der Wirtschaftslobby, available under: https://www.amnesty.ch/de/kontakt/medien/kommentare/2019/der-staenderat-kuscht-vor-der-wirtschaftslobby (last accessed: 9 April 2020).

129 *Shamir*, Between Self-Regulation and the Alien Tort Claims Act: On the Contested Concept of Corporate Social Responsibility, in: Law & Society Review 38 (2004), p. 635–664; see however *Dederer*, Extraterritorial Possibilities of Enforcement in Cases of Human Rights Violations, in: Bungenberg/Hobe (eds.), Permanent Sovereignty over National Resources (2015), pp. 187 (201) stressing that legislation of corporates' extraterritorial conduct requires the home state to take into account the host state's territorial jurisdiction as well.

130 *Henkin*, Human Rights and State "Sovereignty", in: Georgia Journal of International and Comparative Law 25 (1995), p. 31 (32) on the traditional notion of sovereignty.

tification under international law.[131] In case of the companies mentioned, though, the principle of territoriality and personality might serve as justification.[132]

The pivotal question remains, however, if states are obliged by international human rights law to regulate the activities of their companies with the aim of protecting human rights abroad. The extraterritorial application of human rights obligations is nothing new for public international law.[133] Even though the application clauses of most treaties can be interpreted as having a territorial scope in general,[134] the European Court of Human Rights has for instance declared that the state parties to the convention are bound by human rights obligations when they effectively exercise public authority over a region or a person.[135] Concerning the International Covenant on Civil and Political Rights, the International Court of Justice has affirmed that irrespective of its wording the treaty might be applied in extraterritorial situations.[136] It is important to stress that these extraterritorial effects of human rights concern the states' duty to respect, *i.e.* the situation where the states themselves are acting. However, even if a state itself or via state-owned companies is engaged in business activities abroad, public authority will most likely not be exercised as this could infringe the sovereignty of the other state and the principle of non-intervention.[137] The UN Guiding Principles, however, contribute to the assumption that states should refrain from human rights abuses abroad even when acting in a private capacity or by state-owned companies.[138] The assumption that companies, which are significantly owned or influenced by public authorities,

---

131 *Donovan/Roberts*, The emerging recognition of universal civil jurisdiction, in: American Journal of International Law 100 (2006), pp. 142–163.

132 *Krajewski* (fn. 73), pp. 113 *et seq.*

133 *Milanovic*, Extraterritorial application of human rights treaties: law, principles, and policy (2011).

134 Concerning Art. 2 ICCPR see *Schabas*, Nowak's CCPR Commentary (2019), pp. 46–52; a comparable reading for Art. 1 ECHR is provided for by the ECtHR, see *European Court of Human Rights*, Guide on Article 1 of the European Convention on Human Rights (2019), paras 11–72.

135 Summarising *European Court of Human Rights*, Application no. 27765/09 (Hirsi Jamaa and others v. Italy), paras. 71–75.

136 *International Court of Justice*, Legal Consequences of the Construction of a Wall in the Occupied Palestinian Territory, I.C.J. Reports (2004), p. 136 paras. 107–111.

137 See *Jamnejad/Wood*, The Principle of Non-Intervention, in: Leiden Journal of International Law 22 (2009), p. 345 (375 *et seq.*).

138 *Backer*, The Human Rights Obligations of State-Owned Enterprises (SOEs): Emerging Conceptual Structures and Principles in National and International

are directly bound by human or fundamental rights is increasingly becoming recognized in domestic legal orders as well.[139]

The question of whether states – in addition to their duty to respect – are also obliged to extraterritorially apply their duty to *protect* human rights against private abuses (by their companies) remains controversial. The UN Guiding Principles do not require home states to regulate the extraterritorial activities of their companies, stating that no such general obligation under international law exists while also stressing that states are not generally prohibited from doing so.[140] In 2011, a group of 40 experts adopted the Maastricht Principles on Extraterritorial Obligations of States in the Area of Economic, Social and Cultural Rights.[141] Calling extraterritorial obligations the missing link in the universal human rights protection regime, these principles affirm extraterritorial obligations of home states towards regulating the conduct of their companies (paras. 9 lit. b and c; 23 *et seqq*., in particular para. 25 lit. c). The *Human Rights Committee* in its General Comment No. 31[142] interprets Art. 2 ICCPR narrowly in that respect. Though not confined to a state's territory, the Committee holds that the duty to respect and *ensure* human rights might have extraterritorial effects only in connection with the state exercising power or effective control outside its territory (para. 10). That would not justify the assumption of a general obligation to ensure the protection of human rights abroad. However, concerning the right to life, the Committee in its General Comment No. 36[143] has recently recognized that Art. 2 in conjunction with Art. 6 ICCPR also covers military or other activities of states if these have a

Law and Policy, in: Vanderbilt Journal of Transnational Law 50 (2017), p. 827 (827 *et. seqq*.).

139 For Germany see German *Federal Constitutional Court*, Decision of 21 February 2019, 2 BvR 2456/18, para. 8 (not yet officially published); Judgment of 22 February 2011, BVerfGE 128, 226 (244 *et seq*.); this understanding is also confirmed by the *Committee on the Rights of the Child*, General Comment No. 16 on State obligations regarding the impact of the business sector on children's rights (2013), UN Doc. CRC/C/GC/16, para. 27.

140 UN Guiding Principles (fn. 91), para. 2 commentary.

141 Available under: https://www.etoconsortium.org/nc/en/main-navigation/library/maastricht-principles/?tx_drblob_pi1%5BdownloadUid%5D=23 (last accessed: 9 April 2020).

142 *Human Rights Committee*, General Comment No. 31 (2014), The Nature of the General Legal Obligation Imposed on States Parties to the Covenant, UN Doc. CCPR/C/21/Rev.1/Add.

143 *Human Rights Committee*, General Comment No. 36 (2018) on article 6 of the International Covenant on Civil and Political Rights, on the right to life, UN Doc. CCPR/C/GC/36.

direct and reasonably foreseeable impact on the rights of the Covenant abroad (para. 63). The Committee, then, applied this impact-approach to the regulation of transnational business, stating that states must "also take appropriate legislative and other measures to ensure that all activities taking place in whole or in part within their territory and in other places subject to their jurisdiction, but having a direct and reasonably foreseeable impact on the right to life of individuals outside their territory, including activities taken by corporate entities based in their territory or subject to their jurisdiction, are consistent with article 6 [...] (para. 22)." While previously the Committee has only "encouraged" Germany "to set out clearly the expectation that all business enterprises domiciled in its territory [...] respect human rights throughout their operations",[144] it is now using the language of a general obligation to protect human rights with regard to transnational business activities having a foundation in their country. That is in line with the reasoning of other treaty bodies, in particular the quite active Committee on Economic, Social and Cultural Rights[145] and the Committee on the Rights of the Child.[146] For the extractive industry and mining-related risks, the Committee on Economic, Social and Cultural Rights detects well-documented risks that make human rights abuses reasonably foreseeable, meaning that particular due diligence is required.[147]

Some authors refer to the '*neminem laedere*'- or 'no harm'-rule (as specifically developed in international environmental law) to establish an obligation for states to regulate the external business activities of their companies,[148] *i.e.* according to the principles of territoriality states shall ensure that no extraterritorial harm is inflicted on other people if such harm is

---

144 *Human Rights Committee*, UN Doc. CCPR/C/DEU/CO/6 (2012), para. 16.

145 *Cp.* General Comment No. 14 (2000), The Right to the Highest Attainable Standard of Health (Art. 12), UN Doc. E/C.12/2000/4, para. 39; General Comment No. 15 (2003), The Right to Water (Arts. 11 and 12 of the Covenant), UN Doc. E/C.12/2002/11, para. 33; General Comment No. 24 (2017) on State obligations under the International Covenant on Economic, Social and Cultural Rights in the context of business activities, UN Doc. E/C.12/GC/24, paras. 30–35.

146 *Cp.* General Comment No. 16 on State obligations regarding the impact of the business sector on children's rights (2013), UN Doc. CRC/C/GC/16, paras. 39–43.

147 General Comment No. 24 (2017) on State obligations under the International Covenant on Economic, Social and Cultural Rights in the context of business activities, UN Doc. E/C.12/GC/24, para. 32.

148 *Krajewski* (fn. 73), pp. 121 *et seqq.*; also, but more reluctantly in favour: *Dederer* (fn. 129) pp. 199 *et seq.* defining the state's extraterritorial duties as such of 'due diligence' with regards to activities that are typically prone to human rights violations abroad.

foreseeable and avoidable. Even though the link between the territory and the harm might be quite indirect and mediate concerning supply chains if human rights abuses are committed by subsidies or mere contractual partners, the obligations of due diligence for parent companies find their foundation in territorially defined jurisdiction. Another approach invokes the very idea of universal human rights and the need to protect them against any potential threat irrespective of its source or matters related to questions of jurisdiction.[149] While this is an interesting theoretical consideration, it seems, however, that legal obligations can hardly be based on a mere idea deprived of textual underpinnings[150] in existing treaties. Some link is needed to the concept of jurisdiction which is still of the utmost importance in public international law when determining competencies and obligations, as well as to prevent conflicts.

Undoubtedly, there might be a momentum towards regulation of business activities abroad. However, still only a few states have adopted respective legislation, and proposals such as the initiative in Switzerland remained highly controversial and finally failed. It remains doubtful whether these states have reacted to an assumed obligation or rather to demands from the public. Consistent state practice can hardly be deduced from these examples – *e.g.* Germany, as the world's fourth biggest economy, in its National Action Plan only expresses the expectation of the federal government that companies will meet their responsibility to protect human rights in and outside the country,[151] even though discussions concerning the enactment of a fair-supply-chain-law are gaining momentum as the voluntary-approach seems unsatisfying.[152] Furthermore, the ongoing

149 *Kanalan*, Extraterritorial State Obligations Beyond the Concept of Jurisdiction, in: German Law Journal 19 (2018), p. 44 (53 *et seqq*.).

150 According to *Kanalan* (fn. 149), p. 51 "it is not convincing to base an argument on the texts of the conventions" if justice cannot be done. In fact, to ignore positive international law, *i.e.* the text of legal norms, is not convincing, though (*cp.* Art. 31 Vienna Convention on the Laws of Treaties, stressing the importance of the text and the terms of treaty interpretation).

151 *Bundesregierung*, Nationaler Aktionsplan: Umsetzung der VN-Leitprinzipien für Wirtschaft und Menschenrechte, 2016 – 2020 (2017), p. 19; available under: https://www.csr-in-deutschland.de/SharedDocs/Downloads/DE/NAP/nap-im-original.pdf?__blob=publicationFile&v=3 (last accessed: 9 April 2020).

152 *Riedel*, Bundesregierung arbeitet an Gesetz für faire Lieferketten, in: Handelsblatt v. (10 December 2019), available under: https://www.handelsblatt.com/politik/deutschland/menschenrechte-bundesregierung-arbeitet-an-gesetz-fuer-faire-lieferketten/25318754.html?ticket=ST-1344422-sfMdkCbnbgX2osVrs9Q7-ap3 (last accessed: 9 April 2020).

opposition against the draft treaty on business and human rights, which intends to intensify regulation of transnational business activities, demonstrates that many states still do not accept an obligation to regulate their companies' responsibilities concerning extraterritorial effects. Even an evolutionary interpretation of treaties – in particular those containing an explicit jurisdiction or territoriality clause (as Art. 1 ECHR and Art. 2 para. 1 ICCPR) – cannot fully ignore this situation. Accordingly, doubts remain as regards a general obligation of states to regulate the extraterritorial effects of business activities.

iii. Claims for Damages and Application of Domestic Tort Law

With regard to judicial remedies and potential respondents one might consider claims against the host state and the home state of the company, as well as against the company itself – before the home state's, the host's states or foreign courts. Each claim has its specific challenges,[153] in the present paper a closer look shall be taken at claims against the companies under the domestic tort law of the home or a foreign state.

The application of domestic tort law to extraterritorial situations might help the victims of human rights abuses and create incentives for business corporations to take care of their subsidiaries and contractual partners abroad. In the first place, jurisdiction has to be established and the applicable law determined.[154] In the past, the United States Alien Tort Statute (ATS)[155] has been regarded as an important tool for international strategic litigation. It grants original jurisdiction to the U.S. district courts for any civil action brought by an alien for a tort committed in violation of the law of nations or a treaty of the United States. It was widely held that human rights violations committed abroad, without any link to the United States, might nevertheless be brought before domestic courts. As a result, the United States promised to be the best option for *forum shopping* concerning suits against corporations. The Supreme Court, though, has recently rejected such an interpretation. In its *Kiobel*-decision the Court significantly restricted jurisdiction under the ATS and required that claims must

---

153 For a concise overview: *Dederer* (fn. 129), pp. 194 *et seqq*.

154 On these questions, the relevance of EU law and the application of foreign law by domestic courts in Europe see *Spitzer*, Human Rights, Global Supply Chains, and the Role of Tort, in: Journal of European Tort Law 10 (2019), p. 95 (99 *et seqq*.).

155 28 U.S. Code § 1350.

touch and concern the territory of the United States.[156] In a more recent decision, *Jesner v. Arab Bank*, the Court confirmed that foreign corporations without any link to the United States cannot be sued under the ATS.[157] Whether a foreign victim of business-related human rights abuses may sue a U.S. company under the ATS has however, not yet been decided. This proves, irrespective of whether legal actions against parent companies in their home states might be successful, a certain reluctance of states to become arbitrators for the world without any genuine link to them. If such a link exists, the situation changes dramatically. Thus, a landmark decision of a Dutch court in May 2019 confirmed that it has jurisdiction to decide whether Royal Dutch Shell, based in the Netherlands, was complicit *i.a.* in the execution of members of the Ogoni People – including Mr. *Barinem Kiobel* – who protested against the widespread oil pollution of the Niger Delta.[158] The decision on the merits, *i.e.* whether the parent company actually is responsible for human rights abuses in Nigeria, is pending. Even before, in 2015, a Dutch court accepted its comprehensive jurisdiction concerning claims regarding environmental damages and corresponding cleaning obligations of Royal Dutch Shell, as well as of its Nigerian subsidy, because of sufficient cohesion between the claims.[159]

If jurisdiction has been established and the applicable law identified, domestic tort law might become relevant in three dimensions: (1) the corporate veil might be lifted to hold the parent company directly liable for the misconduct of their subsidiaries; (2) the misconduct and fault of subsidiaries might be attributed to the parent company; (3) and finally the parent company might be held liable for its own wrongdoings. The last approach, which offers the best chance to achieve accountability,[160] shall be addressed here. Obviously, national tort law varies: In some countries, an enumerated list of protected goods exists (life, physical integrity, personali-

---

156 *Kiobel v. Royal Dutch Petroleum Co.*, U.S. Supreme Court, 569 U.S. 108 (2013); for further discussion *cp. Dederer* (fn. 129) pp. 206 *et seqq*.

157 *Jesner v. Arab Bank, PLC*, U.S. Supreme Court, 584 U.S. ___ (2018).

158 *Hodal*, Dutch court will hear widows' case against Shell over deaths of Ogoni Nine, The Guardian (1 May 2019) available under: https://www.theguardian.com/global-development/2019/may/01/dutch-court-will-hear-widows-case-against-shell-over-deaths-of-ogoni-nine-esther-kiobel-victoria-bera-hague?CMP=share_btn_tw (last accessed: 9 April 2020).

159 *Court of Appeal*, Judgment of 18 December 2015, No. C/09/337058 / HA ZA 09-1581 and C/09/365482 / HA ZA 10-1665; an English version of the judgment is available: https://uitspraken.rechtspraak.nl/inziendocument?id=ECLI:NL:GHDHA:2015:3586 (last accessed: 9 April 2020).

160 *Spitzer* (fn. 154), pp. 101 *et seq.*, 107.

ty rights, or property), so that a potential violation of human rights has to be subsumed under these goods. In other countries, the focus lies more on conduct and negligence without concretizing the protected interest. Furthermore, the conception of a principal's liability and the possibility of exculpation might vary, which is of special importance for parent companies. While some countries opt for strict liability without the necessity of misconduct of the principal, others know forms of vicarious liability, and still others have confined their tort law to a liability of the principal for its own fault.[161] In the latter cases, the decisive questions are whether the principal has shown due care and met the expectation towards its partners. Accordingly, the determination of the duty of a parent company towards its subsidiaries and even contractual partners is of the utmost importance. If a state has regulated the human rights compliance of business actors (see above lit. (ii)), the respective laws might specify a company's obligation, provide for liability clauses and grant effective access to domestic courts. However, even in the case when concretizing domestic regulation is absent, national tort law might apply in such cases and be interpreted in reaction to human rights violations committed abroad to establish accountability of companies and offer compensation. To define the duties of parent companies, a court can refer to general interpretation methods under national law. Furthermore, the due diligence principles developed by the OECD and the UN Guiding Principles might be of great importance as they can be invoked to define the duties that a company has towards its subsidiaries and contractors in order to "respect human rights" as stated by the aforementioned *Ruggie*-Principles.[162] Although these principles do not oblige states to enact strict liability, they sanction violations of due diligence and report obligations with compensation duties.

Some national courts already have applied their domestic tort law to establish responsibility of the parent undertaking for negligence concerning the behaviour of subsidiary companies.[163] The total number of respective

161 Briefly on the following *Werro*, The Swiss Responsible Business Initiative and the Counter-Proposal, in: Journal of European Tort Law 10 (2019), p. 166 (170 *et seq.*).

162 *Cp. Ruggie*, Report, Report of the Special Representative of the Secretary-General on the Issue of Human Rights and Transnational Corporations and other Business Enterprises on Promotion and Protection of all Human Rights, Civil, Political, Economic, Social and Cultural Rights, Including The Right To Development – Clarifying the Concepts of "Sphere of influence" and "Complicity", UN Doc. A/HRC/8/16 of 15 May 2008; *Dederer* (fn. 129), p. 205.

163 *Chandler v. Cape*, England and Wales Court of Appeal (Civil Division), EWCA Civ. 525 (2012).

judgments remains limited, though, and many cases have been settled before a formal judgment has been rendered. Therefore, it is not possible to deduce current trends from settled case law.

3. Supranational Entities as Addressees of Human Rights Obligations

While in the past states have been regarded as being the main – or even exclusive – addressees of human rights obligations, the rise of supranational authorities has broadened the view in so far as it is accepted that supranational organisations, the European Union in particular, are themselves bound by human rights[164] as they exercise such public authority that states have transferred to them. The range of obligations follows from the transfer of authority,[165] so that the supranational organisation is in a situation comparable to the states. The EU, *e.g.*, is entrusted with broad and partially even exclusive competencies in the economic sphere[166] and the organisation has adopted several measures to protect human rights in that respect, including the protection of workers within the EU.[167] In general, though, human rights violations with respect to resource mining are hardly a problem within the EU, especially because most natural resources are imported from other countries. Accordingly, the external dimension of human rights protection is of particular importance. Remarkably, the EU has adopted various instruments to protect human rights abroad, some of which shall be addressed here.

164 *Cp.* Art. 6 TEU and the Charter of Fundamental Rights of the European Union, both building the foundation for the human rights obligations of the European Union under primary law.

165 *European Court of Human Rights,* Application no. 24833/94 (Matthews v. United Kingdom), paras. 36–44; Application no. 26083/94 (Waite and Kennedy v. Germany), para. 67.

166 *Cp.* Art. 3 para. 1 lit. a) and e) TFEU for the exclusive competence of the EU concerning custom unions and the common commercial policy which is accompanied by a far-reaching external competence after Art. 207 para. 1 TFEU.

167 See *e.g.*, Council Directive (89/391/EEC) of 12 June 1989 on the introduction of measures to encourage improvements in the safety and health of workers at work, OJ L 183, 29.6.1989, p. 1 and Directive 96/71/EC of the European Parliament and the Council of 16 December 1996 concerning the posting of workers in the framework of the provision of services, OJ L 18, 21.1.1997, p. 1.

a) Trade Incentives

One approach of the EU policy on the protection of human rights abroad is to provide economic incentives to third countries as offered by its preference system concerning tariffs. Under the law of the World Trade Organization, tariffs shall be the only instrument to regulate and restrict trade (Art. XI GATT), with the aim being to substantially reduce them (Art. XXVIII*bis* GATT). Any advantage granted concerning custom duties shall be accorded immediately and unconditionally to the like product originating in or destined for the territories of all other contracting parties (Art. I:1 GATT). This Most-Favoured-Nation clause provides for equal treatment among all contracting parties, however, unilateral and non-reciprocal trade preference might be granted to developing countries due to the enabling clause (*cf.* No. 1 and 2 lit. b).[168] The EU has implemented this special and differential treatment through the Generalised Scheme of Preferences, the Generalised Scheme of Preferences+, and the "Everything but arms" (EBA) special arrangement for the least developed countries, each of which contains a human rights component.[169] The Standard GSP reduces EU import duties for about 66% of all product tariff lines and is applied automatically to eligible developing countries. The preferential arrangement can be temporarily withdrawn in case of serious and systematic violations of enumerated core human and labour rights conventions of the United Nations and the International Labour Organization (Art. 19 Regulation (EU) No 978/2012 in conjunction with Annex VIII part A). In addition to the GPS, respective countries might request to benefit from the special incentive arrangement for sustainable development and good governance (GPS+) to further privileges amounting to full removal of tariffs on over 66% of EU tariff lines. Such countries, *first*, have to ratify 27 conventions on human and labour rights, environmental protection and good governance. They, *second*, must not have formulated reservations prohibited by these treaties and, *finally*, must have accepted monitoring mechanisms under the convention by treaty bodies. These bodies must not have identified any serious failure to effectively implement the treaties (Art. 9 *et seqq*. Regulation (EU) No 978/2012 in conjunction with Annex VIII part A and B). An EU monitoring mechanism has also been established to ensure the effective fulfil-

168 Decision by the Contracting Parties of 28 November 1979 (L/4903).

169 *European Commission*, Generalised Scheme of Preferences (GSP), available under: https://ec.europa.eu/trade/policy/countries-and-regions/development/generalised-scheme-of-preferences/index_en.htm (last accessed: 9 April 2020).

ment of human rights obligations in exchange for additional trade preferences. Accordingly, privileges under the GPS+ are dependent on a request (not automatically granted), a broader scope of accepted obligations and the willingness to accept monitoring mechanisms. They serve a far reaching interest in protecting human rights. Finally, the EBA scheme grants full duty free and quota free access to the EU Single Market for all products with the exception of arms and armaments stemming from least developed countries. Additional human rights commitments from the concerned states are not required, however – as with the GPS scheme – participating in the EBA arrangement can be temporarily withdrawn in case of serious and systematic violations of enumerated core human and labour rights conventions. In its GPS report, the Commission has declared that trade preferences to promote universal values of human rights, social justice and environmental protection are an integral part of the Commission's "Trade for All" strategy. This strategy is based on the three key principles of effectiveness, transparency, and values (including human rights).[170] Although there is no data specifically addressing resource mining, interlinked topics such as child labour, health issues, and the rights of indigenous peoples have been addressed and the Commission detects progress.[171]

b) *Trade and Investment Agreements*

Another means for the protection of human rights by trade policy can be the conclusion of free trade and investment agreements. Most agreements contain a general reference to the Universal Declaration of Human Rights in their preamble and some agreements also contain concrete human rights provisions. Whereas the EU–Japan Economic Partnership Agreement, which entered into force on 1 February 2019, does not further elaborate on human rights issues, under Art. 12.3 para. 3 of the EU-Singapore Free Trade Agreement,[172] another recent example, the parties commit to respecting, promoting and effectively implementing fundamental rights at work, including the elimination of all forms of forced or compulsory

170 *European Commission*, Trade for all – Towards a more responsible trade and investment policy (2014), available under: https://trade.ec.europa.eu/doclib/docs/2015/october/tradoc_153846.pdf (last accessed: 9 April 2020).

171 *Cf. European Commission* (fn. 170).

172 The text of the EU–Singapore Free Trade Agreement is available under: http://trade.ec.europa.eu/doclib/press/index.cfm?id=961 (last accessed: 9 April 2020).

labour (lit. b) and the effective abolition of child labour (lit. c). The parties further commit to effectively implementing the ILO Conventions that Singapore and the Member States of the Union have ratified respectively. This is comparable to Art. 13.4 para. 2 of the EU–Vietnam Free Trade Agreement,[173] which the parties agreed upon in July 2018. This FTA will also contain a legally binding link with the EU–Vietnam Partnership and Cooperation Agreement (PCA), signed in June 2012. The PCA includes a general human rights clause (Art. 1 para. 1) and obliges the parties to foster cooperation including in the human rights sector (Art. 2 lit. f; Art. 35). Accordingly, it will be ensured that human rights are also part of the trade relations between the parties. Finally, investment agreements or the investment chapters of more comprehensive "new generation" free trade agreements contain substantive provisions to protect investments and the rights of foreign investors, *i.a.* by the obligation not to discriminate between foreigners and nationals (national treatment) and between foreigners (most favoured nations treatment), as well as by protection from unlawful direct and indirect expropriation and the right to fair and equitable treatment.[174] Often the protection of these rights is accompanied by the procedural right of investors to file a suit against the state before an arbitrational tribunal. That grants investors a strong position towards concurring interests and claims by local communities and might lead to a "regulatory chill" even before the stage of formal arbitration proceedings.[175] Particularly when the mining industry is of essential interest to a state's economy, host states might refer to investors' protection to justify omissions.[176] That underlines the importance of human rights clauses in such agreements and of the willingness of the investors' home state to monitor the human rights compliance of its enterprises acting abroad.

The instruments mentioned intend to induce other states to meet their human rights obligations, including the duty to protect, *i.e.* to enact human rights and enforce them toward private persons. The protection of human rights by the EU is not limited to its relations towards other states but might also be directed against private persons engaged in economic activi-

---

173 The text of the EU–Vietnam Free Trade Agreement is available under: http://trade.ec.europa.eu/doclib/press/index.cfm?id=1437 (last accessed: 9 April 2020).

174 *Dolzer/Schreuer*, Principles of International Investment Law (2012), pp. 130–215.

175 *Tienhaara*, Regulatory Chill and the Threat of Investment Arbitration in: Brown/Miles (eds.), Evolution in Investment Treaty Law and Arbitration (2011), p. 606 (606 *et seqq.*).

176 *Williams*, Investor-State Arbitration in Domestic Mining Conflicts, in: Global Environmental Politics 16 (2016), p. 32 (33 *et seq.*).

ties that potentially infringe human rights. Some recent examples should be addressed here.

c) Regulation concerning the Supply Chain

Quite recently, the EU has adopted the *Conflict Minerals regulation*[177] that addresses importers of tin, tantalum, and tungsten, their ores, and gold from conflict-affected and high-risk areas; and is to become fully effective from 1 January 2021. By this EU secondary law, the respective OECD Due Diligence Guidance for Responsible Supply Chains of Minerals from Conflict-Affected and High-Risk Areas[178] is transferred to hard law enforceable towards enterprises.[179] The regulation requires EU companies to ensure that in their supply chain they import the minerals and metals from responsible and conflict-free sources only. Following a five-step approach, the companies have to establish strong company management systems; to identify and assess risk in the supply chain; to design and implement a strategy to respond to identified risks; to carry out an independent third-party audit of supply chain due diligence; and, finally, to report annually on supply chain due diligence. The regulation differentiates between downstream and upstream companies, the latter encompassing mining companies, traders, smelters and refiners. The latter have to comply with mandatory rules on due diligence when they import. Even though the regulation primarily intends to break "the nexus between conflict and illegal exploitation of minerals", thereby guaranteeing peace, development and stability (recital 1), the indirect prevention of human rights abuses – such as child labour, sexual and gender-based violence, the disappearance of people, forced resettlement, and the destruction of ritually or culturally significant sites – is also covered, as shown by recital 2. The regulation is

177 Regulation (EU) 2017/821 of the European Parliament and of the Council of 17 May 2017 laying down supply chain due diligence obligations for Union importers of tin, tantalum and tungsten, their ores, and gold originating from conflict-affected and high-risk areas, OJ L 130, 19.5.2017, p. 1.

178 *OECD*, OECD Due Diligence Guidance for Responsible Supply Chains of Minerals from Conflict-Affected and High-Risk Areas (3rd edition 2016).

179 On the drafting history and for a first appraisal see *Nowrot*, The 2017 EU Conflict Minerals Regulation: A Promising European Rite to Remove the Natural Resource Curse, in: Feichtner/Krajewski/Roesch (eds.), Human Rights in the Extractive Industries, 2019, p. 51 (51 *et seqq.*)

inspired by Sec. 1502 of the US-Dodd-Frank-Act of 2010[180]. However, this regulation has a more limited field of application due to its referral to minerals from the Democratic Republic of Congo and neighbouring states and the fact that it only foresees annual disclosures but does not impose due diligence obligations on concerned companies.[181]

Another approach is chosen by the *Kimberley Process Certification Scheme*.[182] Established in 2003, this mechanism is intended to prevent rough 'conflict diamonds' from entering the general market after it had been shown that diamonds serve as an important financial instrument for rebel groups to fight (legitimate) governments and thereby to fuel violent ongoing conflict.[183] By a coalition of governments, civil society and the diamond industry, an international certification scheme for rough diamonds has been established,[184] which depends on a system of warranties and certificates, updated by the World Diamond Council recently in 2018.[185] All buyers and sellers of rough, as well as polished diamonds are obliged to make an affirmative declaration on all their invoices that the concerned diamonds have been purchased from legitimate sources not involved in funding conflict and in compliance with United Nations resolutions. The seller has to guarantee that these diamonds are conflict free, based on his personal knowledge and/or written guarantees provided by the supplier of these diamonds. It shall be ensured that trade in rough diamonds is com-

180 Public Law 111–203 — Juli 21, 2010; for a favourable assessment *cp. Martin-Ortega*, Human Rights Due Diligence for Corporations: From Voluntary Standards to Hard Law at Last, in: Netherlands Quarterly of Human Rights 32 (2014) pp. 44, 64 *et seq*.; a sceptical assessment is given by *Harline*, Can we Make Them Obey? U.S. Reporting Companies, Their Foreign Suppliers, and the Conflict Minerals Disclosure Requirements of Dodd-Frank, in: Northwestern Journal of International Law & Business 35 (2015), p. 439 (439 *et seqq*.)

181 *Martin-Ortega* (fn. 180), pp. 64 *et seq*., which refers specifically to Section 1502 of the US Dodd-Frank Act of 2010.

182 The KPCS Core document is available under: https://www.kimberleyprocess.co m/en/kpcs-core-document (last accessed: 9 April 2020).

183 See *United Nations General Assembly*, UN Doc. A/RES/55/56 of 1 December 2000.

184 Supported by *United Nations Security Council*, UN Doc. S/RES/1459 (2003) and regularly by the *United Nations General Assembly*, most recently by UN Doc. A/RES/73/283 of 5 March 2019, on the topic of "The role of diamonds in fuelling conflict: breaking the link between the illicit transaction of rough diamonds and armed conflict as a contribution to prevention and settlement of conflicts."

185 World Diamond Council, System of Warranties Guidelines (2008), available under: https://www.worlddiamondcouncil.org/downloads/WDC%20SoW%20Guid elines.pdf (last accessed: 9 April 2020).

mitted only between participating partners of the KPCS (Sec. III lit. e). The participating states must meet "minimum requirements" (Sec. IV; V); they have to put in place national legislation and institutions to establish export, import, and internal controls; and, finally, commit themselves to transparency and the exchange of statistical data. The intention is to drain the illicit trade in 'blood diamonds' and thereby deprive conflict parties of their financial ability to remain engaged in a conflict and thereby to prevent systematic and gross human rights violations that have been perpetrated in such conflicts.[186]

V. Conclusion and Outlook

The extractive industry, and resource mining in particular, pose specific challenges for human rights: Be it the question of who is entitled to conduct resource mining and how to share the benefits of national resources, be it the detrimental impact resource mining can have on a broad array of human rights and individuals. Furthermore, as states remain the duty bearers of human rights with an obligation to protect human rights against private abuses, the situation of the weak, authoritarian, unstable or even corrupt states in which many of the world's natural resources are located give cause for concern.

Thus, the interest in imposing direct human rights obligations on powerful business players does not come as a surprise. In resource mining, this would mean that companies themselves, regardless of the legal order of the host state, have to ensure safe working conditions, protect the environment, ensure that no children are among their workforce, engage in a dialogue with local and regional communities, establish monitoring and auditing systems, etc. Yet, there is insufficient support for an obligatory extension of the personal scope of human rights obligations on the international level.

Rather, current approaches adopt different steering instruments, including 'soft' ones. An increasingly prominent approach consists of fostering corporate social responsibility, *i.e.* self-regulation by concerned companies which goes beyond mere compliance with existing rules. The law could favour such supplementary efforts but also react to the violation of respec-

186 See recital 2 of the preamble of the Kimberley Process Certification Scheme Core document, available under: https://www.kimberleyprocess.com/en/kpcs-core-document (last accessed: 9 April 2020).

tive voluntarily accepted duties by domestic tort law. Correspondingly, transparency has become an important aspect for addressing human rights abuses and can be imposed by the law. The rationale behind this is the expectation that the consumer will take the social consequences of business behaviour and the respective performance of companies into consideration when deciding upon the purchase of a product or service. Thus, a market logic (attaining a competitive advantage) might induce companies to increase their human rights friendly corporate policy. Finally, obligations for companies to respect human rights might become 'hard law', meaning that competent states have transformed obligations for companies into positive domestic law. This is the standard approach under the duty to protect under international law. But the mentioned dilemmas with the operating state remain. Accordingly, the legal order of the (still mostly western) home states and their extraterritorial range have come to the fore in recent years. However, in general, states seem to be reluctant to impose extraterritorial obligations on companies hosted in their territory and try to prevent their jurisdiction from becoming a preferred forum in a game of "international forum shopping". With the Conflict Minerals regulation, the EU has adopted a tougher stance with regard to the regulation of business companies, their supply chains, and contractual partners. Though the scope of application remains limited, it could serve as a legislative example for potential future regulation of the extraterritorial dimension of business activities. Recent legal changes in France and the Netherlands go in the same direction; and in December 2020 the Council of the EU has finally asked the Commission to launch an EU Action Plan that is focusing on shaping global supply chains sustainably, promoting human rights, social and environmental due diligence standards and transparency by 2021.[187] However, due to potential and feared competitive disadvantages it is far from being certain that other states or organisations follow this approach. The Trump administration had declared that it e. g., wented to pull the Dodd-Frank's Act's teeth. In addition, the ongoing discussions about the Business and Human Rights Treaty show that in particular industrial states still lay low. Furthermore, it also remains to be proven whether consumers will sustainably put a stronger emphasis on the social responsibilities of

187 *Council of the European Union*, Council Conclusions on Human Rights and Decent Work in Global Supply Chains (13512/20) of 1 December 2020.

companies than on the price.[188] And with particular regard to natural resources it seems they often hardly have knowledge or even a choice – both of which are a precondition to play out the consumers' might in order to potentially influence the behaviour of companies.

An international approach bringing together all stakeholders, such as governments, enterprises, consumers, and NGOs might seem promising. The Extractive Industries Transparency Initiative (EITI)[189] could serve as an example. Established in 2003 with support of the UK government, it intends to fight corruption – as an assumed threat to human rights – by ensuring transparency with regard to payments from enterprises to officials in the operating countries. It optionally provides for further information to be covered by the transparency rules and establishes a verification regime. Yet, there are no tough sanctions offered, so the actual relevance and achievements remain limited. Such an approach can, however, be one additional tool to create awareness and provide for a broader basis of sectors, countries, companies, and civil society that are involved in the issue.

In the end, protecting human rights in the sector of resource mining is an ongoing process and depends on various approaches and – bearing in mind the pivotal role of the states – on the cooperation of many actors, including companies as well as consumers. Reiterated by the difficulties and challenges presented here: There isn't just one way of doing it.

188 For a study attesting substantial consumers' support for a fair-trade label *cp. Hiscox/Sequeira*, Consumer Demand for the Fair Trade Label: Evidence from a Multi-Store Field Experiment (2014), available under: https://www.hbs.edu/faculty/conferences/2014-launching-the-star-lab/Documents/FT_final_2_20.pdf (last accessed: 9 April 2020).

189 On this initiative see *Feldt*, The Extractive Industries Transparency Initiative (EITI) as a Human Rights Instrument: Potentials and Shortcomings, in: Feichtner/Krajewski/Roesch (eds.), Human Rights in the Extractive Industries (2019), pp. 11 *et seqq*.

Crimes against the Environment? The Deliberate Destruction of the Natural Environment and Natural Resources during War

*Steven Freeland**

Abstract

Acts perpetrated during the course of warfare have, through the ages, led to significant environmental destruction. These have included situations where the natural environment and natural resources have intentionally been targeted as a 'victim' of warfare. Until recently, such acts were generally regarded as an unfortunate but unavoidable element of armed conflict, despite their potentially disastrous impacts. The existing international rules have largely been ineffective and inappropriate, and have in practical terms done little to deter deliberate environmental destruction, particularly when measured against perceived military advantages. However, as the significance of the environment and the need for access to natural resources have come to be more widely recognised, this is no longer acceptable, particularly given the ongoing development of weapons capable of widespread and significant damage. This chapter discusses the current international legal regime relevant to the intentional destruction of the environment during warfare, and argues that such acts should, in appropriate circumstances, be recognised as an international crime and should be subject to more effective rules giving rise to international criminal responsibility.

---

* Emeritus Professor of International Law, Western Sydney University; Professorial Fellow, Bond University; Visiting Professor, University of Vienna; Permanent Visiting Professor, iCourts Centre of Excellence for International Courts, Denmark; Visiting Professor, Universite Toulouse1 Capitole; Adjunct Professor, University of Hong Kong; Associate Member, Centre for Research in Air and Space Law, McGill University; Senior Fellow, London Institute of Space Policy and Law; External Examiner, Universiti Teknologi MARA (UiTM), Malaysia; Director, International Institute of Space Law; Member of the Space Law Committee, International Law Association and International Bar Association.

Overview

I. Intentional Destruction of the Environmental and Natural Resources as a Part of Warfare

History has been witness to many deliberate acts aimed at destroying the natural environment and natural resources in order to achieve strategic goals during the course of a military conflict. Herodotus described how, in the fifth century BC, the retreating Scythians scorched the earth and poisoned the water wells in an effort to slow the advancing Persian army led by Darius. In 146 BC, Roman troops razed the city of Carthage and poisoned the surrounding soil with salt to prevent its future fertilisation. More recent warfare has seen countless further examples including:

i) During the Vietnam War, the United States implemented 'Operation Ranch Hand' to devastating effect to destroy vegetation used by the enemy for cover and sustenance, through the use of chemicals such as Agent Orange.[1]
ii) Few can forget the haunting images of over 700 burning Kuwaiti oil well heads, which had been deliberately ignited by retreating Iraqi forces towards the end of the Gulf War in 1991, and the emptying of millions of barrels of oil into the Gulf waters. These actions galvanized

1 It has been estimated that Operation Ranch Hand destroyed 8 per cent of Vietnam's croplands, 14 per cent of its forests, and 50 per cent of its swamp areas: *Yuzon*, Deliberate Environmental Modification Through the Use of Chemical and Biological Weapons: "Greening" the Environmental Laws of Armed Conflict to Establish an Environmentally Protective Regime, in: American University Journal of International Law and Policy 11 (1996), p. 793 (795-796).

the international community to address deliberate attacks on the environment during armed conflict,[2] and gave rise to almost universal condemnation.[3] The then German Chancellor, Helmut Kohl, for example, asserted that this constituted a 'crime against the environment'.[4]

iii) It has been estimated by Human Rights Watch that, during the course of the 2003 invasion of Iraq, United States and British forces used almost 13,000 cluster bombs – containing almost two million munitions – and over 1.9 tonnes of depleted uranium,[5] causing very significant environmental and resources-related damage, the extent of which may not be known for a considerable period of time.[6]

iv) The western region of Darfur in Sudan has seen the poisoning of vital water wells and drinking water installations,[7] as part of a deliberate government-supported strategy by the Arab Janjaweed Militia to eliminate or displace the ethnic black Africans living in that region.

II. Impact of Environmental and Resources Destruction on Human Security

These few (of many) examples indicate how the intentional destruction of the natural environment and natural resources has already been a part of many warfare situations. Such actions can have catastrophic effects, not on-

---

2 *Seacor*, Environmental Terrorism: Lessons from the Oil Fires of Kuwait, in: American University Journal of International Law and Policy 10 (1994), p. 481 (488).

3 For example, shortly afterwards, the Parliamentary Assembly of the Council of Europe called for the establishment of a war crimes tribunal to prosecute those responsible for 'this disgraceful attack on the environment': Anthony Leibler, Deliberate Wartime Environmental Damage: New Challenges for International Law , in: California Western International Law Journal 23 (1992), p. 67 (68).

4 *Kohl*, Statement by the German Chancellor, Bulletin (Bonn), 9 April 1991, p. 255.

5 *Haavisto*, in Symposium, The International Responses to the Environmental Impacts of War, in: Georgetown International Environmental Law Review 17 (2005), p. 565 (581).

6 Depleted uranium is a by-product of the process of 'uranium enrichment', which involves the separation of the three different uranium isotopes (uranium-238, uranium-235 and uranium-234) as a preliminary step towards the use of nuclear fission as a source of energy (uranium-235 is the most suitable for nuclear fission): *Koppe*, The Use of Nuclear Weapons and the Protection of the Environment During International Armed Conflict (2006), p. 18.

7 See *United Nations Commission on Human Rights*, Report of the United Nations High Commissioner for Human Rights and Follow-Up to the World Conference on Human Rights: Situation of Human Rights in Darfur Region of the Sudan (2004), UN Doc. E/CN.4/2005/3, paras. 50, 73.

ly in human, but also in ecological terms. They may also represent a breach of the fundamental human rights of the targeted individuals.[8] The relationship between human security and a safe and habitable environment is vital, particularly in relation to access to natural resources.

In addition, access to natural resources – or the lack of access – can itself be the trigger for conflict. In both the Democratic Republic of Congo and Haiti, the United Nations Environment Programme (UNEP) has reported that environmental damage has been a major cause of political unrest and conflict.[9] It has been estimated that, during the 1990s, approximately five million people were killed in armed conflicts that related to the exploitation of natural resources,[10] and that one quarter of the 50 active armed conflicts in 2001 were largely 'motivated' by resources.[11]

Environmental degradation also results in increasing numbers of refugees. In an interview in 2008, the then High Commissioner, António Guterres (now UN Secretary-General), stated that climate change led to the dislocation of people 'by provoking conflicts over increasingly scarce resources, such as water' and that its impact on the environment 'was a trigger of extreme poverty and conflict'.[12]

The Iran-Iraq War, the events in Kuwait at the end of the 1991 Gulf War, and the conflicts in African countries such as Sierra Leone, the Democratic Republic of Congo and Liberia, all serve to illustrate how armed conflict that is (partially) driven by disputes over natural resources can also subsequently result in significant destruction to the natural environment.[13] In the latter cases, not only were the conflicts fought over natural resources, but the resources themselves (for example, timber and dia-

8 For example, Principle 1 of the Declaration of the United Nations Conference on the Human Environment (16 June 1972) UN Doc. A/CONF.48/14/Rev.1 (Stockholm Declaration) provides that '[m]an has the fundamental right to freedom, equality, and adequate conditions of life, in an environment of a quality that permits a life of dignity and well-being'.

9 *Doyle*, UN Aims to Study Link Between Environment, Wars, reproduced in United Nations Environment Programme, in: The Environment in the News (14 January 2004).

10 *Salo*, When the Logs Roll Over: The Need for an International Convention Criminalizing Involvement in the Global Illegal Timber Trade, in: Georgetown International Environmental Law Review 16 (2003), p. 127 (142).

11 *Francis*, Fuelling the Fire: "Resource Wars" Spurred by Assets of Developing Nations, Christian Science Monitor (6 December 2002), p. A3.

12 *Borger*, Conflicts fuelled by climate change causing new refugee crisis, warns UN, The Guardian (17 June 2008), p. 15.

13 *Baker*, Legal Protections for the Environment in Times of Armed Conflict, in: Virginia Journal of International Law 33 (1993), p. 351 (351 *et seqq.*).

monds) became sources of funding for the combating parties, to be used to acquire weapons for the conflict. In 2002, a panel of experts appointed by the United Nations Security Council concluded that many of the serious crimes committed in the Democratic Republic of Congo were both in aid of, and financed by, the profits of the illegal appropriation of natural resources in that country.[14]

These examples illustrate a phenomenon sometimes referred to as 'resource wars', where the economic value of natural resources serves to fuel or trigger conflict. Exploitation of these resources represents a source of funding for military activities, giving rise to an unvirtuous circle.[15] The misuse of natural resources such as diamonds, or the scarcity of resources like water, may facilitate potential conflict, a situation which then becomes self-perpetuating and protracted.[16] Environmental degradation and destruction of natural resources can thus be both a cause and a consequence of armed conflict. In addition, during the course of conflict there are further 'knock-on' effects flowing from such destruction arising from the actions of the combatants.[17]

Moreover, the very nature of armed conflict and its adverse effects on the livelihood of communities, and the destruction of the natural environment and natural resources, fuel a spiralling vicious cycle of poverty and further violence, leaving desperate individuals, who are often children, with no choice but to themselves become active participants in the conflicts,[18] thus adding to the tragically high number of 'child soldiers' en-

---

14 *United Nations Security Council*, Final Report of the Panel of Experts on the Illegal Exploitation of Natural Resources and Other Forms of Wealth of the Democratic Republic of the Congo (16 October 2002) UN Doc. S/2002/1146.

15 *Ezekiel*, The Application of International Criminal Law to Resource Exploitation: Ituri, Democratic Republic of the Congo, in: Natural Resources Journal 47 (2007), p. 225 (234).

16 *United Nations General Assembly*, Report of the Special Representative of the Secretary-General for Children and Armed Conflict (13 August 2007), UN Doc. A/62/228, para. 12. See also the section entitled 'Diamonds' in the Trial Chamber decision of the *Special Court of Sierra Leone*, Judgment of 18 May 2012, Prosecutor v. Charles Gankay Taylor, Case No. SCSL-03-01-T, Trial Chamber II, paras. 2046-2173.

17 *Nebehay*, Dirty Water Provokes Hepatitis Outbreak in Darfur, Reliefweb (2004), available under: http://reliefweb.int/report/sudan/sudan-dirty-water-provokes-hepatitis-outbreak-darfur (last accessed: 4 December 2018).

18 *Freeland*, Mere Children or Weapons of War - Child Soldiers and International Law, in: University of La Verne Law Review 29 (2008), p.19 (27-28).

gaged in conflicts.[19] Environmental degradation and destruction of natural resources can also lead to social upheaval and tensions, thus representing a threat to national security.[20] This is one reason why combatants in a conflict may seek to intentionally 'target' natural resources and many States view environmental and resource-related concerns 'in strategic terms'.[21]

In some respects, therefore, the intentional destruction of the environment and natural resources may be a precursor or trigger point for conflict. In other circumstances, such intentional damage may be perpetrated as a part of the conduct of warfare. Whilst we must, naturally, remain cognisant of the impacts of the former, it is the latter that this chapter is primarily concerned with.

III. Intentional Destruction of the Environment and Resources during Warfare and the Development of International Criminal Justice

Notwithstanding (or perhaps because of) its significance to human populations, the targeting of the environment and natural resources has, increasingly, become a part of the conduct of armed conflict. Such acts represent not only a feature of conflict strategy, but also, as noted, a root cause for the further escalation of the conflict itself.[22] Given the increasingly diverse

---

19 In a 2004 report, the NGO Coalition to Stop the Use of Child Soldiers found that 'hundreds of thousands of children have fought and died in almost every major conflict in the world': *Coalition to Stop the Use of Child Soldiers*, Child Soldiers: Global Report 2004 (2004), available under: https://reliefweb.int/sites/reliefweb.int/files/resources/7951D366562987B4C1256F50004D9C23-child_soldiers_CSC_nov_2004.pdf (last accessed: 15 May 2020), p.13. In addition to an estimated 300,000 children who engage in actual military conflict, another 500,000 are 'conscripted' into paramilitary organisations, guerrilla groups and civil militias in over 85 countries. See also *Freeland*, Child Soldiers and International Crimes – How Should International Law be Applied?, in: New Zealand Journal of Public and International Law 3 (2005), p. 303 (304).

20 *Brunneé*, Environmental Security in the Twenty-First Century: New Momentum for the Development of International Environmental Law, in: Fordham International Law Journal 18 (1995), p. 1742 (1742 *et seqq.*).

21 *Parsons*, The Fight to Save the Planet: U.S. Armed Forces, "Greenkeeping," and Enforcement of the Law Pertaining to Environmental Protection During Armed Conflict, in: Georgetown International Environmental Law Review 10 (1998), p. 441 (444).

22 *Nordquist*, Panel Discussion on International Environmental Crimes: Problems of Enforceable Norms and Accountability, in: ILSA Journal of International Law 3 (1997), p. 697 (*et seqq.*).

ways in which armed conflict might be conducted, particularly in light of the development of weapons technology, there is even greater scope for such destructive actions in future warfare, perhaps even in ways that we cannot at this time completely fathom.

Indeed, actions taken during previous armed conflicts illustrate that the environment and natural resources have been targeted as a 'victim' of armed conflict – in the sense that it is deliberately destroyed. This is not only unacceptable, but also may result in irreversible and unpredictable consequences, irrespective of the manner in which the environment and natural resources are involved. It is submitted that such intentional damage should be appropriately regulated, and that the existing legal frameworks are inadequate in this regard, since environmental damage has historically been overlooked when assessing the toll wrought by warfare.[23] This approach is not sustainable, particularly, as noted, in light of the ongoing development of weapons with unimaginable and ever increasing destructive capability.[24]

It is submitted, therefore, that the deliberate nature of such actions requires stringent legal regulation and accountability. The relevant legal measures must 'stigmatise' such acts, so as to properly reflect the unsustainable risks they entail. Intentional damage to the environment and natural resources during armed conflict cannot be regarded as immaterial or of secondary importance. The International Court of Justice has affirmed that, 'the environment is not an abstraction but represents the living space, the quality of life and the very health of human beings, including genera-

---

23 A committee established by the Office of the Prosecutor of the International Criminal Tribunal for the former Yugoslavia (ICTY) to consider whether any crimes falling within the jurisdiction of that Tribunal had been committed by NATO forces during Operation Allied Force failed to consider the full environmental consequences of the operation: *Freeland*, The Bombing of Kosovo and the Milosevic Trial: Reflections on Some Legal Issues, in: Australian International Law Journal (2002), p. 150 (164).

24 For example, it has been asserted that many thousands of children born in Vietnam to war veterans and exposed civilians after the Vietnam war had physical and mental deformities that could be directly linked to the widespread spraying of the herbicide Agent Orange by the United States, as well as the continuing presence in the destroyed regions of its poisonous residue, dioxin: *Mydans*, Vietnam Sees War's Legacy in Its Young, The New York Times (16 May 1999), available under: http://www.nytimes.com/1999/05/16/world/vietnam-sees-war-s-legacy-in-its-young.html (last accessed: 4 December 2018).

tions unborn'.[25] This is a truism even during times of warfare and certainly extends to the preservation of, and access to, natural resources.

Of course, warfare by its very nature results in damage to the natural environment and to natural resources, as well as to other 'protected sites'.[26] However, this alone cannot be justification for the *intentional* targeting of them. The increasing concern regarding the state of the environment and the need for a system of greater culpability for intentional environmental and natural resources destruction has previously given rise to proposed crimes such as 'ecocide'[27] and 'geocide',[28] as well as calls for an Ecocide Convention, to be enforced by an International Environmental Court.[29] Whilst these proposals have generally not been limited to situations of armed conflict, they are demonstrative of the need to at least address those circumstances more comprehensively. The appropriate regulation of unjustified damage to the environment during armed conflict has been described as the 'unmet challenge of the 20th century'.[30]

It is argued that the most appropriate method to address the issue is not through environmental protection measures but rather under international criminal law (although it is hoped that this will have positive consequences for the environment and for natural resources), so that those who intentionally instigate such destruction during armed conflict can be made criminally liable. This approach is both timely and appropriate. International criminal law has been developing rapidly, particularly over the past two decades. This has principally been through the operation of the United Nations *ad hoc* international criminal tribunals, as well as a number of

---

25 *International Court of Justice*, Legality of the Threat or Use of Nuclear Weapons (Advisory Opinion), I.C.J. Reports (1996), p. 242, para. 29. See also *International Court of Justice*, Judgment of 25 September 1997, Gabcíkovo-Nagymaros Project (Hungary v. Slovakia), I.C.J. Reports 7 (1997), para. 53.

26 For example, similar concerns arise from the deliberate destruction of cultural property during armed conflict: see the Hague Convention for the Protection of Cultural Property in the Event of Armed Conflict 249 UNTS 240.

27 See, for example, *Teclaff*, Beyond Restoration - the Case of Ecocide, in: Natural Resources Journal 34 (1994), p. 933 (933 *et seqq.*); *Gray*, The International Crime of Ecocide , in: California Western International Law Journal 26 (1996), p. 215 (*et seqq.*).

28 See, for example, *Berat*, Defending the Right to a Healthy Environment: Toward a Crime of Genocide in International Law, in: Boston University International Law Journal 11 (1993), p. 327 (327 *et seqq.*).

29 *Drumbl*, Waging War against the World: The Need to Move from War Crimes to Environmental Crimes, in: Austin/Bruch (eds.), The Environmental Consequences of War: Legal, Economic, and Scientific Perspectives (2000), p. 620 (641).

30 *Parsons* (fn. 21), p. 442, fn. 344.

'hybrid' or 'internationalised' courts, established to deal with international crimes perpetrated during specific conflicts.[31] More recently, of course, the world's first *permanent* international criminal institution, the International Criminal Court (ICC), was established in 2002. The development of this system of international criminal justice has been described as 'one of the few bright spots in the recent history of international law.'[32]

The process of articulating the crimes that exist under international (criminal) law has generally been subject to the traditional principle of legality (*nullum crimen sine lege*), which is reiterated in the Rome Statute.[33] Partially in response to arguments (which were inconclusively dealt with by the judges) by the defendants at the Nuremberg trials, that the *ex post facto* punishment of the crimes in the Charter of that Tribunal[34] offended the *nullum crimen sine lege* principle,[35] the ICTY was established to prose-

31 The United Nations *ad hoc* Tribunals are the ICTY (established by United Nations Security Council Resolution 827 (25 May 1993) UN Doc S/RES/827/1993 and the International Criminal Tribunal for Rwanda (established by United Nations Security Council Resolution 955 (8 November 1994) UN Doc. S/RES/955/1994) (ICTR). In December 2010, the Mechanism for International Criminal Tribunals (MICT) was established to continue the 'obligations and essential functions' of the ICTR and the ICTY: United Nations Security Council Resolution 1966 (22 December 2010) UN Doc. S/Res/1966/2010 on the ICTY and ICTR. The 'hybrid' or 'internationalised' criminal tribunals include those that operate or have operated in East Timor (established in 2000 by the United Nations Transitional Administration in East Timor (UNTAET), pursuant to UNTAET Regulations 2000/11 and 2000/15 (6 March 2000 and 6 June 2000 respectively)), Sierra Leone (established by an agreement between the United Nations and the Government of Sierra Leone dated 16 January 2002, pursuant to United Nations Security Council Resolution 1315 (14 August 2000) UN Doc. S/RES/1315/2000), and Cambodia (established by an agreement between the United Nations and the Government of Cambodia dated 6 June 2003, pursuant to United Nations General Assembly Resolution 57/228 B (13 May 2003) UN Doc. A/RES/57/228 B. There is also The Special Tribunal for Lebanon, which operates in The Netherlands and was established by United Nations Security Council Resolution 1757 (30 May 2007) UN Doc. S/RES/1757/2007 on the Situation in the Middle East.

32 *Jessberger/Geneuss*, Down the Drain or Down to Earth? International Criminal Justice under Pressure, in: 11 Journal of International Criminal Justice 501 (2013), p. 501.

33 See Rome Statute, Art. 22(1).

34 Charter of the Nuremberg International Military Tribunal, annexed to the 1945 London Agreement for the Establishment of an International Military Tribunal 82 UNTS 279 (Nuremberg Charter), Art. 6.

35 For example, the concept of 'crimes against humanity' was first codified in the Nuremberg Charter (Art. 6(c)), and then applied to actions that took place at an

cute only crimes that were 'doubtless part of customary international law.'[36]

However, this may not always be the case,[37] since the definition of the crimes specified in (some of) the statutes of the international criminal tribunals may differ from the crime as it existed at the relevant time under customary international law. In addition, the development of these crimes is, in reality, a 'reactive' process. As Theodor Meron has noted in the context of discussing the evolving principles of international humanitarian law, '[c]alamitous events and atrocities have repeatedly driven the development of [...] law'.[38]

This is equally the case with respect to the development of international crimes and the principles of international criminal law. In other words, the acceptance by the international community that certain behaviour is unacceptable and illegal under international criminal law is a responsive act, perhaps also stemming from changing views regarding the conduct of armed conflict. As such, international criminal law is a dynamic area of legal regulation and continues to evolve over time. It is therefore important to assess the appropriateness of the existing rules of international criminal law from time to time.[39] For a crime to fall within the classification of international crimes – which have been described as *crimen contra omnes*[40] – it is to be regarded as an affront to us all, violating fundamental norms

---

earlier time. It is unclear whether such a crime existed coincidentally under customary international law: see, for example, the judgments of Justice Brennan (587-590) and Justice Toohey (664-677) of the High Court in Australia in Polyukhovich v. Commonwealth and Another (1991) 172 CLR 501.

36 *United Nations Security Council*, Report of the Secretary-General Pursuant to Paragraph 2 of Security Council Resolution 808 (3 May 1993) UN Doc. S/25704, paras. 33-5. See also *International Criminal Tribunal for the Former Yugoslavia*, Decision on Dragoljub Ojdanić's Motion Challenging Jurisdiction – Joint Criminal Enterprise, Prosecutor v. Milan Milutinović, Nikola Šainović and Dragoljub Ojdanić, Case No. IT-99-37-AR72, Appeals Chamber (21 May 2003), para. 9.

37 With respect to the ICTR, see *Gallant*, Jurisdiction to Adjudicate and Jurisdiction to Prescribe in International Criminal Courts 48 Villanova Law Review 764 (2003), p. 783.

38 *Meron*, The Humanization of Humanitarian Law, in: American Journal of International Law 94 (2000), p. 239 (243).

39 *Scovazzi*, State Responsibility for Environmental Harm, in: Yearbook of International Environmental Law 12 (2001), p. 43 (43 *et seqq.*).

40 *Beres*, Iraqi Crimes and International Law: The Imperative to Punish, in: 21 Denver Journal of International Law and Policy (1993), p. 335 (338).

that regulate the peaceful co-existence of the international community.[41] The factors underlying such a determination are, however, dynamic, and will change and evolve over time.

The establishment of, and resort to these international(ised) criminal courts indicates a broad acceptance of international criminal law as an appropriate legal mechanism to address grave violations of human rights and crimes that conflict with humanity. The ICC seeks to address 'the most serious crimes of concern to the international community as a whole'.[42] Such institutions help to further shape and develop important norms that seek to regulate the behaviour of those engaged *inter alia* in armed conflict.

A clear example of the evolving nature of international criminal law (and its codification) is the elaboration of an increasing number of acts involving sexual violence that can constitute the international crime of crimes against humanity.[43] Similarly, we have seen the relatively recent characterisation of rape as an act of genocide[44] – the 'crime of crimes'[45] – representing a significant further extension of the scope of international criminal law within the context of an armed conflict.[46]

---

41 *Orellana*, Criminal Punishment for Environmental Damage: Individual and State Responsibility at a Crossroad, in: Georgetown International Environmental Law Review 17 (2005), p. 689 (673).

42 Rome Statute, Preamble, para. 4.

43 Compare article 5(g) of the ICTY Statute (Statute of the International Tribunal for the Prosecution of Persons Responsible for Serious Violations of International Humanitarian Law Committed in the Territory of the Former Yugoslavia since 1991, 32 ILM 1159) and article 3(g) of the ICTR Statute (Statute of the International Criminal Tribunal for the Prosecution of Persons Responsible for Genocide and Other Serious Violations of International Humanitarian Law Committed in the Territory of Rwanda and Rwandan Citizens Responsible for Genocide and Other Such Violations Committed in the Territory of Neighbouring States, between 1 January 1994 and 31 December 1994, 33 ILM 1598), both of which specify 'rape' as an act that might constitute a crime against humanity, with article 7(1)(g) of the Rome Statute, which refers not only to rape, but also to 'sexual slavery, enforced prostitution, forced pregnancy, enforced sterilization, or any other form of sexual violence of comparable gravity'.

44 *International Criminal Tribunal for Rwanda*, Judgement of 2 September 1998, (Prosecutor v. Jean-Paul Akayesu), Case No. ICTR-96-4-T, Trial Chamber, para. 734.

45 *International Criminal Tribunal for Rwanda*, Judgement and Sentence of 4 September 1998, (Prosecutor v. Jean Kambanda), Case No. ICTR 97-23-S, Trial Chamber, para. 16.

46 The crime of genocide requires the existence of a special intent (*dolus specialis*) 'to destroy, in whole or in part, a national, ethnical, racial or religious group, as

It is submitted that a similar shift in sentiment is taking place in relation to the intentional destruction of the environment and natural resources during armed conflict. The universal condemnation of the acts committed by the Iraqi forces in 1991 – involving not only the igniting of the oil wells, but also the dumping of up to four million barrels of crude oil into the Persian Gulf[47] – galvanised significant support among the broader community for the establishment of stronger criminal sanctions. Although some commentators regarded such acts as constituting a violation(s) of article 53 of the Fourth 1949 Geneva Convention,[48] no action was initiated under that instrument.[49] Others called for the finalisation and implementation of a 'Fifth Geneva Convention' specifically directed towards such acts,[50] arguing that the assumption that the existing legal regime was shown to be incapable of providing appropriate protection and enforcement in the circumstances.[51]

In the *Legality of the Threat or Use of Nuclear Weapons* Advisory Opinion, one relevant issue was whether, and to what extent, environmental considerations restricted what could be regarded as legitimate military actions. In essence, as articulated by Edith Brown Weiss, the International Court of Justice was faced with three options on this question:

> "*that environmental considerations apply directly to armed conflicts; that environmental considerations do not apply to armed conflicts unless specifically provided for in an international agreement governing armed conflicts; or, third, in addition to any express provisions in international agreements governing armed conflicts, environmental considerations must be taken into account in applying laws related to armed conflict*".[52]

The Court affirmed that environmental issues *do* play a role in the overall assessment of military necessity, so that even though:

---

such': article II of the Convention on the Prevention and Punishment of the Crime of Genocide 78 UNTS 277 (Genocide Convention); Rome Statute, Art. 6.

47 *Yuzon* (fn. 1), p. 794.

48 Geneva Convention Relative to the Protection of Civilian Persons in Time of War 75 UNTS 287.

49 *Beres* (fn. 40), fn. 16.

50 This was, for example, suggested at a conference sponsored by the London School of Economics and the British Centre for Defence Studies in June 1991.

51 *Sharp*, The Effective Deterrence of Environmental Damage During Armed Conflict: A Case Analysis of the Persian Gulf War, in: Military Law Review 137 (1992), p. 1 (3).

52 *Weiss*, The International Responses to the Environmental Impacts of War, in: Georgetown International Environmental Law Review 17 (2005), p. 565 (569).

> *"existing international law relating to the protection and safeguarding of the environment does not specifically prohibit the use of nuclear weapons [...] States must take environmental considerations into account when assessing what is necessary and proportionate in the pursuit of legitimate military objectives. Respect for the environment is one of the elements that go to assessing whether an action is in conformity with the principles of necessity and proportionality"*.[53]

It has been suggested that this conclusion indicates that the protection of the environment and natural resources during armed conflict 'is an object and purpose of international law.'[54] However, it remains for examination as to whether the overarching criteria of military necessity – which is itself often an extremely difficult concept to quantify in the circumstances of decision-making – dilutes, within the context of an armed conflict, the importance to be attached to the environment.

This poses some complex questions: do the existing legal rules provide the appropriate level of deterrence, and do they readily create mechanisms that allow for accountability and for sufficient condemnation of the perpetrators? Moreover, do they emphasise sufficiently the gravity and stigma that is associated with acts that intentionally target the environment as a victim, or use the environment as a weapon?

What is clear is that international law increasingly recognises the links between environmental and ecological rights, including access to natural resources, and fundamental human rights.[55] It is broadly accepted that customary international law requires that one's actions do not cause significant destruction to the environment so as to threaten fundamental human rights.[56] It logically follows that international legal regulation intended to protect the environment should lead to accountability in appropriate circumstances for those individuals who intentionally set out to significantly

---

53 *International Court of Justice*, Legality of the Threat or Use of Nuclear Weapons (Advisory Opinion), I.C.J Reports (1996), p. 242, paras. 33, 30.

54 *Parsons* (fn. 21), p. 448.

55 *McCallion*, International Environmental Justice: Rights and Remedies, in: Hastings International and Comparative Law Review 26 (2003), p. 427 (427 *et seqq.*).

56 *McCallion/Sharma*, Environmental Justice Without Borders: The Need for an International Court of the Environment to Protect Fundamental Environmental Rights, in: George Washington Journal of International Law and Economics 32 (2000), p. 351 (354).

damage the environment and natural resources.[57] As a consequence, the intentional targeting of the environment and natural resources as an act of warfare can *and should* give rise to individual criminal responsibility at the international level. Such acts can constitute an international crime that 'shocks the conscience'[58] of humankind as a whole. Indeed, the Universal Declaration of Human Rights affirms that 'disregard and contempt for human rights have resulted in barbarous acts which have outraged the conscience of mankind'.[59]

To reiterate, the author does not argue here for an *environmental* mechanism to address such actions, but rather one under international *criminal* law, although there will clearly be the expectation that additional environmental protection may also be achieved in this way.[60]

IV. The Need for Legal Regulation

Law has traditionally been used to regulate acts that may affect the environment. In addition to those *jus in bello* treaties that may be relevant to environmental destruction during armed conflict, there are many hundreds of multilateral treaties and bilateral instruments[61] that have been concluded by States in an effort to regulate the state of the environment, primarily in times of peace. To the extent, however, that some of the principles in those instruments might also apply during armed conflict, some parallel wartime environmental protections may emerge.[62]

The conclusion of many of these environmental instruments has coincided with a greater environmental consciousness that emerged in the 1960s and 1970s, when it was recognised that international law could (and

57 *McLaughlin*, Improving Compliance: Making Non-State International Actors Responsible for Environmental Crimes, in: Colorado Journal of International Environmental Law and Policy 11 (2000), p. 377 (386).

58 *International Court of Justice*, Reservations to the Convention on the Prevention and Punishment of the Crime of Genocide (Advisory Opinion), I.C.J. Reports 16 (1951), p. 23.

59 *United Nations General Assembly*, Resolution 217A (III) (10 December 1948) UN Doc. A/810 on the Universal Declaration of Human Rights, Preamble, para. 2.

60 See also *Faure/Visser*, How to Punish Environmental Pollution? Some Reflections on Various Models of Criminalization of Environmental Harm, in: European Journal of Crime, Criminal Law and Criminal Justice 3 (1995), p. 316 (317).

61 *McCallion/Sharma* (fn. 56), p. 355.

62 *Baker* (fn. 13), p. 354.

should) assume practical relevance in terms of environmental issues.[63] This coincided with a growing awareness of the potential for future 'risks' to human health and the environment, and the uncertainties as to their effects, that could arise from the (in)action of States.[64] This trend has since continued as illustrated, for example, by the increasing efforts over the past decade to implement legally binding standards to curb the effects of climate change. This is, as those efforts demonstrate, a complex, difficult and constantly evolving process. In some circumstances, even those international environmental agreements that historically have been 'successful' may no longer continue to remain effective without further refinement and expansion.[65]

In addition to legal regulation, there are a number of other mechanisms that may contribute to greater protection of the environment, perhaps even in armed conflict situations. Examples include important guidelines established through an 'increasing resort to the so-called "soft law" approach' to international environmental law,[66] as well as greater education of military personnel as to the long-term effects of environmental damage. However, although it has been argued that the use of binding legal sanctions and standards actually exacerbates environmental damage, by entrenching an expectation that *some* degradation is acceptable or anticipated,[67] it would be naive to assume that a system comprising primarily of non-compulsory 'regulation', without the concurrent application of legally binding (and enforceable) standards of behaviour, would be sufficient to establish appropriate sanctions directed against the intentional targeting of

63 *van Niekerk*, Environmental Pollution – The New International Crime, in: South African Law Journal 93 (1976), p. 68 (73).

64 *Peel*, The Precautionary Principle in Practice: Environmental Decision-Making and Scientific Uncertainty (2005), p. 1.

65 For example, it has been suggested that the terms of the Montreal Protocol on Substances that Deplete the Ozone Layer 26 ILM 154, described as 'one of the world's most successful multilateral environmental agreements', must be reconsidered in light of the threats posed by climate change: see *Kaniaru et al.*, Strengthening the Montreal Protocol: Insurance Against Abrupt Climate Change, in: Sustainable Development Law and Policy Journal 7 (2007) p. 3 (*et seqq.*).

66 *Birnie/Boyle*, International Law and the Environment (1st edition, 1992), p. 10. See also *Freeland*, For Better or For Worse? The Use of 'Soft Law' within the International Legal Regulation of Outer Space, in: Annals of Air and Space Law XXXVI (2011), p. 409 (409 *et. seqq.*).

67 See, for example, *Halsey*, Environmental Crime: Towards an Eco-Human Rights Approach, in: Current Issues in Criminal Justice 8 (1996), p. 217, who (at p. 235) suggests that there is a '*structural embeddedness* of environmental harm' implicit in the current general approach to environmental crime (emphasis in original).

the environment. This is particularly so in the circumstances of an armed conflict, where, in the mindset of those involved, (real or perceived) military and strategic issues would almost certainly outweigh most (if not all) environmental concerns.

V. International Law and the Destruction of the Environment and Resources

The inter-relationship between intentional environment and natural resources destruction, human security and armed conflict requires that effective enforcement measures exist at the international level. As indicated, both national law and regional law can only play a very limited role in addressing such acts. This author therefore advocates for the application of *international* law – principally international criminal law – to the issue of intentional environmental damage during armed conflict.

International law – and more particularly international criminal law – is particularly suited to regulating such acts since, even though some international crimes such as genocide and crimes against humanity can (theoretically) occur in times of 'peace', the principles of international criminal law were developed principally within the context of armed conflict.[68] This is so even where the armed conflict may be non-international (as opposed to international) in character, since the consequences of such damage do not necessarily end at the borders of any one country. There is no overarching moral or legal justification for treating perpetrators of very serious 'international' crimes in internal conflicts differently from those engaged in international armed conflicts.[69] For example, during the conflict in Rwanda during the 1990s, culminating in the genocide that took place during 1994,[70] significant amounts of agricultural land were destroyed in order to force groups of people to move, both within the country and beyond its

---

68 *Orellana* (fn. 41), p. 689.

69 See *Frowein*, Book Review – Theodor Meron, The Humanization of International Law, in: 101 American Journal of International Law 680 (2007), p. 681.

70 The ICTR has held that the conflict in Rwanda was an internal armed conflict under international law: *International Criminal Tribunal for the Former Yugoslavia*, Judgment of 2 September 1998, Prosecutor v. Akayesu, Case No ICTR-96-4-T, Trial Chamber, para. 627.

borders.[71] Moreover, many of the more recent conflicts have been internal in nature.[72]

It is true that the distinction between non-international and international armed conflicts is still important in the context of various international crimes,[73] a consequence of the traditional adherence of the 'non-intervention' principle that still pervades in international law and international relations.[74] However, it is equally clear that international criminal law already does apply to 'armed conflict not of an international character',[75] as do the *jus in bello*.[76] In circumstances where intentional environmental damage during armed conflict is sufficiently serious to warrant criminalisation, the same imperatives should apply irrespective of the legal nature of the armed conflict. Yet, the existing war crime relating to damage to the natural environment in the Rome Statute only applies in international armed conflict.[77]

The argument in this chapter does not distinguish between armed conflict of an international and non-international character, and the call for criminal accountability regulating crimes against the environment applies to both types of armed conflict. In fact, there have been calls from time to time to 'unify' the *jus in bello*, so that they are equally applicable 'in all forms' of armed conflict.[78]

There is already a body of *jus in bello* treaties that deal with certain aspects of intentional environmental damage during armed conflict. These

71 *Weinstein*, Prosecuting Attacks that Destroy the Environment: Environmental Crimes or Humanitarian Atrocities?, in: Georgetown International Environmental Law Review 17 (2005), p. 697 (700).

72 See *Bruch*, All's Not Fair in (Civil) War: Criminal Liability for Environmental Damage in Internal Armed Conflict, in: Vermont Law Review 25 (2001), p. 695 (698) and the corresponding footnotes.

73 Certain international crimes within the jurisdiction of the international criminal tribunals can only be committed where the conflict is characterised as an international conflict: compare, for example, articles 8(2)(a) and 8(2)(b)) of the Rome Statute with articles 8(2)(c) and 8(2)(e). See also *International Criminal Tribunal for the Former Yugoslavia*, Decision on Defence Motion for Interlocutory Appeal on Jurisdiction, Prosecutor v. Duško Tadić, Case No. IT-94-1, Appeals Chamber (2 October 1995).

74 See also Charter of the United Nations, 1 UNTS 16 (United Nations Charter), Art. 2(7).

75 See, for example, Rome Statute, Arts. 8(2)(c) and 8(2)(e).

76 See, for example, 1977 Additional Protocol II, as well as Article 3 common to the four Geneva Conventions of 12 August 1949 for the Protection of War Victims.

77 See Rome Statute, Art. 8(2)(b)(iv).

78 See, for example, *Bruch* (fn. 72), pp. 738-43, 750 and the corresponding footnotes.

instruments must be analysed to determine whether they adequately reflect the heinous nature associated with the *intention* to destroy the environment. On the other hand, the United Nations Charter, which is concerned with the maintenance of international peace and security,[79] makes no mention of the problem of environmental degradation. This goes some way towards explaining why the environment has not been of particular focus to the main organs of the United Nations, particularly the Security Council.[80] This is not particularly surprising given that, at the time that the United Nations Charter was drafted, the issue of environmental protection was not regarded at all as a priority.[81]

As a result, legal regulation aimed at promoting criminal law to enforce important international environmental principles has only been a relatively recent phenomenon.[82] International law has been even 'slower' to recognise the need to address environmental destruction during armed conflict situations.[83] It was not until 1977, following the television broadcasts of the environmental destruction wrought during the Vietnam War, that the concept of the 'natural environment' appeared in the treaty principles that set out the rules of international humanitarian law, although the overriding principle of 'military necessity' still generally applies in any assessment of environmental damage caused during armed conflict. There are some *jus in bello* instruments that do not specifically refer to military necessity in this context,[84] but it is necessary to critically consider the level of environmental damage required before a breach of those treaties is achieved, described by Carl Bruch as 'extreme'.[85]

In terms of many international environmental agreements that have emerged since the 1970s, most do not refer to armed conflict, although some may be applicable in wartime. However, while many of these treaties

---

79 See United Nations Charter, Art. 1(1).

80 Of course, there are some United Nations agencies that are directed towards the environment, such as UNEP.

81 *van Niekerk* (fn. 63), p. 70.

82 *Hedemann-Robinson*, Enforcement of European Union Environmental Law: Legal Issues and Challenges (2007), p. 516.

83 *Gasser*, For Better Protection of the Natural Environment in Armed Conflict: A Proposal for Action, in: American Journal of International Law 89 (1995), p. 637 (638).

84 See Protocol I Additional to the Geneva Conventions of August 12, 1949, and relating to the Protection of Victims of International Armed Conflicts, 1125 UNTS 3 (1977 Additional Protocol I); Convention on the Prohibition of Military or Any Other Hostile Use of Environmental Modification Techniques 1108 UNTS 151.

85 *Bruch* (fn. 72), p. 703.

– and the relevant principles of customary international law – may provide for the *prohibition* of certain forms of environmental destruction, even during armed conflict, they have been wholly ineffective in terms of the *prevention* of such action. With some exceptions, the general focus of these international environmental agreements has instead been in relation to principles between States *inter se* – the breach of which gives rise to principles of State responsibility under the traditional rules of general international law. As the International Court of Justice has noted:

> "*in the field of environmental protection, vigilance and* prevention *are required on account of the often irreversible character of damage to the environment and of the limitations inherent in the very mechanism of reparation of this type of damage*". [86]

What appears to be lacking is a mechanism that provides sufficient *deterrence* and 'facilitates condemnation and accountability' in a more effective manner.[87] There have been virtually no prosecutions of individuals for intentional environmental destruction in such circumstances,[88] notwithstanding the inclusion in the *jus in bello* of the so-called 'Martens clause', which was first incorporated into the 1899 Hague Convention II with Respect to the Laws and Customs of War on Land,[89] and has been included in a number of subsequent treaties.

There have, in the past, been general calls – in non-binding instruments – for the *absolute* protection of the environment during times of war. The 1982 World Charter for Nature declares that '[n]ature *shall* be secured against degradation caused by warfare or other hostile activities',[90] and that '[m]ilitary activities damaging to nature *shall* be avoided'.[91] Ten years later,

86 *International Court of Justice*, Judgment of 25 September 1997, Gabcíkovo-Nagymaros Project (Hungary v. Slovakia) I.C.J. Reports (1997), para. 140 (emphasis added).

87 *Sharp* (fn. 51), p. 5.

88 One reason for this is that 'environmental crimes [have been] overshadowed by other atrocities': *Weinstein* (fn. 71), p. 698.

89 Hague Convention II with Respect to the Laws and Customs of War on Land 26 Martens (2nd) 949.

90 *United Nations General Assembly*, Resolution 37/7 (28 October 1982) UN Doc. A/RES/37/7, Annex, principle 5 (emphasis added). There were 110 States who voted in favour of this resolution, 1 (United States) against, with 18 abstentions.

91 *United Nations General Assembly*, Resolution 37/7 (28 October 1982) UN Doc. A/RES/37/7, Annex, principle 20 (emphasis added).

the Rio Declaration on Environment and Development[92] called for the protection of the environment during armed conflict, with principles 23 and 24 providing *inter alia*:

> *"[t]he environment and natural resources of people under oppression, domination and occupation shall be protected (Principle 23);*
>
> *[w]arfare is inherently destructive of sustainable development. States shall therefore respect international law providing protection for the environment in times of armed conflict and cooperate in its further development, if necessary (Principle 24)".* [93]

It has been somewhat optimistically asserted by one commentator that principle 23 establishes 'an absolute right to environmental protection',[94] thus sidestepping 'the pitfall of military necessity'.[95] Yet, only a few months after the Rio Declaration was adopted, the United Nations General Assembly, while taking note of the Declaration, stressed that 'destruction of the environment, *not justified by military necessity* and carried out wantonly, is clearly contrary to existing international law'.[96] A few years later, the International Court of Justice affirmed that the *jus in bello* prohibited 'harm greater than that unavoidable to achieve *legitimate military objectives*'.[97]

The Rome Statute currently continues along the same path, incorporating military advantage into a consideration of whether a war crime involving damage to the environment has been committed.[98] Whilst some support this approach, the impact of the military necessity factor upon the

92 *United Nations General Assembly*, Declaration of the United Nations Conference on Environment and Development (14 June 1992) UN Doc. A/CONF.151/26 (Volume 1), 31 ILM 874 (Rio Declaration).

93 *United Nations General Assembly*, Declaration of the United Nations Conference on Environment and Development (14 June 1992) UN Doc. A/CONF.151/26 (Volume 1), 31 ILM 874 (Rio Declaration), principles 23 and 24.

94 *Hourcle*, Environmental Law of War, in: Vanderbilt Law Review (2001), p. 653 (678).

95 *McManus*, Civil Liberty for Wartime Environmental Damage: Adapting the United Nations Compensation Commission for the Iraq War, in: Boston College Environmental Affairs Law Review 33 (2006), p. 417 (428).

96 *United Nations General Assembly*, Resolution 47/37 on the Protection of the environment in times of armed conflict (25 November 1992) UN Doc. A/RES/47/37, Preamble, para. 5 (emphasis added).

97 *International Court of Justice*, Legality of the Threat or Use of Nuclear Weapons (Advisory Opinion), I.C.J. Reports (1996), p. 242, para. 78 (emphasis added).

98 Rome Statute, article 8(2)(b)(iv).

current international criminal legal regime regulating intentional destruction of the environment during armed conflict, as well as the existing thresholds of permissible damage, warrant, in the opinion of this author, a more circumspect analysis. The risks associated with allowing for weak accountability mechanisms can only become graver as weapons technology continues to evolve.[99]

VI. *International Criminal Law as a Regulatory Mechanism*

It is submitted that international criminal law can play a leading role in addressing intentional destruction of the environment during armed conflict. To do so, the regulatory framework must be structured such that it does not, as is the current position, require a 'balancing test stacked heavily against the environment'.[100]

International criminal accountability on this issue results in the 'individualisation' of responsibility for intentional destruction of the environment during armed conflict, in that a guilty person(s) is held culpable without entire groups, or the State itself, deemed to be responsible.[101] This may aid in seeking external assistance to help remediate the environmental damage. International criminal law is also an appropriate form of regulation in this area because it more directly expresses the outrage that such acts give rise to as well as the imperative of global compliance with appropriate standards of behaviour.[102]

That said, the concept of an 'environmental crime' has not, until quite recently, been a point of focus in the otherwise rapid evolution of international criminal law. However, it is now accepted that international criminal law *is* an appropriate mode to deal with this issue, and it is already addressed in one provision of the Rome Statute, which is regarded by many as the most up-to-date codification of the nature and scope of international crimes, even though it does not reflect existing customary international

---

99 In this regard, see, for example, Commentary by the International Law Commission on Article 19 'Articles on State Responsibility for Internationally Wrongful Acts', in: Yearbook of the International Law Commission Part II (1976), UN Doc. A/CN.4/SER.A/1976/Add.l (Part 2), p. 96 *et seq.*

100 *Sharp* (fn. 51), p. 241.

101 Transitional Justice in the Twenty-First Century: Beyond Truth versus Justice, Roht-Arriaza/Mariezcurrena (eds.) (2006), p. 6.

102 *Cho*, Emergence of an International Environmental Criminal Law?, in: UCLA Journal of Environmental Law and Policy 19 (2001), p. 11 (13-14).

law in every respect.[103] Article 8(2)(b)(iv) of the Rome Statute provides that a war crime within the context of an international armed conflict and 'within the established framework of international law' may have been committed in the event that an accused:

> "*[i]ntentionally launch[es] an attack in the knowledge that such attack will cause [...] widespread, long-term and severe damage to the environment which would be clearly excessive in relation to the concrete and direct overall military advantage anticipated*".[104]

This specific provision draws on principles also found in the 1977 Additional Protocol I, which proscribe methods or means of warfare that are intended, or may be expected to cause 'widespread, long-term and severe' environmental damage. At the time that the 1977 Additional Protocol I was concluded, those provisions were regarded as an important step forward in acknowledging the issue of environmental damage during conflict. Article 8(2)(b)(iv) of the Rome Statute has already been considered by the respective Offices of the Prosecutor of both the ICTY and the ICC,[105] but, for various reasons, was not used as a basis of any charges in either case. In analysing claims relating to the use of cluster bombs in the situation in Iraq, Luis Moreno-Ocampo, the then Prosecutor of the ICC, concluded *inter alia* that, on the basis of the information available to his office at that time, there was 'a lack of information indicating clear excessiveness in relation to military advantage'.[106]

Tara Weinstein has suggested that the environmental pollution wrought by Saddam's forces in 1991 would probably not have been sufficient to

---

103 A Trial Chamber of the ICTY has described the Rome Statute as follows: 'Depending on the matter at issue, the Rome Statute may be taken to restate, reflect or clarify customary rules or crystallise them, whereas in some areas it creates new law or modifies existing law. At any event, the Rome Statute by and large may be taken as constituting an authoritative expression of the legal views of a great number of States': *International Criminal Tribunal for the Former Yugoslavia*, Judgment of 10 December 2998, Prosecutor v. Furundzjia, Case No. IT-95-17/1, Trial Chamber, para. 227.

104 Rome Statute, Art. 8(2)(b)(iv).

105 See, for example, Final Report to the Prosecutor of the International Criminal Tribunal for the former Yugoslavia by the Committee Established to Review the NATO Bombing Campaign Against the Federal Republic of Yugoslavia, 13 June 2000, 39 ILM 1257, para. 21; *Office of the Prosecutor*, The International Criminal Court, Iraq Response, (9 February 2006), p. 5, available under: http://www.iccnow.org/documents/OTP_letter_to_senders_re_Iraq_9_February_2006.pdf (last accessed: 4 December 2018).

106 *Office of the Prosecutor* (fn. 105), p. 6.

constitute a breach of article 13(b)(5) of the Statute of the Iraqi Special Tribunal, which, as noted, is identical with article 8(2)(b)(iv) of the Rome Statute.[107] The applicability of the existing legal regime to such acts will be the subject of detailed analysis in the remaining chapters of this book. In undertaking this examination, it will do well to bear in mind the words of the International Court of Justice:

> "[...] *one of the most effective ways of preventing criminal acts, in general, is to provide penalties for persons committing such acts, and to impose those penalties effectively on those who commit the acts one is trying to prevent*".[108]

Seen in this context, it is argued that the most appropriate mechanism of international criminal justice to prosecute such acts is the first permanent international criminal court, the ICC, acting in accordance with the terms of the Rome Statute. Moreover, this may also 'incentivise' States – at least those that have ratified the Rome Statute – to 'upgrade' their respective domestic laws, in order to ensure that their respective national courts would have jurisdiction to deal with any alleged act that constituted an international crime within the mandate of the Court, thus minimising the risk of falling within the 'unable' criteria for complementarity set out in article 17 of the Rome Statute.[109]

Although there are, undoubtedly, some uncertainties as to precisely how aspects of the complementarity principle may apply in practice, it does represent a safeguard for those States who would otherwise be concerned that its nationals would face trial before the Court.[110] Even though a number of State Parties to the Rome Statute have yet to pass appropriate implementing legislation, as the international system of criminal justice evolves and the acceptance of the ICC broadens, national governments will come under increasing pressure to recognise the international crimes

107 *Weinstein* (fn. 71), p. 710.

108 *International Court of Justice*, Judgment of 26 February 2007, Case Concerning the Application of the Convention on the Prevention and Punishment of the Crime of Genocide (Bosnia and Herzegovina v. Serbia and Montenegro) I.C.J. Reports 43 (2007), para. 426 (Application of the Genocide Convention Case).

109 Under the system of complementarity established by the Rome Statute, a case is inadmissible *inter alia* where it 'is being investigated or prosecuted by a State which has jurisdiction over it, unless that State is unwilling or unable genuinely to carry out the investigation or prosecution': Rome Statute, Art. 17(1)(a).

110 See *Goh* and *Freeland*, Australia and the International Criminal Court, in: Moens/Biffot (eds.), Convergence of Legal Systems in the 21st Century – An Australian Approach (2002), p. 285.

within their own legal systems. As has been suggested, the Rome Statute itself plays 'a powerful trendsetting role'[111] in articulating and shaping the actions of States.

It is therefore argued that a new crime, 'crimes against the environment' be included within the terms of the Rome Statute so as to create international criminal responsibility in appropriate circumstances for those who deliberately target the environment and/or natural resources as a strategy of armed conflict. This author has elsewhere elaborated on this argument and provided a detailed draft of the terms of this crime.[112]

VII. Conclusions

As a result of the author's broader research, parts of which are highlighted in this chapter, the following conclusions can be raised:

1) There is an imperative to appropriately regulate against the intentional destruction of the environment and natural resources during warfare;
2) The existing *jus in bello*, international environmental law treaties, and customary law, do not meet this imperative;
3) International criminal law is a tool that is well suited to providing the context for regulation of this issue, and can assist in a peacebuilding function post-conflict;
4) The existing provisions of the Rome Statute of the International Criminal Court – a 'trendsetting' and highly influential instrument in the area of international criminal law – are not adequate in this regard; and
5) A *sui generis* crime of 'crimes against the environment' should therefore be included in the Rome Statute of the International Criminal Court.

111 *Drumbl*, Reimagining Child Soldiers in International Law and Policy (2012), p. 121.

112 For a more detailed discussion of all of the issues canvassed in this chapter, including the author's suggestion for the terms of the crime of 'crimes against the environment' to be inserted into the Rome Statute, see *Freeland*, Addressing the Intentional Destruction of the Environment during Warfare under the Rome Statue of the International Criminal Court (2015).

Resource Mining and Law of the Sea: Evolving Issues and Challenges for the Indian State Practice

Bimal N. Patel[*]

Abstract

Resource mining in the deep seabed requires novel thinking than traditional legal and regulatory approaches. Several countries including India have been struggling to put in place a framework which not only matches the country-specific requirements but also remains compatible with the proposed framework of the International Seabed Authority (ISA). Indian exploitation of natural resources shall be based on the benefit of mankind as a whole but specifically the developing countries and shall foster commercially viable and sustainable exploitation operations. The priority shall be given to Indian operators, even at the expense of higher investment and subsidisation to contribute to their capacity-building and reap long term strategic economic and security benefits for the nation.

Overview

* Bimal N. Patel is Professor of International Law and Vice Chancellor of the Rashtriga Raksha University in Gandhinagar. He is a member of the National Security Advisory Board and a former Vice Chancellor of Gujarat National Law University in Gandhinagar from 2008–2019.

India will continue to have significant increase in demand for metal (copper, cobalt, nickel and manganese) and at the same time it is unable to afford high price due to profitability margin sought by other supplier nations and companies to procure metal at higher prices.[1] Indian companies have limited mining experience abroad, however, the recent explorations suggest that they can be encouraged to engage in high profit mining sectors in the world with the sovereign intervention and help. Furthermore, the country is experiencing a decline in the tonnage and grade of land-based nickel, copper and cobalt sulphide deposits. India is seriously considering initiating technological advancements for deep seabed mining and processing. India does not yet have any successful example seabed mining licences; however, recent licensing by Papua New Guinea to Nautilus Mining Company of Canada sets a good example for India to take a public-private partnership approach to seabed mining. Papua New Guinea gave deep seabed mining licence to Nautilus Company of Canada for territorial Bismarck Sea operations – available now to be adopted as a prototype.[2] Based on the assessment of the licence and terms of contract between Papua New Guinea and Nautilus, India can develop its own model. This model shall consider the various options: an exclusive licence to a foreign company or Indian company or a Joint Venture between Indian sovereign and foreign company or a JV between Indian sovereign and Indian company. India has recognised that ISA has approved Plans of Work for several companies, in-

---

1 According to the Indian Minerals Yearbook 2016 on nickel, released by the Indian Bureau of Mines, entire nickel demand is met through imports. Although cobalt is available in a few states, IBM lists the seabed nodules as resources for cobalt and nickel. ISA allotted 1.5 million square kilometers in the Central Indian Ocean Basin (CIOB) to India, half of which was returned after the initial survey. It is estimated that there are 380 million metric tonnes of polymetallic nodules in the CIOB. Of these, nickel makes up 4.7 mmt, copper 4.29 mmt, cobalt 0.55 mmt and manganese 92.59 mmt – reason enough for the government's ambition to harvest them. Samuel, Can India Mine Deep-Sea Resources Without Disturbing the Indian Ocean Bed Ecosystem? (2018) available at: https://india.mongabay.com/2018/02/09/can-india-mine-deep-sea-resources-without-disturbing-the-indian-ocean-seabed-ecosystem.

2 However, local communities and civil societies are fighting towards cancelling all licences given to Natulis. See, Call for Nautilus Seabed Mining Licences to be cancelled in Papua New Guinea, Deep Sea Conservation Coalition, 11 March 2019.

cluding Nauru, Tonga (Polymetallic Nodules) and China, Russia (Polymetallic Sulphides). Seventeen exploration contracts have been already approved by the ISA. The first PN exploration expired in 2016 – plan of work or action is imperative.

I. Gradual Approach to Exploitation

Like any state endowed with sea-minerals, India shall decide which option it will adopt: (a) relatively small but high-grade nodule areas with a rapid payback; (b) limited, but significant number of large and high-grade nodule occurrences or (c) similar sized deposits but of relatively low grade. These are three options; however, the available knowledge is limited within India, therefore, and strategic priority will have to decide upon an available and verifiable robust knowledge base. India may opt for the whole of the deposit approach which would include a comprehensive resources and reserve assessment of the proposed mining area, adoption of a sequential mining plan which will maximise reserve recovery, utilisation and metal recovery, provision for periodic review and updating of the mining plan and performance guarantee and failure to perform penalties with the latter escalating over time.

II. Regulatory Regime

Due to abundance of land-based mineral resources and available regulatory framework, India can largely compare its existing land-based mineral resource regulatory framework to adopt with the seabed mining. It is important that it takes into account the problems and new initiatives implemented by China, the Russian Federation and Indonesia, in particular. Environmental issues, unique technical and logistical issues are important for such consideration. However, this issue is mitigated because ISA will play the main role as the regulator. What roles, and why, India would like the ISA to play in its specific role as the regulator needs to be deliberated at this stage before other countries, especially China, the Russian Federation and other developed states take a lead. It can be assumed that China will have a supportive role towards the Indian initiatives, however, unlike other areas of cooperation, China has direct economic interests in the Indian Ocean, so India needs to be cautious in cooperation with China in this regard. Therefore, India needs to be ready with a predominantly statutory framework along with a limited standardised contract, detail site, contractor-specific and India-specific terms.

1. *Environmental Issues*

ISA is pursuing research and efforts on environmental regime. There is a need to proactively participate in this regime as the feedback from the discussions in the environmental groups will play a crucial role in developing the whole framework. One way to address this gap is to invite Indian scientists and economists working in the field of ocean resources to participate and give specific thematic inputs to the government on a regular basis. ISA has already identified specific key environmental issues which would be developed and included in the overall framework. ISA has collected a large volume of environmental data. Two fundamental issues that any government encounters are: Does India have any position on these specific environmental issues? Has India carried out an internal assessment to see whether the analysis of the data and conclusions support the long-term interests of India?

2. *Provisional Mining Licence*

ISA has proposed the following elements for provisional licence:

a. Technical, fiscal and environmental qualification of the proposed operator: India shall ensure that these elements are based on the prevailing capacity of developing countries instead of adopting the model based on the capacities of industrialised nations. Here, experiences from China could be very useful and therefore calls for bilateral cooperation.
b. Approved funding: India may consider inviting bids and provide funding.
c. A prefeasibility study: This study would be based on the contractor's previous exploration, transportation, processing and testing data, and analysis including an environmental impact assessment based upon the contractor's work during the exploration stage. While governmental institution may have carried out such study, it is imperative that more private actors are encouraged as government constraints and vision may become stumbling blocks. In any case, commercial private partners will play crucial role, so it is fitting into the scheme of current eco-

nomic developments, that private actors, after following due legal procedure, are encouraged.

Plans of work will include plans for undertaking a detailed feasibility study based upon a pilot commercial site; expenditure schedules; development schedules; mining methods; production estimates for the pilot site during the term of the provisional licences and tenured mining licence; environmental management plans including closure and rehabilitation; transportation and logistical specifics (including accident prevention) for the operation; performance assurances and guarantees; government specific terms; training and corporate social responsibility and size and area of concession. Like the International Seabed Authority Indian government would be able to determine whether based on the prefeasibility study, environmental impact assessment, economic analysis, it would be able to support the grant of a provisional mining licence to undertake a pilot commercial operation.

3. Tenured Mining Licence

Depending upon the success and effectiveness of the conclusions reached above, the next phase will be the tenured mining licence which would be conditional upon (a) successful completion of pilot commercial study under provisional licence; (b) ISA approval of a detailed bankable feasibility study and a full environmental impact assessment; (c) technical, fiscal and environmental qualifications of the proposed operator; (d) approved funding operation; (e) work plan including, *inter alia,* expenditure schedules, development schedules, mining methods, production estimate for the tenured term, environment management plan including closure and rehabilitation as well as transportation and logistics; (f) performance assurances and guarantees; (g) host and India specifics; (h) training and CSR; and (i) size and area of concession.

India needs to prepare a staged or phased licensing process including the prefeasibility study for a provisional licence to allow ISA to make an intermediate decision whether or not to allow a pilot project to fully demonstrate viability and safety, and provisional licence would provide an important measure of control and power to claw back the project should unforeseeable problems arise, without having to suspend or terminate a full-scale mining project. Licensing options shall include types of exploitation licensing such as production sharing and contractors of work and auctions for some blocks. It is pertinent to mention that the impact of the international trade and competition law needs a special study.

4. *Fiscal Regime*

Fiscal regime for deep seabed minerals will differ from land-based minerals. Detailed inter-disciplinary study, *i.e.* law and finance focusing on the setting of fiscal rates based on comparable land-based minerals, identifying tax and cost accounting codes on which fiscal calculations and concept that a simple system can be developed that does not burden the ISA or mining investors, need to be prioritised. It is unclear which royalty options other countries have adopted but the unit-based royalties based on units of volume or weight, *ad valorem* royalties based on value of sales, hybrid royalties and profit-based royalties are the most important ones. Accordingly, India needs to decide which royalty approach it wants ISA to adopt. ISA's choice will be influenced by the size and diversity of the mining operations and strength of the regulatory regime. In this regard, some critical questions require further financial research such as the question of division of profit and risk is equally important including resource rent questions about capturing windfall profits and rents in the name of social justice. Fiscal package should take care of these conflicting priorities. Can the Indian government and sea-mineral industry develop a fiscal model that is simple, equitable, transparent, defensible and responsive to change? India shall work towards ensuring that while ISA receives its fair share of resource rent after deductions, its commercial policies are not subjected to unfair advantages by industrial nations mining companies nor they shall be too in favour of host mining companies as to attract lawsuits at the WTO or under competition laws. While the arm's length principle is important, India shall closely monitor its national interests especially if it agrees with royalty-based resource rent capture scheme. While preparing the fiscal regime for marine mining, issues such as royalty, concept of economic rents, effective tax rates will be important.

5. *Corporate Social Responsibility*

India shall propose its own indigenous corporate social responsibility ('CSR') model before industrialised nations impose models suiting their needs and interests for the deep seabed mining. The ISA model emphasises specific positive social impacts and returns, and specific baseline financial returns. ISA has prepared a CSR model – the Hybrid Social Business ('HSB') on the basis of lost benefits which includes: (a) focus on sustainable development of deep seabed resources is essential to preserve the marine environment and to reduce poverty while meeting the return on investment requirements of investors; (b) HSB is directly applicable to supporting the extant ISA endowment fund for collaborative marine scientific research; (c) HSB has significant appeal to potential investors and shareholders who wish to invest in socially responsible corporations; (d) Although the model is claimed to be a win-win for ISA, industry and developing nations, a developing-country approach to the CSR/HSB is imperative. In particular, the CSR/HSB model shall have an obligatory character instead of a recommendatory nature which is widely prevalent in most international instruments; (e) the 2013 Companies Act of India is capable to provide CSR regime which suits the needs of India and shall be developed accordingly.

6. *Overall framework*

There would be a need for creation of internal mining inspectorate consisting of mining registry, compliance office, data and archive centre and inspector general office. This will be the most important strategic unit within the ISA. India shall play an active role in ensuring the composition, mandate, role and responsibilities, reporting mechanisms, overall accountability structure and rules of procedure of functioning of this unit and a Permanent Committee: for environmental rules, regulations and requirements. Thus, it is recommended to move from an *ad hoc*/standing committee to a permanent well-structured committee with liaison with the industry and stakeholders – the above observation (a) is also applicable.

7. *PN Development*

India also needs to ascertain in concrete terms the challenge of three issues namely – how much is available (resource recovery), when it can utilise resources (when) and resource sustainability. This is important to keep in mind while developing a long-term permanent sustainable program. Resource recovery: viable and bankable PN mining enterprise is a long way to go. In fact, ISA assumptions are based on the very limited number of areas that have explored in detail, large areas with limited exploration and the vast majority of the area remaining largely unexplored in terms of nodule distribution and grade. It may be noted that even Clarion Clipperton Fracture Zone (CCZ) impressive statistics are being classified as hypothetical and undiscovered resources with unknown economic potential. Compared to land-based viability, a very small percentage of the licence area will have commercially viable reserves. Unlike land-mineral resources, PN exploitation and resource recovery will proceed sequentially. This is an important reminder while developing a gradual approach framework. Mining companies will be tempted to exploit selective high grading individual mine sites – this shall be avoided. Instead, India shall assess and offer mining companies on the basis of the "whole deposit mining plan" that can ensure long-term and sustainable exploitable nodules in various grades over the life of a defined mine area.

8. *Legal Framework*

Investors can only operate within the economic reality of externally set commodity pricing and they require internal rates of return sufficient to justify the exploitation operation. While mining companies of advanced countries can afford relatively longer break-even period, heavy subsidisation of Indian mining companies is must. Hence, a proper subsidy structure has to be kept in mind throughout the progress. Certain assumptions of ISA merit a political and strategic critical review as these assumptions are tilted in favour of industrialised nations. While land-based mining experience will be very useful, the primary difference – needed to be kept in mind for the ocean bed mining – is that the international legal instruments will play a more crucial role compared to domestic laws. Various political and security risks need to be kept in mind while preparing the PN mining operation plan developed by foreign mining companies. UNCLOS is largely silent on the legal regime between a mining company and sponsoring state. Thus, the *travaux preparatoires* of the United Nations Convention on the Law of the Sea as well as Agreement relating to the implementation of Part XI of 1994 will be a useful legal guide in understanding the intentions of the developing nations. Issues such as double taxation treaties, *in rem* over the PN resources jurisdiction, overall state's jurisdiction over mining operations, state certification, which are typically applicable on land-based resources will be applicable for India in a different version, though.

India should start delineating the scope of overall ISA authority regarding the PN exploitation regime. In addition, the country could prepare the regime which would include regulations, contracts, licences and inter-linking relations between them. India shall think in clear terms the legal relationship it prefers to have between the ISA, operators, contractors, the government, sponsoring states and other third parties. India has apparently the reserving authority in place but this authority needs a clear mandate with regard to managing and safeguarding the PN resource by issuing licences and permits and to monitor, inspect and enforce the regulatory regime. A national authority (as discussed above) shall be set up to make additional rules, regulations, procedures including emergency cease and desist orders as well as the power and resources to immediately direct adequate resources to a given area under its control. While it seems that ISA would like to keep the substantial power and authority to manage, regulate and oversee the exploitation regime based on various principles, India needs to ensure that interests of developing countries are fully and completely protected while rendering the necessary authority to the ISA.

As ISA plans to work on licensing procedure in addition to the approval of work plans, India shall ensure that the licensing procedure developed by the ISA protects and promotes developing countries interests. ISA has identified 18 preliminary issues which would define the form, scope and constitute parts of the regulatory regime. Each of the issues needs to be deliberated and a preliminary set of legal rules needs to be adopted. The regulatory regime and the bilateral relationship between ISA and states significantly differ between the exploration and PN exploitation. The exploitation part will require more deliberations due to the possibility of multilateral contracts covering several jurisdictions, ISA and international legal instruments. A draft National Authority Framework and Manual to implement the Exploration and Exploitation Regime is imperative. This will enable developing and developed countries alike. The manual will address, *inter alia*, the structure, project and site-specific issues, stability and certainty of agreements and legislation, monitoring and administration, as well as enforcement issues. The ISA is also considering a Model Mining Development Agreement (MMDA). India is well advised to play a key role in development of the MMDA to protect and promote developing countries interests at this thinking stage itself. Operators from industrialised nations versus developing nations may have diametrically different interests, negotiation of package, options to transfer, convey or pledge project interests, security and stabilisation of terms, dispute resolution form and choice of law.

As International Financial Institutions (IFIs) will play a crucial role in financing the mining operations for foreign and domestic mining companies, IFIs preferences for regulatory regime and contracts will differ and hence a protected cautious careful approach is imperative. India has to decide which types of contract it prefers ISA to adopt and which types of contract it prefers for domestic companies – a one-size-fit-for-all approach although may be preferred by the ISA, but may not be most suitable for India. The same applies with regard to the concession or lease agreements, service contracts, common versus civil law system-based contracts, joint ventures, production sharing agreements, speciality and other agreements, model community development agreements. Each of these types and systems of contracts have their own pros and cons. While taking a position on any of these contractual systems, India shall keep in mind a three-tiered approach *vis-à-vis* (1) the ISA; (2) industrialised nations; and (3) developing nations or a combination of industrialised and developing nations. Security of tenures, administrative and lease fees, regime to safeguarding the resources, environmental regulations for exploration with the mining code, grant of concession via auction, tendering process and platforms, international trade issues all need an India-specific thinking at the earliest.

III. Conclusion

The Indian and select international state practice leads to the following conclusion. First, India needs to proactively contribute to the development of the overall activities framework of the ISA in view of potential PN developers and member countries that will require establishing internal ISA structure and capacity to manage PN exploitation. Second, the current taxation infrastructure needs to be prepared for incorporating rules, procedures and administrative staff, audits, legal decisions, etc. in order to determine project profits and ensure resource development and financial flows. Indian participation is imperative in the international discussion concerning the taxation structure. India needs to develop robust framework to understand cost-benefit analysis to determine sensitivity levels for fees and costs associated with PN exploitation. As the number of legal, financial, operational, administrative issues are overwhelming, India shall consider establishing ISA National Authority at the earliest to develop domestic laws and procedures but also participate in the ISA discussion with the whole-of-government coordinated approach.

Space Resources and Property Rights – Unilateral and Multilateral Approaches

Irmgard Marboe[*]

Abstract

The exploitation of space resources still faces big technical and financial challenges. Even according to optimistic estimates there will be many more years of research and preparation necessary to make it happen. Nevertheless, questions about the legality of such activities have already attracted much attention because of increased efforts by space agencies and private companies to initiate projects aiming at the exploration and eventually exploitation of natural resources of the Moon, Mars, and asteroids. The reasons for this interest are manifold. They include the argument of an alleged shortage of natural resources on Earth, the creation of new business opportunities, the facilitation of space exploration into deep space, and visions on human settlement on the Moon and on Mars. The new initiatives create important legal questions because the legal status of space resources is not clear. The Outer Space Treaty of 1967 does not explicitly address space resources but contains only general principles for the conduct of human activities in outer space. These principles allow different interpretations according to which the exploitation of space resources is allowed or, on the contrary, prohibited. Some States have taken the view that the appropriation of space resources is allowed and enacted national space legislation to authorize respective activities under their jurisdiction. Other States have criticised these unilateral initiatives and asked for a multilateral approach. This chapter will discuss the different options and show that innovative solutions are necessary to balance the right to the free use of outer space with the need to avoid conflicts and consider the interests of all countries.

* *Irmgard Marboe*, ao.Univ.-Prof. Mag. Dr., Associate Professor of International Law, University of Vienna, Austria.

Overview

I. Historical Review

The beginning of human activities aiming at the exploration and use of outer space was closely followed by the development of international legal rules governing such activities. One year after the successful launch of Sputnik 1 by the Soviet Union on 4 October 1957, the UN General Assembly passed Resolution 1348(XIII) in which it recognized that outer space should be used for peaceful purposes only and expressed its wish to avoid the extension of present national rivalries into this new field.[1] This immediate reaction was due to the "Sputnik shock" which arouse fear that outer space would become a new battlefield and add a new dimension to the arms race between the two super-powers at the time of the Cold War, the United States and the Soviet Union. The UN General Assembly, also in 1958, established the Committee on the Peaceful Uses of Outer Space (UNCOPUOS) as a body for international cooperation and information exchange and requested the UN Secretary-General to render appropriate

1 *United Nations General Assembly*, Resolution 1358(XIII) of 13 December 1958, preamble.

assistance.[2] In 1961, the UN General Assembly gave a mandate to UNCOPUOS to *"study and report on the legal problems which may arise from the exploration and use of outer space"*[3]. For this purpose, UNCOPUOS established a Legal Subcommittee dedicated to the elaboration of legal principles governing human space activities.

The first milestone was reached with the adoption of the "Declaration of Legal Principles Governing the Activities of States in the Exploration and Use of Outer Space" by the UN General Assembly in 1963.[4] It contained a set of fundamental principles which should be respected and applied by all States carrying out space activities. These principles represented the basis for the subsequent elaboration of a binding treaty, the Treaty on Principles Governing the Activities of States in the Exploration and Use of Outer Space, including the Moon and Other Celestial Bodies (Outer Space Treaty) of 1967.[5] Some of the important principles contained in the Outer Space Treaty have been the subject of further elaboration in more specialized treaties. The four subsequent treaties are the Agreement on the Rescue of Astronauts, the Return of Astronauts and the Return of Objects Launched into Outer Space (Rescue Agreement) of 1968,[6] the Convention on International Liability for Damage Caused by Space Objects (Liability Convention) of 1972,[7] the Convention on Registration of Objects Launched into Outer Space (Registration Convention) of 1975,[8] and the

---

2 *United Nations General Assembly*, Resolution 1358(XIII) of 13 December 1958, paras. 1 and 2.

3 *United Nations General Assembly*, Resolution 1721(XVI) of 20 December 1961, para. 2.

4 *United Nations General Assembly*, Declaration of Legal Principles Governing the Activities of States in the Exploration and Use of Outer Space, Resolution 1962(XVIII) of 13 December 1963.

5 Treaty on Principles Governing the Activities of States in the Exploration and Use of Outer Space, including the Moon and Other Celestial Bodies of 27 January 1967, entered into force on 10 October 1967, 610 UNTS 205.

6 Agreement on the Rescue of Astronauts, the Return of Astronauts and the Return of Objects Launched into Outer Space, opened for signature 22 April 1968, entered into force 3 December 1968, 672 UNTS 119.

7 Convention on International Liability for Damage Caused by Space Objects, opened for signature 29 March 1972, entered into force 1 September 1972, 961 UNTS 187.

8 Convention on Registration of Objects Launched into Outer Space, opened for signature 14 January 1975, entered into force 15 September 1976, 1023 UNTS 15.

Agreement Governing the Activities of States on the Moon and Other Celestial Bodies (Moon Agreement) of 1984.[9]

After this period of treaty-making, the UNCOPUOS Legal Subcommittee addressed legal issues connected to new technological, political, and economic developments which resulted in a series of "Principles" resolutions. Between 1982 and 1996, the UN General Assembly adopted the "Broadcasting Principles",[10] the "Remote Sensing Principles",[11] the "Nuclear Power Principles",[12] and the "Benefits Declaration".[13] Further technological progress and the increased privatization and commercialization of space activities raised new legal questions. Three UN General Assembly resolutions containing recommendations in this context should be highlighted, namely the Resolution elaborating the concept of the *"launching State"*,[14] the Resolution enhancing the practice of States in registering space objects,[15] and the Resolution on recommendations on national space legislation.[16] In addition, the Resolution endorsing the Space Debris Mitigation Guidelines developed by the Committee on the Peaceful Uses of Outer Space[17] should be mentioned as evidence of the increasing problem

9 Agreement Governing the Activities of States on the Moon and Other Celestial Bodies, opened for signature on 18 December 1979, entered into force on 11 July 1984, 18 ILM 1434, 1383 UNTS 3.

10 *United Nations General Assembly*, The Principles Governing the Use by States of Artificial Earth Satellites for International Direct Television Broadcasting, Resolution 37/92 of 10 December 1982.

11 *United Nations General Assembly*, The Principles Relating to Remote Sensing of the Earth from Outer Space, Resolution 41/65 of 3 December 1986.

12 *United Nations General Assembly*, The Principles Relevant to the Use of Nuclear Power Sources in Outer Space, Resolution 47/68 of 14 December 1992.

13 *United Nations General Assembly*, The Declaration on International Cooperation in the Exploration and Use of Outer Space for the Benefit and in the Interest of All States, Taking into Particular Account the Needs of Developing Countries, Resolution 51/122 of 13 December 1996.

14 *United Nations General Assembly*, Application of the concept of the "launching State", Resolution 59/115 of 12 December 2004.

15 *United Nations General Assembly*, Recommendations on enhancing the practice of States and international intergovernmental organizations in registering space objects, Resolution 62/101 of 17 December 2007.

16 *United Nations General Assembly*, Recommendations on national legislation relevant to the peaceful exploration and use of outer space, Resolution 68/74 of 11 December 2013.

17 *United Nations General Assembly*, Resolution 62/217 of 22 December 2007, para. 26.

of space debris present in outer space, which endangers the long-term sustainability of outer space activities.[18]

On the basis of this framework the new initiatives aiming at the exploration and eventual exploitation and ownership of space resources by space agencies or private companies shall be assessed with respect to their legal and regulatory aspects.

II. The Exploitation of Space Resources and Their Legal Challenges

The exploitation of space resources still faces big technical and financial challenges. Even according to optimistic estimates there will be many more years of research and preparation necessary to make it happen.[19] Against this backdrop the discussion about property rights in outer space has some surreal connotation.[20] While the issue of ownership of "plots on the Moon" has meanwhile been clarified as nonsense and legally null and

---

18 The long-term sustainability of outer space activities is an important topic on the agenda of UNCOPUOS since 2010. At the fifty-ninth session of the Committee, in June 2016, a first set of guidelines for the long-term sustainability of outer space activities was agreed upon (*United Nations General Assembly*, Report of the Committee on the Peaceful Uses of Outer Space (2016), A/71/20, Annex). In 2018, consensus was reached on a preamble and nine additional guidelines (*United Nations General Assembly*, Report of the Scientific and Technical Subcommittee on its fifty-fifth session, held in Vienna from 29 January to 9 February 2018, A/AC.105/1167, Annex III). The last step in this process was the agreement on a preamble and 21 guidelines in June 2019 (*United Nations General Assembly*, Report of the Committee on the Peaceful Uses of Outer Space on its Sixty-second Session (2019), A/74/20, para. 163 and Annex II). Nevertheless, the topic remained on the agenda of UNCPUOS, which should discuss the implementation and review of the guidelines. It decided that a working group under the Scientific and Technical Subcommittee should be established (see ibid, para. 165). See *United Nations Office for Outer Space Affairs*, Long-term Sustainability of Outer Space Activities, available under: http://www.unoosa.org/oosa/en/ourwork/topics/long-term-sustainability-of-outer-space-activities.html (last accessed: 8 May 2021).

19 Taylor, The Asteroid Boom, in: Mashable (2019), available at: https://mashable.com/feature/asteroid-mining-space-economy/?europe=true (last accessed: 8 May 2021); Abrahamian, How the Asteroid-Mining Bubble Burst (26 June 2019) in: MIT Technology Review (July 2019), available at: https://www.technologyreview.com/2019/06/26/134510/asteroid-mining-bubble-burst-history/ (last accessed: 8 May 2021).

20 See for example *von der Dunk et al.*, Surreal Estate: Addressing the Issue of "Immovable Property Rights on the Moon", in: Space Policy 20 (2004), p. 149 (149 *et seqq.*).

void,[21] the question whether the resources of the Moon and other celestial bodies can be appropriated is less clear. It also appears not any more mere surreal in view of increased attempts by space agencies and private companies to explore and eventually also to exploit such resources.[22] Even if the realization of such plans has seen some setbacks and proceeds slowlier than expected,[23] certainty about the legality of space resource activities is required earlier, as otherwise planning and financing cannot continue. It is therefore important to know, the sooner the better, whether and under which conditions the exploration and exploitation of space resources will legally be possible.

The Outer Space Treaty of 1967 represents the most important legal framework governing human activity in outer space and sets out the main "Principles Governing the Activities of States in the Exploration and Use of Outer Space, including the Moon and Other Celestial Bodies", as its full title says.[24] It is ratified by a large number of States, including the most relevant space faring countries,[25] and its main provisions are generally accepted as representing customary international law.[26] Yet, the Outer Space Treaty does not contain any specific rule on the legal status of space resources. By contrast, the treaty which explicitly deals with the exploitation

---

21 See *von der Dunk et al.*, Surreal Estate: Addressing the Issue of "Immovable Property Rights on the Moon", in: Space Policy 20 (2004), p. 149 (149 *et seqq.*), and *International Institute of Space Law*, Statement by the IISL Board of Directors on claims to property rights regarding the Moon and other celestial bodies (2004), available under: https://iislweb.org/statement-by-the-iisl-board-of-directors-on-claims-to-property-rights-regarding-the-moon-and-other-celestial-bodies/ (last accessed: 8 May 2021); see also *International Institute of Space Law*, Further statement by the IISL Board of Directors on claims to lunar property rights (2009), available under: https://iislweb.org/further-statement-by-the-iisl-board-of-directors-on-claims-to-lunar-property-rights/ (last accessed: 8 May 2021).

22 See further below, at section II.2.

23 In the US, the two pioneer companies, Planetary Resources and Deep Space Industries, were taken over, in 2018 and 2019 respectively, by other companies, whose interest in the continuation of space resource exploration and exploitation is uncertain. See below (fn. 47).

24 Treaty on Principles Governing the Activities of States in the Exploration and Use of Outer Space, including the Moon and Other Celestial Bodies of 27 January 1967, entered into force on 10 October 1967, 610 UNTS 205.

25 110 ratifications as of 1 January 2020, see *Committee on the Peaceful Uses of Outer Space*, Status of International Agreements relating to activities in outer space as at 1 January 2020, available at: https://www.unoosa.org/documents/pdf/spacelaw/treatystatus (last accessed: 8 May 2021).

26 *Lyall/Larsen*, Space Law, A Treatise (2nd edition 2018), pp. 50-52.

of natural resources of celestial bodies, the Moon Agreement of 1979,[27] has received only a few ratifications and is not widely accepted.[28] In view of this uncertainty and in response to an increased interest of commercial and other actors two countries have enacted national space legislation addressing specific legal issues related to activities aiming at the exploration and use of space resources, namely the United States[29] and Luxemburg.[30]

In the following, it will be analysed to what extent these unilateral initiatives at the national level are in accordance with international law, most importantly with the principles set out in the Outer Space Treaty, and whether they may provide legal certainty. This will be contrasted with arguments for a multilateral approach aiming at the resolution of the problem uncertainty and avoiding future conflicts. Before this discussion, a short overview will be given about allegedly existing natural resources on the Moon and other celestial bodies, and about recent initiatives aiming at exploring or exploiting them.

1. *Valuable Resources on the Moon and other Celestial Bodies*

Scientific research suggests that the Moon and asteroids contain natural resources that are valuable for humankind, in particular in view of the increasing need for such resources on Earth with its growing population and declining reserves.[31] The Moon, in particular, has created interest for the so-called lunar regolith – the dust layer on its surface – and the Helium 3 it contains, an isotope of helium that can be used for the generation of non-polluting energy in large quantities.[32] While the nuclear fusion reactors which would be needed for this to happen are not developed sufficiently

---

27 Agreement Governing the Activities of States on the Moon and Other Celestial Bodies, opened for signature on 18 December 1979, entered into force on 11 July 1984, 18 ILM 1434, 1383 UNTS 3.

28 18 ratifications as of 1 January 2020, see *Committee on the Peaceful Uses of Outer Space*, Status of International Agreements relating to activities in outer space as at 1 January 2020, https://www.unoosa.org/documents/pdf/spacelaw/treatystatus (last accessed: 8 May 2021).

29 Commercial Space Launch Competitiveness Act of 25 November 2015, H.R. 2262, Title IV, Space Resource Exploration and Utilization Act.

30 Loi sur l'exploration et l'utilisation des ressources de l'éspace, 20 July 2017, Official Journal of the Grand Duchy of Luxembourg of 28 July 2017.

31 *Jakhu/Pelton/Nyampong*, Space Mining and Its Regulation (2017), pp. 15-18.

32 *Bilder*, A Legal Regime for the Mining of Helium-3 on the Moon: U.S. Policy Options, in: Fordham International Law Journal 33 (2009), p. 243 (246 *et seq.*).

yet, fusion energy could allegedly reduce the world's dependences on fossil fuels and nuclear fission reactors.[33] Furthermore, the Moon contains significant resources in its crust, such as uranium, thorium, potassium, oxygen, silicon, magnesium, iron, titanium, calcium, aluminium, and hydrogen.[34] The lunar soil supposedly preserves important platinum-group metals, such as platinum, palladium, osmium, and iridium.[35] The detection of ice-water reserves in some of the Moon's craters has further created incentives for returning to the Moon, even with the purpose of human settlement.[36]

Asteroids are also composed of material that can be valuable for human life depending on their composition. Near-Earth asteroids may contain large amounts of platinum, iron, and nickel.[37]

While respective research is still ongoing and only a few exploration missions have so far returned material in small quantities, the promising prospects continue to motivate scientists and entrepreneurs to continue evaluating ways for the eventual exploitation of resources of the Moon and other celestial bodies.

2. *Recent Initiatives by Space Agencies and Private Companies*

The Moon and other celestial bodies are the target of various scientific missions of national space agencies and the European Space Agency (ESA) in

---

33 *Bilder*, A Legal Regime for the Mining of Helium-3 on the Moon: U.S. Policy Options, in: Fordham International Law Journal 33 (2009), p. 243 (247); see also *Schmitt*, Return to the Moon: Exploration, Enterprise, and Energy in the Human Settlement of Space (2006), pp. 25 *et seqq.*; see also *Tronchetti*, The Exploitation of Natural Resources of the Moon and Other Celestial Bodies (2009), pp. 5 *et seq.*; sceptical however *Crawford*, Lunar Resources: A Review, in: Progress in Physical Geography 39 (2015), p. 136 (136 *et seqq.*).

34 See *Tronchetti*, Legal Aspects of Space Resource Utilization, in: von der Dunk/Tronchetti (eds.), Handbook of Space Law (2015), p. 771 with further references.

35 See *Tronchetti*, Legal Aspects of Space Resource Utilization, in: von der Dunk/Tronchetti (eds.), Handbook of Space Law (2015), p. 771. See also *Crawford*, Lunar Resources: A Review, in: Progress in Physical Geography 39 (2015), p. 136 (140-145).

36 *Crotts*, The New Moon, Water, Exploration, and Future Habitation (2014), pp. 227 *et seqq.*

37 See *Tronchetti*, Legal Aspects of Space Resource Utilization, in: von der Dunk/Tronchetti (eds.), Handbook of Space Law (2015), p. 772; *Elvis*, Prospecting Asteroid Resources, in: Badescu (ed.), Asteroids, Prospective Energy and Material Resources (2013), p. 81, 88 *et seqq.*

order to investigate the physical nature and composition of the soil. While science and research is in the focus of the respective programmes and projects, the space agencies are increasingly open to other actors and encourage private engagement. It is not a secret that these would not always satisfy themselves with mere research activities but also look for new business opportunities. The combination of science projects with commercial aims is not new in the space sector. On the contrary, many programmes have been developed by space agencies and eventually lead to profitable businesses. The commercial communication satellite industry is one of the best examples. Such a result is frequently not only welcomed but even intended. In view of this, the recent initiatives by space agencies to return to the Moon and to explore asteroids may not coincidently lead to commercial activities by private entities.

The US lunar programme, with its launch of the Lunar Reconnaissance Orbiter in 2009, aims at the study of the physical nature of the polar regions of the Moon.[38] China's Moon exploration programme Chang-e, carried out by the Chinese National Space Agency CNSA, achieved a remarkable success with the landing of Chang-e 4 on the far side of the Moon on 2 January 2019.[39] In 2007, Japan's JAXA launched the Selene mission whose purpose is to analyze the Moon's origin and physical conditions and to find out whether there are potential sites for lunar base construction.[40] The Indian Space Research Organisation ISRO launched its mission to the

---

38 See *Nasa*, Lunar Reconnaissance Orbiter, available under: https://lunar.gsfc.nasa.gov/science.html (last accessed: 8 May 2021). The Lunar Reconnaissance Orbiter (LRO) sends images from the lunar surface to Earth on a regular basis. After a change in the US administration a more ambitious lunar programme was cancelled in 2010, but the White House Space Policy Directive 1 of December 2017 provided for a U.S.-led, integrated programme with private sector partners which shall enable human return to the Moon, followed by missions to Mars and beyond. See *Nasa*, New Space Policy Directive Calls for Human Expansion Across Solar System (11 December 2017), available under: https://www.nasa.gov/press-release/new-space-policy-directive-calls-for-human-expansion-across-solar-system (last accessed: 8 May 2021).

39 See *Space.com*, Photos from the Moon's Far Side! China's Chang'e Lunar Landing in Pictures (3 January 2019), available under: https://www.space.com/42887-china-moon-far-side-landing-photos-chang-e-4.html (last accessed: 8 May 2021).

40 In 2017, the research team published its finding that intact lava tubes, shielded from the hostile outside environment, offer potential sites for lunar base construction. See *Japan Aerospace Exploration Agency*, SELENE: SELenological and ENgineering Explorer "KAGUYA", available under: https://global.jaxa.jp/projects/sas/selene/ (last accessed: 8 May 2021). See also *Tronchetti*, The Exploitation of Natural Resources of the Moon and Other Celestial Bodies (2009), p. 3.

Moon, Chandrayaan-1, in 2008 to get a better knowledge of the minerals contained on the Moon and to facilitate the future permanent presence of human beings on its surface.[41] ESA completed its Rosetta-mission to the comet 67P/Churyumov-Gerasimenko in 2016.[42] The successful landing of the lander Philae in 2014 can be regarded as an important milestone for the future landing of instruments aiming at the exploitation of asteroid resources.

In addition to these efforts by space agencies, private companies have started to engage in the study of Moon and asteroid resources for the purpose of exploration and future commercial exploitation.[43] The US pioneer companies included Planetary Resources, based in Redmond, Washington,[44] and Deep Space Industries, based in San José, California.[45] The company iSpace was founded in Japan and later opened offices in the United States and in Luxembourg.[46] Maxar Technologies (USA), the Asteroid Mining Corporation (UK), Stellar Space Industries (NL) and Gedex Sstems Inc (CAN) are other examples of companies dedicated to the exploration and exploitation of lunar or asteroid resources. They all form part of the so-called "New Space" industry, start-ups with highly innovative ideas but risky when it comes to funding and sustainable business plans.[47]

41 See *Datta and Chakravarty*, Chandrayaan-1. India's First Mission to the Moon (2008), available under: https://www.issdc.gov.in/docs/ch1/Chandrayaan-1.pdf (last accessed: 8 May 2021). See also *Tronchetti*, The Exploitation of Natural Resources of the Moon and Other Celestial Bodies (2009), pp. 2-3. The follow-up mission Chandrayaan-2 was launched in July 2019 and reached lunar orbit in August 2019. During the landing attempt in early September 2019, contact with the Moon lander was lost. *Howell*, Chandrayaan-2: India's Orbiter-Lander-Rover Mission (8 October 2019), available under https://www.space.com/40136-chandrayaan-2.html (last accessed: 8 May 2021).

42 See *European Space Agency*, Comet 67P/Churyumov-Gerasimenko, available under; https://www.esa.int/Our_Activities/Space_Science/Rosetta/Comet_67P_Churyumov-Gerasimenko (last accessed: 8 May 2021).

43 See *Jakhu/Pelton/Nyampong*, Space Mining and Its Regulation (2017), pp. 3-6.

44 *Lewicki et al.*, Planetary Resources—The Asteroid Mining Company, in: New Space 1 (2013), p. 105 (105 *et seqq.*).

45 *Shaer*, The Miner's Guide to the Galaxy, in: Foreign Policy (May/June 2016), p. 44 (44–51).

46 See the company's website, available under: https://ispace-inc.com/ (last accessed: 8 May 2021).

47 See *Jakhu/Pelton/Nyampong*, Space Mining and Its Regulation (2017), pp. 3-6. However, Planetary Resources was acquired by ConsenSys, Inc., a blockchain venture production studio in October 2018, and Deep Space Industries was acquired by Bradford Space, Inc. in January 2019. It is not certain whether the new owners will continue space resource exploration and exploitation. See *Abrahamian*, How

3. The International Legal Framework

The most important obstacle against space resource exploitation and property rights on space resources can be seen in the principle of "non-appropriation" as contained in Article II of the Outer Space Treaty:

> *"Outer space, including the Moon and other celestial bodies, is not subject to national appropriation by claim of sovereignty, by means of use or occupation, or by any other means."*

While it is generally accepted that this principle prohibits claims of sovereignty and thus appropriation of outer space or (parts) of celestial bodies as such,[48] there is no agreement whether it also prohibits the appropriation of space resources.[49] Such activities could arguably be covered by the principle of "free use" which is contained in Article I of the Outer Space Treaty and provides that outer space, including the Moon and other celestial bodies, *"shall be free for exploration and use by all States"*.[50] This "freedom of outer space", similar to the "freedom of the high seas" in the law of the sea as stipulated in the United Nations Convention on the Law of the Sea of 1982 (UNCLOS),[51] represents a fundamental principle of space law. However, the exercise of this "freedom" is considerably limited by other provisions of the Outer Space Treaty, as Article I in its first paragraph sets out:

> *"The exploration and use of outer space, including the Moon and other celestial bodies, shall be carried out for the benefit and in the interests of all*

---

the Asteroid-Mining Bubble Burst (26 June 2019), in: MIT Technology Review (July 2019), available at: https://www.technologyreview.com/2019/06/26/134510/asteroid-mining-bubble-burst-history/ (last accessed: 8 May 2021).

48 *Freeland/Jakhu*, in: Hobe/Schmidt-Tedd/Schrogl (eds.), Cologne Commentary on Space Law, Volume 1 (2009), Article II, pp. 49 *et seqq*.

49 *Hobe*, Space Law (2019) 70-71; *Hobe / Chen*, Legal Status of Outer Space and Celestial Bodies, in: *Jakhu / Dempsey* (eds.), Routledge Handbook of Space Law (2017) p. 25 (29-30).

50 *Su*, Legality of Unilateral Exploitation of Space Resources Under International Law, in: International and Comparative Law Quarterly 66 (2017) p. 991 (999-1001).

51 See, most importantly, Article 87 UN Convention on the Law of the Sea, according to which the freedom of the high seas is open to all States, whether coastal or land-locked, and includes, for example, the freedom of fishing and of scientific research. See also *Treves*, High Seas, in: Max Planck Encyclopedia of Public International Law (ed.), available under: http://opil.ouplaw.com (last accessed: 8 May 2021) (last updated: January 2009).

> *countries, irrespective of their degree of economic or scientific development, and shall be the province of all mankind."*

It is not clear what "the benefit and the interest of all countries" really are, but the formulation indicates that space activities should not be planned and carried out in the interest or to the benefit of only one State or a few States – presumably wealthy and developed ones who are in the position to invest and engage in space activities.[52] Article IX of the Outer Space Treaty, first sentence, formulates a principle of "due regard" even more explicitly which requires taking into account the interests of other countries including present and future space faring nations:

> *"In the exploration and use of outer space, including the Moon and other celestial bodies, States Parties to the Treaty shall be guided by the principle of co-operation and mutual assistance and shall conduct all their activities in outer space, including the moon and other celestial bodies, with due regard to the corresponding interests of all other States Parties to the Treaty."*

The concept of "the province of all mankind" in the first paragraph of Article I of the Outer Space Treaty lacks clarity, also because of diverse formulations in other authentic languages.[53] Whether it is comparable to the similar sounding principle of the "common heritage of mankind" stipulated in Article 11 (1) of the Moon Agreement,[54] is contested.[55] According to the Moon Agreement, the exploitation of the natural resources of the

52 *Hobe*, in: *Hobe/Schmidt-Tedd/Schrogl* (eds.), Cologne Commentary on Space Law, Volume 1 (2009), Article I, pp. 36 *et seqq*.; *Su*, Legality of Unilateral Exploitation of Space Resources Under International Law, in: International and Comparative Law Quarterly 66 (2017) p. 991 (1002-1003); *Feichtner*, Mining for Humanity in the Deep Sea and Outer Space: The Role of Small States and International Law in the Extraterritorial Expansion of Extraction, in: Leiden Journal of International Law 32 (2019) p. 255 (265-266).

53 In French, it reads: *"L'exploration et la utilisation de l'espace.... sont l'apanage de l'humanité toute entière."* The formulation in Spanish is *"[…] e incumben a toda la humanidad."*

54 See Article 11 (1) of the Moon Agreement: *"The Moon and its natural resources are the common heritage of mankind, which finds its expression in the provisions of this Agreement, in particular in paragraph 5 of this article."*

55 See *Tronchetti*, The Commercial Exploitation of the Natural Resources of the Moon and Other Celestial Bodies: What Role for the Moon Agreement?, in: International Institute of Space Law (ed.), Proceedings of the International Institute of Space Law 2010 (2011), p. 614 (614-624).

Moon is permitted,[56] but an international regime to regulate space resource activities must be developed, as paragraph 5 of Article 11 stipulates:

> *"States Parties to this Agreement hereby undertake to establish an international regime, including appropriate procedures, to govern the exploitation of the natural resources of the Moon as such exploitation is about to become feasible. [...]."*

This situation is similar to the law of the sea under UNCLOS, according to which the deep seabed and its resources are also qualified as the "common heritage of mankind".[57] The minerals recovered from the deep seabed may only be alienated in accordance with international rules, regulations and procedures of the Deep Seabed Authority.[58]

An important provision with respect to private space activities is Article VI of the Outer Space Treaty, which provides for the "international responsibility" of States for their national activities in outer space and requires that they are authorized and continuously supervised:

> *"States Parties to the Treaty shall bear international responsibility for national activities in outer space, including the moon and other celestial bodies, whether such activities are carried on by governmental agencies or by non-governmental entities, and for assuring that national activities are carried out in conformity with the provisions set forth in the present Treaty. The activities of non-governmental entities in outer space, including the moon and other celestial bodies, shall require authorization and continuing supervision by the appropriate State Party to the Treaty. [...]."*

This provision is essential for ensuring that all space activities, private or governmental, are conducted in conformity with the provisions of the

---

56 *Jakhu et al.*, in: *Hobe/Schmidt-Tedd/Schrogl* (eds.), Cologne Commentary on Space Law, Volume 2 (2013), Article 11 Moon Agreement, pp. 396 *et seqq*.

57 See Article 136 UNCLOS. However, the clarification of what this actually means needed some time, so that UNCLOS could only enter into force in 1994, when the Implementation Agreement of Part XI of UNCLOS was finalized and ratified by a sufficient number of State parties.

58 According to Article 137, para. 2 UNCLOS. However, in view of the specific context this issue was discussed at the 3rd UN Conference on the Law of the Sea and subsequently elaborated in the Implementation Agreement of Part XI of UNCLOS, it is arguable that the concept has a special meaning for the scope of UNCLOS which cannot simply be transferred to the Moon Agreement. See also *Wolfrum*, Common Heritage of Mankind, in: Max Planck Encyclopedia of Public International Law (ed.), available under: http://opil.ouplaw.com (last accessed: 8 May 2021) (last updated: November 2009).

Outer Space Treaty.[59] In case of uncertainty, the State must take a decision to allow or prohibit the space activity and bear the consequences on the international level.

Even though outer space in general is not subject to national jurisdiction, States have the right to exercise jurisdiction over space objects carried in their national registry of space objects, which can be regarded as a form of active personal jurisdiction.[60] Art. VIII of the Outer Space Treaty allows them to prescribe certain behaviour of their space actors:

> *"A State Party to the Treaty on whose registry an object launched into outer space is carried shall retain jurisdiction and control over such object, and over any personnel thereof, while in outer space or on a celestial body."*

This brief overview of relevant provisions in the international space law shows that States have the right and – in view of Article VI of the Outer Space Treaty – even an obligation to regulate space activities at the national level. However, it is controversial whether this includes the authorization of activities in outer space the lawfulness of which is uncertain and, in particular, the granting of property rights on space resources.

4. *Unilateral Regulatory Initiatives at the National Level*

In response to an emerging interest of private companies in engaging in the discovery and eventual exploitation of space resources,[61] the United States engaged in the development of national legislation to create a legal framework for such activities. After an unsuccessful attempt of an "Asteroid Act" in 2014,[62] the "Commercial Space Launch Competitiveness Act" which amended and complemented several aspects of US national space legislation included, as its Part IV, the "Space Resource Exploration and

---

59 *Gerhard*, in: *Hobe/Schmidt-Tedd/Schrogl* (eds.), Cologne Commentary on Space Law, Volume 1 (2009), Article VI, pp. 111 *et seqq.*

60 *Hobe/de Man*, National Appropriation of Outer Space and State Jurisdiction to Regulate the Exploitation, Exploration and Utilization of Space Resources, in: German Journal of Air and Space Law 66 (2017), p. 460 (469).

61 See above, II.2.

62 American Space Technology for Exploring Resource Opportunities in Deep Space Act, H.R.5063 – 113th Congress. For a preliminary assessment see *Tronchetti*, Private Property Rights on Asteroid Resources: Assessing the Legality of the Asteroids Act, in: Space Policy 30 (2014), p. 193 (193 *et seqq.*).

Utilization Act"[63] which entered into force in November 2015. As a reaction to these developments in the United States, Luxembourg initiated its "SpaceResources.lu" to provide a legal, regulatory, and business environment enabling private investors and companies to explore and use space resources in Europe.[64] After circulating a draft text in 2016,[65] the Luxembourg Law on the Exploration and Utilization of Space Resources was enacted in July 2017.[66]

These two national acts on space resources triggered a debate among experts and practitioners about the conformity with international law of such national legislation, in particular with the Outer Space Treaty.

a) *The US Commercial Space Launch Competitiveness Act*

The purpose of Title IV, the Space Resource Exploration and Utilization Act, of the US Act is foremost to establish a reliable legal framework for space resources activities and to encourage entrepreneurship. Accordingly, § 51302 of the Act provides:

> "(a) *In GENERAL – The President, acting through appropriate Federal agencies shall*
>
> (1) *facilitate commercial exploration for and commercial recovery of space resources by United States citizen;*
>
> (2) *discourage government barriers to the development in the United States of economically viable, safe, and stable industries for commercial exploration for and commercial recovery of space resources in manners consistent with the international obligations of the United States; and*
>
> (3) *promote the right of the United States citizens to engage in commercial exploration for and commercial recovery of space resources free from harmful interference, in accordance with the international obligations of the United States and subject to authorization and continuing supervision of the Federal Government."*

63 Commercial Space Launch Competitiveness Act of 25 November 2015, H.R. 2262, Title IV, Space Resource Exploration and Utilization Act.

64 See the website of SpaceResources.lu, available under: https://spaceresources.public.lu/en.html (last accessed: 8 May 2021).

65 See *Economic Commission of the Parliament of Luxembourg*, Report No. 7093 of 6 July 2017.

66 Loi sur l'exploration et l'utilisation des resources de l'éspace, 20 July 2017, Official Journal of the Grand Duchy of Luxembourg of 28 July 2017.

These obligations of the President aim at facilitating the commercial recovery of space resources, but also explicitly refer to the international obligations of the United States, which must not be violated. The authorization and continuing supervision by the Federal Government, a literal reflection of the formulation of Article VI of the Outer Space Treaty, can be regarded as an indication that the authority will exercise its task in a way that ensures that the commercial activities will be in accordance with international law.[67] However, the next provision of the Act goes further and explicitly grants property rights over the recovered space resources. § 51303 reads:

> *"A United States citizen engaged in commercial recovery of an asteroid resource or a space resource under this chapter shall be entitled to any asteroid resource or space resource obtained, including to possess, own, transport, use, and sell the asteroid resource or space resource obtained in accordance with applicable law, including the international obligations of the United States."*

It depends on the interpretation of the non-appropriation principle in Article II of the Outer Space Treaty, whether the United States has the right to accord such ownership rights or not. According to the US legislator, the ownership over space resources is distinct from ownership rights over a celestial body or parts thereof. Section 403 of the Act reads in this respect:

> *"It is the sense of Congress that by the enactment of this Act, the United States does not thereby assert sovereignty or sovereign or exclusive rights or jurisdiction over, or the ownership of, any celestial body."*

At first sight, the Act seems to assume the right of the United States to grant property rights on space resources straightforward. However, the repeated reference to the international obligations of the United States also entails the possibility that the Federal agency, in exercising its authorizing and supervising function, takes into account international efforts and agreements providing for conditions under which such ownership rights are granted and protected. [68] It is thus possible that the implementation of the US Act can be brought in line with an international legal regime governing the exploitation of space resources, depending on the success of multilateral efforts in this respect. On the other hand, it seems to be the

---

67 *Tronchetti*, The Space Resource Exploration and Utilization Act: A move forward or a step back?, in: Space Policy 34 (November 2015), p. 6 (6 *et seqq.*).

68 *Su*, Legality of Unilateral Exploitation of Space Resources Under International Law, in: International and Comparative Law Quarterly 66 (2017) p. 991 (999).

position of the United States that, as long as such efforts are not successful, it may proceed unilaterally and grant such property rights. It will then depend on the reaction of other States whether such property rights will be recognized and protected.

b) *The Luxembourg Law on the Exploration and Utilization of Space Resources*

The development of the Luxembourg Law on the Exploration and Utilization of Space Resources is remarkable as it included an international consultation process whereby a first draft text was translated into English and circulated among interested experts and governments with the invitation for comments.[69] Article 1 of the first draft text stipulated: "*Space resources are capable of being appropriated in accordance with international law.*"

The formulation of this provision reminds of the US approach to grant property rights on space resources under the conditions of international law, if any. The report annexed to the draft text provided a detailed explanation of why the national commercial exploitation of space resources complies with international law. As a preliminary point, it emphasizes that even the Civil Code, which was enacted in 1804 (still valid in Luxembourg today), states that the ownership of mines can fall apart with the ownership of the surface. In addition, it is argued that one can draw an analogy between the resources of the sea ("fish and shellfish") which is used in a commentary on French Civil Law of 1878 (by *Francois Laurent*).[70] Furthermore, the report states that Article II of the Outer Space Treaty prohibits national appropriation of celestial bodies, but is silent on the question of resources. In that vein, Article 1 of the draft text only speaks of the exploitation of space resources without claiming possession of the celestial bodies. In addition, it highlights that exploitation is open to all States in accordance with Article I para. 2 of the Outer Space Treaty. Interestingly, the report does not mention the equally conceivable analogy between resource exploitation in space and resource exploitation in the deep seabed,

---

69 Projet de loi sur l'exploration et l'utilisation des ressources de l'espace, Projet de Loi No 7093, presented to the Parliament on 15 November 2016; see also the English translation, Draft law on the Exploration and Use of Space Resources, dated 11 November 2016.

70 Projet de loi sur l'exploration et l'utilisation des ressources de l'espace, Projet de Loi No 7093, presented to the Parliament on 15 November 2016; see also the English translation, Draft law on the Exploration and Use of Space Resources, dated 11 November 2016.

which is considered the "common heritage of mankind" and subject to an international regime that prohibits purely national mining.[71]

After a series of consultations with various commissions and committees, including the State Council, the law was presented to the parliament for adoption in July 2017 and entered into force on 1 August 2017.[72] Interestingly, Article 1 had been changed during consultation process, and the final text now reads: "*Space resources are capable of being appropriated.*"

The explanation of this surprising change can be found in the criticism by the State Council, which opined that, since international law would be above national law anyway, such a reference would be superfluous or questionable.[73] The reference was therefore moved to Article 2 (3), according to which space resources exploitation need prior authorisation, which is to be given to the applicant under certain conditions and in accordance with the international obligations of Luxembourg. Article 2 (3) shall therefore ensure that Luxembourg complies with its obligations under the Outer Space Treaty, including the principle of "due regard" with respect to the corresponding interests of other countries and the prohibition of harmful contamination of the outer space environment.[74]

The removal of the explicit reference to international law remains nevertheless surprising as the current formulation gives the impression that Luxembourg asserts the right to legislate on the legal status of space resources, which is in contradiction to Article II of the Outer Space Treaty.[75] The rather hidden and complicated construction through the authorization process cannot be deemed fortunate. That the national authority must comply with international law in the authorization process is different from the obligation of the legislator not to enact a law, which is contrary

71 See *Feichtner,* Mining for Humanity in the Deep Sea and Outer Space: The Role of Small States and International Law in the Extraterritorial Expansion of Extraction, in: Leiden Journal of International Law 32 (2019) p. 255 (265).

72 See *Economic Commission*, Report of 6 July 2017, Projet de loi sur l'exploration et l'utilisation des ressources de l'espace, Projet de Loi No 7093.

73 *Economic Commission*, Report of 6 July 2017, Projet de loi sur l'exploration et l'utilisation des ressources de l'espace, Projet de Loi No 7093, pp. 3-4.

74 *Hofmann / Bergamasco,* Space Resources Activities from the Perspective of Sustainability: Legal Aspects, in: Global Sustainability 3 (2020) p. 1 (3-4).

75 See the criticism by *Hobe/de Man*, National Appropriation of Outer Space and State Jurisdiction to Regulate the Exploitation, Exploration and Utilization of Space Resources, in: German Journal of Air and Space Law 66 (2017), p. 460 (468); *Feichtner,* Mining for Humanity in the Deep Sea and Outer Space: The Role of Small States and International Law in the Extraterritorial Expansion of Extraction, in: Leiden Journal of International Law 32 (2019) p. 255 (265-266).

to international law. In contrast to the apparent assumption of the State Council, a national law, which violates international law is not by itself null and void, but must be corrected or set aside.

On the other hand, Luxembourg is engaged in promoting the development of a multilateral legal regime on the exploitation of space resources. It has actively participated in various pertinent multilateral fora and recently signed a bilateral declaration with Belgium, an active State party to the Moon Agreement, to collaborate on the development of an international framework for the exploration and utilisation of space resources.[76]

5. *Multilateral Approaches*

a) *The Outer Space Treaty*

The uncertainty about property rights on space resources stems primarily from the unclear relationship between paragraphs 1 and 2 of Article I, Article II, and Article IX of the Outer Space Treaty. The State parties to the Outer Space Treaty could clarify this relationship by subsequent agreements or subsequent practice according to Article 31 paragraph 3 of the Vienna Convention on the Law of Treaties.[77] A more formal solution could be an amendment to the Outer Space Treaty in accordance with Article XV, which any State party may propose and which shall enter into force, when a majority of the States parties has accepted them. The amendment will, however, only enter into force for each State party that has accepted it, which may even increase legal uncertainty.

More difficult than the procedural questions are the substantive issues which need to be clarified. Discussions and negotiations on the possible contents of an international agreement are necessary on how to interpret, or maybe even change, the provision in the Outer Space Treaty. Commentators have put forward the proposal to distinguish between "large/impor-

---

76 *Kingdom of Belgium*, The Grand Duchy of Luxembourg and Belgium join forces to develop the exploration and utilisation of space resources, Press Release of 23 January 2019, available under: https://diplomatie.belgium.be/en/newsroom/news/2019/grand_duchy_luxembourg_and_belgium_join_forces_to_develop_exploration_and_utilisation_space_resources (last accessed: 8 May 2021).

77 Art. 31 (3) VCLT provides: "*There shall be taken into account, together with the context: a) any subsequent agreement between the parties regarding the interpretation of the treaty or the application of its provisions; (b) any subsequent practice in the application of the treaty which establishes the agreement of the parties regarding its interpretation.*"

tant" and "small/less important" celestial bodies taking into account the classification by the International Astronomical Union (IAU) of objects in our solar system as "planets", "dwarf planets" and "small solar system bodies".[78] Only the large and important objects would fall under the non-appropriation principle, but smaller and less important objects could be taken by States and private entities under the "freedom of use"-principle.[79] Similar differentiations were proposed to the International Institute of Space Law (IISL) in the context of the discussion on the legality of actions against asteroid threats.[80] According to a draft resolution, "celestial bodies" could be defined as *"natural objects in Outer Space, including their eventual gaseous coronas which cannot be artificially moved from their natural orbits."*[81] The distinction between "large/important" and "small/less important" celestial bodies is somehow taken up in the US Space Resource Exploration and Utilization Act of 2015, which contains different definitions of "asteroid resources" and "space resources",[82] without however treating them legally any differently.

---

78 See IAU Res GA 26-B5, adopted at the 26th General Assembly of the IAU, August 2006.

79 See *Capurso*, The Non-Appropriation Principle: A Roman Interpretation, Paper presented at the 69th International Astronautical Congress in Bremen, Germany, 1-5 October 2018, available under: https://iislweb.org/wp-content/uploads/2019/01/The-NonAppropriation-Principle-A-Roman-Interpretation.pdf (last accessed: 8 May 2021); *Marboe/Friedl*, What are Space Resources? What are Celestial Bodies? – The Need for Refined Definitions in View of Recent Regulatory Efforts at the National and International Level, Paper presented at the 69th International Astronautical Congress in Bremen, Germany, 1-5 October 2018, in: International Institute of Space Law (ed.), Proceedings of the International Institute of Space Law 2018 (2019), p. 749 (750, 755).

80 *Smirnoff*, Report for Working Group Three of the IISL, Proceedings of the Seventh Colloquium on the Law of Outer Space (1964), p. 352; see also *Fasan*, Asteroids and other Celestial Bodies – Some Legal Differences, in: Journal of Space Law 26 (1998), p. 33 (33, 36); *Su*, Legality of Unilateral Exploitation of Space Resources Under International Law, in: International and Comparative Law Quarterly 66 (2017) p. 991 (997, 998).

81 Draft Resolution of Working Group Three of the IISL of 15 March 1964.

82 See § 51301 Commercial Space Launch Competitiveness Act of 25 November 2015, H.R. 2262, Title IV, Space Resource Exploration and Utilization Act, according to which the term "space resource" means *"an abiotic resource in situ in outer space", and "asteroid resource" means "a space resource found on or within a single asteroid."*

b) The Moon Agreement

The Moon Agreement has left it for the future to determine the rules governing the exploitation of space resources in accordance with its Article 11 paragraph 5.[83] Yet, it also gave a time limit until which the United Nations should consider a review of the Moon Agreement, namely 10 years after the entry into force.[84] This means, since 1994, such a review of the Moon Agreement is overdue. Nevertheless, at any time, one third of the States parties, with the concurrence of the majority of the States parties, could request the UN Secretary-General to convene a conference of the States parties to review the Agreement. According to Article 18, such a review conference shall also consider the question of the implementation of the provisions of Article 11, paragraph 5, on the basis of the principles referred to in paragraph 1 of that Article and taking into account in particular any relevant technological developments. It might be tempting for the State parties to the Moon Agreement to take advantage of the small number of them and to initiate the process for a review conference. As there are currently 18 State parties,[85] only 6 of them would be required to put the request forward to the UN Secretary-General, and 4 more to approve such an initiative.

However, similar as to what has been said with respect to the possible agreement on the interpretation or the amendment of the Outer Space Treaty, to achieve an understanding on the substantive contents of the revision of the Moon Agreement seems to be the bigger challenge.

c) UNCOPUOS

UNCOPUOS, established by the UN General Assembly as the body for international cooperation and information exchange, and its Legal Subcom-

---

83 See *Jakhu et al.*, in: *Hobe/Schmidt-Tedd/Schrogl* (eds.), Cologne Commentary on Space Law, Volume 2 (2013), Article 11 Moon Agreement, pp. 396 *et seqq*, and subsequent text.

84 Art. 18 Moon Agreement provides: *"Ten years after the entry into force of this Agreement, the question of the review of the Agreement shall be included in the provisional agenda of the General Assembly of the United Nations in order to consider, in the light of past application of the Agreement, whether it requires revision."*

85 As of 1 January 2018, see *Committee on the Peaceful Uses of Outer Space*, Status of International Agreements relating to activities in outer space as at 1 January 2018 (2018), UN Doc. A/AC.105/C.2/2018/CRP.3 10.

mittee with the mandate to *"study and report on the legal problems which may arise from the exploration and use of outer space"*[86] seem to be the most appropriate and representative fora to discuss legal issues relating to the exploitation of space resources and the granting of property rights. It can therefore be welcomed that consensus could be reached to put a new "Single Issue Item" on the agenda of the UNCOPUOS Legal Subcommittee entitled "General exchange of views on potential legal models for activities in exploration, exploitation and utilization of space resources" in 2016.[87] After the initial decision, the agenda item was renewed in the subsequent years and, in 2019, included the possible establishment of a working group.[88] However, as UNCOPUOS has more than 90 member States and works by consensus it remains to be seen whether true progress can be made as regards the substance of a potential legal model for activities in exploration, exploitation and utilization of space resources. In addition, in UNCOPUOS and its Legal Subcommittee only governments are represented as members. Permanent observers include international governmental and non-governmental organisations, but private industry is not represented by itself. It can only make an indirect input to the discussion as members of national delegations or permanent observers.

d) The Hague International Space Resource Governance Working Group

The initiative of the Hague International Space Resource Governance Working Group tries to offset the disadvantages of merely governmental representation, which is characteristic for the three multilateral approaches mentioned above. Even though the Working Group is financially supported by the Dutch government, representing a State party to the Moon

86 *United Nations General Assembly*, Resolution 1721(XVI) of 20 December 1961, part A, para. 2; UNCOPUOS previously had been established by *United Nations General Assembly*, Resolution 1348(XIII) of 13 December 1958, paras. 1 and 2.

87 *United Nations General Assembly*, Report of the Legal Subcommittee on its fifty-fifth session, held in Vienna from 4 to 15 April 2016, UN Doc. A/AC.105/1113, para. 250.

88 *United Nations General Assembly*, Report of the Legal Subcommittee on its fifty-sixth session, held in Vienna from 27 March to 7 April 2017, UN Doc. A/AC.105/1122, para. 269; *United Nations General Assembly*, Report of the Legal Subcommittee on its fifty-seventh session, held in Vienna from 9 to 20 April 2018, UN Doc. A/AC.105/1177, para. 268; *United Nations General Assembly*, Report of the Legal Subcommittee on its fifty-eight session, held in Vienna from 1 to 12 April 2019, UN Doc. A/AC.105/1203, paras. 271, 278-280.

Agreement, and, in the second phase, by the government of Luxembourg, it is not a governmental initiative.[89] Other sponsors have also contributed, and the meetings were held at the University of Leiden and the University of Luxembourg. Members and observers include ministries, space agencies, universities, industry, and individuals.[90] The Working Group aimed to pursue an inclusive and practical approach. Its purpose was to create an enabling legal environment for space resource activities. At the end of the second phase of its work, 20 "building blocks" were agreed upon.[91] According to the drafters, the future regime should incrementally regulate space resource activities at the appropriate time, an approach, which is called "the principle of adaptive governance".[92]

The "building blocks" have the potential to represent the cornerstones of a future international regime. However, it is not entirely clear whether all aspects of the proposed elements are in accordance with international law, even though this is purported and reflected in several parts of the text. Several "building blocks" are rather vague and need further elaboration.[93] However, the cooperative efforts of different stakeholders provided the opportunity of an open exchange of information, needs, and concerns. The result contains a number of ideas and concepts, which are innovative, but may raise questions about their compatibility with international space law. These include the registration and protection of "priority rights", the establishment of "safety zones" around space resource activities, and "response measures" to address harmful impacts. Nevertheless, the "building blocks" provide an interesting input to the discussion and could be used as a basis for the more formal multilateral processes of international agreements indicated further above.

---

89 *Committee on the Peaceful Uses of Outer Space*, The Hague Space Resources Governance Working Group, Information provided by the Netherlands, Factsheet, UN Doc. A/AC.105/C.2/2018/CRP.18 (12 April 2018).

90 *The Hague Space Resources Governance Working Group*, Final Report of 27 January 2020, HSRGWG/FR/1/27012020, Annex 1.

91 *The Hague Space Resources Governance Working Group*, Building Blocks for the Development of an International Framework on Space Resource Activities, November 2019, available at: https://www.universiteitleiden.nl/binaries/content/assets/rechtsgeleerdheid/instituut-voor-publiekrecht/lucht--en-ruimterecht/space-resources/bb-thissrwg--cover.pdf (last accessed: 8 May 2021).

92 *The Hague Space Resources Governance Working Group*, Final Report of 27 January 2020, HSRGWG/FR/1/27012020, p. 11.

93 See Bittencourt Neto, Hofmann, Masson-Zwaan, Stefoudi (eds.), Building Blocks for the Development of an International Framework for the Governance of Space Resources Activities. A Commentary (2020) p. 1-2.

III. Summary

In view of the lack of clear international rules on the legal status of space resources and pertinent legislation at the national level some arguments can be summarized which support the unilateral and the multilateral approach respectively. Justifications for the unilateral approach include Article I of the Outer Space Treaty which provides for the freedom of exploration and use and the carrying out of space activities for the benefit and in the interests of all countries. It can be argued that, if nobody carries out space activities, including space resource activities, this would be for the benefit and in the interest of no country. Furthermore, Article II of the Outer Space Treaty prohibits national appropriation of celestial bodies, but does not explicitly prohibit the appropriation of their resources. Moreover, Article VI requires authorization and continuous supervision of non-governmental space activities so that governments need to act, when such activities are planned by commercial companies. Governments have the right and possibility to do so because Article VIII provides for jurisdiction over space objects of the State of registry. With respect to the desired international regime over space resources, only few States have ratified the Moon Agreement. The reluctance to do so by many States is an indication that broad international consensus may not be reached in the foreseeable future. Instead of waiting for multilateral solutions, which are not in sight, States could argue that they need to take the first steps at the national level. Such unilateral initiatives may trigger reactions by other States and start a dynamic, which otherwise would not exist. This dynamic ultimately could lead to international cooperation and coordination in order to avoid conflicts.

By contrast, arguments against a unilateral approach and in favour of a multilateral approach from the outset include that Article I of the Outer Space Treaty provides for exploration and use of outer space for the benefit and in the interests of all countries, without discrimination of any kind and on a basis of equality. This excludes a "first come-first serve"-approach which privileges technologically highly developed countries. In addition, Article I of the Outer Space Treaty makes clear that there shall be free access to all areas of celestial bodies, which represents an obstacle against areas on celestial bodies for exclusive use. Article II of the Outer Space Treaty prohibits national appropriation of celestial bodies not only by explicit claims of sovereignty, but also by means of use or occupation, or by any other means. Some sort of occupation of a celestial body will inevitably be necessary if one exploits its resources. Art. II furthermore prohibits legislating on the legal status of celestial bodies and their resources, because legislation is exercise of sovereignty. Most importantly, such legislation cannot provide legal certainty, because property rights so conferred may not be recognized by other countries. While the concept of "common heritage of mankind" contained in the Moon Agreement is yet to be developed and defined, the Outer Space Treaty already contains the concept of "province of all mankind" which implies that the benefit of space activities for humanity as a whole needs be taken into consideration. In this vein, Article IX contains the principle of "due regard" of the interests of other States and explicitly talks about the need to avoid harmful contamination of the environment of celestial bodies.

Against this background, further efforts seem to be needed to provide clarity and avoid conflicts. As has been shown, there are various ways to achieve a reliable legal framework on the international level. While such a framework must be developed by States in order to grant legal certainty cooperative efforts which include also other stakeholders may pave the way for an evolving understanding of the needs and problems, rights and obligations of all actors concerned.

Natural Resources and Investment Law, in particular Investor-State Contracts

Marc Bungenberg[*]

Abstract

Parallel to the development of PSNR as a principle of customary international law, investment contracts not only in regard to their typical contents changed but also the type of specific contract used. Concession agreements were partly replaced by Production Sharing Agreements and "modern" types of concession agreements have been developed. These include taxation or minimum work obligations, the use and again specific content of stabilisation clauses – not to be in contradiction to the right to regulate – has changed fundamentally. Also a stronger implementation of obligations in regard to sustainable development as well as to corporate social responsibility (CSR) in ISCs is taking place.

Overview

* *Marc Bungenberg* is Director of the Europa-Institut and Professor of Public Law, European Law and Public International Law at University of Saarland in Germany, Permanent Visiting Professor at the University of Lausanne, Switzerland, and inter alia member of the scientific advisory board to the International Investment Law Centre in Cologne.

I. Introduction

As the development, character and content of the general principle of Permanent Sovereignty over Natural Resources (PSNR) has evolved over time, so has the interplay between natural resources law, especially PSNR, and international investment law. This interplay on its turn can be demonstrated in various sectors – investment agreements, investment admission, investment guarantee programs or also investment contracts. Since the evolution of the principle of PSNR has been analysed by *Stephan Hobe* in his publications,[1] this short contribution will only focus on the interplay aspects, particularly the interrelation of investment contracts and natural resources law.

Firstly, it will be shown that especially investment contracts in the natural resources sector have brought about some of the landmark cases of international investment law (II.). Secondly, the focus will be on the development of investment contracts: it will be important to discuss their agreed changing content, especially as mentioned reflecting the elements and the growing importance of PSNR (III.1.). Furthermore, the use of different types of contracts reflects that not only the clauses, but even the choice of type of contract itself has undergone influence of PSNR (III.2.).

II. Investment Contract Arbitration in the Natural Resources Sector as one of the Origins of International Investment Law

Disputes in the natural resources sector have a long history. Only lately the majority of the investment disputes are submitted to treaty-based arbitration, however, contract-based arbitration was the rule for a long time – if arbitration was at stake at all and not "gunboat diplomacy" was the means to solve disputes. The interrelation of a lack of effective investment protection and gunboat diplomacy becomes obvious by taking a look at the example of oil extraction in Iran in the past century, where, after arbitration failed, the secret service became active and a *coup d'État* followed, with the installation of an investor-friendly new government.[2]

---

1 *E.g. Hobe*, Evolution of the Principle on Permanent Sovereignty over Natural Resources, in: Bungenberg/Hobe (eds.), Permanent Sovereignty over Natural Resources (2015), p. 1 (1 *et seqq*).

2 *Weiner*, CIA, p. 125 *et seq.*

Hence, landmark arbitration cases show the close link between natural resources and the need for effective investment protection mechanisms. Part of international investment law forms parts of the international regulatory body of natural resources law. Numbers prove the importance of investment contracts as an integral part of a more general natural resources and especially oil, gas and minerals law. At least 150 investor-state arbitrations were based on investment contracts in the period between 1972 and 2018,[3] but even in the past decade there was a relatively high number of solely contract-based arbitrations, mostly in the field of oil, gas and mining.[4] The nationalisation of the Anglo Persian Oil Company (APOC) in 1951 and of foreign oil companies in Libya in the 1970s are probably the most discussed examples in this regard.

A concession agreement between Persia and APOC was already cancelled in 1932. Requests for arbitration by the investor as foreseen in the 1901 agreement were unsuccessful. The dispute was considered by the Council of the League of Nations and was resolved via a renegotiation of the concession agreement in 1933. This agreement again was terminated by the Persian Government. Until 1951, the Anglo Persian Oil Company controlled the domestic oil industry; the company was granted various long-time exploration and extraction concessions with only small royalty payments to the government of Persia. After the company resisted demands for a greater share of profits, the Iranian parliament voted to nationalise the Anglo Iranian Oil Company (AIOC) and its holdings.[5] The Anglo Iranian Oil Company requested arbitration under Article 22, and named also the company's arbitrator, whereas the Iranian Minister of Finance, rejecting the proposal for arbitration, replied:

> *"First: The nationalization of industries is based on the right of the sovereignty of nations, such as exercised by other governments, including the British Government itself and the Mexican Government in different cases.*

---

3 *Pitad*, Case Map, available under: https://pitad.org/index#static/illustrations (last accessed: 1 April 2020).

4 *ICSID*, Spotlight on Contract-based Disputes at ICSID, available under: https://icsid.worldbank.org/en/Pages/resources/Spotlight-on-Contract-based-Disputes-at-ICSID.aspx. (last accessed: 1 April 2020).

5 See on this in general *Duval et al.*, International Petroleum Exploration and Exploitation Agreements: Legal, Economic and Policy Aspects (2nd edition 2009), p. 45; *Mulack*, Rechtsprobleme der Erdölkonzessionsabkommen im Nahen Osten (1972), p. 15.

> *Second: A private agreement cannot obstruct the enforcement of this right, which is based on the principles of international rights.*
>
> *Third: The nationalization of the oil industry, which is based on the enforcement of the right of sovereignty of the Persian people, is not subject to arbitration, and no international authority is qualified to investigate this matter."*[6]

Against this rejection of arbitration, the company then initiated a claim against Iran before the International Court of Justice (ICJ).[7] In its application, it asked the Court to decide that the Iranian Government was under a legal obligation to submit its dispute with the Anglo Iranian Oil Company to arbitration or, alternatively, to decide that the Iranian Government was not entitled to alter the Concession Agreement, even by legislation, except by mutual consent with the Company. The above already mentioned Iranian *coup d'État* in 1953 – generated by the CIA – finally led to a change in government with a new consortium and an American leadership taking over the Iranian oil production.[8] Even though AIOC was finally compensated for its losses, this nationalisation in the field of natural resources gives a perfect example for the interplay of (early discussions of) PSNR at that time – with a lot of emphasis on sovereignty and little on property rights – as well as the need of an effective investment protection. Furthermore, it demonstrates the deficits in times before the first international investment agreements were concluded.

Another example are the "Libyan Cases" of the 1970s. By that time, the PSNR principle had developed into an integral part of public international law. Between 1971 and 1974, the Libyan Government nationalised the foreign oil production, following suit the previous examples of other countries – especially Mexico and Iran, but parallel, in regard to other resources, also Chile. In all Libyan cases, the Libyan Government refused to arbitrate and did not appoint its arbitrator in accordance with the concession agreements. Nevertheless, three arbitration tribunals were established and rendered awards on the issue; all awards also dealt with the UN Resolutions on Permanent Sovereignty over Natural Resources.

---

6 Cited after American Journal of International Law 45 (1951), pp. 749-754.

7 *International Court of Justice*, Judgment of 22 July 1952, Anglo Iranian Oil Company (United Kingdom v. Iran), I.C.J. Reports (1952), pp. 93-171.

8 See *Weiner*, CIA, Die wahre Geschichte (2008), pp. 122 *et seqq.; Kinzer*, All the Shah's Men (2003), pp. 195 *et seqq.*

The awards (BP,[9] Texaco Overseas Petroleum Co.,[10] Liamco[11]) differ considerably in their argumentation and final outcome and are to be seen as some of the most mentioned arbitral awards, at least in the field of natural resources and investment law. Libya's only appearance was in the Texaco Overseas Petroleum Co. case in which it filed a memorandum with the President of the ICJ contending that the disputes were not subject to arbitration because the nationalisations were acts of sovereignty, and thereby of course basing its argumentation on the PSNR principle. In all arbitrations, this argument was rejected.

In the Texaco Overseas Petroleum Co. case, it was stressed that contracts between states and private persons can be "internationalised" in the sense of being subjected to international law or international arbitration. In regard to Resolution 1803, Arbitrator *Dupuy* stressed in the Texaco Overseas Petroleum Co. Case that:

> *"On the basis of the circumstances of adoption mentioned above and by expressing an opinio juris communis, Resolution 1803 (XVII) seems to this Tribunal to reflect the state of customary law existing in this field. Indeed, on the occasion of the vote on a resolution finding the existence of a customary rule, the States concerned clearly express their views. The consensus by a majority of States belonging to the various representative groups indicates without the slightest doubt universal recognition of the rules therein incorporated, i.e., with respect to nationalisation and compensation the use of the rules in force in the nationalising State but all this in conformity with international law."*[12]

In the BP case,[13] Arbitrator *Lagergren* excluded single municipal law, and instead applied general principles of international law, including those principles applied by international tribunals. Paragraph 7 of the contract specified the choice of law:

9 *B.P. Exploration Co. (Libya) Ltd. v. Government of Libyan Arab Republic*, Award of 10 October 1973, 53 ILR 297 (1979).

10 *Texaco Overseas Petroleum Co. and California Asiatic Oil Co. v. Government of Libyan Arab Republic*, Award on the Merits of 19 January 1977, 17 ILM 1 (1978).

11 *Libyan American Oil Company v. Government of Libyan Arab Republic*, Award of 12 April 1977, 20 ILM 1 (1981).

12 *Texaco Overseas Petroleum Co. and California Asiatic Oil Co. v. Government of Libyan Arab Republic*, Award on the Merits of 19 January 1977, 17 ILM 1 (1978), p. 30, para. 87.

13 *B.P. Exploration Co. (Libya) Ltd. v. Government of Libyan Arab Republic*, Award of 10 October 1973, 53 ILR 297 (1979).

> *"This Concession shall be governed by and interpreted in accordance with the principles of the law of Libya common to the principles of international law and in the absence of such common principles then by and in accordance with the general principles of law, including such of those principles as may have been applied by international tribunals."*[14]

The nationalisation law provided for compensation to be determined by a Committee to be established, but no action to calculate the amount of compensation had been taken by the time the arbitrator had been appointed. In the Liamco case, Arbitrator *Mahmassani* applied the "principles of international law" – including the sanctity of property and contracts, respect for acquired or vested rights, a prohibition of unjust enrichment, and the obligation to pay compensation for expropriation.

These examples show, firstly, the permanent risk of expropriation that is especially high in resource rich countries – very often also politically unstable States with little interest in environmental protection, respect of human rights or the promotion of good governance structures – and secondly, the reflection of the development of the law of aliens in general as well as of international investment law in particular in international arbitral awards. Nevertheless, it was made clear in all arbitrations that States have an absolute right to control their natural resources and this right cannot be given away by any agreement with any non-State entity. However, whenever States do expropriate foreign owned assets, they have to do so for a public purpose. Furthermore, expropriation also for a public purpose must be accompanied by "appropriate compensation", which will be determined having regard to the economic development of the host State. An investor whose assets have been unlawfully expropriated is entitled to "full" compensation meaning the full value of his losses – as Arbitrator *Lagergren* concludes in the BP case.[15] Today, we find again ideas of this approach when discussing indirect expropriation under for example the Comprehensive Economic and Trade Agreement (CETA) Investment Chapter: a regulatory measure might not even count as indirect expropriation if taken for a public purpose and in some circumstances followed by a payment to the investor to make the measure proportional in the specific case. However, in the rare circumstance that the regulatory measure is not

---

14 *B.P. Exploration Co. (Libya) Ltd. v. Government of Libyan Arab Republic*, Award of 10 October 1973, 53 ILR 297 (1979), para. 23.

15 *B.P. Exploration Co. (Libya) Ltd. v. Government of Libyan Arab Republic*, Award of 10 October 1973, 53 ILR 297 (1979).

proportional, it may be considered an indirect expropriation leading to a full market value compensation.

III. PSNR Elements and Types of Investor-State Contracts

Investor-State Contracts are country-specific, generally motivated by the desire to increase foreign investment balanced against key priorities of the host government.[16] They are, in general and their content in particular, motivated by inter alia investment protection and a certain stability on the one side as well as the protection of the environment, public policy issues, adherence to the domestic legal order of the host State, the distribution of resources or the altogether revenue on the other side. Therefore, the basic rationale is to allow foreign enterprises to operate in the country and to determine their rights and obligations. There is no specific model Investor-State Contract used, but there is a region- and country-specific as well as a resources-specific approach, that also undergoes changes in time. Nevertheless, not only the identification of evolution of typical (natural resources law) elements and their evolution (1.) throughout time somehow is possible, but even the type of contract has undergone influence of the developing PSNR concept (2.).

1. PSNR Specific Elements in Investor-State Contracts

Typical elements of investment contracts – also in the natural resources sector – are stabilisation clauses, economic equilibrium clauses, transparency obligations, arbitration clauses, articles on profit sharing, choice of law clauses and finally, also contract renegotiation clauses. All these different clauses of investment contracts have undergone a dramatic change because of the invention and development of other principles in domestic as well as in public international law.

The "inclusion of a renegotiation clause" ensures for example that throughout the contract duration as well as exploration and extraction

16 In general on investor-state contracts see *Fischer*, Die internationale Konzession (1974), *passim*; *Besch*, Schutz von Auslandsinvestitionen – Risikovorsorge durch Investitionsverträge (2008), *passim*; *El Chiati*, Protection of Investment in the Context of Petroleum Agreements, 204 Recueil des Cours: Collected Courses of The Hague Academy of International Law (1987), pp. 9-169.

phase, the parties can react to unforeseen circumstances arising at different stages of the contract to avoid unfair and unintended impact on the weaker party.[17] A typical example here would read:

> *"This Agreement shall be subject to periodic review once every five (5) years after the date of [the start of production] for the purpose of good faith discussions to effect such modifications to this Agreement as may be necessary or desirable in the light of any substantial changes in circumstances which may have occurred during the previous five (5) years."*

Finally, also "profit or production sharing" might be an element of these agreements. Already the concession given to *Knox d'Arcy* in 1901 foresaw some kind of revenue sharing: a concession of 500.000 square miles for a duration of 60 years at a relatively low price.[18] For sixty years of exclusive rights to oil exploration in the entire country (apart from the five northern provinces of Azerbaijan, Gilān, Mazandarān, Astarābād, and Khorasan), *Knox D'Arcy* agreed to pay the Persian government twenty thousand pounds in cash, with another twenty thousand pounds worth of shares, as well as an annual royalty which was defined somewhat vaguely as equal to 16 percent of "annual net profits".[19]

Here, the example of "stabilisation clauses" and "transparency" issues especially in natural resources-related investment contracts is taken. Stabilisation clauses vary regarding their legal effect, depending on whether they actually freeze the law and hence make future legislation inapplicable to the investment governed by the contract (freezing clauses) or rather only state an obligation to compensate the affected investor if new laws are enacted (economic equilibrium clauses).[20] In investment contracts in the nat-

---

17 *Besch*, Schutz von Auslandsinvestitionen – Risikovorsorge durch Investitionsverträge (2008), pp. 178 *et seqq.*; *Berger*, Äquivalenzstörungen, Neuverhandlungsklauseln und Vertragsanpassung bei internationalen Konzessionsverträgen sowie Probleme der Streitschlichtung, in: Baur/Hobe (eds.), Rechtsprobleme von Auslandsinvestitionen (2003), pp. 65 *et seqq.*

18 Knox d'Arcy-concession, cited in *Hurewitz*, Persian Gulf: After Iran's Revolution (1979), pp. 482 *et seqq.*

19 British Petroleum Archives at the University of Warwick, U.K.; for the terms see *Hurewitz*, Persian Gulf: After Iran's Revolution (1979), pp. 483-484.

20 *Shemberg*, Stabilization Clauses and Human Rights (11 March 2008), para. 22, available under: http://documents.worldbank.org/curated/en/502401468157193496/pdf/452340WP0Box331ation1Paper01PUBLIC1.pdf (last accessed: 1 April 2020). Finally, there are hybrid clauses combining elements from both types. See also *Faruque*, Validity and Efficacy of Stabilisation Clauses, in: Journal of International Arbitration 23 (2006), p. 317 (318-321).

ural resources sector, different degrees of stabilisation clauses are used. The extreme ones are freezing clauses, meaning that the host State is actually not allowed to apply any new law with view to the project covered by the specific investor-state contract.[21] Freezing clauses tend to leave no room for regulatory change. Such "absolute" freezing clauses were for example used in the Libyan Oil concessions. The already mentioned concession agreement between the Royal Libyan Government and oil extraction companies gave the exclusive rights for fifty years to search for, extract and sell oil from specific areas of Libyan territory. The relevant provisions in the different concession agreements were negotiated in identical terms since they were based upon a model concession set out in a schedule to the Libyan Petroleum Law of 1955. Clause 16, the stabilisation clause, excluded the contract from the ambit of any subsequent changes in Libyan law. It reads as follows:

> *"1. […]*
> *2. This Concession shall throughout the period of its validity be construed in accordance with the Petroleum Law and the Regulations in force on the date of execution of the agreement of amendment by which this paragraph 2 was incorporated into this concession agreement. Any amendment to or repeal of such Regulations shall not affect the contractual rights of the Company without its consent."*

"Economic equilibrium clauses" on the other hand require the restoration of the economic equilibrium including through compensation – but they do not actually freeze applicable law.[22] A typical example would be:

> *"In the event of the occurrence of a Change in Law […] that requires a material modification of [the investment project], or an increase or decrease in operating costs […], the investor is entitled to receive Recovery Allowance payments […]. The amount of any Recovery Allowance shall be determined pursuant to Article […]."*

---

21 *Faruque*, Validity and Efficacy of Stabilisation Clauses, in: Journal of International Arbitration 23 (2006), p. 317 (319); *Gjuzi*, Stabilization Clauses in International Investment Law (2018), p. 39; *El Chiati*, Protection of Investment in the Context of Petroleum Agreements, 204 Recueil des Cours: Collected Courses of The Hague Academy of International Law (1987), para. 132; *Waelde/Ndi*, Stabilizing International Investment Commitments: International Law Versus Contract Interpretation, in: Texas International Law Journal 31 (1996), p. 215 (260).

22 *Gjuzi*, Stabilization Clauses in International Investment Law (2018), pp. 46 *et seqq*.

A policy recommendation by different institutions now is to avoid strict freezing clauses under all circumstances. They are seen as "unfair" and not being in line with fundamental democratic principles. The democratic legitimicy of investment contracts has to be assessed. In general, however, the procedure of concluding an investor-state contract will vary. Hence, a state contract cannot be qualified as an international agreement, although various forms of "internationalisation" are assumed in academic literature.[23] If an investor-state contract affects competences of the parliament or can serve as consent to arbitration resulting in a likely "regulatory chill", the question of a necessary participation of the legislative branch arises. A significant (potential) impact on the right to regulate can be argued if the investor-state contract includes a stabilisation clause. The main purpose of stabilisation clauses is to introduce some restrictions on the host government when it comes to changing national law in a way that has an impact on the investor-state contract, including the provision that the investor will be compensated in the event of adverse changes in the law.[24] A stabilisation clause might lead to an unconstitutionality of the investment contract even if the parliament is involved in its conclusion. Particular concerns are raised with regard to stabilisation clauses, which usually state that the municipal law in force will apply for the investment in its entire duration, notwithstanding later changes in the national law of the host State.[25] The legislative branch therefore enters into a contractual commitment not

23 *Voss*, The Impact of Investment Treaties on Contracts Between Host States and Foreign Investors (2011), pp. 25 *et seqq.*; *Dumberry*, International Investment Contracts, in: Gazzini/De Brabandere (eds.), International Investment Law. The Sources of Rights and Obligations (2012), p. 215 (217 *et seqq.*); *Nassar*, Internationalization of State Contracts: ICSID, The Last Citadel, in: Journal of International Arbitration 14 (1997), p. 185 (185 *et seqq.*); *Bernardini*, Investment Protection under Bilateral Investment Treaties and Investment Contracts, in: The Journal of World Investment 2 (2001), p. 235 (236).

24 *Crockett*, Stabilisation Clauses and Sustainable Development: Drafting for the Future, in: Brown/Miles (eds.), Evolution in Investment Treaty Law and Arbitration (2001), p. 516.

25 *Comeaux/Kinsella*, Reducing Political Risk in Developing Countries: Bilateral Investment Treaties, Stabilization Clauses, and MIGA & OPIC Investment Insurance, in: New York Law School Journal of International and Comparative Law 15 (1994), p. 1 (23); *Shemberg*, Stabilization Clauses and Human Rights (11 March 2008), para. 15, available under: http://documents.worldbank.org/curated/en/502401468157193496/pdf/ 452340WP0Box331ation1Paper01PUBLIC1.pdf (last accessed: 1 April 2020).

to exercise its constitutional and thereby sovereign right to regulate.[26] Although a stabilisation clause might oblige the State to freeze its laws in relation to the investment, factually, it cannot prevent the government or parliament from enacting legislation since this has to be assessed exclusively under the constitutional order, even if a breach of the clause causes the obligation of the State to compensate the investor concerned in the sphere of public international law.[27] This could also be seen as exercising the State's permanent sovereignty in the field of natural resources.

Definitely, the biggest topic in a developing international natural resources law is the issue of "transparency". Currently, the main point here is that payments of the extraction industry have to be published on an annual basis. The next topics of interest in this field will be the publication of contracts themselves[28] as well as working on more transparent and thus public awarding procedures. The movement for contract transparency is supported by an increasing number of organisations and institutions. The Extractive Industries Transparency Initiative[29] and the Publish What You Pay[30] campaign are asking for further openness, and so are the World Bank, the International Monetary Fund (IMF) and the International Finance Corporation as promoters of good governance in the extractive industries. Some countries support contract transparency as a fundamental

---

26 *Waelde/Ndi*, Stabilizing International Investment Commitments: International Law Versus Contract Interpretation, in: Texas International Law Journal 31 (1996) p. 215 (239).

27 See also *Waelde/Ndi*, Stabilizing International Investment Commitments: International Law Versus Contract Interpretation, in: Texas International Law Journal 31 (1996) p. 215 (238-239), pointing out that neither a state contract as such nor a stabilisation clause can achieve a binding effect on the legislature which is incompatible with the constitution. See in that sense also *Comeaux/Kinsella*, Reducing Political Risk in Developing Countries: Bilateral Investment Treaties, Stabilization Clauses, and MIGA & OPIC Investment Insurance, in: New York Law School Journal of International and Comparative Law 15 (1994), p. 1 (25), who emphasise that a breach of a stabilisation clause will most likely affect the quantum phase. Critical regarding the effectiveness of stabilisation clauses also *Bernardini*, The Renegotiation of the Investment Contract, in: ICSID Review 13 (1998), p. 411 (415), referring to the public international law principle of permanent sovereignty over natural resources.

28 See *Pitmann*, Mongolia's Missiong Oil, Gas and Mining Contracts, Natural Resource Governance Institute, Briefing (January 2019), available under: https://resourcegovernance.org/sites/default/files/documents/ mongolias-missing-oil-gas-and-mining-contracts.pdf_(last accessed: 1 April 2020).

29 https://eiti.org/ (last accessed: 1 April 2020).

30 https://www.pwyp.org/ (last accessed: 1 April 2020).

principle in managing their extractive sector. Contract transparency is seen essential for the responsible management of natural resources and the potential for growth and economic development that those resources can provide. Furthermore, in most countries sub-soil resources such as minerals, oil and gas are the property of the nation, which means that the relationship with private contractors should fulfil legitimacy conditions – from which transparency can be derived as a key one. Because it is a somehow "public" contract, the award of such a contract is also to be governed by public, thus, constitutional concerns, that in a lot of cases and countries will still have to be developed.

2. *Types of Investor-State Contracts*

As mentioned, there is no "one size fits all" contract, but different models that are used on a case-by-case basis. There are, as the most relevant types of investment contracts in the natural resources sector, concession agreements, (risk) service contracts, built-operate-transfer contracts or also production sharing agreements. Here again, we can identify a changing application of contract type usage.

A widely applied type of Investor-State Contract is the so-called and already mentioned "concession agreement". The probably most famous one is the concession granted to *William Knox d'Arcy* by the Shah of Persia in 1901: No wonder that out of this fairly unbalanced agreement without renegotiation clauses some disputes arose in the long run. These first concession agreements contained few – if any at all – obligations for the oil companies.[31] Nevertheless, the oil companies owned all the oil in the concession area and government revenues were more often based on a flat fee, rather than on the value of the production.[32] Therefore, these agreements can be summarised from today's perspective as being unbalanced and unfavourable contracts with the oil companies harnessing government revenue by controlling or regulating the production. These concessions placed severe constraints on national sovereignty over resources and the

31 *Cf. Duval et al.*, International Petroleum Exploration and Exploitation Agreements: Legal, Economic and Policy Aspects (2nd edition 2009), p. 43.

32 *Cf. Duval et al.*, International Petroleum Exploration and Exploitation Agreements: Legal, Economic and Policy Aspects (2nd edition 2009), p. 43.

wealth these resources could mean for a country.[33] However, these concessions were the predominant model used until at least World War II.

Many States that originally used concessions shifted then to "Production Sharing Agreements" (PSAs). This model is closely associated with the idea of PSNR; it was first developed in the early 1960s in Indonesia and then spread out over the world.[34] Under such PSA, the "sovereign State" retains the ownership over the natural resources,[35] and the production is shared between the investor and the host State, at a certain contractually agreed stage of the production process.[36] Furthermore, the investor has generally the right to take "cost oil" for cost recovery.[37] If the extraction in-

---

33 *Cf. Duval et al.*, International Petroleum Exploration and Exploitation Agreements: Legal, Economic and Policy Aspects (2nd edition 2009), p. 63.

34 *Dolzer*, Petroleum Contracts and International Law (2018), para. 5.04; *Hauert*, Ergebnis- und prozessorientierte Stabilisierungsmechanismen und staatliches Regulierungsinteresse (2016), p. 51; *Talus/Looper/Otillar*, Lex Petrolea and the Internationalization of Petroleum Agreements: Focus on Host Government Contracts, in: Journal of World Energy Law and Business 5 (2012), p. 181 (187).

35 *Asante*, Restructuring Transnational Mineral Agreements, in: American Journal of International Law 73 (1979), p. 335 (364); *Dolzer*, Petroleum Contracts and International Law (2018), para. 5.06; *Duval et al.*, International Petroleum Exploration and Exploitation Agreements: Legal, Economic and Policy Aspects (2nd edition 2009), pp. 70 *et seq.*; *Fabrikant*, Production Sharing Contracts in the Indonesian Petroleum Industry, in: Harvard International Law Journal 16 (1975), p. 303 (331); *Pongsiri*, Partnerships in Oil and Gas Production-Sharing Contracts, in: International Journal of Public Sector Management 17 (2004), p. 431 (432 *et seq.*); *Smith*, From Concessions to Service Contracts, in: Tulsa Law Journal 27 (1991-1992), p. 493 (515); *Talus/Looper/Otillar*, Lex Petrolea and the Internationalization of Petroleum Agreements: Focus on Host Government Contracts, in: Journal of World Energy Law and Business 5 (2012), p. 181 (187).

36 *Asante*, Restructuring Transnational Mineral Agreements, in: American Journal of International Law 73 (1979), p. 335 (364); *Dolzer*, Petroleum Contracts and International Law (2018), paras. 5.09 *et seqq.*; *Mikesell*, Foreign Investment in Copper Mining (1975), p. 60; *Talus/Looper/Otillar*, Lex Petrolea and the Internationalization of Petroleum Agreements: Focus on Host Government Contracts, in: Journal of World Energy Law and Business 5 (2012), p. 181 (187).

37 *Asante*, Restructuring Transnational Mineral Agreements, in: American Journal of International Law 73 (1979), p. 335 (364); *Dolzer*, Petroleum Contracts and International Law (2018), para. 5.10; *Duval et al.*, International Petroleum Exploration and Exploitation Agreements: Legal, Economic and Policy Aspects (2nd edition 2009), p. 70; *Fabrikant*, Production Sharing Contracts in the Indonesian Petroleum Industry, in: Harvard International Law Journal 16 (1975), p. 303 (312, 321); *Leung/Wang*, State Contracts in the Globalized World, in: Journal of World Investment and Trade 7 (2006), p. 829 (831); *Markert*, Streitschlichtungsklauseln

dustry is not successful, the investor assumes all the costs associated with its exploration.[38]

Similarly to the move from concessions to PSAs, the politicisation has led nations to look at the "service model" as a way to maintain sovereignty. Under a service contract, the ownership of the petroleum remains with the host State at all times, including after production.[39] The distinction between the service contract and the PSA is less clear, where the investor is compensated by a royalty-in-kind of the produced oil. The first form of service contract, where the exploration risk is borne by the State, is a pure service contract and the extraction industry is paid according to agreed terms, notwithstanding the discovery or production of oil and gas – that remains "state property".[40] The second form of service contract is where the exploration risk is borne by the industry; the investor is compensated for its services through payments that are dependent on and limited by the amount of profits from hydrocarbons produced from the contract area.[41] From the author's perspective, given the risk element, this is almost to be categorised

---

in Investitionsschutzabkommen (2010), p. 41; *Pongsiri*, Partnerships in Oil and Gas Production-Sharing Contracts, in: International Journal of Public Sector Management 17 (2004), p. 431 (432 *et seq.*); *Smith*, From Concessions to Service Contracts, in: Tulsa Law Journal 27 (1991-1992), p. 493 (517); *Talus/Looper/Otillar*, Lex Petrolea and the Internationalization of Petroleum Agreements: Focus on Host Government Contracts, in: Journal of World Energy Law and Business (2012), p. 181 (187).

38 *Hauert*, Ergebnis- und prozessorientierte Stabilisierungsmechanismen und staatliches Regulierungsinteresse (2016), p. 52; *Talus/Looper/Otillar*, Lex Petrolea and the Internationalization of Petroleum Agreements: Focus on Host Government Contracts, in: 5 Journal of World Energy Law and Business (2012), p. 181 (188).

39 *Talus/Looper/Otillar*, Lex Petrolea and the Internationalization of Petroleum Agreements: Focus on Host Government Contracts, in: Journal of World Energy Law and Business 5 (2012), p. 181 (188); *Stompfe*, Gestaltung und Sicherung internationaler Investor-Staat-Verträge in der arabischen Welt am Beispiel Libyens und Katars (2016), p. 181; *Theodorou*, Investitionsschutzverträge vor Schiedsgerichten (2001), p. 44.

40 *Duval et al.*, International Petroleum Exploration and Exploitation Agreements: Legal, Economic and Policy Aspects (2nd edition 2009), p. 86; *Markert*, Streitschlichtungsklauseln in Investitionsschutzabkommen (2010) pp. 41 *et seq.*; *Talus/Looper/Otillar*, Lex Petrolea and the Internationalization of Petroleum Agreements: Focus on Host Government Contracts, in: 5 Journal of World Energy Law and Business (2012), p. 188.

41 *Duval et al.*, International Petroleum Exploration and Exploitation Agreements: Legal, Economic and Policy Aspects (2nd edition 2009), p. 86; *Smith*, From Concessions to Service Contracts, in: Tulsa Law Journal 27 (1991-1992), p. 493 (520).

as a concession agreement. Generally, service contracts are well suited for States with sufficient capital but a need for the expertise of the international oil companies or for fields where there is little or no exploration risk. Risk service contracts have traditionally been used in countries such as Iraq in fields that have been producing for many years with limited exploration risk.

However, very often, hybrid models somewhere in between these categories are set up in practice.

IV. Conclusion: New developments in the world of Investor-State Contracts

After World War II, a move away from unfavourable contracts was witnessed. Concessions were partly replaced by PSAs, but are also still used. Furthermore, "new" or "modern" types of concession agreements have been developed. These are, for example foreseeing state or state owned entities participation, royalties, taxation or minimum work obligations. Stabilisation clauses are to be seen in a slight tension with the right to regulate; they have limits especially in countries where sovereign states as contracting parties are bound to follow democratic principles. Also a stronger implementation of obligations in regard to sustainable development as well as to corporate social responsibility (CSR) in ISCs can be witnessed.

It is possible to select investment contract types under PSNR considerations; the thesis is put up that the selection of specific contract types changed over time because of the growing importance of taking into consideration of the principle of PSNR also in investment contracts. As *Stephan Hobe* pointed out, the principle actually did not exist until even after World War II and then only slowly emerged as a principle of public international law, first only being existent in soft law standards, but then being incorporated also in different international treaties, domestic law and then being recognised as an element of customary international law. Today it is also an at least inherent element of investment contracts.

Resources and Investment – Understanding and Misunderstanding the Friction between the Right to Regulate and Investor Protection

August Reinisch[*]

Abstract

This chapter demonstrates that under most international investment agreements (IIAs) host states incur only weak admission obligations, whereas they are usually subject to rather high protection standards once investments have been made. In regard to the right to regulate the natural resources industry this implies that states normally enjoy much discretion to determine the conditions under which they allow foreign investors to make an investment in the first place.

Once investments have been made they are usually guarded by rather protective rules against uncompensated expropriation and, most importantly, guarantees of fair and equitable treatment. In regard to the latter, recent jurisprudence of investment tribunals has scaled down overly protective approaches in regard to the stability of the legal framework expected under the fair and equitable treatment standard. They have done so by relying on a balancing of the interests of host states and investors and mitigating investor expectations by what appears reasonable and thus legitimate. Such balancing often specifically addresses the regulatory interests of host states by using elements like fairness, consistency, predictability, substantive and procedural propriety.

Interestingly, parts of this fair and equitable treatment jurisprudence have had a spill-over effect towards expropriation cases. Increasingly, reasonable investment-backed expectations are taken into account when determining whether host states regulatory measures may amount to indirect

---

* *August Reinisch* is a Professor of International and European Law at the University of Vienna, Member of the International Law Commission, President of the German Society of International Law and the Austrian Branch of the ILA, expert and arbitrator in investment cases; listed on the ICSID lists of arbitrators and conciliators. The author would like to thank *Michael Moffatt* and *Céline Braumann* for their research assistance.

expropriation. Most importantly, the police powers doctrine, according to which bona fide, non-discriminatory, regulatory measures in the public interest are not deemed expropriatory, has gained wider acceptance by investment tribunals. This doctrine which was first prominently relied upon by the *Saluka* and *Methanex* tribunals is now often also reflected in IIA clauses referencing "public welfare objectives".

Overview

I. Introduction

The exploration and exploitation of natural resources has been a major issue in public international law since the mid-20th century. It is a field which has been dominated by the discourse on national sovereignty over natural resources.[1] This was meant as a concept challenging the dominance of foreign investors in the field, such as the seven sisters[2] and others

---

1 *Schachter*, Sharing the World's Resources (1977), *passim*; *Hossain/Chowdhury* (eds.), Permanent Sovereignty over Natural Resources in International Law – Principle and Practice (1984), *passim*; *Schrijver*, Sovereignty over Natural Resources: Balancing Rights and Duties (1997), *passim*.

2 The term refers to a group of corporations which chiefly controlled global fossil fuel production and distribution after World War II: Standard Oil of New Jersey, British Petroleum, Royal Dutch-Shell, Standard Oil of California, Texaco, Standard

dominating the oil extraction business via long-term concession agreements.[3]

While the sovereign rights over resources situated in the territory or under the jurisdiction of coastal states has been repeatedly affirmed,[4] the fact remains that many states need foreign investment and know-how to actually explore and exploit such resources.[5]

There is thus a clear convergence of interests of the actors involved that is host states having sovereignty over natural resources and foreign investors having the required capital and know-how to actually extract them. There are competing, if not conflicting interests though when it comes to sharing the profits.

Often it is not only the commercial outcome or profits that need to be allocated. Rather, it is the resources controlling process, such as making decisions of whether, how and which resources to actually use, where frictions between investors and states may arise.

Important economic, environmental, social, and other concerns may lead states to regulate, limit or even prohibit the exploitation of natural resources which may conflict with the interest of foreign investors to do so. States are clearly empowered under the concept of permanent sovereignty over their natural resources to make these decisions. Investment law, including investment protection treaties, does not provide for a right of foreign investors to have access to particular resources. Rather, they protect investments once made and these investments may actually consist in rights of exploration or exploitation.

Oil Co of New York and Gulf Oil. See *Moos*, Organization of the Petroleum Exporting Countries (OPEC), in: *Wolfrum* (ed.), Max Planck Encyclopedia of Public International Law (2008).

3 *Fischer*, Die internationale Konzession (1974), *passim*; *Maniruzzaman*, State Contracts in Contemporary International Law: Monist versus Dualist Controversies, in: European Journal of International Law 12 (2001), p. 309 (309 *et seqq.*); *Leben*, La Théorie du Contrat d'Etat et l'Evolution du Droit International des Investissements (2004), *passim*.

4 *United Nations General Assembly*, Resolution 1803 (XVII) on Permanent Sovereignty over Natural Resources UN Doc A/RES/1803(XVII), UN Doc A/5217, 15, GAOR 17th Session Supplement 17, 15; *United Nations General Assembly*, Resolution 3016 (XXVII) on Permanent sovereignty over natural resources of developing countries UN Doc A/PV.2113 (XXVII), UN Doc A/8963, 12, GAOR 27th Session Supplement 30, 12.

5 *Busse/Königer/Nunnenkamp*, FDI Promotion through Bilateral Investment Treaties: More than a Bit?, in: Review of World Economics 146 (2010), p. 147 (147 et *seqq.*); *Rugman/Doh*, Multinationals and Development (2008), p. 18.

It is at that particular stage that investment disputes may arise where a host state decides to change, limit or stop the foreign investors' rights to explore or exploit natural resources. In such a situation the investment may be considered directly or indirectly expropriated or affected in a manner contrary to some of the other guarantees contained in bilateral investment treaties (BITs) such as fair and equitable treatment or the prohibition of arbitrary or unreasonable measures.

Finding the right balance between the host state's right to regulate, taking interests into account such as human rights, the rights of indigenous peoples, social and labour rights, health and safety aspects, *etc.* and respecting the protected rights of foreign investors under existing investment agreements is sometimes a voyage between Scylla and Charybdis.

The competing interests between the state's right to regulate in order to meet these interests and the level of protection afforded to foreign investors will be the focus of this contribution. It aims at highlighting a few aspects only, and contributing to a better understanding of the underlying frictions and thereby also at addressing some misunderstandings.

II. The right to regulate resource investments and the right of access to certain investments

The crucial sovereign decision concerning natural resources is whether certain resources should be extracted at all and, if so, in which form. It is here that states usually have large discretion and freedom of decision-making.

Investment law plays only a minor role. International investment agreements (IIAs) cannot be used to demand access to the resource extraction industry because typical investment treaties do not contain any admission obligations. Thus, while foreign investors may have a keen interest in accessing certain resources, they usually do not have a right to do so.[6] Many

6 *Newcombe/Paradell*, Law and Practice of Investment Treaties: Standards of Treatment (2009), p. 127; *United Nations Conference on Trade and Development (UNCTAD)*, Admission and Establishment, p. 18, available under: https://unctad.org/en/Docs/iteiit10v2_en.pdf (last accessed: 1 April 2020), citing *Dolzer/Stevens*, Bilateral Investment Treaties (1995), pp. 50-57 (*"BITs are the most frequent international investment agreements. With some notable exceptions, as a matter of law, they do not accord positive rights of entry and establishment to foreign investors from the other contracting party. Such treaties have, in general, expressly preserved the host State's discretion through a clause encouraging the contracting parties to promote favourable investment conditions between themselves but leaving the precise conditions of entry and establishment to the laws and regulation of reach party."*).

European BITs express this approach by qualifying their admission obligations to the effect that host states are only obliged to admit foreign investments in accordance with their own law.[7]

Some IIAs contain further reaching admission clauses, though, in particular, those which form part of free trade agreements (FTAs).[8] However, such admission rights are usually tied to non-discrimination standards; this means that foreign investors benefitting from such admission clauses usually do so only in a non-discriminatory fashion.

1. *Implicit admission obligations in non-discrimination clauses*

The typical admission clauses of this type are found in US and Canadian BITs as well as in Chapter 11 of NAFTA, intentionally containing such a right of admission, mostly through extending the national treatment obligations to the pre-establishment phase of an investment, *i.e.* admission, acquisition and expansion.[9]

---

7 See *e.g.* Article 3 Netherlands-India 1995 or Article 2 Netherlands-Bolivia BIT 1992 ("*Either Contracting Party shall, within the framework of its laws and regulations, promote economic cooperation through the protection in its territory of investments of nationals of the other Contracting Party. Subject to its right to exercise powers conferred by its laws or regulations, each Contracting Party shall admit such investments.*"); Article 2 Afghanistan-Germany BIT 2005 ("*Each Contracting State shall in its territory promote as far as possible investment by Investors of the other Contracting State and admit such investment in accordance with its legislation.*"); Article 2 Japan-Kenya BIT 2016 ("*Each Contracting Party shall, subject to its applicable laws and regulations, including those with regard to foreign ownership and control, admit investment of investors of the other Contracting Party.*"); Article 3 Colombia-India BIT 2009 ("*Each Contracting Party shall promote in its territory investments of investors of the other Contracting Party. Each Contracting Party shall admit these investments in accordance with its laws, regulations and policies.*").

8 See infra text in fn. 9.

9 Article 3(1) US Model BIT 2012 and Article 3(1) Canadian Model FIPA 2014 ("*Each Party shall accord to investors of the other Party treatment no less favorable than that it accords, in like circumstances, to its own investors with respect to the establishment, acquisition, expansion, management, conduct, operation, and sale or other disposition of investments in its territory.*"); Articles 1102(2) and 1103(2) North American Free Trade Agreement (NAFTA), signed 17 December 1992, entered into force 1 January 1994 ("*Each Party shall accord to investments of investors of another Party treatment no less favorable than that it accords, in like circumstances, to investments of its own investors with respect to the establishment, acquisition, expansion, management, conduct, operation, and sale or other disposition of investments […] Each Party shall accord to investments of investors of another Party treatment no less favorable than that its*

As a result, the foreign origin of a particular investor may not constitute a ground for exclusion. However, that does not grant an unconditional right to be active in the resources industries. The required licences, concessions and permits still have to be issued by the state. The state maintains the degree of discretionary power it has defined within national law and merely stipulates that such discretion shall be exercised in a manner which does not discriminate against nationals of the other treaty party or parties.

More importantly, treaties containing such non-discriminatory admission clauses often contain specific exception clauses as well. States have employed a variety of techniques in this context. One is to specify excluded sectors within a treaty annex.[10] Another, to exempt existing[11] or future[12] conflicting laws and regulations. A further approach relates to exceptional circumstances.[13]

2. *Admission in accordance with host state law clauses*

Admission "in accordance with host state law"-clauses equally ensure the right of host states to decide whether and under what conditions foreign

accords, in like circumstances, to investments of investors of any other Party or of a non-Party with respect to the establishment, acquisition, expansion, management, conduct, operation, and sale or other disposition of investments.").

10 See *e.g.* Article 2 Azerbaijan/United States BIT, signed 1 August 1997, entered into force 2 August 2001 (*"With respect to the establishment […] of covered investments, each Party shall accord treatment no less favorable than that it accords, in like situations, to investments in its territory of its own nationals […] A Party may adopt or maintain exceptions […] in the sectors or with respect to the matters specified in the Annex to this Treaty."*).

11 Article 9(1) 2004 Canadian Model BIT (*"[...] shall not apply to: (a) any existing non-conforming measure that is maintained by (i) a Party at the national level, as set out in its Schedule to Annex I."*).

12 Article 9(2) 2004 Canadian Model BIT (*"[…] shall not apply to any measure that a Party adopts or maintains with respect to sectors, subsectors or activities, as set out in its schedule to Annex II."*).

13 Article 6 Japan/Viet Nam BIT, signed 14 November 2003, entered into force 19 December 2004 (*"Notwithstanding the provisions of paragraph 4 of this Article, each Contracting Party may, in exceptional financial, economic or industrial circumstances, adopt any exceptional measure in the sectors or with respect to the matters specified in Annex II."*).

investors will be admitted to invest in a particular host state; they do not oblige host states to admit them.[14]

Interesting in many of these "admission" provisions is the obligatory language "shall admit". Nevertheless, tribunals seem to adopt the view that this obligation is qualified by the right to exercise powers conferred by its laws or regulations which include the decision whether or not to admit.[15]

With regard to the second sentence of Article 2 of the Netherlands-Bolivia BIT, providing that *"[s]ubject to its right to exercise powers conferred by its laws or regulations, each Contracting Party shall admit such investments"*, the *Aguas del Tunari* tribunal[16] found *"[...] that the inclusion of the term 'subject to' indicates that the duty to admit investments is limited by 'the right to exercise powers conferred by its laws or regulations'."*[17] Thus, the *Aguas del Tunari* tri-

---

14 See *e.g.* Article 3 Netherlands-India 1995 or Article 2 Netherlands-Bolivia BIT 1992 (*"Either Contracting Party shall, within the framework of its laws and regulations, promote economic cooperation through the protection in its territory of investments of nationals of the other Contracting Party. Subject to its right to exercise powers conferred by its laws or regulations, each Contracting Party shall admit such investments."*); Article 2 Afghanistan-Germany BIT 2005 (*"Each Contracting State shall in its territory promote as far as possible investment by Investors of the other Contracting State and admit such investment in accordance with its legislation."*); Article 2 Japan-Kenya BIT 2016 (*"Each Contracting Party shall, subject to its applicable laws and regulations, including those with regard to foreign ownership and control, admit investment of investors of the other Contracting Party."*); Article 3 Colombia-India BIT 2009 (*"Each Contracting Party shall promote in its territory investments of investors of the other Contracting Party. Each Contracting Party shall admit these investments in accordance with its laws, regulations and policies."*).

15 See *Schrijver/Prislan*, The Netherlands, in: Brown (ed.), Commentaries on Selected Model Investment Treaties (2013), p. 535 (559), commenting on Article 2 Netherlands Model BIT (*"The duty to admission remains subject to the host State's 'right to exercise powers conferred by its laws and regulations'. This allows the host State to apply any admission and screening mechanisms it may have enacted in its legislation, as well as to determine the conditions under which foreign investments may enter, if at all."*).

16 *Aguas del Tunari, S.A., v. Bolivia*, Decision of 21 October 2005 on Respondent's Objections to Jurisdiction, ICSID Case No. ARB/02/3.

17 Ibid., para. 147 (*"As to the second sentence, the Tribunal observes that if it omits the reference to Bolivian law, the second sentence states that both Bolivia and the Netherlands 'shall admit' the investments of nationals of the other Contracting Party. This obligation to allow the entry of foreign investment is a common provision in bilateral investment treaties, and is often termed an 'admission clause'. The obligation to admit is 'subject to' the decision of Bolivia ('its right') to 'exercise powers conferred by its laws or regulations'. The Tribunal concludes that the inclusion of the term 'subject to' indicates that the duty to admit investments is limited by 'the right to exercise powers conferred by its laws or regulations'. The Tribunal notes that the reference specifically subjects the*

bunal found that the reference subjected or limited the host state's duty to cooperate and to admit foreign investments.

"In accordance with host state law"-clauses in BITs are often contained in the definitions of "investments".[18] Their main function is to limit the scope of BIT protection to investments made in conformity with the law of the host state.[19] Alternatively, "in accordance with host state law"-clauses may be contained in other BIT articles, such as those relating to the applicability of the treaty, the admission of investments or those dealing with substantive protection standards.[20]

Thus, host states generally enjoy a large measure of discretion before natural resources investments have actually been made. This implies that

---

State's duty to admit investments not to the laws and regulations of Bolivia, but rather to the 'right to exercise powers' conferred by such laws or regulations. The Tribunal finds this language significant as it implies an act at the time of admittance in accordance with the laws or regulations in force at that time.").

18 See e.g. Article 1(1) Germany-Philippines BIT 1997 ("*The term 'investment' shall mean any kind of asset accepted in accordance with the respective laws and regulations of either Contracting State […].*"). This clause was in issue in *Fraport AG Frankfurt Airport Services Worldwide v. Philippines*, Award of 16 August 2007, ICSID Case No. ARB/03/25. See also Article 1(1) Israel/Uzbekistan BIT 1994 ("*The term 'investments' shall comprise any kind of assets, implemented in accordance with the laws and regulations of the Contracting Party in whose territory the investment is made, including, but not limited to: […]*"); a clause that was in issue in *Metal-Tech Ltd. v. Uzbekistan*, Award of 4 October 2013, ICSID Case No. ARB/10/3.

19 As the clause in *Gustav F W Hamester GmbH & Co KG v. Republic of Ghana*, Award of June 18 2010, ICSID Case No. ARB/07/24, Article 10 Germany-Ghana BIT (1995), signed 24 February 1995, entered into force 23 November 1998 ("*This Treaty shall also apply to investments made prior to its entry into force by nationals or companies of either Contracting Party in the territory of the other Contracting Party consistent with the latter's legislation.*").

20 See *Inceysa Vallisoletana S.L. v. Republic of El Salvador*, Award of 2 August 2006, ICSID Case No. ARB/03/26, para. 189, quoting Respondent El Salvador in these proceedings ("First, many investment treaties incorporate limitations into their definition of investment [...] Alternatively or in addition, State Parties sometimes incorporate a requirement of compliance with the host State's laws into provisions addressing the applicability of the treaty [...] A common variation in applicability provisions of investment treaties is to specify the prerequisite of investment legality for the extension of treaty protections to investments made prior to the date the treaty entered into force [...] Third, State Parties frequently incorporate 'in accordance with law' limitations into treaty provisions requiring host States to admit or accept foreign investments [...] Finally, State Parties frequently incorporate 'accordance with law' requirements in the provision pledging protection and non-impairment of qualifying investments, which is usually the first substantive obligation section of the investment treaties.").

they can take into account environmental and human rights concerns, as well as rights of indigenous peoples and other public interests that may be negatively affected by investments in the natural resources field.

Of course, this conclusion only relates to the potential impact of investment law. The fact that many developing countries may be factually heavily dependent upon income-generating natural resources investments will be a major factor pushing them to accept investment projects with sometimes questionable quality.[21] But in order to ensure that this does not happen, one would have to enable host states to improve their decision making process, possibly including a better screening process when it comes to admitting foreign investments, but more generally to have the required legal framework in force that safeguards the public interests.

III. The right to regulate existing resources investments

More relevant in the context of trying to regulate already existing resources investments that are also protected by the typical investment treatment standards contained in IIAs is the "right to regulate" of host states and its potential limits.

It is obvious that the right to regulate understood as including the right of host states to change the regulatory environment for natural recourses investments may pose a major challenge to the interests of foreign investors. This can lead to a potential friction with the guarantees usually contained in IIAs, such as protection against uncompensated expropriation, fair and equitable treatment, full protection and security, *etc.*

But such friction is not necessarily the unavoidable outcome. Rather, balancing exercises have become crucial and tribunals have increasingly not only recognized, but actually applied a balancing of the competing interests and also fine-tuned the protection according to what a host state has agreed to.[22]

---

21 *Smith/Wells*, Mineral Agreements in Developing Countries: Structures and Substance, The American Journal of International Law 69 (1975), p. 560 (560 *et seqq.*).

22 See *Henckels*, Proportionality and Deference in Investor-State Arbitration: Balancing Investment Protection and Regulatory Autonomy (2015), *passim*; *Vadi*, Proportionality, Reasonableness and Standards of Review in International Investment Law and Arbitration (2018), *passim*.

1. Fair and equitable treatment

Investment tribunals have recognized that while investors may – as an element of the protection afforded under fair and equitable treatment – expect a minimum level of stability in terms of the legal environment of the host state, such stability does not override regulatory needs.

Investment tribunals have emphasized this thought by developing two interrelated strands of jurisprudence, one emphasizing the objective element of stability and the other concentrating more on the subjective element of investor expectations.

a) Balanced stability

Since investment protection largely concerns a predictable and stable investment framework, IIAs mainly aim at reducing political risk and strengthening the 'reliability of the respective investment climates.'[23]

Investment tribunals have clarified that the stability inherent in fair and equitable treatment should not work as a surrogate to an express stabilization clause whereby a host state explicitly undertakes not to change its law.[24] Rather, they have recognized that investors should be protected against drastic and unforeseeable changes of the legal environment and that any stability must be balanced against the regulatory interests of host states. The tribunal in *Electrabel* v. *Hungary* made this very clear when it stated that

> *"[w]hile the investor is promised protection against unfair changes, it is well established that the host State is entitled to maintain a reasonable degree of regulatory flexibility to respond to changing circumstances in the public interest. Consequently, the requirement of fairness must not be understood as the immutability of the legal framework, but as implying that subsequent*

---

23 *Jacob/Schill*, Fair and Equitable Treatment: Content, Practice, Method, in: Bungenberg *et al.* (eds.), International Investment Law: A Handbook (2015), p. 700 (728), relying on *Rubins/Kinsella*, International Investment, Political Risk and Dispute Resolution (2005), p. 1 *et seq.*

24 See, *e.g.*, *AES Summit Generation Limited and AES-Tisza Erömü Kft v. Hungary*, Award of 23 September 2010, ICSID Case No. ARB/07/22, para. 9.3.29 (*"The stable conditions that the ECT mentions relate to the framework within which the investment takes place. Nevertheless, it is not a stability clause. A legal framework is by definition subject to change as it adapts to new circumstances day by day and a state has the sovereign right to exercise its powers which include legislative acts."*).

changes should be made fairly, consistently and predictably, taking into account the circumstances of the investment."[25]

In a similar way, the tribunal in *Micula* v. *Romania*[26] insisted that

"[…] the state may always change its legislation, being aware and thus taking into consideration that: (i) an investor's legitimate expectations must be protected; (ii) the state's conduct must be substantively proper (e.g., not arbitrary or discriminatory); and (iii) the state's conduct must be procedurally proper (e.g., in compliance with due process and fair administration)."[27]

And recently, the ICSID tribunal in *Eiser* v. *Spain*[28] started its fair and equitable treatment analysis with an endorsement of the investment jurisprudence affirming the right to regulate:

"Absent explicit undertakings directly extended to investors and guaranteeing that States will not change their laws or regulations, investment treaties do not eliminate States' right to modify their regulatory regimes to meet evolving circumstances and public needs. As other tribunals have observed, '[i]n order to adapt to changing economic, political and legal circumstances the State's regulatory powers still remain in place.' '[T]he fair and equitable treatment standard does not give a right to regulatory stability per se. The state has a right to regulate, and investors must expect that the legislation

25 *Electrabel S.A. v. Republic of Hungary*, Decision of 30 November 2012 on Jurisdiction, Applicable Law and Liability, ICSID Case No. ARB/07/19, para. 7.77.

26 *Ioan Micula, Viorel Micula, S.C. European Food S.A, S.C. Starmill S.R.L. and S.C. Multipack S.R.L. v. Romania*, Final Award of 11 December 2013, ICSID Case No. ARB/05/20.

27 Ibid., para. 529 ("*[…] the fair and equitable treatment obligation is not an unqualified guarantee that regulations will never change. Investors must expect that the legislation will change from time to time, absent a stabilization clause or other specific assurances giving rise to a legitimate expectation of stabilization. The BIT's protection of the stability of the legal and business environment cannot be interpreted as the equivalent of a stabilization clause. In the Tribunal's view, the correct position is that the state may always change its legislation, being aware and thus taking into consideration that: (i) an investor's legitimate expectations must be protected; (ii) the state's conduct must be substantively proper (e.g., not arbitrary or discriminatory); and (iii) the state's conduct must be procedurally proper (e.g., in compliance with due process and fair administration). If a change in legislation fails to meet these requirements, while the legislation may be validly amended as a matter of domestic law, the state may incur international liability.*").

28 *Eiser Infrastructure Limited and Energía Solar Luxembourg S.à r.l. v. Kingdom of Spain*, Award of 4 May 2017, ICSID Case No. ARB/13/36.

will change, absent a stabilization clause or other specific assurance giving rise to a legitimate expectation of stability'."[29]

b) Legitimate expectations

Legitimate expectations are probably among the most important and controversial aspects of the fair and equitable treatment standard that may serve investor interests. They embody a concept closely linked to stability and predictability.[30] While investment tribunals have generally upheld the idea that the reasonable and legitimate expectations of investors at the time of the making of an investment deserve protection, they have also made clear that such expectations have to be reasonable[31] and must thus recognize a certain probability of potential changes to the regulatory environment resulting from the need of host states to exercise its regulatory powers. This notion was well captured by the tribunal in *Perenco* v. *Ecuador* which held that

> *"[t]he expectations are not those exclusively of the investor and an undue reliance upon a claimant's subjective expectations expressed in the context of adversarial proceedings years after the investment's making, can result in a skewed view of what it could reasonably have expected when it made the investment. […] The search is for a balanced approach between the investor's reasonable expectations and the exercise of the host State's regulatory and other powers."*[32]

---

29 *Eiser Infrastructure Limited and Energía Solar Luxembourg S.à r.l. v. Kingdom of Spain*, Award of 4 May 2017, ICSID Case No. ARB/13/36, para. 362, relying on *Parkerings* v. *Lithuania*; *EDF (Services) Ltd. v. Romania*; *BG Group Plc. v. Argentine Republic*; *Micula v. Romania* (footnotes omitted).

30 *Frontier Petroleum Services (FPS) v. Czech Republic*, Final Award of 12 November 2010, UNCITRAL, para. 285 (*"The protection of the investor's legitimate expectations is closely related to the concepts of transparency and stability."*).

31 *Saluka Investments BV (The Netherlands) v. The Czech Republic*, Partial Award of 17 March 2006, para. 309 (*"[…] the investor's underlying legitimate and reasonable expectations."*); *Electrabel S.A. v. Republic of Hungary*, Decision of 30 November 2012 on Jurisdiction, Applicable Law and Liability, ICSID Case No. ARB/07/19, para. 7.74 (*"[…] the investor's reasonable and legitimate expectations […]"*); *Rumeli Telekom A.S. and Telsim Mobil Telekomunikasyon Hizmetleri A.S. v. Kazakhstan*, Award of 29 July 2008, ICSID Case No. ARB/05/16, para. 609 (*"[…] the State must respect the investor's reasonable and legitimate expectations."*).

32 *Perenco Ecuador Limited v. The Republic of Ecuador*, Decision of 12 September 2014 on Jurisdiction and Liability, ICSID Case No. ARB/08/6, para. 560.

This implies that investors have to act reasonably and have to exercise due diligence when assessing a business environment on which they intend to rely. The *Parkerings* tribunal very well connected this thought back to the degree of stability that may legitimately be expected by an investor:

> *"In principle, an investor has a right to a certain stability and predictability of the legal environment of the investment. The investor will have a right of protection of its legitimate expectations provided it exercised due diligence and that its legitimate expectations were reasonable in light of the circumstances. Consequently, an investor must anticipate that the circumstances could change, and thus structure its investment in order to adapt it to the potential changes of legal environment."*[33]

Thus, it is clear that in the absence of express promises of stability, host states are free to change their regulatory framework, including the one applying to existing foreign investors as long as it does not amount to radical changes.

2. *Expropriation*

The balanced approach of fair and equitable treatment cases has had a spill-over effect on the indirect expropriation jurisprudence, and vice versa. Whether this is sufficient to rebalance perceived pro-investor bias remains to be assessed. But first it is important to understand how a balancing of host state and investor interests has entered the field of expropriation.

While the initial wave of indirect expropriation jurisprudence focused on the effect of state measures on an investment (sole effects doctrine),[34] more recently both the so-called police powers doctrine as well as legitimate expectations have also become crucial in the balancing exercise to be undertaken in order to assess whether an indirect expropriation has occurred at all.

---

33 *Parkerings-Compagniet AS v. Lithuania*, Award of 11 September 2007, ICSID Case No. ARB/05/8, para. 333.

34 *Saipem S.p.A. v. The People's Republic of Bangladesh*, Award of 30 June 2009, ICSID Case No. ARB/05/07, para. 133 (*"[…] according to the so-called 'sole effects doctrine', the most significant criterion to determine whether the disputed actions amount to indirect expropriation or are tantamount to expropriation is the impact of the measure. As a matter of principle, case law considers that there is expropriation if the deprivation is substantial, as it is in the present case."*).

a) Police powers doctrine

One of the major jurisprudential developments in expropriation law was the establishment of the so-called *Saluka/Methanex* doctrine to rebalance the "sole effects" doctrine.[35] By claiming a carve-out for measures taken under the "police powers" of host states and complying with certain criteria from the broad potential scope of indirect expropriation,[36] it effectively led to a substantial recovery of regulatory space by host states.

Subsequently, investment tribunals have started to engage in a balancing test in order to establish whether State measures constitute expropriation.[37]

Beyond *ad hoc* dispute settlement, states have in turn taken up the concept of police powers and integrated it into the wording of IIAs. Starting with the understandings annexed to the 2004 US and Canada Model BITs many states have adopted treaty language clarifying that

> *"[e]xcept in rare circumstance, non-discriminatory regulatory actions by a Party that are designed and applied to protect legitimate public welfare objectives, such as public health, safety, and the environment, do not constitute indirect expropriations."*[38]

---

35 *Dolzer/Schreuer*, Principles of International Investment Law (2012), p. 114; *McLachlan/Shore/Weiniger*, International Investment Arbitration Substantive Principles (2017), p. 387.

36 *Methanex Corporation v. United States of America*, Final Award of 3 August 2005 on Jurisdiction and Merits, NAFTA Arbitral Tribunal, IV D para.7 (*"[...] as a matter of general international law, a non-discriminatory regulation for a public purpose, which is enacted in accordance with due process and, which affects, inter alios, a foreign investor or investment is not deemed expropriatory and compensable unless specific commitments had been given by the regulating government to the then putative foreign investor contemplating investment that the government would refrain from such regulation."*); *Saluka Investments BV (The Netherlands) v. The Czech Republic*, Partial Award of 17 March 2006, UNCITRAL, para. 262 (*"[...] the principle that a State does not commit an expropriation and is thus not liable to pay compensation to a dispossessed alien investor when it adopts general regulations that are 'commonly accepted as within the police power of States' forms part of customary international law today."*).

37 *LG&E Energy Corp., LG&E Capital Corp., LG&E International Inc. v. The Argentine Republic*, Decision of 3 October 2006 on Liability, ICSID Case No. ARB/02/1, para. 189 (*"In order to establish whether State measures constitute expropriation [...], the Tribunal must balance two competing interests: the degree of the measure's interference with the right of ownership and the power of the State to adopt its policies."*).

38 See *e.g.*, Annex B (4)(b) U.S. Model BIT of 2012; Annex B.13(1)(c) Canada Model BIT of 2004; Annex B.13(1)(c) Canada/Jordan BIT, signed 28 June 2009, entered into force 14 December 2009; Annex B.13(1)(c) Canada/Peru BIT, signed 14

b) Reasonable investment-backed expectations

Legitimate expectations, with their inherent balancing, have also found their way into expropriation law.

The inclusion of "reasonable investment-backed expectations" into expropriation clauses may be an example for such a "migration" of concepts. Some U.S. and Canadian investment treaties refer to "investment-backed expectations" amongst the factors to be considered in order to determine whether a certain state measure constitutes indirect expropriation[39] and tribunals like the NAFTA panel in *Fireman's Fund* v. *Mexico*[40] were ready to accept this notion by stating that also *"[t]he investor's reasonable 'investment-backed expectations' may be a relevant factor whether (indirect) expropriation has occurred."*[41]

Both the police powers doctrine as well as the concept of reasonable "investment-backed expectations" can be viewed, not only as investment protection concepts having "migrated" from fair and equitable treatment law, but also as jurisprudentially developed ideas that have been quickly adopted and incorporated into treaty-making.

Of course, this latter trend is most visible in recent investment chapters of free trade agreements negotiated by the EU. For instance, the provision on fair and equitable treatment in the Comprehensive Economic and Trade Agreement between Canada and the EU (CETA)[42] is clearly intended to reduce fair and equitable treatment protection and ensure that the regulatory space of host states remains largely unfettered. The obligation is expressly limited to the elements listed in the clause, which does not con-

---

November 2006, entered into force 20 June 2007; Annex A(c) Canada/Slovakia BIT, signed 20 July, 2010, entered into force 14 March 2012; Annex 11-B(4)(b) Australia/United States FTA, signed 18 May 2004, entered into force 1 January 2005; Annex 10-D(4)(b) Chile/United States FTA, signed 6 June 2003, entered into force 1 January 2004; Annex 10-B (4)(b) Morocco/United States FTA, signed 15 June 2004, entered into force 1 January 2006.

39 See, *e.g.*, U.S. Model BIT of 2012, Annex B(4)(a)(ii) (requiring, for a finding of indirect expropriation, consideration of *"the extent to which the government action interferes with distinct, reasonable investment-backed expectations"*). Similarly, Canada Model BIT of 2003, Annex B.13(1)(b)(ii); Australia-Chile FTA 2008 Annex 10-B(3)(a)(ii).

40 *Fireman's Fund Insurance Co. (U.S.) v. Mexico*, Award of 17 July 2006, ICSID ARB(AF)/02/01.

41 *Fireman's Fund Insurance Co. (U.S.) v. Mexico*, Award of 17 July 2006, ICSID ARB(AF)/02/01, para. 176 (footnotes omitted).

42 Consolidated Comprehensive Economic and Trade Agreement (CETA) Text, revised text of 29 February 2016.

tain a separate stability element and ensures that legitimate expectations are narrowly interpreted. Article 8.10 CETA provides as follows:

> "1. *Each Party shall accord in its territory to investors and to covered investments of the other Party fair and equitable treatment and full protection and security in accordance with paragraphs 2 through 6.*
> 2. *A Party breaches the obligation of fair and equitable treatment referenced in paragraph 1 if a measure or series of measures constitutes:*
>   a) *denial of justice in criminal, civil or administrative proceedings;*
>   b) *fundamental breach of due process, including a fundamental breach of transparency, in judicial and administrative proceedings;*
>   c) *manifest arbitrariness;*
>   d) *targeted discrimination on manifestly wrongful grounds, such as gender, race or religious belief;*
>   e) *abusive treatment of investors, such as coercion, duress and harassment; or*
>   f) *a breach of any further elements of the fair and equitable treatment obligation adopted by the Parties in accordance with paragraph 3 of this Article.*"[43]

This cross-fertilization of jurisprudence demonstrates a growing awareness of the need to balance expectations of a stable investment environment and the protection of the ownership position of investors with the right to regulate of host states.

IV. Conclusion

It seems that the major challenge in regard to the right to regulate and investor protection in the resources industry is a proper understanding of what obligations host states usually incur by agreeing to abide by investment protection standards in IIAs.

This contribution has demonstrated that admission obligations are usually weak, whereas protection standards once (often highly capital and risk intensive) investments have been made are normally rather high.

Thus, the liberty of states to decide whether and by whom their natural resources are exploited remains largely unhampered by investment treaties. When states decide to conclude IIAs that govern not only the treatment of established investments, but also conditions of admission, usually little dis-

---

43 Article 8.10 CETA ("*Treatment of investors and of covered investments*").

cretion is ceded. Even the most generous terms do not venture beyond stipulating that investors from the other contracting state will be subject to the same procedures as nationals. Whether by reference to domestic law, sectoral exclusion or exceptional circumstances, host states usually maintain a high degree of flexibility.

Though host states are free not to admit investments, once rights to explore or exploit natural resources are granted and then denied in violation of investment protection standards, compensation and/or damages may be owed. One misunderstanding in this regard relates to the limits of the freedom of a state to regulate under investment treaties. BITs and other IIAs do not aim at limiting the regulatory space of states. Rather, they aim at protecting investors against such exercises of regulatory measures that may amount to indirect expropriation or other interference with legitimate investor expectations.

Two interesting trends can be perceived in recent treaties and relevant case-law. First, the conflation of fair and equitable treatment tests with those relating to expropriation and, second, the widening of the already substantial appreciative margin of host states.

The concept of (investment-backed) legitimate expectations, stemming from fair and equitable treatment jurisprudence, is employed to identify instances of indirect expropriation. Informing the extent of the right to regulate, expectations of investors are balanced with regulatory needs of host states by reference to fairness, consistency, predictability, substantive and procedural propriety, as well as an *ex ante* evaluation of legitimate expectations.

The police powers doctrine, coming to prominence in investment arbitration in the *Saluka* and *Methanex* awards, is now often reflected in IIA clauses referencing "public welfare objectives".

Thus, to a host state fearing that the exploitation of natural resources might conflict with its public interest, three principal conclusions are likely to provide a certain degree of comfort: First, enacting appropriate national statutes and screening relevant projects, rather than avoiding obligations under international investment protection standards, remains decisive in limiting negative impacts of natural resource exploitation. Second, even if certain admission terms have been stipulated in IIAs, these will usually not demand that foreign investors be afforded better treatment than that owed to nationals. Third, subsequent to establishment, even where regulatory exceptions have not been anticipated *pro futuro,* widely accepted balancing approaches under both fair and equitable treatment and expropriation standards have further broadened the discretionary regulatory space of host states.

Reforming International Investment Treaties for an Equitable Natural Resource-Related Investment Governance Regime

Manjiao Chi[*]

Abstract

Natural resource-related investments are a major form of transnational investments. A distinct feature of these investments is that they are closely linked to local communities, and are often prone to cause environmental and social damages. IIAs are the major component of international investment law, but they are designed primarily for protecting foreign investments. The strong "pro-investor bias" of IIAs makes them insufficient in the governance of natural resource-related investments. With the global expansion of natural resource-related investments and the proliferation of IIAs, such insufficiency of IIAs should be improved. To achieve this purpose, merely correcting the "pro-investor bias" of IIAs is not enough; IIAs should be made more inclusive to support an equitable state-investor-community relationship.

Overview

* Professor of international law & Founding Director, Center for International Economic Law and Policy (CIELP), Law School, University of International Business and Economics (UIBE), Beijing. This research is an outcome of a China National Social Science Funding project (Grant Number: 17ZDA144). The author can be contacted at chimanjiao@uibe.edu.cn.

I. Introduction

There is a lack of a uniform definition of the term "natural resource" at the global level in the field of international economic law, but no one would deny the importance of natural resources for economic development. It has been suggested that, along with physical and human capital, natural resources should also be viewed as important economic assets for economic development, and that "economies that have a greater endowment of natural resources must surely have a much better chance of attaining higher economic growth rates and prosperity than relatively resource-poor economies".[1] The natural resource sector is a major industrial sector appealing to transnational investments. Not only many resource-rich developing countries rely heavily on the natural resource-related (NR-related) industries for economic development, but investors also find NR-related industries attractive, since global access to natural resource is an advantage in international competition and a potential source of profit. Natural resources are geographically unevenly distributed around the world, but the demand for natural resources is global. Such a situation not only necessitates transnational NR-related trade and investments, but also provokes international disputes and conflicts.[2] Furthermore, environmental pollution, population growth, climate change and many other factors further escalate the global tension between the access to natural resources and the control over natural resources.[3]

International investment agreements (IIAs), national laws and investment contracts are the major sources of norms for the existing global investment governance regime.[4] This regime is also supported by various soft

1 See *Barbier*, The Role of Natural Resources in Economic Development, in: Australian Economic Papers 42 (2003), p. 253 (263).

2 See *Bannon/Collier (eds.)*, Natural Resources and Violent Conflict: Options and Actions (2003), *passim*; *United States Institute of Peace*, Natural Resources, Conflict and Conflict Resolution, available under: https://www.usip.org/sites/default/files/file/08sg.pdf (last accessed: 1. April 2020); *United Nations Environmental Program*, 40% of Conflicts Linked to Use of Natural Resources, available under: https://reliefweb.int/report/world/40-conflicts-linked-use-natural-resources (last accessed: 28 April 2020).

3 See, *e.g.*, *Njuguna Mwanika*, Natural Resources Conflict: Management Processes and Strategies in Africa, in: ISS Paper 216 (2010), available under: https://www.files.ethz.ch/isn/136685/PAPER216.pdf (last accessed: 1 April 2020).

4 See *Salacus*, The Three of International Investment Law (2013), *passim*.

law instruments.[5] Among these different sources, IIAs are the main supplier of binding norms, which include a large number of bilateral investment treaties (BITs), the investment chapters of free trade agreement (FTAs), and some multilateral treaties, such as the Energy Charter Treaty (ECT). Since the first modern BIT was concluded in the 1950s,[6] states around the world have concluded a huge number of IIAs. Up to the present, there are over 3300 IIAs, with nearly 3000 BITs and over 300 other types of IIAs.[7] The number is still on the rise as states are negotiating more IIAs at bilateral and regional levels.

Given the important role of IIAs in global investment governance, investors routinely take IIAs into account when making investment decisions. Such consideration could be especially necessary in making NR-related investments, because such investments often last for a long period and are environmentally sensitive, while IIAs may help provide a long-term and stable legal environment for the investments.[8] Here, two questions are raised. First, can IIAs provide sufficient protection to NR-related investments, given the distinct features of such investments? Second and perhaps more important, can IIAs create an equitable governance regime for NR-related investments? While it is widely acknowledged that IIAs are primarily designed for investment protection, it remains unclear whether and to what extent they are sufficient and effective in protecting non-investor interests which are typical and important in many NR-related investment projects, such as the cultural interest of the local communities and the environment.

This paper tries to present a preliminary study of the above questions. In addition to Part A (Introduction), this paper introduces typical risks of the investors, host states and local communities respectively in a typical NR-related investment project (Part B). It then argues that although IIAs are designed to offer protection to foreign investments, they have an inherent "pro-investor bias" (Part C), and raises proposals for making IIAs more

5 See *Hirsch*, Sources of International Investment Law, in: Bjorklund/Reinisch (eds.), International Investment Law and Soft Law (2012), p. 9 (37).

6 See *Germany-Pakistan BIT* (1959), available under: https://investmentpolicy.unctad.org/international-investment-agreements/treaty-files/1387/download (last accessed: 1. April 2020).

7 *UNCITAD*, Most recent IIAs, available under: http://investmentpolicyhub.unctad.org/IIA (last accessed: 1. April 2020).

8 See, *e.g.*, *Crowell&Moring*, How Mining Companies Can Mitigate Risks and Protect their Investments, available under: https://www.crowell.com/NewsEvents/AlertsNewsletters/all/How-Mining-Companies-Can-Mitigate-Risks-and-Protect-their-Investments-Part-I-International-Investment-Agreements (last accessed: 1. April 2020).

suitable for equitable governance of NR-related investments (Part D). Finally, this paper concludes that proper governance of NR-related investments calls for IIAs that are able to foster and maintain an equitable state-investor-community relationship, which would go beyond making "balanced IIAs" (Part E).

II. The state-investor-community relationship

Compared with investments in many economic sectors, NR-related investments bear some distinct features, such as environmental sensitiveness, geographical fixation, community involvement and long duration, to list a few.[9] It is important to note that NR-related investments could profoundly impact local communities, and prompt a delicate relationship among the main stakeholders, *i.e.* state-investor-community relationship.[10] In comparison, investments in many other economic sectors, especially in service sectors, are often less environmentally sensitive and have less impacts on local communities. Thus, at the outset, it is necessary to present a brief analysis of the potential risks of the various stakeholders in a typical NR-related investments project.

First, when engaging in NR-related investment projects, foreign investors often undertake greater risks than investing in other economic sectors.[11] This can be viewed from different perspectives. From an investor-state perspective, as NR-related investments are typically made on the basis of long-term contracts between foreign investors and host states or state entities, sometimes in the form of public-private partnership (PPP), political risks are likely to occur during this long period, due to possible changes of policy and legislation of the host states and the situation of national and international security. In some countries, natural resources are often con-

9 See *Cameron*, International Energy Investment Law: The Pursuit of Stability (2010), *passim*; *Pinto*, Settlement of Disputes Concerning New Natural Resources, in: Dupuy (ed.), The settlement of disputes on the new natural resources (1982), p. 19 (20).

10 See *Viñuales*, International investment law and natural resource governance, in: Morgera/Kulovesi (eds.), Research Handbook on International Law and Natural Resources (2016), pp. 26-45.

11 See *Tabari*, Lex Petrolea and International Investment Law: Law and Practice in the Persian Gulf (2017), pp. 133-135; *Cotula*, Human Rights, Natural Resource and Investment Law in a Globalized World: Shades of Grey in the Shadow of the Law (2012), pp. 79-104.

ceived with a strong sense of sovereignty,[12] and "resource nationalism" is growing and may escalate the risks on foreign investors.[13] Some developing countries have recently enacted new laws and policies to enhance state control over natural resources for national security reasons,[14] or environmental protection reasons.[15] While it is legal and understandable for the states to take such measures, it is possible that these measures would make the prospect of NR-related investments in these states more uncertain.

From an investor-market perspective, NR-related investments face greater commercial unpredictability, largely due to the frequent change of the demand and price of natural resources in the global market, the complicated structure of the investment projects and the huge amount of financial and technological input for obtaining the license or conducting initial exploration.

From a community perspective, as NR-related investments are often made in environmentally-vulnerable regions and labor-intensive industries, they are closely connected with local communities, especially the indigenous groups of the region. Such investments may incur strong opposition and criticisms for negatively influencing the livelihoods of the local communities or for neglecting the sustainable development of the region.[16] It may particularly be the case in countries where the "local-central

---

12 See, *e.g.*, *United Nations*, General Assembly Resolution 1803 (1962), available under: https://digitallibrary.un.org/record/204587/files/A_RES_1803%28XVII%29-EN.pdf (last accessed: 1. April 2020); *Schijver*, Sovereignty over Natural Resources: Balancing Rights and Duties (1997), *passim*.

13 See *Ng'ambi*, Recourse Nationalism in International Investment Law (2016), pp. 13-43.

14 *UNCTAD*, The Prospect of National Security in IIAs, p. 135, available under: http://unctad.org/en/docs/diaeia20085_en.pdf (last accessed: 1. April 2020).

15 See *Masamba*, Government Regulatory Space in the Shadow of BITs: The Case of Tanzania's Natural Resource Regulatory Reform, in: IISD Investment Treaty News 8 (2017), p. 5 (*5 et seq.*), available under: https://www.iisd.org/sites/default/files/publications/iisd-itn-december-2017-english.pdf (last accessed: 1 April 2020).

16 See, *e.g.*, *Viscidi/Fargo*, Local Conflicts and Natural Resources: A Balancing Act for Latin American Governments, in: Energy Working Paper (2015), available under: https://www.thedialogue.org/wp-content/uploads/2015/05/Local-Conflicts-and-Natural-Resources-FINAL.pdf (last accessed: 1. April 2020); *Dhont*, Opposition to extractive industry in Colombia, available under: https://ihsmarkit.com/research-analysis/opposition-to-extractive-industry-in-colombia.html (last accessed: 1. April 2020); *González Porras*, Stakeholder Opposition in a Foreign Direct Investment: Case Botnia's Pulp Mill in Uruguay, available under: https://tampub.uta.fi/bitstream/handle/10024/100401/GRADU-1482401608.pdf?sequence=1 (last accessed: 1. April 2020).

relationship" is vulnerable or where the protection of the environment and human rights of the local communities are at a low level.

Second, host states may face a high pressure in properly regulating NR-related investments for reasons of IIAs. A typical reason is that IIAs are traditionally and primarily designed for the purpose of protecting foreign investors and investments. Such a purpose is not only manifested from the preambles and titles of IIAs, but is also enshrined in the core provisions of IIAs, such as the expropriation clause and the fair and equitable treatment (FET) clause. While IIAs in general prevent and prohibit host states from improperly treating foreign investors, they also incur profound restraining effects on state regulatory power in taking measures for public interest purposes, resulting in "regulatory chill".[17]

Besides, many IIAs also allow foreign investors to sue host states through investor-state arbitration (ISA). Many ISA cases target at host states' regulatory measures for public interest purposes, which are frequently seen in NR-related industries. As a matter of fact, the recent years have witnessed a growing number of NR-related investment disputes.[18] According to a study of the International Center for Settlement of Investment Disputes (ICSID), as of 30 June 2017, out of the 619 ICSID registered cases, 4% are in agriculture, fishery and forestry sector, 24% are in oil, gas and mining sector, 5% in water, sanitation and flood protection sector, and 17% are in electric power and other energy sector.[19] The number of such disputes is likely to grow along with the global expansion of NR-related investments.

Third, local communities, especially indigenous groups, inhabiting the area where the natural resources are located and exploited, are often vulnerable to the environmental and social impacts of NR-related investment activities. The perceptions of local communities and foreign investors of the value and significance of natural resources and NR-related investments could be quite different. While foreign investors control and use natural

---

17 See *Tienhaara*, Regulatory Chill and the Threat of Arbitration: A View from Political Science, in: Brown/Miles (eds.), *Evolution in Investment Treaty Law and Arbitration* (2011), pp. 606-628; *Chi*, Integrating Sustainable Development in International Investment Law: Normative Incompatibility, System Integration and Governance Implications (2018), p. 155 *et seq*.

18 See *de Trazegnies Granda*, Arbitration and Natural Resources, Transnational Dispute Management 5 (2007), available under: www.transnational-dispute-management.com/article.asp?key=1133 (last accessed: 1. April 2020).

19 *ICSID*, The ICSID Caseload Statistics (2017), p. 12, available under: https://icsid.worldbank.org/en/Documents/resources/ICSID%20Web%20Stats%202017-2%20(English)%20Final.pdf (last accessed: 1. April 2020).

resources to make profits, local communities rely on natural resources for livelihoods, including economic, cultural, social and religious lives.[20] Investment activities may be detrimental to the local communities in at least two senses. First, they may cause serious environment and social damages to the local communities, which has been revealed in some African and Latin American countries.[21] Second, as a result of the "regulatory chill" of IIAs and ISA, the host states may confront profound impediments in taking regulatory measures for protecting the environment and local communities.

The distinct features of NR-related investments, especially their environmental, cultural and religious sensitivity, essentially requires that the governance of NR-related resource should be conductive in forming and maintaining an equitable state-investor-community relationship. This relationship is not merely an expansion of the investor-state relationship, but is a dynamic relationship forged among the major stakeholders. The involvement of local communities in NR-related investment governance raises a number of challenges for states in their future IIA-making and implementation in an equitable manner.

III. The structural imbalance of IIAs

It is almost undoubted that IIAs should be applied in regulating transnational NR-related investment activities. However, the existing IIAs in general are structurally imbalanced in allocating rights and obligations of the major stakeholders, including but not limited to states (host and home states), foreign investors, the impacted groups and local communities and the general public. Such imbalance will be discussed in detail.

---

20 See *Winter*, Conservation and Culture: Natural Resource Management and the Local Voice, in: Journal of Ecological Anthropology 1 (1997), p. 42 (42 *et seqq.*); *Roe*, in: Nelson/Sandbrook (eds.), Community Management of Natural Resources in Africa: Impacts, Experiences and Future Directions (2009), pp. 1-5.

21 See *Mabe/McNally*, Foreign Direct Investment and the Environment: From Pollution Havens to Sustainable Development, in: WWF-UK Report (1999), available under: http://www.oecd.org/investment/mne/2089912.pdf (last accessed: 1. April 2020); *Boocock*, Environmental Impacts of Foreign Direct Investment in the Mining Sector in Sub-Saharan Africa, available under: https://www.oecd.org/env/1819582.pdf (last accessed: 1. April 2020); *Shinn*, The Environmental Impact of China's Investment in Africa, in: Cornell International Law Journal 49 (2016), p. 25 (25 *et seqq.*).

First, there is an "investor-state imbalance". IIAs in general fail to draw a proper balance between the rights of foreign investors and of host states. IIAs primarily aim at protecting foreign investors and investments, even though they are negotiated by states. IIAs are often silent on preservation and exercise of the regulatory power by host states and engagement of other non-state actors. For such reason, it has been argued that IIAs contain only rights for foreign investors and very limited rights, if any, for host states.[22] It is not until the recent decade that a consensus has been gradually formed to make "balanced" IIAs to help better preserve state regulatory power for public interest protection purpose.

Second, there is an "investors' right-obligation imbalance". IIAs in general fail to draw a proper balance between the rights and obligations of foreign investors. This can be typically shown by the fact that IIAs seldom incorporate provisions that impose obligations on investors. The conducts of foreign investors are largely left to be regulated through the national laws of the host states. Though an increasing number of IIAs nowadays starts to incorporate corporate social responsibility (CSR) provisions to help regulate investor conducts, these CSR provisions are often in the form of soft law rules and have limited enforceability in practice.[23] Such an imbalance also exists in the procedural aspects of IIAs. Many IIAs provide foreign investors broad access to ISA, but they neither provide sufficient access for non-disputing parties (third parties) to ISA (despite that IIAs are becoming increasingly friendly towards *amicus curiae* participation in ISA), nor grant sufficient access for states in raising counterclaims against investors, not to mention allowing affected groups, such as local communities and indigenous groups, to sue foreign investors through ISA. Such an ISA system cannot be deemed as an equitable one since the procedural rights of the various key stakeholders are not equitably guaranteed.

Third, there is a "private-public imbalance". IIAs in general fail to draw a proper balance between the protection of foreign investment and the protection of public interest. To put it differently, IIAs are mainly designed to regulate the relationships between foreign investors, host states and home states,[24] while non-investment values and/or public interest are often insufficiently reflected in IIAs. This design substantively marginalizes

---

22 *Dolzer*, The Impact of International Investment Treaties on Domestic Administrative Law, in: NYU Journal of International Law and Policy (2005), p. 953 (954).

23 See *Bantekas*, Corporate Social Responsibility in International law, in: Boston University International Law Journal 22 (2004), p. 309 (309).

24 *Salacuse*, Three Laws of Investment Treaties: National, Contractual and International Frameworks for Foreign Capital (2013), p. 35.

the protection of public interest that may be adversely affected by foreign investments. Compared with investments in many other economic sectors, NR-related investments seem more prone to give rise to "non-investment" concerns due to their distinct features, such as the concerns over the environment, human rights, work safety, investor liability and interests of indigenous groups. All these concerns are inherently associated with public interest protection. IIAs often do not contain sufficient provisions to effectively address these concerns. Even if some IIAs contain public interest provisions, these provisions are often in the form of soft law rules or merely declaratory or aspirational in nature, which cannot produce a sufficient binding force on states and foreign investors. As a matter of fact, the recent years have witnessed a number of ISA cases and other undesirable situations in which irresponsible investors and investments gave rise to serious public interest damages.[25]

The structural imbalance of IIAs leads to a strong "pro-investor bias". To put it differently, while IIAs try to provide protection to foreign investors, they largely fail to provide sufficient protection to other stakeholders, especially host states and local communities. This bias heavily restricts IIAs in playing a more constructive role in creating an equitable investment governance regime, and is not supportive in achieving a proper state-investor-community relationship. The incompatibility between the "pro-investor bias" of IIAs and an equitable state-investor-community relationship should be addressed in future IIA-making.

IV. Suggestions for reforming the existing IIAs

The international community has come to realize the structural imbalance of IIAs, and has taken measures to address this issue. In recent years, there has emerged a growing call to make existing IIAs more "balanced".[26] Such

---

25 See, generally, *Fung/Law/Yau*, Socially Responsible Investment in Global Environment (2010); *Richardson*, Socially responsible Investment Law: Regulating the Unseen Polluters (2008).

26 See, *e.g.*, *Tuerk/Rosert*, The Road towards Reform of the International Investment Agreement Regime: A Perspective from UNCTAD, in: Bungenberg/Herrmann/Krajewski/Terhechte (eds.), European Yearbook of International Economic Law (2016), pp. 769-786; *UNCTAD*, Reform of the IIA Regime: Four Paths of Action and A Way Forward, in: IIA Issue Note (No.3, June 2014), p. 7, available under: https://unctad.org/en/PublicationsLibrary/webdiaepcb2014d4_en.pdf (last accessed: 1. April 2020) ; See, *e.g.*, *Dorf*, Making an Offer They Can't Refuse: Corporate Investment in Africa and the Divestment of Indigenous Land Rights, in:

a balance is struck mainly by preserving state regulatory power to allow states to take a wider range of measures for public interest purposes that are otherwise inconsistent with their IIA obligations. Such a "balance" addresses the state-investor relationship, but does not necessarily address the concerns over local communities and public interest. In this sense, even a "balanced" IIA could only play a limited role in striking an equitable state-investor-community relationship. More profoundly, the inadequacy of IIAs can be partly attributed to their limit as international treaties between states. When discussing the limit of international law in natural resource allocation, it has been proposed that a "peoples-based" approach should be taken into account in the making and application of treaties:

> *"[…] while international law may have only been originally concerned with the allocation of natural resources in an interstate context, it plays a distributive role today in an intrastate context. […] [A]n emerging human rights approach to the allocation of land and natural resources supports a peoples-based development model potentially capable of more readily alleviating conditions of inequity and continued subordination for historically marginalized communities."*[27]

To be more peoples-based, IIAs need to be reformed. Indeed, IIA reform is not a novel term. Over the past decade, it has received global attention. A number of proposals have been put forward, often aiming at making IIAs more compatible with sustainable development goals and more helpful in preserving state regulatory power.[28] It seems that the main purpose and the greatest merit of the existing proposals lie in striking a better state-investor

---

British Columbia International and Comparative Law Review 38 (2015), p. 65 (86 *et seqq.*).

27 *Miranda*, The Role of International Law in Intrastate Natural Resource Allocation: Sovereignty, Human Rights, and Peoples-Based Development, in: Vanderbilt Journal of Transnational Law 45 (2012), p. 785 (785 *et seq.*).

28 See *International Institute of Sustainable Development*, A Model International Investment Agreement for the Promotion of Sustainable Development (2004), available under: https://www.iisd.org/publications/model-international-investment-agreement-promotion-sustainable-development (last accessed: 1. April 2020); *UNCTAD*, Investment Policy Framework for Sustainable Development (2012), available under: http://unctad.org/en/PublicationsLibrary/diaepcb2012d5_en.pdf (last accessed: 1. April 2020); *UNCTAD*, Investment Policy Framework for Sustainable Development (2015), available under: http://unctad.org/en/PublicationsLibrary/diaepcb2015d5_en.pdf (last accessed: 1. April 2020); *South African Development Community*, SADC Model Bilateral Investment Treaty Template with Commentary (2012), available under: http://www.iisd.org/itn/wp-content/uploads/2012/10/sadc-model-bit-template-final.pdf (last accessed: 1. April 2020).

balance, which is helpful in correcting the "pro-investor bias" of IIAs. While recognizing these merits, however, one may find that the existing proposals is not sufficiently successful in constructing an equitable state-investor-community relationship. In this sense, it seems fair to say that the IIA reform up to the present remains insufficient in making IIAs truly supporting for equitable governance of NR-related investments. Further reform measures need to be taken. Here, a few suggestions are put forward.

First, local communities often seem to be the "weak end" in the state-investor-community relationship, as they are often the affected group or victims of NR-related investment activities. They have inadequate influence on the making and implementation of IIAs in many states. Thus, IIAs should be reformed to enhance the engagement of local communities in NR-related investment governance. Admittedly, whether local communities should be engaged in a state's economic governance regime and what role they could play in this regime is primarily a national political issue. It is difficult to design IIA provisions for this purpose. However, efforts could be made at different levels. At policy level, it is necessary for states to be aware that local communities deserve more systematic consideration in IIA-making and ISA practice.

In IIA-making, a sensible suggestion is to incorporate more and better public interest provisions in IIAs. Though there is almost no IIA provision expressly titled as "public interest clause" or "sustainable development clause", several types of IIA provisions may serve the purpose of protecting public interest. Typically such provisions include clauses of general exceptions, environmental measures, public health and safety and labor rights, to list some.[29] In future IIA-making, such provisions should harnessed, especially with regard to their enforceability. This could be helpful in addressing outstanding concerns raised in the governance of NR-related investments, such as environmental and labor rights concerns.

In ISA practice, even though the growing allowance of third party participation seems to provide broader access to local communities to engage in the dispute settlement proceeding,[30] such participation is subject to some important restraints. The decision of third party participation is often at the discretion of the arbitral tribunals and must satisfy the condi-

---

29 *Chi*, Integrating Sustainable Development in International Investment Law: Normative Incompatibility, System Integration and Governance Implications (2018), p. 19 *et seqq.*

30 See *VanDuzer*, Enhancing the Procedural Legitimacy of Investor-State Arbitration through Transparency and Amicus Curiae Participation, in: McGill Law Journal 52 (2007), p. 681 (723).

tions laid down in the applicable arbitration rules. Thus, such decisions are often made on a case-by-case basis with all contending circumstances taken into consideration. Besides, even if the tribunal allows third party participation, third parties are only in a position to provide the court or the tribunal with its special perspective or expertise in relation to the dispute.[31] Further, under most existing arbitral rules, arbitral tribunals typically award monetary compensation to the grieved investors, while non-monetary damages, such as specific performance of a certain obligation, are infrequently seen.[32] For these reasons, it seems fair to say that the current third party participation mechanism could not sufficiently address the concerns of the affected local communities.

Second, IIAs aim primarily at protecting foreign investors and investments. Host states are left to implement IIAs. Therefore, how well (or badly) foreign investors and investments are protected, or more broadly, governed, depends partly on the how the host states honor and enforce their IIA obligations. Some states, particularly developed states may have a high rule-of-law level, but this is not the reality in many developing states. As many NR-related investments are made in developing states with a low rule-of-law level, damages of these investments are often left insufficiently dealt with in these states. Thus, a sensible suggestion is to make IIAs more effective in holding foreign investors accountable for the environmental and social damages associated with the investments.[33] Recently, some states have taken to deal with such situation through IIA-making in different approaches. For instance, Tanzania tries to revise and enact national laws to discourage investors from abusing IIAs,[34] and India tries to include investor obligation provisions in its IIAs.[35] Some organizations propose

31 *Bartholomeusz*, The *Amicus Curiae* before International Courts and Tribunals, in: Non-State Actors and International Law 5 (2005), p. 209 (211).

32 See, generally, *Schneider*, Non-Monetary Relief in International Arbitration: An Overview of Principles and Arbitration Practice, in: Schneider/Knoll (eds.), ASA: Performance as a Remedy (2011), pp. 3-48.

33 *Bottini*, Extending Responsibilities in International Investment Law, in: ICTSD Think Piece (2015), available under: http://e15initiative.org/wp-content/uploads/2015/09/E15-Investment-Bottini-Final.pdf (last accessed: 1. April 2020).

34 *Masamba*, Government Regulatory Space in the Shadow of BITs: The Case of Tanzania's Natural Resource Regulatory Reform, in: IISD Investment Treaty News 8 (4) (2017), p. 5, available under: https://www.iisd.org/ sites/default/files/ publications/iisd-itn-december-2017-english.pdf (last accessed: 1 April 2020).

35 See *Model Text for the Indian BIT* (2015), Chapter III, available under: https://www.mygov.in/sites/default/files/master_image/Model%20Text%20for%20the%20Indi

that more enforceable CSR norms should be incorporated in IIAs,[36] or that IIAs should be made more constructive in promoting "socially responsible investments".[37] Despite their merits, these proposals do not form the mainstream of the existing IIA reform proposals and have limited influence on IIA-making practice.

Third, as NR-related investments may have profound social and environmental impacts, the restraining effects of IIAs and ISA on state regulatory power may pose serious challenges to host states and local communities. For such reason, IIAs should be reformed to preserve more state regulatory power, which essentially means to strike a better public-private balance under IIAs. This suggestion is not novel. A number of IIA-making proposals have been put forward. A large portion of the proposals focuses on reforming the core substantive provisions of IIAs, particularly indirect expropriation and FET clauses. The main purpose is to exclude certain state regulatory measures from the ambit of these clauses. For instance, some IIAs have an annex that explicitly excludes environmental measures from being deemed as an act of indirect expropriation.[38] Some IIAs incorporate GATT Article XX-style clause of general exceptions, which could exempt host states from being held liable for taking a broad range of regulatory measures that are otherwise inconsistent with their IIA obligations.[39]

Fourth, the procedural rules of IIAs should also be reformed for better governance of NR-related investments. As discussed, although existing IIAs and ISA practices allow, to varying extents, local communities to participate in ISA as non-disputing third party (*amicus curiae*), such engagement

---

an%20Bilateral%20Investment%20Treaty.pdf (last accessed: 1. April 2020); *Hanessian/Duggal*, The 2015 Indian Model BIT: Is This the Change the World Wishes to See?, in: ICSID Review 30 (2015), p. 729 (731).

36 See *UNCTAD*, World Investment Report (2011), p. 111 *et seq.*, available under: http://unctad.org/en/PublicationsLibrary/wir2011_en.pdf (last accessed: 1. April 2020).

37 See *IAWG*, Promoting Standards for Responsible Investment in Value Chains, in: Report to the High-Level Development Working Group (2011), available under: http://unctad.org/sections/dite_dir/docs//diae_G20_CSR_ Standards_Report_en.pdf (last accessed: 1. April 2020); *The US SIF Foundation*, The Impact of Sustainable and Responsible Investment (2016), available under: https://www.ussif.org/files/Publications/USSIF_ImpactofSRI_FINAL.pdf (last accessed: 1. April 2020); *Johan/Cumming*, Socially Responsible Institutional Investments in Private Equity, in: Journal of Business Ethics 75 (2007), p. 395 (395 *et seqq.*).

38 *U.S. Model BIT* (2012), Paragraph 4 (b), Annex B, available under: https://2009-2017.state.gov/e/eb/ifd/bit//index.htm (last accessed: 1. April 2020).

39 *Canadian Model FIPA* (2004), Article 10, available under: https://www.italaw.com/sites/default/files/files/italaw8236.pdf (last accessed: 1. April 2020).

could be insufficient in protecting the rights of the affected local communities and the public interest. It seems necessary for IIAs to incorporate improved procedural provisions that could better engage local communities in ISA. For instance, the UNCITRAL Rules on Transparency in Treaty-Based Investor-State Arbitration (UNCITRAL Transparency Rules, effective as of 1 April 2014),[40] and the United Nations Convention on Transparency in Treaty-Based Investor-State Arbitration (Mauritius Convention on Transparency, effective as of 18 October 2017),[41] could be expected to improve the transparency of ISA. Greater transparency of ISA is helpful in engaging local communities and other stakeholders in the governance of NR-related investments. Aside from this, other procedural aspects, such as the rules of counterclaim, preliminary objection may also be reformed. On the broader issue of ISDS reform, as the UNCITRAL Working Group III is currently charged with the study of the reform, it is yet to see what resolution the international community would propose to improve the existing ISDS, and whether and how the proposals could influence the governance of NR-related investments.

To sum up, it has to be noted that the above suggestions are in no way exhaustive. These proposals not only aim at correcting the "pro-investor bias" of IIAs, but also try to strike a balance of the state-investor-community relationship. Though it remains premature to assess the real effects of these proposals at present, one may reasonably expect that the proposals could be helpful in making IIAs more supporting to equitable governance of NR-related investments.

V. Summary

Natural resources are important to states, investors, local communities and the general public in many senses. NR-related investments are an important form of transnational investments in the globalized world. Recognizing the commonalities shared by NR-related investments and investments in other economic sectors, one may clearly observe that NR-related investments are closely associated with local communities and may cause environmental and social damages to the host states. Such features give rise to a

40 *UNCITRAL,* Transparency Rules (2014), available under: https://uncitral.un.org/en/texts/arbitration/contractualtexts/transparency (last accessed: 1. April 2020).

41 *UNCITRAL,* United Nations Convention on Transparency in Treaty-based Investor-State Arbitration (2014), available under: https://uncitral.un.org/en/texts/arbitration/conventions/transparency (last accessed: 1 April 2020).

pressing need for an equitable state-investor-community relationship in the governance of NR-related investments.

IIAs are a major source of norms for global investment governance. The global governance of NR-related investments based on IIAs seems insufficiently satisfactory, due largely to the fact that IIAs have a strong "pro-investor bias", and that they are also ill-suited for an equitable state-investor-community relationship. IIAs should be reformed. In recent years, some IIA reform proposals have been put forward. Besides, UNCITRAL Working Group III has also been set up to facilitate the study of ISDS reform.

The focus of the existing IIA and ISA reform proposals have so far been set largely on the restoration of the investor-state balance, while insufficient consideration has been paid to local communities. To transform IIAs to be suitable for equitable NR-related investment governance, merely correcting the "pro-investor bias" of IIAs is not enough. More efforts need to be made to create an equitable state-investor-community relationship. This essentially requires that IIAs to be made more inclusive. Particularly, due consideration should be paid to the rights and risks of the local communities in IIA-making and IIA-enforcement.

Authority over Natural Resources: No End of Geography

Christian J. Tams[*]

Abstract

This chapter offers concluding reflections on the legal regimes governing natural resources, as discussed in this Volume. Stepping back from the details offered in the preceding chapters and seeking to spell out assumptions informing them, it makes three points. First, it notes the diversity and fragmentation of the various regimes, which typically address a particular resource or resource-related activity, or lay down rules for a particular area. Second, it emphasises the continuing relevance of geographical factors for the allocation of authority over resources, and in this respect draws a distinction between (i) resources within a State's sphere of influence, (ii) resources located outside spheres of State influence, and (iii) resources 'straddling' spheres of influence. Finally, third, it notes the contingency of these three categories, and highlights how in the course of the 20th century, international law has evolved to recognise expanded spheres of State influence, often driven by a quest for control over resources.

Overview

* Professor of International Law, University of Glasgow, Academic Member, Matrix Chambers London.

I. Introduction

The preceding chapters provide insightful perspectives on the legal regime governing the exploration and exploitation of natural resources. In these brief concluding remarks, I have no intention of summarising the (often rich) findings. Instead, my aim is to step back and reflect on assumptions and premises that inform the preceding chapters, but often have remained hidden. The result is a fairly abstract set of comments that avoids the nitty-gritty, but that hopefully can contribute to an understanding of key parameters structuring the international law of natural resources.

II. Bric-à-brac

This attempt has to start with a trite observation—which, while trite, is important to make, as it so obviously shapes our approach to the topic. It is this: in assessing the legal rules governing natural resources, international lawyers have to confront diversity and fragmentation. Rosalyn Higgins' comment, offered 25 years ago, remains as pertinent as ever:

> *"To study the international law of natural resources is rapidly to discover that it is not a single, monolithic topic. Almost everything depends, if not on the specific resource, [then] on the category of resource that one is studying."*[1]

And further: "Not only the answers, but indeed the questions that it is necessary to ask, will depend on that initial matter."[2] While hardly ever expressly mentioned in the preceding chapters, this "initial matter" is indeed vital, if only because it complicates our understanding of the field, which —in Jean Combacau's juxtaposition—is more 'bric-à-brac' than 'system'.[3]

There are different aspects to the fragmentary and complex character of the rules governing natural resources. Perhaps most fundamentally, it means that international lawyers engaging with the topic have to engage with regimes that, for the most part, address a particular resource or a particular activity relating to it, or indeed a particular area or situation in which such activities take place. The choice and focus of the preceding chapters reflects the point and illustrates the diversity of the field. They dis-

1 *Higgins*, Problems and Process. International Law and How We Use It (1994), p. 129.

2 *Higgins* (fn. 1), p. 129.

3 Cf. *Combacau*, Le droit international: bric-à-brac ou système?, in: Archives de philosophie du droit 31 (1986), p. 85.

cuss dedicated treaty regimes addressing mining in space and mining on the seabed.[4] They assess provisions found in general treaty regimes (such as those relating to trade,[5] or international security[6]) to the extent that they apply to specific features of resources—which they, naturally, do from the particular vantage point of the general treaty, i.e. with a focus on trade or security issues. Some of the regimes referred to have a long history (fisheries comes to mind, a driver of international legal developments for centuries), others are more recent. As Nico Schrijver points out in his contribution,[7] some resources have been addressed in relatively detailed, specific conventions (such as those bearing on fisheries, tropical timber and water), while in other fields the regulation is sketchy,[8] or in fact it focuses only on particular situations which are felt to require a focused approach (the Kimberley rules[9] concerning 'conflict diamonds' being an example in point). Some regimes have stood the test of time; others have had their time and today seem in decline. (One might think of international commodities agreements, now rather out of favour, but at some point, thought to be a central pillar of the international resources regime.[10] Their almost complete absence from the preceding chapters is indicative.)

All these forms of specificity and fragmentation mean that there is no coherent, overarching international regime governing resources. The preceding chapters do not claim that there should be; reading them (or just glancing at their titles and introductory passages), one indeed "rapidly discovers" that our topic is anything but "monolithic", that answers and relevant questions vary from resource to resource.[11] But does that mean that

---

4 See especially the chapter by *Irmgard Marboe* and comments in section 2 of *Nico Schrijver's* chapter.

5 See the contribution by *Hans-Georg Dederer*.

6 See the contributions *Heike Krieger* and *Jonas Püschmann* (*ius ad bellum*) and by *Thilo Marauhn* and *Barry de Vries* (the law of belligerent occupation).

7 See *Schrijver*, p. 79-80.

8 *Schrijver* mentions mining (p. 79); one could equally point to oil, gas or rare earths.

9 See https://www.kimberleyprocess.com/ for details; and further *Dam-de Jong*, International Law and Governance of Natural Resources in Conflict and Post-Conflict Situations (2015).

10 For a helpful overview see *Desta*, Commodities, International Regulation of Production and Trade, in: Max Planck Encyclopedia of Public International Law, available under: www.mpepil.com (last accessed: 7 April 2020) describing international commodity agreements as "the most prominent international law instruments for the management of commodity markets over the past several decades", and noting their "progressive decline" paras. 16, 40.

11 *Cf. Higgins* (fn. 1), p. 129.

everything depends on the resource or category of resource in question? The subsequent sections suggest that the different resource-specific regimes, notwithstanding their diversity, at least start from a shared premise: that authority over a particular resource depends on its localisation, as part of international law's fundamental attempt to allocate authority over geographical spaces. It is to this aspect that I now turn.

III. Allocating Authority: The Continued Relevance of Spatial Ordering

This premise is rarely mentioned explicitly in the preceding chapters; for the most part, contributors seem to take it for granted in their discussion of the various regimes. This is perfectly understandable, because it is hardly particular to natural resources. Regulating their subject-matter 'at source', regimes governing particular resources are governed by international law's general rules of allocating authority over different parts of the globe and extra-terrestrial space. Put differently, in the absence of special provisions opting out of the general regime, the law governing natural resources partakes in the spatial ordering of international authority which has been one of the international law's key functions for centuries, and remains so, notwithstanding popular proclamations of an 'end of geography'.[12] As many resources are 'grounded' in the most immediate sense, and thus easily localisable, spatial ordering remains dominant.[13]

On the basis of the general rules, the various regimes governing particular natural resources can be grouped into three categories, which reflect the different *locus* of resources and resource-related activities. A basic dis-

12 See *e.g.*, *Bethlehem*, The End of Geography: The Changing Nature of the International System and the Challenge to International Law, in: European Journal of International Law 25 (2014), p. 9 (listing 'six broad areas of challenge that have a self-evidently transboundary, geography-defying quality'); and the discussion in *Greig*, The End of Geography? Globalization, Communications, and Culture in the International System, in: Journal of Conflict Resolution 46 (2002), p. 225. For refreshing commentary see *Landauer*, The Ever-Ending Geography of International Law, in: The Changing Nature of the International System and the Challenge to International Law: A Reply to Daniel Bethlehem, in: European Journal of International Law 25 (2014), p. 31.

13 As is discussed in section IV, this spatial ordering proceeds from an overarching principle of territorial sovereignty, which has significance well beyond the field of natural resources. At the same time, as noted below (section VII), the quest for resources has been a factor shaping the general principles governing territorial authority.

tinction is between (i) natural resources and activities located within a state's sphere of influence; and (ii) natural resources and activities located beyond national jurisdictions. (iii) A third category—comprising resources "straddling" this basic divide between—raises peculiar challenges. These three categories will be highlighted in the subsequent sections. Following that, I will offer brief comments on their contingency, emphasising that none of these three categories is inherently fixed: they depend on the geographical scope of a State's authority, which has undergone significant changes over the course of the past decades.

IV. Natural Resources Located within a State's Sphere of Influence

For the first category of resources, those located within a State's sphere of influence, the situation is straightforward: international law vests authority in the State itself. For the most part,[14] this is can be easily explained. Resources located on the territory of a State come within its economic sovereignty. As Ian Brownlie observed in his 1979 Hague Lectures, under the classical approach, "[t]he disposition of resources [is] assumed to follow the delimitation of sovereignty in spatial terms between States".[15] There is little unusual about this: the territorial state enjoys regulatory authority over 'its' resources just as much as it enjoys jurisdiction to regulate crimes committed on its territory. In Max Huber's time-honoured phrase, this is part of its claim to sovereignty, which, at least as a starting point, "in regard to a portion of the globe is the right to exercise therein, to the exclusion of any other State, the function of a State".[16]

Significant parts of the preceding chapters are devoted to tracing how territorial States have gone about exercising their "function of a State"[17]—and how international law has sought to mould their conduct. The chapters by Leopold von Carlowitz and Charlotte Kreuter-Kirchhof engage with the United Nations' current attempts to curb excesses of exploitation as part of the SDG agenda.[18] Beyond this high-level initiative, much em-

---

14 See below, section V, for brief remarks concerning resources that are not located on a State's territory, but nevertheless are allocated to it.

15 *Brownlie*, Legal Status of Natural Resources in International Law (Some Aspects), in: Recueil des Cours 162 (1979), p. 245 (253).

16 *Permanent Court of Arbitration*, Arbitral Award of 4 April 1928, Island of Palmas case (Netherlands v. United States), 2 RIAA 828, p. 839.

17 *Permanent Court of Arbitration* (fn. 16), p. 839.

18 See *von Carlowitz*, pp. 98-101; *Kreuter-Kirchhof*, pp. 12-13.

phasis is rightly placed on international legal restrictions on unfettered decision-making: these flow from diverse instruments—among them treaties and contracts in the field of investment and multilateral agreements encouraging cross-border trade,[19] but also international rules imposing obligations *vis-à-vis* individuals and the environment.[20] Each of these rules, to cite another time-honoured passage from the jurisprudence of the inter-war years, "[n]o doubt [...] places a restriction upon the exercise of the sovereign rights of the State, in the sense that it requires them to be exercised in a certain way".[21] But such restrictions are not an "abandonment of [a State's] sovereignty", quite the opposite: "the right of entering into international engagements is an attribute of State sovereignty".[22] None of this, to reiterate, is peculiar to natural resources: the various restrictions imposed by international rules reflect the relative nature of modern-day territorial sovereignty, which exists within the limits imposed by (and self-imposed through) international law.

If the regime of natural resources is peculiar, then in its frequent affirmation, at the level of principle, of a State's authority over its resources. Perhaps because many resources are physically grounded, or perhaps of their economic significance, the territorial nexus is often emphasised, much more commonly than in relation to other objects of regulation. In the decades following World War II, it was often essentialised, notably in debates about the notion of permanent sovereignty over natural resources (PSNR), which came to occupy pride of place in the post-colonial discourse about international law.[23] The preceding chapters reflect as much.[24] Some of them go further and highlight special protections offered by the law of occupation and the *ius contra bellum*,[25] whose prohibition on military force (according to Heike Krieger and Jonas Püschmann) was motivat-

19 On the former, see the trias of chapters by *Bungenberg*, *Reinisch* and *Chi*; on the latter see *Dederer.*

20 See the chapters by *Schrijver* and *Fremuth*.

21 *Permanent Court of International Justice*, Judgment of 17 August 1923, The SS 'Wimbledon' (UK and others v. Germany), PCIJ Series A, No. 1, para. 35.

22 *Permanent Court of International Justice* (fn. 21), para. 35.

23 Prominently affirmed *e.g.*, in United Nations General Assembly Resolution 1803 (XVII), programmatically entitled 'Perrmanent Sovereignty over Natural Resources'. For recent commentary see the contributions to Bungenberg/Hobe (eds.), Permanent Sovereignty over Natural Resources (2015), especially the chapters by *Hobe* (p. 1) and *Schrijver* (p. 15).

24 See *e.g.*, the comments by *Schrijver* (p. 78); *Bungenberg* (pp. 258-262).

25 See notably *Marauhn/de Vries*; and *Krieger/Püschmann*. Steven Freeland's chapter addresses the scope of protection offered by the *ius in bello,* international criminal

ed by a desire "to ban specifically [conflicts over natural resources]".[26] From the perspective adopted here, these rules are best viewed as an attempt to strengthen the allocation of authority over resources; they are ancillary rules that protect the nexus between a territorial State and its resources and that seek to counterbalance the various restrictions flowing from contracts, treaties, and other international rules. Both affirmations and limitations are attempts to fine-tune a mode of spatial ordering that proceeds from a State's control over resources located its territory.

V. Natural Resources Located outside Spheres of State Influence

For natural resources located beyond spheres of State influence, territorial sovereignty-based approaches are of little avail. The starting point is different, there is simply no obvious regulator in whom international law could vest authority: State authority based on territorial sovereignty ends at the State's borders and the limits of its territorial sea, and no international actor enjoys plenary competence over extra-territorial (let alone extra-terrestrial) spaces. This means that regimes governing natural resources outside spheres of State influence are tailor-made. Solutions look at a particular resource, area or activity, and they reflect the balance to be struck between exploitation, protection, and distribution.

The preceding chapters discuss a number of such regimes. Those adopted for the 'global commons' of the deep seabed and Antarctica are mentioned,[27] and in line with current trends in scholarship,[28] there is a particular focus on outer space. As Irmgard Marboe notes,[29] there are indeed "similarities" between the concepts embodying the international community's interest in the areas ('common heritage' and 'province of mankind').

---

law, and international environmental law. These are found to be wanting, leading Freeland to argue for the inclusion of a specific 'crime against the environment' in the Rome Statute (p. 217-220).

26 *Krieger/Püschmann*, p. 31.

27 See *e.g.*, *Schrijver*, p. 76-78; *Marboe*, p. 243.

28 See *Hobe*, Zur Zukunft des Weltraumbergbaus, in: Vereinte Nationen (2019), p. 160; *Wouters/De Man/Hansen*, Commercial Uses of Space and Space Tourism (2017); *Malanczuk*, Investment Protection of Commercial Activities in Space: Treaties, Contracts, Licenses, Insurance, Arbitration, in: Journal of World Investment and Trade 19 (2018), p. 951; *Hofmann/Blount*, Emerging Commercial Uses of Space: Regulation Reducing Risks, in: Journal of World Investment and Trade 19 (2018), p. 1001.

29 *Marboe*, p. 243.

At the same time, the degree of common control varies significantly between the regimes. For the resources of the deep seabed, control is vested in a specialised international institution, the International Seabed Authority (ISA), which enjoys far-reaching rule-making and administrative competences.[30] Its creation, under the Law of the Sea Convention, reflects an ambitious attempt at internationalising and institutionalising control over a particular type of resource. As the on-going debates about a deep-sea mining code indicate,[31] this does not prejudge outcomes, and still less is it a guarantee that community interests (*e.g.* in an equitable sharing out of benefits or in the preservation of the environment) will be duly protected. However, it means that regulatory decisions about the balance between exploitation and protection are taken by an autonomous international body.

In other areas, such degree of institutionalisation has not been reached. Nevertheless, the existing regimes do offer pointers, and these pointers reflect choices for or against access to particular resources. For resources located in outer space and even more so for Antarctica (a special spatial regime that the preceding chapters touch upon rather than explore[32]), the focus is on restraint of unilateral conduct. In both instances, restraint is primarily 'operationalised' through provisions precluding the exercise of sovereign rights by any one State and a commitment to pursuing multilateral solutions.[33] Quite how far the duty of restraint reaches is by no means clear, and the vague language of many of the regime-creating agreements is

30 See United Nations Convention for the Law of the Sea, Arts. 136, 137 , especially Article 137(2), pursuant to which "[a]ll rights in the resources of the Area are vested in mankind as a whole, on whose behalf the Authority shall act." Michael Wood's entry in the Max Planck Encyclopedia provides a very clear account: International Seabed Authority, Max Planck Encyclopedia of Public International Law, available under: www.mpepil.com (last accessed: 7 April 2020); for relevant documents see *International Seabed Authority*, https://www.isa.org.jm/ (last accessed: 7 April 2020).

31 See *e.g.*, *Ranganathan*, Ocean Floor Grab: International Law and the Making of an Extractive Imaginary, in: *Feichtner*, Sharing the Riches of the Sea: The Redistributive and Fiscal Dimension of Deep Seabed Exploitation, in: European Journal of International 30 (2019), p. 573. *Feichtner*, Sharing the Riches of the Sea: The Redistributive and Fiscal Dimension of Deep Seabed Exploitation, in: European Journal of International 30 (2019), p. 601.

32 *Cf.* the brief reference in *Schrijver*, p. 78; and further *Vöneky/Addison-Agyei*, Antarctica, in: Max Planck Encyclopedia of Public International Law, available under: www.mpepil.com (last accessed: 7 April 2020).

33 See Article IV of the Antarctic Treaty (freezing territorial claims), Article II of the Outer Space Treaty.

not conducive to legal clarity.[34] As regards space, Irmgard Marboe's chapters offers insights into ongoing debates about the permissibility of space mining by private actors, an option envisaged—within limits—in a number of national laws.[35] But all these are debates that seek to define the scope of regimes that primarily seek to restrain unilateral conduct.

The point is worth stressing as regimes governing other recourses err on the side of access and exploration. This is notably true for high sea fisheries, which—while not addressed in detail in the preceding chapters—deserve to be mentioned briefly. Fisheries regimes of course are as manifold as they are diverse; but their starting point is anything but restraining. They proceed from the freedom of fishing on the High Seas, enshrined in Article 87(e) and 116 of the UN Law of the Sea Convention. While this freedom is increasingly limited through conservation agreements, marking a move from "freedom of fishing to sustainable use",[36] the express recognition of each and every State's right unilaterally to exploit fish stocks, complemented by the flag State principle,[37] remains significant. It confirms how much, within the law of natural resources, "depends [...] on the category of resource that one is studying",[38] and it illustrates that, with respect to natural resources located outside spheres of State influence, regimes do not follow one blueprint, but are tailor-made.

VI. *'Straddling Resources'*

For the sake of completeness, it is worth briefly mentioning resources that are located neither exclusively within a State's sphere of influence nor exclusively beyond—but that transcend such binary divides. Such resources do not fit easily into a network of regimes built around geographical location, and as few dedicated regimes have been agreed, it is perhaps no coincidence that the preceding chapters treat them rather in passing.

Still, it is interesting to note that existing regimes seem to follow a common rationale: they rely on cooperation between States and impose limits on their control over the 'straddling' resource. This is true notably for the

34 A point made by *Hobe* (fn. 28) and *Marboe*, p. 254 ("lack of clear international rules").

35 See *Marboe*, pp. 244-249.

36 See the title of Francisco Orrego Vicuña's contribution to Stokke (ed.), Governing High Seas Fisheries: The Interplay of Global and Regional Regimes (2001).

37 See United Nations Convention for the Law of the Sea, Art. 92.

38 *Higgins* (fn. 1).

Straddling Fish Stocks Agreement,[39] which encourages States to cooperate with a view to avoiding overexploitation of fish migrating between the High Seas and zones of coastal State control. Such cooperation is to be based on international minimum standards; by strengthening duties of flag States and permitting controls by States other than the flag State, the Convention, in the words of David Freestone, "establish[es] the parameters for the exercise of what could be called a 'conditional' freedom to fish".[40] The straddling character of the resource was a key factor making such condition acceptable to States.

While the subject matter is very different, a very similar strategy informs the international community's approach to regulate non-navigational uses of international watercourses (*i.e.* rivers, canals or lakes, "parts of which are situated in different States"[41]). Here, too, a potentially precious resource — water —straddles a boundary. Here, too, the focus is on inter-State cooperation, aimed at an equitable sharing of resources, which will often translate into a duty of restraint for upstream States.[42] And here, too, it is readily apparent that such restraint is prompted because the resource in question straddles boundaries.

Not too much can be drawn from these two examples. I am not suggesting that they reflect a general approach to the regulation of straddling resources, if only because, even more so than in the case of resources located within the global commons, regimes are tailored to fit the demands of a particular resource. But perhaps the brief comments encourage further research on resources that cut across the divide between national and inter-

39 Or rather, in the official jargon, the Agreement for the Implementation of the Provisions of the United Nations Convention on the Law of the Sea of 10 December 1982 relating to the Conservation and Management of Straddling Fish Stocks and Highly Migratory Fish Stocks, 2167 UNTS 3 ("UNCLOS").

40 *Freestone*, Fisheries, High Seas, in: Max Planck Encyclopedia of Public International Law, available under: www.mpepil.com (last accessed: 7 April 2020), para. 21. See especially Articles 63, 64 UNCLOS as well as Articles 5 and 6 of the Fish Stocks Agreement.

41 See Article 2(2) of the 1997 Watercourses Convention, ILM 36 (1997), p. 700.

42 See Articles 5-9 of the 1997 UN Watercourses Convention. According to Stephen McCaffrey, "[t]he three foundational principles of the law of the non-navigational uses of international watercourses are equitable and reasonable utilization, prevention of significant harm, and prior notification of planned measures": see his entry International Watercourses in: Max Planck Encyclopedia of Public International Law, available under: www.mpepil.com (last accessed: 7 April 2020), para. 21.

nationalised spaces. Their 'straddling' character does set them apart, and seems to inform attempts at international regulation.

VII. Concluding Thoughts: The Contingency of the Categories

The preceding sections apply the basic distinction between categories of resources, based on their geographical location. They illustrate how the different regimes fit within international law's more general attempt at allocating authority. At this (admittedly very general) level, the various regimes, fragmented as they are, do proceed from a common starting point: a starting point that is based on a straightforward distinction based on the location of a resource or resource-related activity.

A final thought — offered lest, in their emphasis on geographical factors, the preceding comments sound rather backward-looking: While the distinction based on geographical location is for the most part straightforward, it is not immune to change. A brief moment of reflection is sufficient to realise that the categories offered here are *contingent:* they depend on the reach of a national State's recognised sphere of influence. This sphere of influence of course has a common core, but its penumbra is constantly adjusted in a process of claim and contestation that significantly affects authority over resources. International law has played a significant role in this adjustment, as the language in which claims have been made and contested, and as the medium embodying the eventual settlement.

These eventual settlements, in turn, reflect divergent trends in the international regime governing authority over resources. The expansion of national state authority over spaces extending from its land territory is the most prominent of these trends. The acceptance, in the course of the 20th century, of a State's air sovereignty is an example in point,[43] though one with limited implications for resource exploitation. This limitation hardly applies to the significant extension of coastal State authority over 'resourceful' maritime spaces, poignantly referred to as 'creeping jurisdiction'.[44] The quadrupling, in width, of the concept of the territorial sea, from three to twelve nautical miles, is part of that process; it has extended coastal State

43 See *Hobe*, Airspace, in: Max Planck Encyclopedia of Public International Law, available under: www.mpepil.com (last accessed: 7 April 2020), highlighting different means of delimiting airspace and outer space, paras. 9-13.

44 See *e.g.*, *Franckx*, The 200-mile Limit: Between Creeping Jurisdiction and Creeping Common Heritage, in: German Yearbook of International Law 48 (2005), p. 117.

sovereignty seawards and concomitantly expanded the reach of States' claims to permanent sovereignty over natural resources.[45] In two more radical steps,[46] law of the sea conventions of the second half of the 20th century have recognised the authority of coastal States over vast stretches of sea and seabed, well beyond the geographical reach of their territorial sovereignty. They have done so by recognising coastal State rights to exploit mineral and non-living resources located in the subsoil of the continental shelf, as well as their control over natural resources within exclusive economic zone.[47] The result is a massive re-allocation of authority over resources towards coastal States, which has come with surprisingly few strings attached.[48]

Movements in the opposite direction are equally significant, at least conceptually. To some extent, they have been mentioned already.[49] While accepting expanded spheres of national State influence, the international regime of resources has ringfenced particular areas from exploitation altogether, and/or from national control. This has resulted in the emergence of global commons regimes of different shapes and sizes (and stringency): in outer space, in Antarctica, in the 'Area'; and it is the main consideration driving calls for fisheries exclusion zones and special zones of restraint in sensitive regions of the globe such as the Arctic.

Both trends — expanding national spheres of influence and the ringfencing of sensitive areas — have been driven in large measure by a quest for resource exploitation and resource preservation. This in turn reflects the formative influence that the international regime governing resources has had on general concepts of international law. "The disposition of resources" not only (as Ian Brownlie noted) "follow[s] the delimitation

45 See *Crawford*, Brownlie's Principles of Public International Law (8th edition 2012), pp. 259-260.

46 As noted by Francisco Orrega Vicuna (writing in 1995), the "expanding exercise of jurisdiction by coastal States over maritime areas" is "[t]he most salient characteristic of contemporary Law of the Sea": see his Coastal States Competences over High Seas Fisheries and the Changing Role of International Law, in: ZaöRV 55 (1995), p. 520.

47 See Articles 56(1)(a) and 77(1) UNCLOS.

48 The dramatic impact of these changes is not always appreciated. David Freestone does appreciate it: as he notes with respect to fisheries, as a consequence of creeping jurisdiction in its different forms, "up to 95% of exploitable fish stocks moved from the regime of the high seas to that of coastal jurisdiction" *Freestone* (fn. 40), para. 3.

49 Section V.

of sovereignty in spatial terms between States",[50] but is a key factor in the spatial ordering of international relations through international law.

50 *Brownlie* (fn. 15).

Final Word: An International Regime for the Exploitation of Natural Resources. Proceedings of an international symposium in March 2018 in Ladenburg

Stephan Hobe

Is there already a robust all-encompassing legal regime for the exploitation of natural resources?

Even if we limit the problem to limited natural resources this is not yet the case. But, as we can clearly decipher from the foregoing, there are necessary fragments of such a legal order.

There should be an international regulation of the problem, (see the contributions of Dederer, Marboe and Schrijver), starting for the exploitation and use with the WTO and GATT (Dederer) and employing peaceful means for the settlement of disputes, be it from the perspective and regulation of the law *ad bellum* (or *contra bellum*), (Krieger), or from the perspective of the law *in bello* (Marauhn/de Vries, Freeland). This is the case for the rule of general international law as well as for special areas of international law like the law of the sea (Patel) as well as the law of outer space (Marboe). And what can be observed as a general tendency in general international law holds true for resources law as well: Not only in times of war, also in times of peace the perspective of good governance with regard to the protection of the environment (Freeland, Schrijver, Kreuter-Kirchhof), as well as with regard to the protection of human rights (Fremuth) must be observed and is on the agenda, e.g. of the German development policy (v. Carlowitz). Here international investment law mirrors the general tendency just dealt with: as much as we can categorize investment contracts (Reinisch, Bungenberg), the need arises and can be observed to arrive at an equitable natural resource related investment governance regime (Chi). And, as has been correctly stated (Schrijver) such an international regime should integrate sustainable management of mineral resources into some coherent regime of international mining law.

It is sincerely hoped that the contributions assembled in this book may give an overview on the present stage of international resource law and may contribute to its further development.